Teaching the Novel across the Curriculum

A Handbook for Educators

Edited by Colin C. Irvine

GREENWOOD PRESS
WESTPORT, CONNECTICUT • LONDON

Library of Congress Cataloging-in-Publication Data

Teaching the novel across the curriculum : a handbook for educators /
[edited by] Colin C. Irvine.
    p. cm.
  Includes bibliographical references and index.
  ISBN 978-0-313-34896-9 (alk. paper)
  1. Fiction—Study and teaching. 2. Youth—Books and reading. 3. Critical
thinking. I. Irvine, Colin C.
  PN3385.T43 2008
  808.3′0711—dc22   2007038718

British Library Cataloguing in Publication Data is available.

Library of Congress Catalog Card Number: 2007038718
ISBN: 978-0-313-34896-9

First published in 2008

Greenwood Press, 88 Post Road West, Westport, CT 06881
An imprint of Greenwood Publishing Group, Inc.
www.greenwood.com

Printed in the United States of America

The paper used in this book complies with the
Permanent Paper Standard issued by the National
Information Standards Organization (Z39.48–1984).

10 9 8 7 6 5 4 3 2 1

Contents

Acknowledgments

This book began when I was a student at Carroll College in Helena, Montana, where I was fortunate to take courses from caring, talented professors who used stories—some told, some written—to help us students to think, truly think, about the world we inhabit and about the subjects we were studying. The voices and the images of these amazing individuals—most especially those of Mr. Hank Burgess, Mr. John Downs, and Dr. Robert R. Swartout—were with me while I worked on this project over the past two years, and I smile now as I picture these teachers up at the front of their classrooms talking and telling stories.

Nearly twenty years later, I have again been blessed to work with a genuine and generous professor and mentor. Michelle Loris, whose essay is included in this collection, was more than instrumental to the completion and success of this project. She is, in many respects, *the* reason it reached this final stage. She has been the kind of colleague everyone in this strange business should be lucky enough to have at least once in his or her career: she is tireless, supportive, and truly selfless; and I envy those at her college who work with her on a daily basis. Thanks, Michelle, for everything.

Many thanks are due to the scholar-teachers who put their time, talent, and faith into this project: Amy C. Branam, Monique van den Berg, Peter Kratzke, Eric Sterling, Yuko Kawai, Lan Dong, Stephanie Li, Ricia Anne Chansky, Christine M. Doran, Stephen E. Severn, Alan Ramón Clinton, John Bruni, John Lennon, Rachel McCoppin, Marshall Toman, Gregory F. Schroeder, Kristina B. Wolff, Peter P. Nieckarz, Jr., Janine DeWitt, Marguerite Rippy, Brent Harger, Tim Hallet, Alexis Grosofsky, Douglas P. Simeone, Lauretta Conklin Frederking, Pamela Black, Marta M. Miranda, and Elizabeth Berg Leer. For all that I have learned from you and for all that you will no doubt teach others who read your essays and follow your examples in and out of the classroom, thank you very much. These pieces printed here are proof of your commitment to teaching and of your profound understanding of our profession's constant need for creativity and collaboration.

To my friends and fellow professors Robert Cowgill and Patrick Mulrooney, you deserve much credit for what has occurred here and what has, at last, resulted. Because of the incisive input you offered free of charge at every stage in the process—tempered as it always was with a hint of humor and a dash of dishonesty—and because of your willingness to answer e-mails at odd hours and to accept phone calls you had to know were coming from your friend the commuter, the manuscript progressed from an idea to an ideal to this reality you hold in your hands. Thanks for being my implied audience and resistant but respectful readers.

To my children, Caleb and Caroline, thanks for your patience. I promise to stop sneaking into the office to check e-mail, I pledge to read you more books before you go to bed, and I pray that you will some day have teachers as good as these whose essays are included here.

Finally, I acknowledge the debt of gratitude I owe my wife, Kelly, and all of the spouses and partners whose names do not appear on this page but whose support was instrumental to the project's success. These collections, drawing as they do on what occurs in our classrooms, are invariably group projects in as much as they involve those important people in our lives who support us in the work we do with and for our students. Thanks.

Introduction

Colin C. Irvine

WHY DO WE HAVE TO READ THIS?

After earning my master's degree in American studies, I changed my name to "Mr." and returned to my old high school, where I taught courses in literature and history for three years. During this time—following the lead of my favorite college professors whom I increasingly idolized the longer I tried my hand at teaching—I incorporated novels into nearly all of my classes. And though, on occasion, this pedagogical strategy proved to be fruitful and effective, there were, nonetheless, always those occasions in which the choice of text, the set of learning outcomes, the cross-section of students, or my limited familiarity with the novel's content proved disastrous. Furthermore, there were—even when the unit seemed to be going well—those smart and exasperating students who insisted on asking the question, "Why do we have to read this?"

Although I could not give what seemed to them or me a satisfactory answer, I remained convinced that there were logically sound and academically rigorous reasons for inviting and enabling my students to wrestle with complicated works of literature. In fact, I was so intuitively confident of these as-yet unarticulated arguments that once I returned to graduate school and completed my doctoral work, which focused on how Wallace Stegner's novels introduce students to ways of thinking about history and about the environment, I found myself constantly searching for compelling and convincing responses to my students' question.

More recently, while incorporating novels into my courses in English education methods, American literature, environmental literature, and freshman composition, I have found repeatedly through casual conversations with other professors that there are many of us in the academy who are using novels in their respective courses. These teachers express their belief in the innumerable and often ineffable benefits of including novels in their courses. And although they, too, often struggle to explain how or why exactly they "use novels," they are, nonetheless, ready to defend their choices.

This handbook allows us to hear from professors across the curriculum who have responded positively to the temptation and corresponding tendency to assign what often prove to be unwieldy, resistant, and yet rewarding texts. It offers an opportunity to hear from effective educators who, in thoughtful, thought-provoking ways, have addressed such important questions as, Why do we (in a particular academic discipline) teach novels? How do we teach them well? What, exactly, do we have our students do with them and why? Which novels, and which teaching techniques associated with those texts, cultivate ways of knowing germane to better understanding issues and problems in our respective disciplines? Which historical novels, for instance, help students comprehend an era, event, issue, or individual and which enable students to begin appreciating historiography and historical inquiry? How do novels help us achieve our objectives and goals in various courses and related disciplines? Finally, and most important, how can we make reading these works a truly meaningful and meaning-making experience for our students?

What follows, then, are the beginnings of a theoretical and practical discussion about the role, the impact, and the import of the novel in higher education and a classroom-based study of sound reasons for and effective ways of teaching these texts.

NAVIGATING A NOVELIZED WORLD

According to Michael Gorman, president of the American Library Association, "[o]nly 31 percent of college graduates can read a complex book and extrapolate from it." Also, as stated in a December 2005 article in *The Washington Post*, "far fewer [students] are leaving higher education with the skills needed to comprehend routine data, such as reading a table about the relationship between blood pressure and physical activity" (Romano 12).

Given these statistics and what they suggest about how well and in what ways high schools, colleges, and universities are preparing students to enter into their respective professions, many people both inside and outside of academic circles have become justifiably anxious. In turn, they have begun to pose and in some cases promote such questions as, Why not, given the failures these statistics seem to reveal, focus more time and resources on teaching students to read less literary, more approachable, more practical works? Why not, given the way things seem to be going, be more realistic and more practical in our approach to teaching students to read? Why not, at the college level, for instance, follow the lead of those elementary- and secondary-education literacy specialists who proclaim that we should stop worrying about what or even how well students read and start celebrating the simple act of reading itself? Why not, in short, be more realistic and meet the students where they are, not where we wish they were?

Eventually, inevitably, this line of inquiry turns its attention to the genre of novel, and not the formulaic kind likely to be converted to a box office blockbuster. With this complicated and often convoluted genre in their sites, these advocates of student learning inquire of those who insist on incorporating novels into their courses, Why not stop clinging to some quixotic notion of reading, let go of the anachronistic novel and the obsolete canon, and move into the twenty-first century? Why not admit, moreover, that the moment of the novel's magisterial import has passed, that this genre is no longer the source for social consciousness, that its mantel has moved on not to the next or to another genre but instead in all directions, that it has no inheritors? Why not at last concede that this novel is out of line and out of step with today's student readers?

Or, to paraphrase the question in a way that, ironically, borrows from one of these erudite and yet irreverent texts, why not accept what Don DeLillo's character Bill Gray proclaims in *Mao II* when he laments of novels and novelists, "in the West we [have] become famous effigies as our books lose the power to shape and influence"? Why not accept as Gray does, that while it "was possible for a novelist to alter the inner life of the culture ... [now] bomb-makers and gunmen have taken that territory. They make raids on human consciousness."

Why? Because the novel requires and cultivates ways of reading and correlative ways of thinking that are sufficiently complex for our increasingly intricate and dynamic world. Because, at its aesthetic best, the novel tells us something more, something elusive and particular about our individual, mutable selves in transcendent and transforming ways. And, most notably, we continue to teach these texts because, as critic Mikhail Bakhtin states, the novel "best reflects the tendencies of a new world still in the making; it is, after all, the only genre born of this world and in total affinity with it" (7).

Speaking from the depths of a Russian prison, more to us in the present it would seem than he was to his peers in our past, Bakhtin, as the above quote illustrates, recognized and reckoned with how the genre of the novel had and would continue to transform culture. He postulated that the novel's greatest strength was its ability to infect and transform every form of communication with which it came in contact. He argued, in essence, that the novel could and would novelize all other genres, including those not yet invented at the time he was writing (7). The result is, as he presciently anticipated, a highly novelized world one cannot escape, at least not permanently. It is a world perhaps best represented by the sensation one gets when walking in Times Square on a busy Friday evening: images, montages, symbolic constructions, and deconstructions wrap around buildings, flutter through the air on updrafts, find their way into your hand from another in the form of pamphlets, ads, and brochures. Every available space presents some part of a story, and one cannot help but conjure images and ideas from *Blade Runner* and other science fiction novels that anticipated these moments and these sensations. And when stepping out of the crush as one might attempt to avoid the spectacle, one finds in the lobby of the hotel or in the rack of magazines in the restaurant waiting area still more texts. Climb to a cruising altitude of 38,000 feet and there, on the seat eighteen inches away are still more texts in the form of inescapable televisions, which often compete for our attention with the ads on the backs and bottoms of everything in sight.

There is, in essence, little reason to assume Bakhtin, with his contention that the novel will eventually make every form of expression immediate, eventful, devalorized, and, if one is not watchful, dangerous, was anything but absolutely accurate. There is, to return to the statistics regarding declining literacy rates, a paramount reason why this handbook is after bigger game than the mere reading of any work as its own end. The handbook represents a concerted, conscious attempt to prepare students to read well, to read both the complex and the seemingly simple texts as part and parcel of larger, more elusive, and often-evolving narratives.

The problem, of course, from a teaching standpoint, is that helping students to recognize that they live in a novelized world does little to prepare them to navigate it. The text(s) have become almost too diffuse and too infused into everything. One cannot stand in Times Square as my mother would stand in the living room and, after peremptorily turning off the television, insist that we have some peace and quiet for a change. The novelized world thus makes it difficult to push back, to read well, to analyze, to gain some semblance of separation, some perspective. Paradoxically, this is the very reason why we must continue to tangle with messy, massive novels; they are—because of the way the world has changed around them since their supposed period of hegemonic dominance in the first half of the last century— more approachable, more manageable. To read these works in a classroom in a college with the help of professor is to participate in Azar Nafisi's select reading group. As Nafisi so eloquently explains in her *Reading Lolita in Tehran: A Memoir in Books*, her students enter her (class)room, remove their "mandatory veils and robes" and then immediately set to the important work of discussing novels, where the "theme of the class [is] the relation between fiction and reality" (6). This defiant act by this teacher and her volunteer students captures what this handbook is about: it is about ingesting (with soothing tea) digestible portions of reality in a safe place in a complicated world so that, when donning their imposed armor and returning to the world, our students will be, if only a little, more prepared. They will, after their labor-intensive respite, be ready, in Thoreau's words, to *meet* life and live it.

At the risk of belaboring the point, I must add here that now, more than ever, we need to teach students not only to read but to read well; we need to help them to negotiate challenging and even resistant novels in most, if not all, of their classes. Teaching our students to read novels will counter the technologies that commonly short circuit their opportunity for and experience of sustained, in-depth reading, thinking, interpreting, and analyzing. Accordingly, in this age of overwhelming information, students must be empowered and enabled to practice inquiry, interpretation, analysis, argumentation, and empathy. They must develop the skills and intellectual sophistication necessary to be able to make their way in a world that bombards them with instant messages, bits of information, and, often times, misinformation. Trained to read and think deeply for sustained periods of time, students can, in a sense, learn to learn in ways relevant to the real and real complex world beyond the books.

But learning to read well and learning to make connections is not the end game, not when it comes to reading novels in the college classroom. Reading *in* collaboration with others *in* the classroom is a collective enterprise, and it is one that entails participating in *shared* attempts at analysis and construction (a fact many of the essays in this handbook address). This collective aspect of reading novels runs counter to what our students are experiencing. Online learning, iPods, high-speed Internet, and even cell phones are reducing college campuses to places peopled by individuals who, in isolation, share a common plot of land but not much else. Squeeze into a crowded elevator in a college dorm, walk across a quad from building to building, or sit down in a bustling student center in almost any campus today and it will quickly become apparent that students are living isolated existences. They are there among others but alone in their own worlds. The infusion of the novel into any course/classroom works against this tendency to seek privacy in all places. In turn, the classroom and, by extension, the college become both an imagined and an empirical meeting place where students share and create new ideas and interpretations in community with others.

WHY THE NOVEL AND WHY NOW IN HIGHER EDUCATION

The principal intent of this text is to share with others in the academy the insights and experiences of those who have successfully incorporated novels into their courses when working toward discipline-specific, epistemology-oriented goals and objectives. The handbook serves those seeking proven ways to instruct and enlighten their students. In so doing, it invites teachers to consider how they teach, what they teach, and why they do so—and although these are admittedly broad considerations, they underline how, in fact, allowing a novel to find its way onto our syllabi and into our classrooms commonly compels us to wrestle with such significant education issues and questions as these.

By virtue of its interdisciplinary nature, this handbook—not despite but because of its focus on the novel—rejects the assumption that only those in English departments know how to teach literature well. It does so because these texts deal with and grow out of issues, ideas, and incidents inside and outside of English and of the academic institutions we inhabit. It is thus worthwhile to note that novels deal in thick detail with history, social issues, personal problems, and a myriad of other aspects of the world college students inhabit. These novels have the capacity to present students with unique perspectives on issues and individuals pertinent to their courses: a history student studying the Vietnam War, for instance, might read Tim O'Brien's *The Things They Carried* or a student in psychology may, for similar but different reasons, read Virginia Wolfe's *To the Lighthouse*. These novels might also help introduce readers to new, discipline-specific ways of thinking. To learn to think as a social worker living in a small town might likely think, one could, for instance, spend some time in Winesburg, Ohio; or, if the reader is searching for subjects and scenarios a little more off the beaten path, she could—with imaginary clipboard in hand—spend a few strange days in Yoknapatawpha County. Likewise, if a student is interested in learning about relationships in a broader, more biological sense of the term—if, in the words of Aldo Leopold, one wants to learn to "Think Like a Mountain"—she could get into the dialogic and environmental mind of a participant narrator in a novel such as Stegner's *All the Little Live Things* or Barbara Kingsolver's *Animal Dreams*. In all of these texts, students are presented with experiences that can cultivate new and keen ways of knowing about the world, ways pertinent to their particular majors.

This emphasis on the epistemology extends beyond the students to their professors, who—like their students—are ever more isolated from each other due to a variety of factors. Increased reliance on technology, on provincial, departmental thinking, and, in general, on proprietary attitudes fueled in large by part by competition for limited funds is creating silos in the academy. In this environment, as a result of these trends and changes, little cross-pollination can occur. So, though we may not be in cubicles, many of us often act like we are. We seldom meet for lunch in large groups or get together to talk, just talk. Instead, we huddle over our keyboards and eat while checking e-mails, all of us in our own worlds tethered tenuously together by Ethernet connections. The novel, and most especially this handbook about its use in higher education, seeks to counter these institutional proclivities. These essays shed light on the importance of interdisciplinary collaboration. As the novel teaches its teachers, those willing to take on this task have much to learn about using these texts from others in other disciplines. In short, all of us stand to learn new ways of learning and teaching from each other through our work on novels.

The novel has an even more subtle and sanguine effect on our place of work and our approach to our profession as professors. At a time when higher education is often narrowly conceived and administered in terms of divisions and departments, and at a time when professors in these departments are under pressure to produce empirical evidence of their efforts to teach and research, it is important we have novels that effectively destabilize and, in the process, enliven our courses, classes, departments, and disciplines. This ability to destabilize and enliven the academy is one of the most subtle and significant side-effects of allowing novels to wick their way into our work. It is proof positive that, not surprisingly, the novel is and has "novelized" higher education.

Finally, as a person who works closely with education majors, I believe that there is much work to be done when it comes to helping teachers and professors alike learn to work with novels. In my English secondary education methods courses, I often have the students participate in mock interviews so that they might prepare for the real thing while also thinking through their philosophies of teaching. Typically, students do well when answering the standard question, "If you could teach any text, what would it be and why would you choose it?" By contrast, they usually struggle when I follow up by asking, "What will your students be doing with that text on the second Tuesday or Wednesday of the unit?" My point is that the idea of teaching a certain work is almost always attractive, especially when it is a novel we know and love. It is the question of what, precisely, will happen in the classroom and among students and teacher after the first day or two of a unit that leaves most teachers-in-training uncertain and uneasy. This book will speak to both questions for all teachers-in-training—which is to say, it will speak to both for all of us.

THE OPEN FILE CABINET

If good teachers are generous teachers, then these essays are the works of excellent educators. These professors have, in effect, invited us into their offices, pulled open their file cabinets, and said, "Here, take what you want." The twenty-seven essays are divided into six sections, and though these sections fall somewhat along divisional lines, any number of different pairings and groupings are possible. The essays speak to common themes, issues, concerns, and ideas, thereby giving the reader multiple perspectives that deepen our understanding of any one theme or idea.

Section One, Teaching the Novel in General Education Classes, addresses the importance of this approach. Amy C. Branam's "Reading Wollstonecraft's *Maria* from Cover to Cover and Back Again: The Novel in the General Education Course" presents a method and rationale for helping students experience the novel "as a powerful space for negotiating complex contemporary issues." Monique van den Berg takes on a similar challenge by selecting what she describes as a fun book whose meaning has not yet been fixed by critics. Berg, in "A Nabokovian Treasure Hunt: *Pale Fire* for Beginners," claims this critical space for her students and provides them with activities and prompts tempered by theory that are anything but boilerplate or pat. The results are student papers that contribute to Nabokovian scholarship and student learning. Using relatively new technologies for teaching, Peter Kratzke also assigns a Gordian text to his students. In "Teaching the Dog's Tale: Vere's 'moral dilemma involving aught of the tragic' in *Billy Budd*," Kratzke braids together a discussion of how he uses the online, readily available version of Melville's *Billy Budd* with an emphasis of genre studies and ethics. Tapping into his students' familiarity with interactive hypertexts, he leads them to confront the ambiguities that are embodied in *Billy Budd* and that are an embedded part of most ethical issues and dilemmas.

Section Two, Using the Novel to Teach Multiculturalism, blends theory and criticism to cultivate ways of knowing requisite for participating intelligently and humanely in a our multicultural world. At a time in higher education when "diversity requirements" and related objectives need to be implemented into our courses and core curriculums, these essays underscore the importance of approaching this concept from the inside out through novels. As Michelle Loris makes apparent in her essay "Using the Novel to Teach Multiculturalism," these texts, when taught in part for the purposes of (re)introducing students to the heterogeneous world they occupy, change one's approach to theory. Theory becomes a means to an end, a part of a pedagogical methodology, rather than a label one wears as a critic. Professors such as Yuko Kawai and Eric Sterling, in their essays titled "Teaching Chinua Achebe's Novel *Things Fall Apart* in Survey of English Literature II" and "Implicating Knowledge with Practice, Intercultural Communication Education with the Novel"—like Loris and like Lan Dong, author of "Teaching Nora Okja Keller's *Comfort Woman* in a Comparative Literature Classroom"—model original, rigorous strategies for making theory available to engage students in appreciating the complexity inherent in texts *and* in individuals. As a case in point, Kawai, who teaches in Japan, uses the novel *Yuhee*, by Korean Japanese Lee Yangi, as a "site for practice in which students engage in internal communication," so that they might, as she explains cogently, "experience living in a different cultural environment."

The next essay in this section, "'Who knows but that, on the lower frequencies, I speak for you?' The Polyphony of Ralph Ellison's *Invisible Man*," by Stephanie Li, continues the conversation by bringing Bakhtin's erudite concept of polyphony to bear on the intersection of Ellison's written work with his affinity for jazz. In doing so, Li underlines the idea that the Invisible Man's crisis stems from his "internalization of social constructs" and from his inability to discern and untangle this hybridized, highly heteroglot discourse. The intent—and one of the many reasons for reading the novel—is to give students the tools and terminology to "join in the Invisible Man's search for identity and find parts of themselves in the story," a sentiment not lost on the other authors in this section.

In Section Three, Teaching the Novel in Literature Classes, Ricia Anne Chansky, in her essay, "Written Images: Using Visual Literacy to Unravel the Novel," and Christine M. Doran, author of "Reading Right to Left: How Defamiliarization Helps Students Read a Familiar Genre," each admit to the unspoken reality that even English teachers face—how to engage students in reading and understanding the novel. Both respond to this reality by developing "creative methods of teaching prose that will excite and interest the beginning students," to quote Chansky. Drawing on the power of the known to help students identify and unravel "symbolic meaning," Chansky uses visual literacy as a bridge away from and back to the novel. Consonantly, Doran's essay on defamiliarization uses the familiar in the form of graphic novels to disabuse students of preconceived, debilitating categorical thinking. Read together, these works enjoin students to reconsider and redefine such enigmatic and elusive concepts and categories as genre and gender.

If, in a new historic vein, we look through Li, Chansky, and Doran's essays at the two that follow in this section—one by Stephen E. Severn titled "Ford Madox Ford's *The Good Soldier*, Creating Writing and Teaching the Introductory-Level Literature Classroom" and the other by Alan Ramón Clinton titled "A. S. Byatt's Finishing School: Literary Criticism as Simulation"—we see Modernist texts as a means and mode for stimulating a similar kind of decentering for our students. Works such as James Joyce's *Ulysses* and Virginia Woolf's *To the Lighthouse* are, in Severn's estimation, "Deliberately abstract and fractured, replete with allusions." They are, thereby, perfect for helping students understand that in this "post-9/11, String Theory" world, reality "never tidies up as neatly as proto-Realists narratives would have us believe." Thus, to plunk down one of these tomes on day one of an introduction to literature class is, according to Severn, to acknowledge the professor's incumbent responsibility "to teach ... students how to read the book," which is precisely what both Severn and Clinton do well.

Section Four, Teaching the Novel in the Humanities, segues from the emphasis on the novel in English courses to the humanities, but the transition here—and the categories this transition occludes—have blurred boundaries. These first essays are written by English professors who are primarily teaching non-English majors. John Bruni, English professor in the Humanities Department at South Dakota School of Mines & Technology, typifies the type of teacher suited for this undertaking. In his essay "Teach the Conflict: Using Critical Thinking to Evaluate Anthony Swofford's *Jarhead*," he outlines his nonlinear, literary approach to enlightening students about metacognition and other aspects of critical thinking. To this end, he uses the novel to "dramatize theoretical concepts that students often find abstract and thus hard to understand." John Lennon, in his humanities classroom, uses another war-related novel for cognate reasons. He moves in the essay, "Novel Truths: *The Things They Carried* and

Student Narratives about History," seamlessly back and forth between his consideration of the student's college-centric world and the otherly world of Tim O'Brien's Vietnam; he also moves equally well in his discussion from the students' often embryonic and simplistic thinking and their concomitant discomfort with ambiguity to the levels of comprehension and kinds of cognition the novel insists on, presenting in the process examples that deftly illustrate the students' internal and external worlds. As is the case with the authors/professors in this handbook, Lennon knows his students well; and like a good gift giver, he knows how to match them with a work that works.

Rachel McCoppin's piece "Questioning Ethics: Incorporating the Novel into Ethics Courses," reaches back to earlier essays by and about English literature and criticism and puts essays such as Loris's, Li's, and Clinton's into conversation with her colleagues in the humanities, most notably those concerned with teaching ethics. She locates her work in a critical context that includes Wayne Boothe, Martha Nussbaum, Lionel Trilling, and others of their ilk and that envelops Kantianism, utilitarianism, care ethics, and pragmatism; and she manages this feat in an intellectually rigorous and simultaneously applicable manner that shows how in a classroom and "in atmosphere of open discourse" novels help students "achieve a greater sense of ethical compassion and understanding."

In the second half of this fourth section, using insights gleaned from his interdisciplinary work, Marshall Toman shows, in "Teaching Dickens's *Hard Times* in a General Education Humanities Course" that, "Just as Dickens's many dialects individualize and bring his characters to life, such language—the many different tones of Dickens—transforms the mechanistic, mathematic, monochromatic world of the Enlightenment and Coketown's factories into the organic world of Wordsworth's 'something far more deeply interfused' ("Tintern Abbey" 98)...." This pattern, one in which the novel engenders insights for teachers and students alike, repeats itself in Gregory F. Schroeder's essay "Novels in History Classes: Teaching the Historical Context." Schroeder commences with the confession that, as a first-year history professor, his maiden attempt at teaching novels floundered when he realized too late that his students were not ready or able to read Milan Kundera's *The Joke*. Schroeder declares in hindsight that he had assigned the text but had not taught it. He then offers numerous techniques and tips, all of which underscore how, in his history courses, novels act "as cultural products of the era and society under study created by someone who lived then and there." Schroeder's brief, concrete case studies are invaluable to all of us who teach the novel.

In Section Five, Teaching the Novel in the Social, Behavioral, and Political Sciences, the authors look through their respective disciplinary lenses at this pliable and applicable genre. As Kristina B. Wolff and Peter P. Nieckarz, Jr., both illustrate in their essays, it is doubly beneficial to find ways to help students look through both the discipline and the novel at the reality that students are preparing to engage as professionals in their field. In Wolff's "Reading Our Social Worlds: Utilizing Novels in Introduction to Sociology Courses," she discusses the discipline-specific reasons to help students imaginatively inhabit communities in fictive but realistic places such as Mango Street and the Chippewa Indian Reservation in North Dakota, where *Love Medicine* unfolds in nonlinear time. In

"Science Fiction as Social Fact: Review and Evaluation of the Use of Fiction in an Introductory Sociology Class," Nieckarz, in keeping with a social science approach, analyzes and evaluates survey data related to students' experiences of this teaching method in different educational situations.

Two cowritten essays, one by Janine DeWitt, an associate professor in the Department of Sociology and Criminal Justice, and Marguerite Rippy, an associate professor of Literature and Languages, and the other by Brent Harger and Tim Hallett, both sociology professors, reify what, in this handbook, is a common refrain: "novels can help students understand complex issues...." And while, like others, they also address how these works bring the convoluted and controversial past into the present and into the present-oriented lives of student readers, they come at these conclusions in ways unique to their fields of inquiry. DeWitt and Rippy's "Insights from the Novel: Good Citizens in Social Contexts" and Harger and Hallett's "Using *The Autobiography of Malcolm X* to Teach Introductory Sociology" each, in its own way, illustrates how—to pluck a phrase from a quote by Lewis Closer in DeWitt and Rippy's introduction—"the trained sensibilities of a novelist" prove to be not unlike those of a sociologist. In both cases, the writer and the sociologist must employ their "sociological imagination[s]" to examine and depict the fictional and factual social situations they see.

The next two essays, one by Alexis Grosofsky and the other by psychology professor Douglas P. Simeone, shift the focus from the community to the individual and, in the process, present exciting findings about the authors' efforts to use novels. Grosofsky's "Stories in Psychology: Sensation and Perception," as the title indicates, spotlights how literature can offer students an insider's approximate encounter with the absence or the accentuation of a particular sense, such as sight or even olfaction. Rather than keeping those with disabilities at arm's length, this activity—facilitated as it is by the novel—places the student in their subject's situation and thus helps the professor accomplish her primary goal. In "Usefulness of *Lord of the Flies* in the Social Psychology Classroom," Simeone talks of teaching texts college students have likely read but not likely read as psychologists. The result, as several of the comments from his students attest, is a more trenchant experience wherein readers are able to identify and understand psychological concepts they previous did not.

The last essay in this section broadens the scope of subject matter with a perspective from political science by examining a specific concept in the context of an equally specific novel. "Demystifying Social Capital through Zola's *Germinal*," by Lauretta Conklin Frederking, establishes for students the experience that they are witnesses to and participants in a precipitous and puzzling decline in altruistic participation in democracy. With the concept of social capital acting as both barometer and key, the students in Frederking's course, in conversation with literature, learn to generalize about human behavior not by "political scientists' more typical generalization from observed patterns of behavior" but, instead, by learning to explicate human connections, an ability nurtured by Zola's *Germinal* and Frederking's teaching of it.

Section Six, Teaching the Novel in Professional Studies, completes the journey from theory to practice but in no way offers the last word on this subject of teaching novels across the curriculum. Similar to the other essays collected here, these touch on, and in some cases delve deeply into, now-familiar themes, strategies, and rationale; however, pressed up firmly against the reality of the working world students will soon engage, these concepts and teaching tactics have an added urgency about them. In Pamela Black and Marta M. Miranda's essay "The Use of Contemporary Novels as a Method of Teaching Social Work Micropractice," the concept of "practice" has that paradoxical quality, wherein practicing means participating fully in one's profession, an undertaking that students of social work can prepare to do by reading novels. In these first case studies, explain Black and Miranda, the students analyze characters in much the same way that they will soon work with clients, and they "practice assessment and intervention in a non-threatening and safe manner."

In line with Black and Miranda's rationale for including novels in her course, Elizabeth Berg Leer, as she outlines in "Multicultural Novels in Education," uses literature to provide case-study type experiences intended to prepare her students for the work they too will soon undertake—in this instance, fittingly, that work involves "The Teaching of English," as stated in the course title. Leer, it should be noted, makes a fine distinction and an important contribution to the discussion concerning how novels can help teachers-in-training to begin to grasp multiculturalism well enough to teach it. She posits persuasively that most students, including those who have read the standard multicultural works in other college courses, are only superficially conversant with this concept, electing, consequently, to attenuate these texts by adopting a universalist stance rather than a more poignant and more pertinent pluralist view, a mistake that in this essay Leer helps other teachers-in-training to avoid.

Directed primarily at preservice secondary education students who have great ideas and tremendous enthusiasm but little in the way of useful, working tricks, tips, and plans, my own "Theories and (Legal) Practice for Teachers-in-Training," presents a new twist on a somewhat familiar approach to teaching these works, especially those that tempt us into customarily taking biographical or historical approaches to the material. Infusing the familiar mock trial with a heavy dose of literary criticism, the essay—the final one in this first edition of *Teaching the Novel across the Curriculum*—answers these questions: How can we teach novels in a manner that makes each day in the unit essential and eventful? And how, moreover, can we use them to nurture ways of thinking that are critical, creative, and—from the students' perspective—relevant?

WORKS CITED

Bakhtin, Mikhail. *The Dialogic Imagination: Four Essays*, translated by Caryl Emerson and Michael Holquist, edited by Michael Holquist. University of Texas Press Slavic Series, No. 1. 1981. Austin: University of Texas Press, 1992.

DeLillo, Don. *Mao II*. New York: Penguin Books, 1991.

Nafisi, Azar. *Reading Lolita in Tehran: A Memoir in Books*. New York: Random House, 2004.

Romano, Lois. "Literacy of College Graduates Is on Decline." *The Washington Post*, December 25, 2005, A12. http://www.washingtonpost.com/wpdyn/content/article/2005/12/24/AR2005122400701_pf.html.

Wordsworth, William. "Lines Composed a Few Miles above Tintern Abbey." 1798.

TEACHING THE NOVEL IN GENERAL EDUCATION CLASSES

Reading Wollstonecraft's *Maria* from Cover to Cover and Back Again: The Novel in the General Education Course

Amy C. Branam

By choosing to enroll in a general education course under the auspices of the English department, students are probably much more likely to expect novels as required readings for this class than those offered in other disciplines.[1] However, by its very nature as an "elective" that meets the requirements for the core curriculum, Women in Literature attracts an eclectic mix of majors: criminal justice, psychology, nursing, elementary education, exercise science, sociology, business administration, Spanish, art, accounting, computer science, and, occasionally, English. In selecting works for the reading list, I take into account numerous factors.[2] In particular, I try to anticipate which works will appeal to these diverse interests while also ensuring that I offer a sufficient representation of female authors. Tantamount to this task is articulating for me and for my students via the syllabus my reasoning regarding what constitutes this sufficient representation. I must consider the length of the novels to avoid inundating these students with too much reading for this 100-level course. Moreover, the general education committee's criteria for this course further limits my choices. The most pervasive element is its emphasis on contemporary issues. Since my approach to literature as a pedagogue and researcher privileges a sociohistorical perspective of literature, I prefer not to exclude entirely earlier works in favor of a syllabus devoted only to the late twentieth and early twenty-first centuries. Instead, when selecting novels, I ask: which female writers and their works best illustrate the idea of women in literature? Although selecting a handful of representative texts is daunting, the first (and last) work emerges clearly: I begin and end this course with Mary Wollstonecraft's posthumously published novel, *Maria* (1798).

SETTING UP THE NOVEL

According to Mary Wollstonecraft in *A Vindication of the Rights of Woman* (1792), "[W]hen I exclaim against novels, I mean when contrasted with those works which exercise the understanding and regulate the imagination."[3] Notwithstanding her objections to what she often referred to as the "silly" novel, this early pioneer for modern feminist politics penned two of these works during her life-time. The second novel, *Maria; or the Wrongs of Woman*, self-consciously inverts her focus on women's *rights* in her political treatise of 1792 to a concentration on the *wrongs*. Through the juxtaposition of these two types of writing, students in my Women in Literature course discover that the novel is not merely a genre, or a neutral form in which to present a story, but a controversial space inherently rife with political implications: in this course, for women.

To set up the novel, I assign chapter thirteen, "Some Instances of the Folly Which the Ignorance of Women Generates; with Concluding Reflections on the Moral Improvement That a Revolution in Female Manners Might Naturally Be Expected to Produce," from *A Vindication of the Rights of Woman* (1792). This chapter familiarizes students with some women's issues that frustrate Wollstone-craft, including their overindulgence of reading sentimental literature. Written in the elevated style of an eighteenth-century political treatise, *A Vindication* imme-diately poses a challenge to most college freshmen and sophomores. The diction and syntax is on a higher level of sophistication, as well as somewhat antiquated for contemporary ears. Rather than allow these obstacles to turn off the students, however, I try to make this initial reading assignment as low stress as possible. I warn the students that this reading will be challenging and explain that my ex-pectation is not that they understand everything in the chapter but that they do their best to extrapolate the main criticisms that Wollstonecraft posits against women and female education. I also tell them to note who Wollstonecraft feels is to blame for these conditions. My final advice is to keep reading the essay to the end even if they feel that they do not understand it.

At the following class, we begin by listing Wollstonecraft's criticisms on the board. Most students discover that they deciphered the essay quite well. They real-ize that no one felt that this was easy to piece together, but, as they persisted, they realized it was easier to cull what she meant to impart. Some students "admit" to looking up words. Through working together as a class, the students derive most of what Wollstonecraft relates to her audience. In my experience, however, Woll-stonecraft's first complaint eludes all of my students. Although they understand that she is trying to say something about religion, I have yet to discover a student who has looked up the meaning of "nativity" in the phrase "pretending to cast nativities," which this section relies on for an accurate understanding. This confu-sion presents a great teaching moment. When I tell the students that this refers to a horoscope based on a person's birthday, they visibly react. After working to-gether on the rest of the work, they are now invested in the text. By revealing the meaning of this word, the puzzle is completed. We list this final criticism on the board, and now the students are equipped with a working list of feminist issues that female writers address in writing. Moreover, the students have learned some key strategies for how to be successful in this course, which include asking basic questions regarding the author's purposes and audiences, trusting in their instincts as they read for meaning, looking up words, persevering in the reading, and col-laborating during our class meetings to understand content.

After the students demonstrate this active engagement with the text, I spend the remainder of class discussing historical context. In particular, I provide some biographical information on Wollstonecraft, some conventions of the political treatise, as well as background on Rousseau's *Emile,* the French Revolution, and the Jacobins.[4] As part of their course requirements, students begin to deliver brief presentations on topics and people relevant to this course. For the subsequent meeting, three students are slotted to discuss Paine's *The Rights of Man* (1791), Burke's *Reflections on the Revolution in France* (1790), as well as Wollstonecraft's earlier work, *A Vindication of the Rights of Man* (1790). These presentations serve to place Wollstonecraft and her works within a vibrant, sociopolitical climate. My goal is to create intrigue regarding her role as a woman in literature rather than to merely read her works apart from their exigency. Discussing the content and form of *A Vindication*, and comparing this treatise with Wollstonecraft's novel, *Maria,* enables us to uncover how genre already contains an ideology. This ideology is revealed through the content changes Wollstonecraft implements in the portrayal of feminist issues in the novel, as well as how the form itself can be used to make points similar to those enumerated in *A Vindication*.[5]

THE FIRST READING: RHETORICAL AND FORMAL CONVENTIONS OF THE NOVEL

During the first reading of *Maria*, the class focuses on the novel as illustration of some of the wrongs outlined in *A Vindication*, as well as some additional twists on that work. I divide the short novel over three class periods. Like *A Vindication*, the 200-year-old text can pose a challenge for many contemporary readers in its syntax and vocabulary. This situation can perplex many students, which is why reviewing the plot and fielding questions at the beginning of each class is essential. We spend a considerable amount of time on unwinding the circuitous narrative, which provides the backstory to the eponymous character's incarceration in a private asylum.

Wollstonecraft drops the reader directly into the confusion that Maria experiences after her abduction and transport to a private madhouse. We learn that she has just given birth to a daughter and that her tyrannical husband, George Venables, has kidnapped this child and, subsequently, committed his wife to the asylum. Maria opens with the deliberate collapse of the boundaries between Gothic tropes and literal experience of this woman—this wife—within the eighteenth-century state of marriage in England. Indeed, as the novel progresses, Wollstonecraft depicts how numerous women are wronged as they attempt to negotiate the current system of male–female sexual relations. Notwithstanding class or education, Wollstonecraft presents an array of women—from the lower-class prostitute Jemima to the merchant-class landlady to the upper-middleclass gentlewoman Maria and many others in between—to illustrate that women's oppression affects all women and that this oppression is directly tied to the institution of marriage, property laws, and reproduction. Moreover, Wollstonecraft indicts sentimental fiction as a means to women's oppression. She illustrates this additional wrong through the title character's inability to realize how strong the patriarchal vision of women's roles as wife and mother influence her desires via her readings of traditionally male sentimental novels.[6] Therefore, the introduction of a new male figure, Darnford, as a sympathetic sharer in her plight, leads the title character to repeat the same mistake with this new paramour as she committed with her first husband, namely falling in love with a romantic image of a truly sympathetic union of minds rather than seeing the man for who he actually is. This repetition results in another form of oppression. Although Maria cannot officially marry her second romantic hero because of divorce laws, they pledge themselves to one another. She promises to receive Darnford as a husband, and he swears to fulfill the role of "protector—and eternal friend."[7] Consequently, the two produce a child, which serves to uncover further the illusive equality in their relationship. Darnford deserts Maria and her child, and Maria's reaction varies depending on which sketched ending one reads. However, the options are overwhelmingly bleak: miscarriage or suicide. Only in the final sketch does Wollstonecraft present a positive vision. Appropriately, after the focus on the oppression of women under the patriarchal institutions of marriage and then of the court, this vision is a homosocial community comprised entirely of females. In this utopia, the mother lives for her child, whom Maria's former jailer, Jemima, has located and returned to her. In reaction to their terrible experiences with men, Jemima and Maria will apparently raise Maria's daughter together in a family without need of a father or husband.

Although the plot is challenging, the students become increasingly confident in their reading abilities with each class meeting, engaging enthusiastically in volleying the plot reconstruction from one student to another. Moreover, I give the class a ten-minute journal prompt so that they can take some time to recall the reading and begin to make connections.[8] For example, during this first meeting on the novel, I ask the students to begin with a comparison and contrast between *A Vindication* and *Maria*:

In *A Vindication of the Rights of Woman*, Wollstonecraft identifies many follies of women, including their susceptibility to astrologers and hypnotists; the ridiculous emotions fostered by the sentimental novel; a frivolous focus on fashion; an inability to feel genuinely for the plight of those who are not themselves, their children, or husbands; and to raise spoiled children. Now, we see her also arguing for women's causes in *Maria*. Compare and contrast the women she describes in *A Vindication* with Maria. How are they similar? How are they different? And, if the tragedy for women in *A Vindication* is the inability to acquire an education that fosters the intellect, what is the tragedy for the semi-educated Maria?

By phrasing the prompt in this manner, I reiterate the main points that the students should have derived from the reading and class discussion of *A Vindication*, as well as allow them to focus on how these ideas are presented in the novel. Moreover, by juxtaposing the women against one another, the students can extrapolate in which ways Maria conforms to *A Vindication*, as well as how it departs from that text's purpose.[9] This leads to a discussion regarding Wollstonecraft's different purposes, which also ties into a discussion of genre and reader expectations for different types of writing. I prepare a series of discussion questions to flush out these ideas during our first meeting on this novel:

1. We have already discussed why and for whom Wollstonecraft writes *A Vindication*, but what is her purpose and who is her audience for Maria?

2. A common practice in literature is to receive an endorsement from a well-respected, authority figure. Who endorses *Maria* and what does he impart in his note?[10]
3. How can we make a meaningful distinction between the type of writing Wollstonecraft condemns in *A Vindication* and the type of writing we find in *Maria*?

This third question is pivotal to tease out ideas regarding women's expectations as readers and as writers, as well as to discuss a deliberate attempt by a woman to change how the novel was and *could be* written. For instance, the author's preface clearly explains that her purpose is to depart from the sentimental tradition in that she will avoid drama to fulfill her main purpose, which is to "[exhibit] the misery and oppression, peculiar to women, that arise out of partial laws and customs of society" (5). Contrary to reality, the sentimental novel turns on the plight of a distressed heroine fleeing from the untoward advances of a libertine, or rake. As these novels unfold, he dramatically reforms (a reform highly unlikely in reality) due to the woman's example of impenetrable chastity. However, Wollstonecraft protests that this situation should not be considered entertainment but rather read for what it is in reality: the stuff fit for tragedy. Wollstonecraft writes:

For my part, I cannot suppose any situation more distressing, than for a woman of sensibility, with an improving mind, to be bound to such a man as I [George Venables] have described for life; obliged to renounce all the humanizing affections, and to avoid cultivating her taste, lest her perception of grace and refinement of sentiment, should sharpen to agony the pangs of disappointment. (5–6)

Indeed, George Venables's lascivious behavior persists after he is united with the virtuous Maria. In a sense, *Maria* is an exposé of what happily ever after really is beyond the sentimental novel.

Wollstonecraft's treatment of the situation may tempt the reader to view the work within the Gothic tradition, because of its departures from the sentimental. However, she discourages the audience from this move in the novel's first two sentences. By discussing these lines in relation to Wollstonecraft's project to urge her (female) readers to reconsider how they read novels, the class can begin to understand how women writers challenge the traditionally male canon. Furthermore, they begin to see how challenging forms of writing serves to underscore the need to challenge patriarchy in its various guises. In this novel, Wollstonecraft not only looks at the wrongs of woman as endemic to marriage and law but also to how women are dealt with in fiction.

As an instructor, I view one of my functions as the repository for supplemental historical information, including laws regarding marriage, property, custody, testimony, insanity, and eighteenth-century asylum management. This information often whets the appetites of most majors in the course, in particular those in criminal justice, history, social science majors, nursing, business, and accounting. In addition to purpose, audience, and the history of the novel, I guide discussion toward other conventions of the novel, such as structure (particularly as it relates to point of view and reliability of narrator), setting, historical and literary allusions, irony, foreshadowing, exposition, rising action, climax, and denouement. In the second and third classes on the novel, I devise prompts for the class that integrate these historical and formal elements into their thinking.[11]

During discussions of the novel, I insist that we look for evidence in the text when students make assertions. I model this for them when I provide my own interpretations and deliver assessments of other scholars. This takes time; however, in my experience, this is time well spent. By modeling how to make a case for an assertion regarding literature, I am able to begin to instill expectations for subsequent class discussions, as well as demonstrate how I want the students to write. This habit does not necessarily discourage a student from saying "I think" or "I feel" when I or a classmate poses a question. However, this practice sets up a climate in which all the students quickly learn that, when they say "I think" or "I feel," they will always receive a version of the follow-up question: "What in the text made you think or feel that way?"

Obviously, this question can fluster some students. They may be used to a class in which the teacher was more interested in getting students to say anything rather than ensuring that they had a reason for their assertions. Clearly, as instructors, we do not want to stunt class discussion. Therefore, I facilitate these exchanges with great care. This is the key to my teaching philosophy because, as my syllabus says, the class is to focus on challenging texts and ideas. In other words, I strive to model academic inquiry as a mode of thinking and to show it as an ongoing conservation. Fortunately, *A Vindication* and *Maria* set this dynamic due to its level of difficulty. As mentioned above, the students volley the plot summaries. What I mean by this technique is that one student volunteers to begin, and then one of three outcomes occurs: (1) the synopsis is too brief; (2) the synopsis contains some inaccuracies; or (3) the synopsis is spot-on and very few, if any, details need to be added.

If the synopsis is too brief, I commend the student on sketching the events. Then I open it to the class, asking which details they would like to add or what else they think is important for us to remember about the reading. This usually works well to flesh out the plot. When the student reports some inaccuracies, the tactic is a bit different. As instructors, we know that handling wrong answers requires some finesse if we want to continue to promote participation. In this case, I respond by reiterating the correct information. Then, I note how some incidents need to be clarified, which is usually the case in this novel. I moderate this carefully. Rather than allow one of the student's classmates to say that the student is wrong, I reiterate that this novel is tricky—in language and in plot presentation—and then I note how other people probably read the passage in the same way as that student did or were confused about that incident altogether. Again, this works well with this novel because of its nature and the fact that very few, if any of these students, are well-versed at reading novels let alone those of the late eighteenth century. Many students do acknowledge to me and their classmates their initial struggles with the reading. However, I would caution against this approach if the plot is more linear or the syntax and vocabulary more up-to-date. Doing so could come across to the student as condescending. Then, similar to the first outcome, the students work together to fill in the correct interpretation. The final likely outcome of this approach is that a student provides a detailed, accurate summary of the events. Granted, this is not as common as the other two outcomes; however, I handle this event similarly to the others. Although I may think that the student has covered all the pertinent events and developments, I think it is extremely important to retain an open mind. Therefore, I commend the student on the thorough reading and well-constructed explanation. Then, I ask if anyone would like to add any more details. Numerous times a student will volunteer to add another detail or observation that either escaped my attention or that I did not think was necessary because I had not noted it as a significant contribution in terms of where I knew I would be guiding discussion that day. However, these additions can be vital for pushing beyond superficial readings. Moreover, the student discloses how something in the text struck them personally. In this way, I learn more about my students and what catches their attentions, as well as challenge myself to avoid the pitfall of concretizing the meaning of a specific text.

Occasionally, students will necessarily disagree on the plot development because it is ambiguous. In addition to providing a compelling reason for active engagement of the text, this also provides an opportune moment to emphasize textual evidence. At these times, the entire class has their noses in their books searching for the evidence in favor or against the two alternatives. By resisting my own impulse to tell them the answer, I put the impetus on them to solve the contradiction. For example, in *Maria*, a question arising from the text is whether the attribute of sensibility is a weakness or strength in a woman.[12] By the time we conclude this text, the answer to this question is difficult to pin down. There are numerous examples in which the third-person narrator clearly points out Maria's folly as byproduct of her propensity to convince herself that she identifies a kindred spirit in her lovers when little to no evidence or, in some cases, contrary evidence is present. The students easily cite passages where this is depicted as it relates to Maria's interpretations of George Venables and Darnford. Near the novel's conclusion, however the narrator says:

There was one peculiarity in Maria's mind: she was more anxious not to deceive, than to guard against deception; and had rather trust without sufficient reason, than be for ever the prey of doubt. Besides, what are we, when the mind has, from reflection, a certain kind of elevation, which exalts the contemplation above the little concerns of prudence! We see what we wish, and make a world of our own and, though reality may sometimes open a door to misery, yet the moments of happiness procured by the imagination, may, without a paradox, be reckoned among the solid comforts of life. Maria now, imagining that she had found a being of celestial mould—was happy,—nor was she deceived. He was then plastic in her impassioned hand—and reflected all the sentiments which animated and warmed her. (122–23)

We know that this "peculiarity" is an apt label because the reader may be exasperated that, after the repeated and gross offenses to her inclination to trust that her husband perpetrated against her, she has not yet learned to withhold her trust—and heart—until more reliable proofs for their care are exhibited by the would-be receiver. Even though the narrator has consistently pointed out Maria's propensity to don her "love goggles" to her own detriment, in this passage, the narrator appears to grant her the boon, perhaps as a consolation prize. This is a challenge for the students. To unravel how this "paradox" is not so much a paradox is to recall the novel's refusal to be a traditional sentimental novel. The novel does not have an unequivocal male hero who rescues the heroine through marriage followed by a happily ever after. Rather, this is the portrayal of reality. Ironically, Maria's female education makes her much more vulnerable to a tendency to sentimentalize than the less-educated women like Jemima. Jemima has no pretenses that a man will prove a valuable asset in her life. However, through sentimental literature, including Rousseau's *Emile*, Maria has been inundated with this myth. She believes that, if she only retains her sensibility, she may yet find that sentimental hero. For this reason, Wollstonecraft's point on sensibility is complex. In *A Vindication* she maligns the novel, but in this work, she presents yet another wrong of woman as it relates to these works. Additionally, the narrator twists this wrong into a morbid right. In essence, the narrator says that Maria has the power to deceive herself through imagination, which she has gathered from her sentimental readings, to obtain the impression of lasting happiness even if it is merely transient in reality. According to our narrator and Maria's experience as Everywoman (which Wollstonecraft notes in her preface), this novel is novel in that, contrary to the judge's verdict in Darnford's trial for criminal conversation, it posits that marriage does not "bear a little hard on a few" but is hard on all women (134).[13] Like the African spirituals, women could resort to the sentimental novel and its imaginative restorative relationships for comfort while suffering under their current bondage. Indeed, Maria compares her situation to that of a slave when she exclaims, "Was not the world a vast prison, and women born slaves?" (11).[14] Also, she likens herself to an unjustly detained prisoner when she asserts, "Marriage had bastilled me for life" (87).[15]

By the time we conclude this novel, the students have uncovered many early feminist issues. In addition to learning specific information regarding Wollstonecraft and the rise of feminism, they also understand the impulsion of women in literature. They begin to see how feminist writers strive to expose and rewrite heretofore exclusively patriarchal constructs. They see through this one novel the potential consequences for women who challenge these constructs, including the repeated denial of personhood, the label of madness, the loss of material wealth, and, in some cases, the loss of life itself. Additionally, in the first two weeks, the students learn the following:

- That discussing literature is much more than merely revealing personal thoughts and feelings.
- That literary forms are not neutral but ideological spaces.
- That purpose and audience greatly affect an author's choices in writing literature, particularly in terms of selecting genre.
- That challenging conventions of a genre simultaneously challenges current ideology that gave rise to and defined those conventions.
- That feminist authors are highly attuned to the male literary tradition and actively seeking ways to adapt the male literary tradition to a female tradition or to expose the male literary tradition as a reification for patriarchal desires.
- That texts respond to historical issues and that historical issues give rise to texts—even (or some say, especially) fiction. Conversely, texts reveal historical issues.
- That students should anticipate the need for textual evidence to support their assertions.
- That texts are rife with ambiguity.

- That students must read to contribute meaningfully to class.
- That utilizing a mode of inquiry creates a much more interesting and meaningful reading of a text.

With the information we cull from *Maria*, the students can pursue the following recurrent sets of questions as the semester progresses:

- Have the issues affecting women changed significantly over centuries?
- What are women's roles? How have these changed/not changed over time? Have they just assumed new forms? How much progress have we made?
- How do women challenge ascribed roles? What are the consequences?
- Who do women blame for their societal setbacks?
- How can they solve these problems? Overcome these barriers?

Wollstonecraft's chapter thirteen from her treatise *A Vindication of the Rights of Woman* and her novel *Maria* lay the foundation for non-English majors to understand how sophisticated readers approach literature and, more generally, how scholars implement inquiry to further knowledge in the humanities. With these two works, the tenor for the entire semester is created, and the class is given the tools to operate at a much higher sophistication level than the high school classroom. In this way, this general education course via the novel introduces the students to what it means to be a *college* student.

SECOND READING: FORMULATING, APPLYING, AND TESTING INTERPRETATIVE THEORIES

Because of the importance of the novel for the inroads women have made in the literary tradition and its predominantly female audience, this course continues to explore how women use the form simultaneously to challenge prevalent ideologies and further alternative views. At the end of the course, we reread *Maria* using the knowledge and approaches we have accumulated over the semester regarding women's writings in general. This time, the students already know how the novel ends, so I shift our approach. Rather than look at the work as a focus on women as oppressed victims, I urge the students to reconsider it more specifically in light of its implications for mother–daughter relationships. After reading Austen's *Pride and Prejudice* (1813), Chopin's *The Awakening* (1899), Woolf's *To the Lighthouse* (1927), Atwood's *The Edible Woman* (1969), Robinson's *Housekeeping* (1981), and Morrison's *Beloved* (1987), these students have been exposed to many elements, including psychoanalytic interpretations, functions of silence, angel–whore dichotomies, suicide and anorexia, the overt and covert power struggles in which women engage with members of the same and opposite sexes, as well as the continued emphasis on the importance of point of view, setting, and motifs, such as food, water, madness, painting, and the supernatural. Yet, one of the main issues that disturbs my students is how mothers relate to or fail to relate to their children.

These books reinforce and challenge our notions of the idyllic Victorian Angel in the House, which many of my students find themselves wanting to believe in today. In *Pride and Prejudice*, Mrs. Bennet's antics to find matches for her daughters may be irksome to the modern reader in that she seems to pursue marriage as a financial rather than an emotional matter. Her concern with her daughters' material welfare is endearing in light of the social customs barring women from adequate means to self-sufficiency. Nevertheless, Austen depicts Mrs. Bennet as riddled with many of the follies her predecessor, Wollstonecraft, observed. Mr. and Mrs. Bennet's relationship showcases the dependence of women on men, and readers see that Mr. Bennet has no respect for his wife, often treating her like a child through the mockery of her frivolities.[16] However, Edna Pontellier poses a whole new set of controversies surrounding the angel figure. Edna's inability to conform to her expectations leads to her ambiguous suicide or, depending on the interpretation, fatal accident that may provide the closest experience to freedom that she can obtain. Her lack of connection with her children is reinforced in the novel when her mother-in-law takes the children. In fact, Edna confides in her friend, Madame Ratignolle, that she will not give up herself for anyone else, including the children. This apparent failure to connect with children is also present in Robison's *Housekeeping*. Helen deposits her daughters with her mother before committing suicide. Conversely, as the dutiful wife and mother in *To the Lighthouse*, Mrs. Ramsay demonstrates another woman who cannot find personal fulfillment in this traditional role. Woolf presents an insidious emotional relationship between husband and wife in which the husband feeds off his wife. This anxiety reappears in *The Edible Woman*. Marian's assessments of Ainsley and her friend Clara represent other manifestations of anxieties surrounding the multiple ways that women can be consumed by others. Unlike her two friends, Marian resists this idea not only through motherhood but also through becoming a wife (a step she sees as placing her on an immutable track to motherhood to the sacrifice of professional employment). Then there is Morrison's *Beloved*. Sethe's response to her imminent recapture challenges readers to reevaluate their expectations of a mother. On the one hand, readers can understand her reaction; on the other hand, they have difficulty wrapping their minds around her actions. When Paul D. refers to Sethe's love as "too thick," we cannot help but wonder whether to attribute her actions to love at all.[17] These novels exhibit the complicated bond between mother and child. More so, they challenge the notion of whether that bond naturally exists or is the result of a cultural construct defining motherhood and the maternal instinct.

The questions raised by these more contemporary novels leads the course back to our starting point: *Maria*. Although we tended to celebrate Maria's courage to leave her tyrannical husband, this time we interrogate the experience of children, particularly daughters, born to these radical mothers. What it meant to be the daughters of these mothers is important to analyze because these daughters suffer the consequences of their mothers' atypical beliefs and subsequent behaviors. These mothers defy norms, and their unusual decisions are difficult to interpret as either selfish or selfless in relation to their children. This paradox is apparent in *Maria* as well. Although she knows her choices may endanger her daughter, she persists in her dangerous course to escape from her husband. This unfortunate situation of oppression demonstrates that, in the end, the price of unconventionality is paid not only by the first generation but also the next. Since young daughters cannot choose whether to suffer for their mothers' causes, the question of how cruel it is for *mothers* (as opposed to women) to challenge the status quo haunts Wollstonecraft's text and must be confronted.

As early as the second novel, *Pride and Prejudice*, the class began to engage in a practice that I called "testing the theory." Basically, I would come to class with a paraphrase of a scholar's interpretation and we would look for textual evidence that supported and refuted the writer's main claim, as well as some of the writer's interpretations of the evidence used in the argument. For this second reading of *Maria*, I set up a similar approach based on a theory I would like the class to test regarding Maria as a model mother.[18] I tell the students to reread this novel in light of what they already know about Maria's predicament and her subsequent choices. Also, I remind them of the laws and customs governing wives as property and child custody laws. Equipped with this knowledge, as well as a healthy distrust regarding taking mothers' testimonies at face value when it comes to their children, we recommence the novel.

Rather than focus on the novel as a story of Maria's victimization within a patriarchal society, the interpretation shifts to the daughter. Showing students how to revisit a text from a different stance with a new set of questions is important to an understanding of how to think in the humanities. Throughout the semester, the students have internalized the expectations for how to make assertions, which means they must be prepared to provide reasons from the text to make their cases. Through this process, I have laid the foundation for them to feel comfortable questioning assertions by citing compelling evidence to the contrary. Many students do this and demonstrate that they understand how knowledge is derived from active conversations between readers (or scholars). Understanding how the experts in humanities arrive at knowledge is important, because it shows the students why writing a report rather than an academic argument does not conform to expectations for how to engage literature at a sophisticated level.

This time through, we focus on Maria's references to her child. Through close reading, the class realizes how difficult casting Maria as *either* victim *or* victor can be. Like the other novels, women's rights are more difficult to assert when the woman who fights for her quality of life is a mother. What I hope that the class realizes in this second reading is that this new theory is also dissatisfactory because it intimates that Maria is a sub par mother because of her assertion of her rights at the expense of another woman's rights, that is, her daughter's. In the final analysis of these novels, the relationship between mother and daughter makes it impossible to isolate selfish from selfless motivations governing a mother's behavior, especially when the mother attempts to reframe her behaviors as her hope to provide a better life for her daughter than the one that she lived. Therefore, rather than either/or assessment, we conclude with ambiguity and an understanding of how ambiguity in the novel often reflects reality.

CONCLUDING THE COURSE: TWENTIETH-CENTURY FEMINIST THEORY APPLIED TO WOLLSTONECRAFT

During our final class meetings, I turn our attention to more sophisticated theoretical ideas regarding feminist issues and writing. Whereas the first reading scratched the surface of the text in that students were learning how to read for content and basic literary devices, this time we can give the text much more critical attention.

Now, I bring in ideas about why the text is presented in a circle. We can discuss more fully the challenges of using the traditional novel form to legitimate female desires. We can interrogate more meaningfully during this reading what Janet Todd means when she refers to Maria as "an unstable story."[19] This question gives rise to many others, including the following:

- Is "unstable" a negative or positive characterization in light of Wollstonecraft's feminist stance and her use of an originally masculine form?
- Do we hunger for the relief of fulfilled expectations? How does Wollstonecraft deny us fulfilled expectations?
- Is one of these expectations fulfilled in Maria's union with Darnford?

Moreover, in *Housekeeping*, we have discussed the notion of female versus male homosocial groups through the writings of Eve Kosofsy Sedgwick and Carroll Smith-Rosenberg.[20] Therefore, we can ask of *Maria*:

- Why can't her story end with a female utopia?[21]
- How are these female bonds undermined?

Plus, in *To the Lighthouse* and *The Awakening*, we have already discussed women's innovative uses of language. Therefore, we can easily glide into a conversation on symbolic versus literal uses of language. Through a basic understanding of Lacan's Law of the Father, the Real, and the Symbolic, we can begin to understand how strongly patriarchy oppresses Maria from this psychoanalytic perspective regarding female ties to the body, feeling, and the inarticulate versus the male privileging of the symbolic, reason, and language.[22] These theorists provide additional explanations for understanding Maria's treatment within the court and the judge's reaction to her plight.

Finally, all of our novelists for the course compel us to consider second-wave feminist ideas on reproduction. As we see, time and time again, dissatisfied mothers and single women terrified to fulfill the expectation of Mother, we can continue to engage ideas from Shulamith Firestone, Mary O'Brien, Catharine MacKinnon, Andrea Dworkin, and Adrienne Rich.[23] By looking at the competing ways in which these women interpret childbirth and motherhood, we can understand why wholeheartedly praising or condemning Maria and the other mothers presented in this course is problematic. Finally, we discuss whether Mary Wollstonecraft can be considered a radical feminist by our modern standards for this label.

Although reading the same novel twice in a single course is unconventional, this reexamination is necessary to illustrate the complexity of feminist writing and issues and to thoroughly address the guiding questions for this course. Though I begin a course on contemporary women's issues with a text that is more than 200 years old, we see that Wollstonecraft's text is relevant today because women continue to strive to make appropriate decisions for themselves and their children within a culture that has strongly articulated expectations for what constitutes a successful woman. Her novel is part of an ongoing tradition of female writers who desire to raise women to the same status of men. These women defy expectations not because being a wife or a mother is an inherently oppressive state but because they want these to be real choices for women among the same array of choices offered for men, which includes husband and father. These writers' marriage of fiction to reality in presenting their ideas exposes the novel for the ideological space it always was and continues to be. By teaching the novel in the general education course, these students see the novel as more than a form of entertainment but as a powerful space for negotiating complex contemporary issues.

END NOTES   .

1. This essay is based on the four-credit course, English 162: Images of Women in Literature offered at Carroll College, Waukesha, Wisconsin, for the general education program as a fulfillment for the liberal studies program, which requires students to complete at least one course in seven areas designed to result in a well-rounded student.

2. Although I prefer to use a series of novels throughout the semester, numerous anthologies have been created for courses in women in literature (see DeShazer; Gubar and Gilbert; Holdstein).

3. Mary Wollstonecraft, *A Vindication of the Rights of Woman*, introduction by Elizabeth Robins Pennell (London: W. Scott, 1892) *University of Virginia Library Electronic Text Center* http://etext.virginia.edu/toc/modeng/public/WolVind.html (August 8, 2006). I provide a link to this electronic version from our class's Blackboard site.

4. Wollstonecraft's responses to Rousseau and Burke in her works have been discussed in detail (see Ty 42; Phillips 270–82).

5. For discussions on Wollstonecraft's revelation of the novel as a patriarchal form and defying readers' expectations of this form, see Mellor, "A Novel of Their Own: Romantic Women's Fiction, 1790–1830" 331–32; Haggerty 103–19; Phillips 227.

6. See Haggerty 105.

7. Mary Wollstonecraft, *Maria; or the Wrongs of Woman*, introduction by Anne K. Mellor (New York: W. W. Norton, 1994) 122. Subsequent references are to the edition and will be provided in the text.

8. Another journal prompt I use relates to the ending. On the day when we complete the novel, I pose the following questions: We are presented with two endings in Maria: one in which our heroine commits suicide and one in which she survives and announces that she will indeed live—for her daughter! Which ending is more effective for portraying Wollstonecraft's concern about the neglect of women as equals to men? Why? These endings spur lively class debates regarding climax and denouement when trying to determine which ending or endings provide a satisfactory resolution for Wollstonecraft's apparent purpose for this novel. Moreover, this discussion provides an entry point to bring in Wollstonecraft's biography and discuss how her personal life, which was revealed by Godwin after her death, adversely affected her personal and professional reputation.

9. In current scholarship, there is some disagreement on how closely connected these two texts are. Hoeveler asserts: "Maria was less conceived as a fiction in its own right than as a fictional presentation of ideologies already presented in prose" (390). However, McGonegal argues that "the two texts are not so intimately bound up in one another as we might initially think" (358).

10. For discussions on Godwin's impact on his wife's posthumous career see Phillips 276; Janet Todd, introduction, xiv; Shaffer 287–88; Myers 299–316.

11. To determine how well my reticent students are reading and understanding the text, I supplement class discussion with brief factual quizzes, as well as design questions for three- to four-member groups to prepare to lead discussion. These questions are also important for preparing for our two exams, which I tell the students in advance.

12. For more on sensibility in this novel, see Haggerty 107–12.

13. For background on criminal conversation and how it operates within this novel, see Komisaruk, 33–64.

14. For parallels between rhetoric used for women's rights and abolition of slavery, see Mellor, "Righting the Wrongs of Woman: Mary Wollstonecraft's *Maria*" 413–14.

15. For a detailed analysis of the use of revolutionary language by 1790s female writers, see Shaffer 283–318.

16. For a discussion of Wollstonecraft's legacy in relation to Austen and other early-nineteenth-century female writers, see Mellor, "A Novel of Their Own: Romantic Women's Fiction, 1790–1830" 327–51.

17. Morrison 164.

18. Indeed, only a few scholars have looked specifically at the mother-daughter relationship presented in this work (see Bagitelli 61–77; Hoeveler 394–96; Maurer 36–54).

19. See treatment of Todd's appellation in Haggerty 107.

20. For more information on the dynamics and cultural views on female homosocial communities, see Faderman 119–43; Smith-Rosenberg 311–42; Todd, *Sensibility: An Introduction*. For male homosocial communities, see Sedgwick, *Between Men*.

21. Although Mellor asserts in "Righting the Wrongs of Woman" that "we must recognize that [both endings] are equally possible" (420), I respectfully disagree. Based on the social customs of England at this time, the ability of this all-female community to survive let alone thrive is highly unlikely.

22. See Haggerty's chapter "Wollstonecraft and the Law of Desire"; Chodorow's chapter "Heterosexuality as a Compromise Formation"; de Lauretis, *Technologies of Gender*.

23. See Firestone, *The Dialectic of Sex: The Case for Feminist Revolution*; MacKinnon, *Toward a Feminist Theory of State,* 184–94. In addition to these primary works, I also recommend Tong, *Feminist Thought: A Comprehensive Introduction*, 71–94. In direct application to the novel, see Keane, *Women Writers and the English Nation in the 1790s*, 125–32.

WORKS CITED

Bagitelli, Anna. "'The Inelegant Complaint': The Problem of Motherhood in Mary Wollstonecraft's *Maria; or the Wrongs of Woman*." *Biography and Source Studies* 6 (2001): 61–77.

Chodorow, Nancy. "Heterosexuality as a Compromise Formation." *Femininities, Masculinities, Sexualities*. Lexington: University Press of Kentucky, 1994: 33–69.

de Lauretis, Teresa. *Technologies of Gender*. Bloomington: Indiana University Press, 1987.

DeShazer, Mary K., ed. *Longman Anthology of Women's Literature*. New York: Longman, 2000.

Faderman, Lillian. *Surpassing the Love of Men: Romantic Friendship and Love Between Women from the Renaissance to the Present*. New York: Morrow, 1981.

Firestone, Shulamith. *The Dialectic of Sex: The Case for Feminist Revolution*. New York: Morrow Quill, 1970.

Gubar, Susan, and Sandra M. Gilbert, eds. *The Norton Anthology of Literature by Women: The Traditions in English*. New York: W. W. Norton, 1996.

Haggerty, George E. *Unnatural Affections.* Bloomington: Indiana University Press, 1998.

Hoeveler, Diane Long. "Reading the Wound: Wollstonecraft's *Wrongs of Woman, or Maria* and Trauma Theory." *Studies in the Novel* 31, no. 4 (1999): 387–408.

Holdstein, Deborah H., ed. *The Prentice Hall Anthology of Women's Literature.* New York: Pearson Education, 1999.

Keane, Angela. *Women Writers and the English Nation in the 1790s.* Cambridge: Cambridge University Press, 2000.

Komisaruk, Adam. "The Privatization of Pleasure: 'CRIM. CON' in Wollstonecraft's *Maria.*" *Law and Literature* 16, no. 1 (2004): 33–64.

MacKinnon, Catherine A. *Toward a Feminist Theory of State.* Cambridge: Harvard, 1989.

Maurer, Shawn Lisa. "The Female (As) Reader: Sex, Sensibility, and the Maternal in Wollstonecraft's Fictions." *Essays in Literature* 91, no. 1 (1992): 36–54.

McGonegal, Julie. "Of Harlots and Housewives: A Feminist Materialist Critique of the Writings of Wollstonecraft." *Women's Writing* 11, no. 3 (2004): 347–62.

Mellor, Anne K. "A Novel of Their Own: Romantic Women's Fiction, 1790-1830." In *The Columbia History of the British Novel*, edited by John Richetti, 327–51. New York: Columbia University Press, 1994.

———. "Righting the Wrongs of Woman: Mary Wollstonecraft's *Maria.*" *Nineteenth-Century Contexts* 19, no. 4 (1996): 413–424.

Morrison, Toni. *Beloved.* New York: Plume, 1998.

Myers, Mitzi. "Godwin's Memoirs of Wollstonecraft: The Shaping of Self and Subject." *Studies in Romanticism* 20, no. 3 (1981): 299–316.

Phillips, Shelley. *Beyond the Myths: Mother-Daughter Relationships in Psychology, History, Literature and Everyday Life.* London: Penguin, 1996.

Sedgwick, Eve Kosofsky. *Between Men.* New York: Columbia University Press, 1985.

Shaffer, Julie. "Ruined Women and Illegitimate Daughters." In *Lewd & Notorious: Female Transgression in the 18th Century,* edited by Katharine Kittredge, 283–318. Ann Arbor: The University of Michigan Press, 2003.

Smith-Rosenberg, Carroll. "The Female World of Love and Ritual." In *A Heritage of Their Own*, edited by Nancy F. Cott and Elizabeth H. Pleck, 311–42. New York: Simon and Schuster, 1979.

Todd, Janet. "Introduction." In *Mary/Matilda,* by Mary Wollstonecraft, vii–xxvii. New York: New York University Press, 1992.

———. *Sensibility: An Introduction.* London: Methuen, 1986.

Tong, Rosemarie. *Feminist Thought: A Comprehensive Introduction.* Boulder: Westview Press, 1989.

Ty, Eleanor. *Unsex'd Revolutionaries: Five Women Novelists of the 1790s.* Toronto: University of Toronto Press, 1993.

Wollstonecraft, Mary. *Maria; or the Wrongs of Woman.* New York: W. W. Norton, 1994.

A Nabokovian Treasure Hunt:
Pale Fire for Beginners
Monique van den Berg

> I could never explain adequately to certain students in my literature classes, the aspects of good reading—the fact that you read an artist's book not with your heart ... and not with your brain alone, but with your brain and spine.
>
> Vladimir Nabokov, Playboy Interview

Pale Fire is not generally viewed as a beginner's novel. It has been described as a "bizarre, three-legged race of a novel" (Grossman), "a somewhat incapacitating text so rich and so perverse that it discourages interpretation by first or tenth time readers," (Naiman), and the "most Shakespearean work of art the twentieth century has produced, the only prose fiction that offers Shakespearean levels of depth and complexity, of beauty, tragedy, and inexhaustible mystery" (Rosenbaum). Brian Boyd, author of Nabokov's *Pale Fire*, agrees. "Because it invites us to discovery, *Pale Fire* also prompts us to disagree radically about what we think we have found ... [it] has become a paradigm of literary elusiveness, a test case of apparent undecidability" (3). Nevertheless, it is the most effective pedagogical tool I have found to create engagement in my introductory literature course. Certainly, this is a counterintuitive choice. My classes include a large percentage of first-year students who are in many cases fresh from their first-ever efforts at college composition. Most are not English majors; when asked to name a favorite book on the first day of class, a depressing percentage of them can't think of a single one. So why assault them with a postmodern book of riddles?

Pale Fire is above all a fun book, a heuristic game with puzzles for students to unlock. As complex as the novel is, they can solve many of its mysteries with satisfaction. Its narrator, Charles Kinbote, is certainly entertaining—albeit in a perverse sort of way. He's delusional, homosexual, suicidal, and possibly a pederast, so utterly and transparently unreliable that students are unable to take him at his word. Furthermore, since the survey class begins with poetry and then moves onto short fiction, it is appropriate that Nabokov's novel is a hybrid of poetry and prose; as such, it's a novel that we can build toward throughout the entire course; the book becomes a synthesis for the students' learning over the course of the semester. It is also relatively short, very funny, and for me, inexhaustible—when I teach it, I hope my enthusiasm will be infectious. There is also no filmed version, no extensive and authoritative body of criticism, and no easy "out" for the students to take. The novel compels students to engage with it on its own terms, even if only because they have no other choice. And despite its immense readability, *Pale Fire* is complex enough to be viewed through many critical lenses, inviting each student to develop her own unique analysis of the text.

Another advantage is the novel's inherent weirdness. It features a commentary to a poem wherein the commentator may have invented the poet (or vice versa), a fabulous (possibly imaginary) kingdom named Zembla, an eccentric narrator, ghosts, crown jewels, word games, amusement parks, suicides—it's unquestionably chock-full of quirky material. Students are absolved from feeling inadequate in their own confusion, since Nabokov definitely intended to confound. When an interviewer accused him of taking "an almost perverse delight in literary deception," Nabokov explained that "deception in chess, as in art, is only part of the game; it's part of the combination, part of the delightful possibilities, illusions, vistas of thought, which can be false vistas, perhaps. I think a good combination should always contain a certain element of deception" (Bookstand). Moreover, I ask my students to consider *Pale Fire* scholarship; Brian Boyd, arguably the foremost scholar of the novel, probably has the most audacious theory of all—that Aunt Maud, John Shade, and Hazel Shade are all working from beyond the grave to help shape Kinbote's commentary. As Daniel Zalewski put it, "Boyd's baroque interpretation sounds every bit as goofy as Kinbote's Zemblan fantasia, especially when distilled into summary" (1). Boyd's theories are far from being canonical; they are still actively debated in critical circles. In explaining this, I underline my most salient point: there's no way you can be more odd than this oddball book or its critics. With no definitive reading, there are still connections and discoveries to be made, and as long as you present evidence, your argument can be as crazy as you want it to be. Students often see this as a meaningful challenge—even as a game.

I treat the semester, in many ways, as a lead-up to *Pale Fire*. The novel takes up roughly four to five weeks toward the end of the course, and students write their final paper on the novel. On the first day of class, as we review the syllabus, I acknowledge the difficulty of the novel, but assure students that they will be given the tools they will need to tackle it throughout the entire semester, not just the critical five weeks. I refer to *Pale Fire* again at key points during the poetry and short fiction sections. For instance, early in the semester, I assign Robert Browning's "My Last Duchess," a dramatic monologue by a narrator, the Duke, who lacks the self-awareness to disguise his true nature: possessive, arrogant, megalomaniacal, and a murderer by proxy. The ensuing discussion is the first time my students hear the name Charles Kinbote; the Duke's lack of self-awareness is, of course, one of Kinbote's major problems as well. When Nabokov makes an allusion to Browning's poem (John Shade's essay collection is entitled "The Untamed Seahorse") and the students discover this "wink," they are delighted to have solved one of Nabokov's puzzles; they know why Browning would be invoked in

Pale Fire, and they understand the irony in Nabokov's doing so. In this one brief reference, Nabokov is simultaneously highlighting Kinbote's unreliability, suggesting personality parallels between Kinbote and the Duke, and providing a fun inside joke for the savvy reader. This is not the first mystery the students solve in the novel, by any means, but it provides that delightful frisson of recognition that shows how active reading can reap rewards.

When we finally do get to the novel itself, I am faced with the problem of how to assign the reading; there are at least five different ways to approach the novel and its four parts (Foreword, Cantos, Commentary, and Index).[1] The first approach is to assign the novel straight through, beginning to end. The student would follow no cross-references, would not match the poem with its accompanying commentary, and in short would do as Neil D. Isaacs suggests when he says, "We read a novel from beginning to end, even if one of its characters tells us otherwise, especially if he is insane" (322). This approach might make the novel less confusing, but the reader loses the interplay between Kinbote's text and Shade's, which arguably comprises the central conflict of the novel. This method also effectively eradicates one of the major themes of the novel, and the source of much of its humor, Kinbote's misreading of the poem. When the American Shade refers to "balls and bats," the European Kinbote assumes he means soccer and cricket. "Shade mentions 'parents,' and after a half a paragraph on Shade's parents . . . Kinbote devotes six pages to Charles II's father and mother; Shade writes 'one foot upon a mountain,' and Kinbote seizes the chance to spend ten pages reliving his own escape over the Bera range" (Boyd 120–21).

An alternative is to assign alternating sections of poem and commentary (the student would read a full Canto before going on to read the applicable commentary in its entirety). This encourages (but does not require) the reader to match the poem with the commentary, and it does promote the tension between the two texts. Nevertheless, the reader's experience may be fractured as he tries to follow several narrative lines simultaneously, switching to Shade's poem in the middle of Kinbote's story and vice versa. This may be the most confusing method to use in reading the novel, and this confusion would detract from, rather than add to, the experience of the novel.

A third approach is to read the novel the way Kinbote tells us to. In the foreword, Kinbote explains that "[T]he reader is advised to consult [my notes] first and then study the poem with their help, rereading them of course as he goes through its text, and perhaps after having done with the poem consulting them a third time so as to complete the picture." This essentially requires the student to read the novel three or four times or, in following all the cross-references and sub-cross-references, to read the whole thing a seemingly infinite number of times. In a real-world situation, it would be difficult to persuade the student to go for this method, or even to treat it as anything other than the mad narrator's joke. Kinbote suggests this method perhaps because Nabokov wants us to do it this way, but more likely because he is hijacking the poem for his own purposes. Indeed, Kinbote is privileging his own text in such a way that it all but ensures the victory of his commentary over Shade's poem. Alternately, a student might tackle John Shade's poem first, from start to finish, skipping Kinbote's foreword until Shade's poem has been read, and then rereading the poem as applicable lines of the commentary are reached. Interestingly, this is the only method that prevents Shade from "losing" the textual conflict, as this is the only method whereby the poem is privileged over the commentary. This also results in one reading the poem multiple times, rather than Kinbote's commentary; in essence, this is the opposite of Kinbote's directive. Instead of focusing on the gradual unfolding of Kinbote's psychosis, we would perhaps be focusing on Shade's themes—nature, love, immortality. However, Nabokov seems to have wanted Kinbote to succeed, to a certain extent, in framing Shade's work, and this approach seems furthest from the novel's intent.

I choose to assign the novel and its associated commentary concurrently, having students read Kinbote's notes to each line as they reach the appropriate line of the poem. This requires readers to match the poem with the commentary, while the nature of the back-and-forth experience will reinforce the continual push and pull of Kinbote's commentary against Shade's poem. Additionally, there are a number of subapproaches relating to Kinbote's cross-references. The reader can follow all or none of them; splitting the difference, a reader might follow Kinbote's initial cross-references, but not those in the notes to which she is sent (in other words, the reader puts a limit on how far she is willing to allow Kinbote to pull her from comment to comment). Finally, the reader might follow a selection of cross-references and subreferences according to which ones seem the most compelling. I do not insist that the students follow any of Kinbote's cross-references, an approach that lends itself to inquiry as deep as each student cares to go. If a student is floundering from the beginning, this method doesn't throw any more at him than he is equipped to handle; if a student is more ambitious or advanced, he can explore the novel in a more sophisticated way. Many students will inevitably be confused by the novel, and asking them to follow cross-references on their first read-through can be daunting enough to put them off *Pale Fire* altogether. Instead, I demonstrate how the cross-references work and what may be gleaned from them, and leave it up to individual students to follow these references if they care to.

The first section that I assign is the foreword; although short, it sets up the major themes of the novel. It introduces all of the novel's major and minor symbols (shadows and shades, "pale fire" and its variations, mirrors and reflections, birds and butterflies, color imagery, and so on) It sets up Kinbote's unreliability—he reveals that he is called "insane" and accused of blackmail—and it also reveals his egocentricity.[2] The foreword sets up his hatred of women, especially Sybil, as well as his sexuality and his propensity for sleeping with his students. It hints at a "Zembla" and at his secret; if the one cross-reference is followed, he flat-out reveals that he is Zembla's dispossessed king. The foreword introduces Kinbote's obsession with Shade and delusions about their friendship. It explains his pathological need for complete control of the manuscript. And finally, it explains how Kinbote wants us to read the novel, thereby setting up its central conflict. His insistence that his notes should be read three times reveals that he is attempting to submerge Shade's poem beneath his commentary, providing the reader with "reality" that "only [his] notes can provide" and setting up his commentary as the dominant text. Indeed, the foreword is so rich that by the end of our initial discussion, many students have forgotten about John Shade altogether, despite the fact that *Pale Fire* is supposedly his.

I initially assigned the foreword without adding my commentary to Kinbote's, leaving the students to make discoveries for themselves. However, some students didn't realize the foreword was part of the novel at all, assuming that Kinbote was a "real" commentator, superfluous and therefore not worth reading. I now explain in advance that the foreword is by the novel's protagonist, who is more or less unhinged. I attempt to pique curiosity about Kinbote's secrets, requiring that students look between the lines of the story for evidence of Kinbote's true nature. To that end, I distribute a worksheet to be completed as students read. The worksheet asks the readers to do a number of things. First, I have them choose one of the symbols used in *Pale Fire*.[3] Students are told to "find one significant instance in your reading where this symbol appears. Give a quote and page number, and explain the significance of the symbol at this stage." Although students do not as yet understand their chosen symbol's significance, they are already formulating theories and possibilities, intrigued by the fact that there is no "right answer" and, as a corollary, no "wrong answer" either. When discussing the symbols in class, the most flippant students are surprised to find that their ideas are not dismissed out-of-hand. Students are instead pressed for evidence, and if they themselves cannot supply it, their colleagues in the classroom can frequently find evidence within the text for some outlandish symbolic ideas; in this way, I attempt to build trust I can draw on at the end of the semester. In the next section of the worksheet, I have them find a quote in the text wherein they question Kinbote's reliability, thus focusing the class on a central hermeneutic impetus: "What does Kinbote want you to believe, and what is the truth?"

On that first day after students read the foreword and complete the worksheet, we have a full discussion about the things they have and have not discovered, invariably relating to each of the novel's major symbols and themes. I also give a brief quiz, designed to make sure they've read the novel and also to offer a conduit into the discussion of the material read. The quiz includes questions designed to test basic reading comprehension ("What is the name of John Shade's poem?"); to note their observations about Kinbote ("In the foreword, Kinbote gives us a "tabulation of nonsense"—things that other people have said about him that we are supposed to believe are untrue. What is one of the things someone else says about Kinbote?"); and to introduce important topics such as the oppositions of Kinbote and Shade ("Is Kinbote a vegetarian? Is Shade?"), Shade's alcoholism ("What does John Shade buy and keep secret from his wife?"), and Kinbote's penchant for spying on his neighbor ("What does Kinbote watch from the second story of his house?")

This pattern—worksheet, quiz, and class discussion—is one I follow throughout the remaining four cantos. As we progress through the novel, my lectures and quizzes attempt to gradually unfold elements of the novel. Shade's poem discusses his youth, his relationship with Sibyl, his daughter Hazel's life and death, and his dedication to discovering what happens after you die. Meanwhile, the commentary tells the story of King Charles Xavier of Zembla, his escape, his pursuit by Gradus, Kinbote's life in New Wye, and the background on Hazel and the haunted barn. In the commentary to the nonexistent one-thousandth line of the poem, we finally discover how Shade died, how Kinbote wrested control of the poem from Sibyl, and Kinbote's motivations for telling his story. Each piece of poem and commentary adds to the students' knowledge about the novel—they watch their symbols evolve, they watch Kinbote's true colors come to light, they nurse their pet theories about authorship, and they enjoy the suspense of what is at core a murder mystery.

As we read, every instance of postmodern intertextuality cannot, obviously, be covered. But the students know these instances exist and are invited to seek them out. "My Last Duchess" is a surefire crowd pleaser, as are the sly references to Hamlet's (and by extension Kinbote's) suicidal tendencies. In Shakespeare's play, Hamlet asks if "he himself might his quietus make / With a bare bodkin"; *Pale Fire*'s Kinbote asks if he might be forgiven "the one sin that ends all sins." In the Index, the entry for Botkin (who, it can be strongly argued, is Kinbote himself) contains a reference to "botkin or bodkin, a Danish stiletto." Those students who are familiar with the "to be or not to be" speech pick up on this reference, but often need the meaning coaxed out of them. When they realize it's another piece of evidence in making the "Kinbote is suicidal" case, they are happy to have ferreted out at least one clue largely on their own.[4] This, I explain, is the point of an intertextual insertion: it provides an allusion that enriches the work one is currently reading. Knowing that work—whether it be *Timon of Athens* or *Lolita*—makes the novel more understandable and more enjoyable. Furthermore, the discussion of these references serves to prove that Nabokov's allusions aren't just, as students put it, "showing off how smart he is" or "trying to be confusing on purpose." I try to prove that the threads of *Pale Fire* are often worth picking up and following, even if they don't always lead in a straight line.

The Index to the novel, which I teach last, also requires a thoughtful approach. Although at first glance, like the foreword, a reader might dismiss it as an "ordinary" index (and who reads an index, anyway?) it actually contains much humor, the answers to several of the novel's key puzzles, and important thematic clues. The Index, focusing almost entirely on Zembla, is a hilarious extension of Kinbote's megalomania—even the entry on Shade refers to Kinbote twenty-five times. The Index plants a number of important clues, for instance, Kinbote's affinity for Hazel, and all the evidence necessary to identify Charles Kinbote as Professor V. Botkin. Furthermore, the Index provides the meat for a deconstructionist reading of the novel in its entry about the crown jewels:

The single greatest evidence that the ambiguity of *Pale Fire* is intentional and purposeful, is the Zemblan crown jewels. Their location is a mystery throughout the text. In the Index, one is directed to see "hiding place," and from there "potaynik," and ultimately "taynik" which is defined as, "Russ, secret place; see Crown Jewels." All clues and evidence only lead back to the beginning in a fruitless circle. Some information is gained, the definition of "taynik," for example, but the journey has no destination. The fruit is in the journey, in the knowledge gained in the exploration. Nabokov invites us to enjoy the exploration, but has placed no treasure at the end of the line. (Pninian)

If the students have not already discovered this circular clue, they are amazed to find what significance it has to the text as a whole. It also gives them permission to approach the novel in a manner both playful and investigative, while beginning to see the Index as an important repository of keys to the novel.

The unit on *Pale Fire* culminates in a research paper that accounts for a sizeable chunk of the final class grade.[5] In guiding students through the paper-writing process, I use the same step-by-step technique that I use in my freshman composition classes. Although we begin laying the groundwork for their final paper as the novel progresses, the first step is really the discussion about critical techniques, many of which lend themselves to a strong reading in *Pale Fire*.

A psychological approach is one of the first critical strategies I discuss, because it is one with which the students are already familiar; we've discussed the evidence of Kinbote's insanity as well as the idea of "classical paranoia" as identified by Brian Boyd (60). The book's primary "hook" is Kinbote himself—seeing his obsession, his narcissism, and his madness gradually unfold is one of the pleasures of the novel. When students are presented with Boyd's cogent psychological "solution" to Kinbote, they can write about him eloquently. Taking this psychological approach a step further, into the Shadean-versus-Kinbotean question of authorship, also holds appeal. In discussion groups one semester, several students decided they were Shadeans, ultimately convincing a sizeable portion of the class that Shade is insane and that Zembla and Kinbote are his inventions. The enthusiasm of these students was palpable as the idea caught fire and many students contributed evidence to support this reading. First, they identified and defined the causes of Disassociative Personality Disorder; next, they provided evidence for Shade's own triggering trauma, the loss of a child. Students supported their theory with a close reading of the poem and commentary, proving the intimacy of the connection between Shade and Kinbote, as well as the oppositions that make the two characters halves of the same whole:

Shade hitting the window "pain" is his daughter's death ... "And from the inside, too, I duplicate / Myself ..." This ... is John Shade directly saying that he has copied his beliefs within himself, [creating his mirror image of Kinbote]. He has created other personalities because of this traumatic event. John Shade is so mentally fragile after the death of his daughter that he wants nothing more than to be his exact opposite, which Kinbote is.

As for the climax of the novel, Shade's assassination, this group went on to present a further theory stemming from the suggestive observation that Shade, Kinbote, and Gradus all share a birthday:

Gradus appears right as Kinbote starts to lose his power in Zembla as Charles Xavier. What truly happens to Kinbote is that he unconsciously creates a third identity, Gradus, to assassinate the personality of Shade. Because Kinbote does not know he has created Gradus for that reason, he believes that Gradus is meant for him. Since John Shade and Kinbote are one [and] the same, Kinbote cannot decipher ... Gradus's target.... The accidental killing was actually Gradus trying to take over Kinbote, and make his identity the prominent one.... With Shade's identity no longer present, Kinbote is the only possible identity to take over.... Kinbote closes his commentary with the idea that his identity will never die.

The development of this theory arose organically from class discussion; throughout our discussion of the novel, I raised the possibility that perhaps either

Shade or Kinbote does not exist. Their resultant papers cited sources focusing not on *Pale Fire* scholarship, but on the literature of psychiatric disorders. Thus, the bulk of the ideas in these papers were generated out of whole cloth by students themselves.

This same semester, another set of students hit on the remarkable theory that, in an act of ultimate parasitism, Kinbote hijacked the poem to write Canto Four (and only Canto Four). Although this hypothesis has a strong counterargument, it is nonetheless a fascinating one that has not, to my knowledge, been put forth in *Pale Fire* scholarship. In her paper, one student writes:

The first time Kinbote reveals himself (as he so often and unintentionally does) in the poem is in the first few lines when he mentions spying. "Now I shall spy on beauty as none has / Spied on it yet. Now I shall cry out as / None has cried out. Now I shall try what none / Has tried. Now I shall do what none has done." Throughout the entire book Kinbote tells the readers himself that he spies on Shade ... and this passage may be referring to spying on a different level. For instance, no one else has seen Shade's poem besides Kinbote himself ... therefore Kinbote has free reign to do whatever he wants with it. These lines seem to suggest, then, that in doing what no other has tried, Kinbote is going to attempt to impersonate Shade and finish his poem.

This student goes on to present a number of plausible pieces of evidence. She points out that the only person who saw Canto Four, before its publication, was Kinbote—Shade died before showing it to Sibyl, as he had done with Cantos One through Three. Furthermore, Kinbote's obsession with Shade and longing for closeness with him (often referring to him as "my poet") may lead to Kinbote's impersonating him, attempting to get close to him in another way. The mundanity of Canto Four compared with the rest of the Cantos—it is about shaving—seems suspiciously Kinbotean. Canto Four mentions Shade in the third person, repeatedly, which does not happen in the first three cantos. Moreover, Canto Four seems too prescient (it predicts Shade's death, and even Kinbote's commentary) to be accidental. Canto Four also contains the only mention, by name, of Zembla. Another student added several other pieces to the puzzle, pointing out that Canto Four refers to the brain "enclosed in a steel cap of pain" and suggesting that "Kinbote is obviously referring to his constant headaches that he goes on to talk about throughout the commentary. He talks about his headaches as these so-called 'assassins' in his brain ..." She goes on to identify instances in the poem in which Kinbote mentions his inability to write poetry, arguing that Kinbote is a known and inveterate liar. She also points out the times when Kinbote refers to the poem as "unfinished," and she draws the reader's attention to the suspicious line in Canto Four, "Man's life as commentary to abstruse / Unfinished poem. Note for further use."

Although psychological papers are popular, another popular approach is symbol, which in *Pale Fire* is an avenue of inquiry both rich and immediately accessible. One student developed a theory wherein he equated the characters in the novel to chess pieces. His paper did not draw heavily on the scholarship that already exists on Nabokov's use of chess in the novel; however, the author's strength was his willingness to devise an independent theory based on his own close reading. His paper presents an interesting theory involving John Shade as the King of Nabokov's chess game, arguing that Shade's death in the commentary to line 1,000 is "Nabokov's checkmate," and the game—the novel—is over. Even more interestingly, he argues that the Queen is Charles Kinbote himself:

The Queen is the most powerful piece in chess ... For the purpose of my argument, the Queen is not a woman, it is Charles Kinbote. Nabokov shows us throughout the book that he has Kinbote move which ever way he wants, no restrictions, no limits, just open board. With Nabokov giving the commentary this much leeway, it allows him to have the upper hand in the story, even over the King ... [T]he entire story is twisted by Kinbote and made about Kinbote. He takes over the story and makes everything about him....

In addition to the main "conventional" symbols of the novel, other students branched out into symbols that the worksheet hadn't suggested. One student developed the innovative argument that music is a referent for Kinbote's social and cognitive abilities, as well as—in the forms of Shade and Charles Xavier—an index of his aspirations. This student writes, "The 'dim distant music' that Kinbote mentions is a metaphor for the potential symbolic meaning that Shade has encrypted in the text. The word selection of Nabokov, using both dim and distant implies that this source of intelligence, the music, is both vague and remote to Kinbote." The paper goes on to point out how Kinbote, Shade, and Charles Xavier are discussed in relationship to technical musical terminology, and it explores the implications of such a reading. Although this paper did not fully flesh out its thesis, I admired its originality of thought and the author's willingness to go out on a limb.

I also lecture on other possible approaches that are underrepresented in *Pale Fire* critical literature, including feminist, mythological, and religious readings. From a feminist standpoint, I point out that the only voices in the novel are male—John Shade's and Charles Kinbote's. Sibyl Shade, for instance, is never given her own voice—she is idealized by Shade, and vilified by Kinbote, but is never allowed to tell her own story. Another major female character, Hazel Shade, is defined by her unwillingness to fit into the normative "feminine" mold. Critics have argued that she is homosexual; certainly she is ugly and unpopular, and her father despairs over this. Shade feels that it's "no use" to expect Hazel to fit in, and he weeps over her inadequacies. In response, one student wrote:

The mood definitely shifts after Shade tells the story of his daughter, but one does not really see any emotion in Shade's words ... Instead of grieving and mourning the loss of his daughter, Shade takes the situation and philosophically tries to understand what is going to occur in his life after he dies ... While Shade loves and respects his wife very passionately ... this passion is void in his relationship with Hazel ... [The] passion and concern that Shade has for his wife is not apparent in his love for his daughter because she does not live up to the qualifications set in his own mind.

As this student argues, the story that Shade tells is essentially that Hazel has drowned herself because she has been rejected by her date; it is more plausible, however, that Hazel kills herself because her father has preemptively rejected her.

In terms of mythology, the novel is concerned with the idea of life after death, so I suggest that students might explore mythological ideas of the underworld. Furthermore, given the novel's love of reflections and mirrored characters, I suggest that Narcissus (who drowns in a pond after seeing his own reflection) might be a mirror to Hazel (who drowns in a pond, not because she is beautiful, but because she is not). One student took this latter idea and wrote that—

their reincarnations are beautiful and delicate creatures; Hazel becomes an Atalanta butterfly ... and Narcissus is converted into a small flower. Hazel's return [is] a warning to John Shade, her father, of his impending death while Narcissus' death is a warning to all that if one is engrossed with their physical appearance ... they will not find love.

She also observes that the settings of their respective deaths are suggestive; Hazel drowns in a pond "half frozen, brown, and overgrown with weeds," while Narcissus dies in a pond "with water like silver ... the grass grew fresh around it, and the rocks sheltered it from the sun." She suggests that the settings reflect the differences in how the pond perceives each of them—Narcissus's pond reflects his beauty, while Hazel's reflects her ugliness.

Teaching at a Catholic college gives me the unique opportunity to discuss the possibility of a religious reading. One singular feature of the novel is that its hero, John Shade, a kind, upright, moral man, does not believe in God; whereas Kinbote, a megalomaniacal homosexual pederast, is a strong believer. Shade has devoted his life to trying to identify what happens in the afterlife but, unlike Kinbote, does not feel he has the answers. On the other hand, Kinbote spends a great deal of time thinking about God and sin, wondering if he will be forgiven "the sin that ends all sins." I ask students to consider the possibilities inherent in these facts—what might Nabokov be trying to say about religious faith? One student argued that the entire novel, including the references to God, stems from one goal, shared by Shade writing his poem, Kinbote writing his commentary, and even Nabokov writing his novel: to respond to the death of a loved one. She argued that Shade was responding to the suicide of Hazel, Kinbote to the death of John Shade, and Nabokov to the death of his father. "The reality of each author is expressed through their masterpieces, motivated by their struggles and questions of death." Another student posited that—

Kinbote is not only making himself the King of Zembla, but also the editor of the poem in order to gain more power on Earth. This is showing the reader that he really [does] not believe in God ... Rather Kinbote uses God as a source for him to gain power over others.

From a queer studies perspective, *Pale Fire* is a problematic novel; Kinbote's homosexuality is conflated with, and often indistinguishable from, madness, hatred of women, and pedophilia. In papers responding to this, some students argue that *Pale Fire* is indeed a homophobic novel, while others assert that Kinbote's homosexuality is an integral component of his insane persona. One student wrote that—

Through his moral upbringing and own personal experience with his brother and pedophilic uncle, Nabokov was left with a sour taste in his mouth. ... So he ... set out to use [homosexuality] as a theme in many of his novels, expressing it as strange and wrong for someone to be or partake in. Whatever his motive, Nabokov's style here presents a case of discrimination.

In contrast, another student argued that together, homosexuality and insanity "create an atmosphere of uneasiness in a creepy way." The student writes:

Not only does [Shade] have to deal with a man that is obsessed and in love with him, but at the same time this man is very unpredictable in what he might do.... This is where the issues of homosexuality and insanity really play an important role with one another. Without the other to back one up, they lose a great amount of effect they have on the reader.... The story needs Kinbote to be unpredictable.

Hashing out these disparate ideas about Nabokov's intentions is an important step in the process of thinking critically about the novel, as homosexuality is a significant and controversial component of the novel's plot. How students react to this is governed in part by their own values, but it is important for them to understand that a novelist may make arguments with which the reader may not be comfortable. As complex as this is for the beginning student, it inevitably leads to an interesting conversation—the homosexuality that has been entertaining the students, as readers, throughout the novel may well reveal a manifestation of the author's own bigotry when unpacked thematically—and what, then, is our obligation in responding to that?

Although we also discuss reader-response, deconstructionalist, Marxist, and formalist criticism, the final approach that students tend to run with is biographical. The danger in writing a biographical paper is that it frequently becomes a regurgitation of facts that doesn't relate to the novel thematically or critically. In the case of *Pale Fire*, many interesting parallels can be drawn between the novel and Vladimir Nabokov's life, specifically the theme of exile, his lepidoptera research, his efforts at critical collaboration, and the circumstances of his family life, particularly his father's accidental assassination. Although it is a well of rich material, students who choose to write a biographical paper about *Pale Fire* are often those who understand the book the least. Rather than doing research on more esoteric critical subjects or generating independent scholarly ideas, they cling to the readily available material at hand. These students merely list the parallels they can find between the novel and Nabokov's life, and they don't explain why Nabokov encoded his life in this fashion, or what it means for the novel that he did so. Some students also take wild guesses but do not present any evidence; one student wrote "Perhaps there is a hidden meaning behind the character King Charles. Maybe, deep down inside Nabokov knew he was homosexual but he didn't want to break his wife's heart." Although, some strong papers and interesting observations arise from a biographical exploration, the most inventive arguments tend to lie elsewhere.

Once we have proceeded through the novel, students have completed their final worksheet, and we've discussed critical strategies, I break the students into small graded discussion groups. In these groups, students are able to share ideas, answer each other's questions, and engage with the novel via the model of synergistic knowledge development (Mu). Based on the quiz grades and my overall sense of each student's comfort level, I assign a facilitator to each group. The facilitators, who tend to be the more dominant students, are in this instance charged with ensuring that each group member has a representative voice, a responsibility that they take seriously in this learning model. I also identify the weakest students, and put one in each group; generally, the remaining students will vary in their facility with the novel. The worksheets ensure that students are prepared before the discussion, and the idea that they are graded on their partici- pation furthers their willingness to contribute. It is during these discussions that students can generate interesting ideas as a group, such as the Canto Four hy- pothesis; students can also express conflicting opinions, still secure in the knowl- edge that no opinion is too outlandish. I give students a simple list of questions and emphasize quality of discussion; groups are welcome to discuss one question for as long as they want. Questions are taken from the final worksheet, which is designed as a launching point for this discussion. If students have any outstand- ing questions about the novel, their groups attempt to answer them. The discus- sion guidelines include such questions as "Is Zembla real?" "What puzzles did the members of your group solve?" "How do you view Kinbote at the end of the novel?" and "What questions does your group still have? Are any of these questions unsolvable?" These discussion groups provide a nice segue into the thesis workshops that follow, allowing students to share and develop ideas communally.

After students have learned about the possible critical approaches to the novel, their assignment is to develop a preliminary thesis to bring to workshop. I give students three criteria for a thesis—it should be clear, arguable, and specific. We review a list of sample *Pale Fire* thesis statements of varying degrees of quality, culled from previous sections of the course as well as from various external sources. I ask where each falls short: Is it too vague? Is it too obvious to be arguable? Is it confusing? We analyze each statement so we can begin to recognize an effective thesis statement as well as what types of arguments can and can't be made in a critical paper. This serves to recap the critical strategies previously discussed—I try to select a wide range of thesis statements that cover each of the strategies. Finally, with twenty plus samples of thesis statements, each with a different critical approach, I hope to demonstrate the near-inexhaus- tible directions in which students can move as they develop their own ideas. After this, the paper progresses in a step-by-step process: outline, bibliography, rough draft, peer evaluation, first draft, a second peer evaluation, and final draft. Throughout the process, students continue to immerse themselves in *Pale Fire*, and the course ends as a sort of literary scavenger hunt, each player following a different, crisscrossing trail to reach his or her own conclusions and present his or her own ideas.

Maurice Couturier says, "in a postmodern novel like *Pale Fire*, the reader does spend a great deal of time hunting for the crown jewels, but he eventually discovers that there are no crown jewels and that the treasure is something else, the text itself." My intent in teaching this novel is first and foremost to convince students to hunt for the crown jewels—that is, the solutions to the many puzzles and riddles that Nabokov presents. Vladimir Nabokov's *Pale Fire* perplexes and eludes even the most advanced readers. It is a labyrinthine Zemblan castle, full of secret doors, hedge mazes, and passageways leading everywhere and nowhere. It subverts its own narrative as it's presented; it has confounded and critically engaged readers for almost fifty years. It is, therefore, an unorthodox choice to attempt to teach to non-English majors in an introductory survey of literature. However, the experiment of teaching *Pale Fire* has developed in the most satisfying way. It is gratifying to find so many students rising to the challenge, developing their ideas, and digging into the novel's multifaceted text with inventiveness and rigor. Over the course of the semester, I invite my students to see the text as Couturier does, as a many-baubled, glittering chest of hidden treasure. These beginning students cannot, in mere weeks, examine every jewel and sift through every gem in Nabokov's inventory. They can, however, bring one or two of their favorites up to the light, squint through their critical loupe, and learn much from them.

END NOTES

1. "In order to be able to make any interpretation of the text, one has ... to make a decision to consciously privilege one reading over the others" (Koskimaa). The reader or student can also, of course, read the book more than once, combining one or two methods; unfortunately, this is impractical when pressed for time.

2. By the end of the foreword, we can already intuit that Kinbote is dropping in these tidbits because he trusts the reader not to believe them; in Kinbote's view the reader will agree that accusations against him form a "tabulation of nonsense" motivated by "the thick venom of envy"; thus Kinbote inadvertently betrays himself.

3. I list the aforementioned symbols and "other" for the intrepid souls who are willing to go out on a limb. Some attempts result in original, excellent work; other attempts fizzle out, which gives me the opportunity to explain the importance of hermeneutic dead ends and blind alleyways.

4. I wait until students have pieced together their case within the text to mention that extratextual evidence supports Kinbote's suicide—in a 1967 interview published in *Wisconsin Studies in Contemporary Literature,* Nabokov said that Kinbote "certainly did" kill himself, "after putting the last touches to his edition of the poem." When I do reveal this to students, it's to demonstrate that not everything in the novel is without a definitive answer—although of course some scholars point out that Kinbote's suicide is not actually in the book, and consider Nabokov's interview noncanonical.

5. I wish to acknowledge the students of English 150, particularly those whose papers and responses are excerpted here—Deanna Bougie, Bobby Covek, Danielle DeGroot, Caitlin Eagan, Elizabeth Gartmann, Christy Gloudemans, Shannon Godfrey, Christy Kuplic, Kevin O'Meara, Steve Petrie, Michael Wallerich, and Jennifer Yerkes.

WORKS CITED

Bookstand (BBC TV program). "Vladimir Nabokov on His Life and Work." Interview with Vladimir Nabokov conducted by Peter Duval-Smith and Christopher Burstall, 1962.

Boyd, Brian. *Nabokov's* Pale Fire*: The Magic of Artistic Discovery.* Princeton, NJ: Princeton University Press, 1999.

Couturier, Maurice. "Nabokov in Postmodernist Land." *Critique: Studies in Contemporary Fiction* 34, no. 4 (Summer 1993): 247–60.

Grossman, Lev. "*Time Magazine*: All-Time 100 Novels." Time.com. 2005. *Time*, Inc. January 4, 2006. http://www.time.com/time/2005/100books/0,24459,pale_fire,00.html.

Isaacs, Neil. "The Riddle of/in *Pale Fire*." *Literature Interpretation Theory* 13 (2002): 317–22.

Koskimaa, Raine. "Digital Literature: From Text to Hypertext and Beyond." University of Jyväskylä. http://www.cc.jyu.fi/~koskimaa/thesis/thesis.shtml (accessed June 15, 2006).

Mu, Shaohua, and Devi R. Gnyawali. "Developing Synergistic Knowledge in Student Groups." *Journal of Higher Education* 74 (2003): 689–711.

Nabokov, Vladimir. *Pale Fire.* New York: Vintage International, 1962.

Naiman, E. NABOKOV-L. University of California at Santa Barbara. http://listserv.ucsb.edu/lsv-cgi-bin/wa?A0=NABOKV-L (accessed June 3, 2006).

Playboy. 1964. "*Playboy* Interview: Vladimir Nabokov—a Candid Conversation with the Artful, Erudite Author of *Lolita*" (conducted by Alvin Toffler) 11, no. 1 (January): 35–45.

Pninian. "Kinbotes of Us All." Writing.Com. Editor. 2001–2006. 21 × 20 Media, Inc. http://www.writing.com/main/view_item/item_id/9216261 (accessed May 14, 2006).

Rosenbaum, Ron. "Pale Fire." *New York Observer*, January 6, 1999.

Wisconsin Studies. "An Interview with Vladimir Nabokov—conducted by Alfred Appel, Jr.," 8, no. 2 (1967): 127–52.

Zalewski, Daniel. "Ghost Story." *New York Times,* March 5, 2000. http://query.nytimes.com/gst/fullpage.html?res=9506E2D91130F936A35750C0A9669C8B63 (accessed August 28, 2007).

Teaching the Dog's Tale: Vere's "moral dilemma involving aught of the tragic" in *Billy Budd*

Peter Kratzke

Whether in high school or college, students face courses designed to orient them to literary analysis. At the core of this orientation are, progressing from reader response to historical appreciation, theme, method, genre, and canon.[1] Because a common teaching approach is to ask students whether they liked the story and then to proceed from this intuitive moment to more formal considerations, part and parcel to today's classroom are theme (beyond its basic plot, what does the story mean? what is it about?), method (how does the author achieve his theme?), and, ultimately, canon (does the story transcend its immediate occasion?). Genre, the third type of criticism and the summation of audience expectations, is more elusive.[2] Still, because it involves relatively stable definitions and traditions, genre is probably the easiest criticism to teach. At first a strange French word, genre snaps into clarity when we remind students that *generic* is the word's adjectival form; generic drugs, for instance, have clear criteria for equivalency, a principle familiar to students when they envision themselves standing in an aisle at Walgreens, comparing ingredients between two boxes of pills. Given this sense of how our expectations are classified into general terms, when an author such as Herman Melville in his *Billy Budd (An Inside Narrative)* is fairly insistent in his sense of genre, we do well to uncover that more lies beneath comedy and tragedy than the laughing or crying so familiar from the classical masks of drama hanging outside school theater departments.

Billy Budd in the classroom works well because the text teaches many aspects of the literary experience. First, students can find the text online (along with synopses, quizzes, and supplementary information) and, with a little guidance, learn that the "search" capability of computers sometimes reveals so much—in this case, about Melville's repeated sense of the tragic. Second, in considering the denotation of *tragedy*, students come not only to a clear sense of genre but an appreciation for semantic edges. Third, Billy's case compels a response at once critical and sympathetic, for students must bring their heads and hearts to reading the novella. Last, I take a somewhat unconventional view of the story that seizes on Billy's peculiar status. As an entry point to estimating the case, a search of canine images provides a reference familiar to students who have experienced "putting down" a beloved pet. Captain Vere's decision to hang Billy is similarly gut-wrenching. We also know that all analogies break at some level: Billy is, after all, not a dog. Regardless, this kind of approach is aimed to make literature matter. Who knows? If we can do that, then maybe some students will join in the feast that is *Moby Dick*.

BILLY BUDD IN THE CLASSROOM AND ON THE COMPUTER

Melville's *Billy Budd* has vexed readers since Raymond Weaver first published it in 1924 (Stern xi). Teachers have not done much better, resorting, for instance, to showing the 1962 film version (starring Peter Ustinov as Vere and Terrence Stamp as Billy). Central to this deceptively simple "inside" story is how to discuss Melville's characterization of Billy, whom the narrator suspiciously praises: Billy is "the Handsome Sailor" (1353),[3] he is "strength and beauty" personified (1345), and he is an un-"citified" man (1362) who "in face showed that humane look of reposeful good nature which the Greek sculptor in some instances gave to his heroic strong man, Hercules" (1360). At the same time, Billy is "in many respects [...] little more than a sort of upright barbarian," a man the narrator likens to Adam "ere the urbane Serpent wriggled himself into his company" (1362). The upshot is that, whatever the image, Billy is innocent. However, Melville ends the novella with a poem he wrote years earlier, "Billy in the Darbies" (Stern viii). The poem, by depicting a dreaming, questioning Billy, retroactively imposes a level of consciousness notably absent from the character who inhabits the preceding book: "But aren't it all sham? [...] The drum roll to grog, and Billy never know?" (1435) This concluding moment is indeed the crux to the whole story.

Melville's text is widely available online, and, although having students hold an "old school" paper-and-binding version in their hands is important, *Billy Budd* is one of those texts that demonstrates the power of "interactive" bullets for comprehension and the "search" function for analysis. By searching "trag" (for "tragedy" or "tragic"), we quickly suspect that Melville has a generic vision pushing his pen: the narrator assures us that the "story in which [Billy] is the main figure is no romance" (1363). However, we should be careful before we equate this "main figure" to a tragic hero. What constitutes the substance of tragedy, in fact, is of a key point to teaching the book in the first place. The evidence accumulates quickly: Vere thinks that the foreboding Nore Mutiny has a "singularly tragical character" (1399), the Surgeon considers the fate of Billy with "an earnest interrogation as to what it was that had resulted in such a tragedy" (1406), and the narrator likens Vere's secrecy of the proceedings "to the policy adopted in those tragedies of the palace which have occurred more than once in the capital founded by Peter the Barbarian" (1408). And, after all is done, the narrator observes that men coveted a piece of the hanging spar "as a piece of the Cross. Ignorant though they were of the secret facts of the tragedy [...] they instinctively felt that Billy was a sort of man as incapable of mutiny as of wilfull murder" (1434). Just what are the "secret facts" of Billy's case and how does his "sort of man" figure are what I see as key questions for the classroom because they demand that students slow down and read carefully. In a world of iPods and video games, that is no easy task.

WHY THE DICTIONARY TRUMPS SPELL-CHECK

To consider *Billy Budd* as tragedy, we must first define the genre, and in that preliminary task the dictionary is the answer and the lesson. A quick glance reveals that, in light of the word's etymology, *tragedy* explores the realm beyond human reason, a realm, from the word's Greek roots, of the *trag(os) oide*, or "goat's song." Anyone who has witnessed a goat's day-to-day habits knows that they can be, in a word, crazy. As it is traditionally enacted in narrative, tragedy dramatizes a hero's encounter with, and ultimate acceptance of, the goat's irrational realm. Acceptance does not, however, mean nihilism, and the tragic hero in his struggles defines the limits, however ambiguous, of his position in the universe. In Melville's vision of tragedy, Edward Rosenberry explains in an essay for *A Companion to Melville Studies* (1986), "the controlling gesture [...] [becomes] the act of penetrating surfaces by stripping away, by digging, by diving. Truth, for Melville, was a tantalizing *raison d'etre*, always hidden and beckoning behind some enigmatic veil [...]" (609). As a result, Rosenberry continues, "Like a victim of some dreadful immune deficiency, Melville had no defenses against failure [...]" (613)—nor, it seems, against tragedy. By writing *Billy Budd*, Melville made a final attempt at overcoming failure.

Although students often feel empty at the book's ending, it is difficult to consider Billy alone as a tragic hero, a diver for truth. More than any other factor in precluding Billy's status as tragic, Billy's sense of choice is less a process of reason than a form of risk aversion. When he sees an afterguardsman punished, Billy "resolved that never through remissness would he make himself liable to such a visitation or do or omit aught that might merit even verbal reproof" (1377). Thereby well trained, Billy is akin to a mascot, and the narrator draws on various domestic animal images to emphasize the point: although Billy's social standing aboard the *Bellipotent* makes him as powerless as "a goldfinch popped into a cage" (1355), the narrator says that in Billy "Noble descent was as evident [...] as in a blood horse" (1361). And, like a horse, "innocence was his blinder" (1395). In contrast, the erudite Vere, whose gray eyes—ambiguously neither bright nor dark—can see the "moral phenomenon" (1385) in the morally guiltless Billy, has different powers of reason and, so, a different heroic potential. It is to Vere's perception of Billy, then, that we must turn.

DEMYSTIFYING THE TIE BETWEEN LOGIC AND LEGALITY

Because tragedy centers on the realm beyond reason, the precise argument of a case—one that ultimately overwhelms the hero—is crucial. Now is the time for a "chalk talk" (that is, a mini-lesson) on logic. Some students have experience with formal logic whereas others only fear it. Narrative examples smooth the waters, and, because students are familiar with the basics of legal procedure and formal logic through television programs (*Law and Order* is virtually its own industry), the classroom moment is perfect for exploiting what they already know and correcting what they already *think* they know—a truly heuristic opportunity. Generally speaking, the starting point of a legal case is considering human actions against an established rule that can be expressed as a mixed hypothetical syllogism. Such a model is a three-part argument comprising a hypothetical major premise (the antecedent and consequent: if P, then Q), a categorical minor premise (the case at hand is confirmed as P), and a categorical conclusion (Q must be implemented to the case at hand).[4] In a nutshell, if a crime occurs, then punishment follows. It all seems so simple, but we also know that abstract logic is one thing while concrete reality is quite another.

When the punishment part of crime and punishment leaves us with a queasy feeling that something is not right, we know, in Oliver Wendell Holmes's famous phrase, that a law's "inarticulate major premise" is to blame.[5] In the rift between our rules and principles (that is, the realities we hope to create by enforcing our rules), we cry foul. Punishing drug users (perpetrators of "victimless crime") is an obvious example: are we really willing to "throw away the key" if, for instance, a drug user's "third strike" is more drug use? Closer to home, students have no trouble grasping this problem that a rule is a rule in reality only as far as we are willing to enforce it. Actions speak louder than words. Classroom attendance policy is an example: will teachers really lower semester grades for an extra missed day? More than a few students have been known to take up the gauntlet on that one. To illustrate this concept still further, I ask students about the difference between the posted speed limit on different roads (campus, residential, freeways) and the realities of driver habits. If, for instance, I were to be ticketed for driving 66 mph in a 65-mph zone (all the while cars rushing by at 75 mph), I might defend myself, "I was only driving at traffic speed" (thus appealing to the principle of public safety). Later, sitting in my car, ticket in hand, I might be forced to mutter about the apparent disjuncture between rules and principles, "Where is the justice?"[6] Envisioning the moment, students can better understand the blindfolded Lady Liberty holding her scales, in the balance (in this interpretation) rules against principles, crimes and punishments against social goals. With that image in mind, students are ready to consider the curious case of Billy Budd, Foretopman.

Billy Budd builds on the rule that if a man kills another man, then the punishment is execution. However, comments the narrator, "In a legal view the apparent victim of the tragedy was he who had sought to victimize a man blameless; and the indisputable deed of the latter, navally regarded, constituted the most heinous of military crimes" (1408). In other words, the guilty Claggart is innocent while the innocent Billy is guilty. Because the social benefit (principle) in executing Billy is thereby unclear, the case becomes difficult. Difficult cases—the kind that make for compelling drama—involve dilemmas that combine hypothetical and disjunctive reasoning. More chalk talk is in order. In their constructive form, dilemmas include a major premise—if P then Q or if R then S; a minor premise—only P or R; and a conclusion—therefore only Q or S (Kelley 290). Fundamental to a dilemma's validity is whether there is complete disjunction between the two premises. For Vere, the apparent premises of his dilemma are that if he acquits Billy (P), then he will override the legal rule against killing (Q); however, if he executes Billy (R), then he will fail to sustain the principle of moral culpability that is integral to justice (S). Neither prospect is satisfying, but he also has no other options by which he might escape "the horns" of his dilemma.

For some readers, what makes the case difficult is exactly *what* rules and principles are applicable to it—military or civilian, wartime or peacetime. Some readers, not knowing "where to stop" in drawing the lines, have focused on what the narrator, in examining the patently evil Claggart, calls "'the space between'" (1382).[7] By this idea, Melville is taken as commenting on the inadequacy of static language (manifest in legal rules) to account for the kaleidoscope of human actions. Other historical examples for the classroom range from the trial and execution of the manifestly insane Charles Guiteau (who assassinated James Garfield) to the "Nuremberg Defense" for Nazi war criminals. Such criticism moves to the issue of legal agency: who writes the rules and what are their principles on which they base those rules? Austin Sarat and Thomas R. Kearns identify this problem in their 1993 essay, "A Journey Through Forgetting: Toward a Jurisprudence of Violence," arguing that legal theorists rarely consider violence as it is integral to the resulting practice of the law:

> There is a deep schism between a jurisprudence of rules and principles, whether traditional or critical, and the practice of legal violence, a schism rarely noted and nowhere bridged. The former is always concerned with law's rhetorical justifications and with the question of whether assent and obedience are warranted, the latter with pain, bloodletting, and the role the pervasiveness of violence plays in the constitution of the legal subject. (265)

Given this schism in the law, the case of *Billy Budd*, in the unequivocal words of Stephen Vizinczey, "fleshes out the grossest, meanest lie in all literature, the lie that a man can love his executioner" (71). On the face of it, Vizinczey's position—expressed in language that hits home with students—is both unnerving and preempts the idea that Billy is a tragic hero. When we further investigate on whom or what Vere casts his sentence, though, the premises of his legal dilemma radically change. Indeed, it is *only* by doing so that the case becomes, in the words of the narrator of the drumhead court, a "moral dilemma involving aught of the tragic" (1409).

THE SCALES OF JUSTICE

Presumed in the rules-versus-principles approach to Vere's dilemma is that Billy is, in fact, a "man" in any conventional sense of the word—again, that "a *man* can love his executioner." In his useful article about the dilemmas informing *Billy Budd*, Lester Hunt summarizes, "the perspective of natural morality is appropriate to beings of a certain sort, while the military perspective is appropriate to beings of another sort" (278). What sort of being Billy might be, exactly, remains unclear, although Melville provides plenty of clues that suggest presuming Billy to be a normal human being might be hasty. The narrator is not long in getting to the clues: in the second paragraph of the novella, he seemingly digresses in recalling a black sailor in Liverpool who was the center of his shipmates' attention. The narrator concludes,

At each spontaneous tribute rendered by the wayfarers to this black pagod of a fellow—the tribute of a pause and stare, and less frequently an exclamation—the motley retinue showed that they took that sort of pride in the evoker of it which the Assyrian priests doubtless showed for their grand sculptured Bull when the faithful prostrated themselves. (1353)

The black sailor, likened at once to an animal and a god, is inscrutable. The narrator begins the third paragraph, "to return [...]" (1354); his transition, however, should not be taken as an apology for digressing but as a continuation of the same topic, thus setting the stage for Billy. Now is the time, especially, for us to help our students read with strict attention to expository detail.

When Billy first appears, there is a quality about him that makes him the *Rights-of-Man*'s "cynosure" (1354)—a word that is, curiously, from the Greek roots *kynos oura*: literally, "dog's tail."[8] The implications are perhaps as semantically coincidental as critically convenient. Billy seems to lead his fellow sailors, but, like a subservient dog, he makes "no demur" to his impressment (1355). Captain Graveling—known as "a respectable man," the narrator emphasizes—"turn[s] a silent reproach at the sailor" (1355), much as would a master when disappointed that his faithful dog obeys someone else. Graveling should not have been surprised: the narrator says, "like the animals [...] [Billy] was, without knowing it, practically a fatalist" (1359). In fact, Lieutenant Ratcliffe calls after Billy (a notably diminutive name) as if calling after a dog: "But where's my beauty?" (1357). And, for some "recondite reason" (1378), the *Bellipotent*'s whole crew follows the Dansker in calling Billy "Baby," a gesture not far in effect from calling him "good boy." In response to these moments of Billy's interaction with others, one cannot help thinking how dogs are now used in American prisons to calm recalcitrant prisoners.

Placed in the *Bellipotent*'s society, Billy is just too friendly to be a normal human being. The critical alternative—to consider Billy as categorically something else—brings the story to where students live. Many will have dogs (or cats), and their relationships with their pets are often their single-most important custodial experiences. They recognize in Billy something familiar from their furry friends. The narrator comments, "of self-consciousness he [Billy] seemed to have little or none, or about as much as we may reasonably impute to a dog of Saint Bernard's breed" (1361). As such, Billy reacts without reason when he is threatened; when he cannot retreat, his only option, like a cornered, wild-eyed animal, is to strike, as he had done, portentously, to Red Whiskers aboard the *Rights-of-Man*. More often, Billy is serenely oblivious to human motivations: in the much-debated soup-spilling scene, Billy does not understand Claggart's unctuous reaction to behavior that is nothing more than "the futile kick of a heifer [...]" (1386). Then, when Billy is approached by the mutinous afterguardsman, the narrator notes that Billy has "an incapacity of plumbly saying *no* to an abrupt proposition not obviously absurd, on the face of it, nor obviously unfriendly, nor iniquitous" (1388). In reaction to the incident, the narrator likens Billy to "a young horse fresh from the pasture suddenly inhaling a vile wiff from some chemical factory [...]" (1390). Dog, heifer, or horse: Melville's use of animal imagery is impossible to ignore.

An important subset of evidence about Billy's animal-like character is his "stutter or even worse" (1362). For Billy, language is a tool of communication but never manipulation, his discourse floating on the denotative level of words. The narrator remarks, "a child's utter innocence is but its blank ignorance, and the innocence more or less wanes as intelligence waxes. But, in Billy Budd, intelligence, *such as it was*, had advanced, while yet his simple-mindedness remained for the most part unaffected" (1393, emphasis added). When Vere calls Billy to face Claggart's accusations of mutiny, Billy's "simple-mindedness" approximates a dog's stream-of-consciousness to its master: "Yes, the Captain, I have always thought, looks kindly upon me. Wonder if he's going to make me his coxswain. I should like that. And maybe now he is going to ask the master-at-arms about me" (1403). During the meeting, Billy, triggered by instinct alone, strikes Claggart dead. Billy's instinct is emphasized when, asked to explain his actions at the drumhead court, he "all at once relinquished the vain endeavor, at the same time turning an appealing glance towards Captain Vere as deeming him his best helper and friend" (1411). When Vere announces his formalist decision, the narrator's use of the double negative alerts us that Billy is not quite human:

[Vere's] utterance [...] caused him [Billy] to turn a wistful interrogative look toward the speaker, a look in its dumb expressiveness not unlike that which a dog of generous breed might turn upon his master seeking in his face some elucidation of a previous gesture ambiguous to the canine intelligence. (1412)

Billy, it is clear by now, is something more ambiguous than a well-trained sailor: in a surreal moment of that ambiguity, when Billy proclaims, "God bless Captain Vere!" it is in "syllables [...] delivered in the clear melody of a singing-bird on the point of launching from the twig [...]" (1426). But, we must emphasize to students, Billy is *not* a bird, dog, or other animal. Rather, he is, in the jargon of postmodernism, *other*.

Placed in the human scales of justice, Billy's status is less of virtue than exemption. Juvenile law offers all sorts of examples for classroom discussion, and students—adolescents themselves—inevitably hold their own opinions. Obviously, Billy is not an adult man in any meaningful sense: the narrator explains that Billy has a "simple nature [that] remain[s] unsophisticated by those moral obliquities which are not in every case incompatible with that manufacturable thing known as respectability" (1361). At the drumhead court, Billy is "non-plussed, evincing a confusion indeed that some observers, such as can readily be imagined, would have construed into involuntary evidence of hidden guilt" (1411). Of course, they would be wrong, for guilt presumes a concern with the past and the future. Lacking that concern, "Not that like children Billy was incapable of conceiving what death really is. No, but he was wholly without irrational fear of it [...]" (1423). Given his simple nature, Billy's death is less an example of martyrdom than what the Purser and the Surgeon call euthanasia. When the Chaplain tries to "impress the young barbarian with ideas of death [,] Billy listened, but less out of awe or reverence perhaps than from a certain natural politeness [...]" (1424). Again, though, Billy is not *just* a barbarian. The Chaplain, feeling "that innocence was even a better thing than religion

wherewith to go to Judgement [...]" (1424), withdraws, but not before kissing
Billy on the cheek. The Chaplain, one might say, could just as well kiss Billy on
the nose. In this light, we almost anticipate that Billy will die more like a dog
given a fatal injection than a man hanged, and, in fact, Billy lacks, unexplain-
ably, any muscular spasm. He seems simply to go to sleep.

If Billy defies legal accountability, what are we to decide of Vere? Although
it may be startling to *consider* (but not, importantly, ultimately to define) Billy as
a sort of *homo caninus*—a dog-man with a canine core and a human body—our
doing so changes the premises of Vere's dilemma and opens the door for meaningful tragedy. Cast in these different terms, Vere's dilemma is that if he acquits
Billy, then he will free a guilty person, but, if he executes Billy, then he will kill
an innocent animal. Vere's decision, however, is foregone: he "vehemently"
exclaims immediately after Billy kills Claggart, "Struck dead by an angel of God!
Yet the angel must hang!" (1406). Beyond the fact that almost every critical
response to *Billy Budd* is some way addresses this line (almost as much as
responses to *Hamlet* address "to be or not to be"), Vere's peremptoriness shows
that the law presumes that human beings like Claggart, no matter how evil, stand
in a category above animals in a moral (and legal) chain of being—a concept perhaps familiar to students through their reading the book of Job or, just as likely,
the argument that slaughtering animals serves a (our) higher purpose, even if the
doomed animals do not understand (muckraking books, such as Eric Schlosser's
Fast Food Nation: The Dark Side of the All-American Meal, might—if the concept
remains unclear—spur industry reform, but they are unlikely to crate a significant
number of vegetarians). At the same time, Billy's ambiguous position between animal and human subverts that presumption, for, observes the narrator, "the con-
demned one suffered less than he who mainly had effected the condemnation
[...]" (1419). Where, we ponder, does the animal stop and the human begin? As
the narrator remarks on the issue of sanity, "Who in the rainbow can draw the line
where the violet tint ends and the orange tint begins?" (1407). Because we cannot
know through logic, the case produces "aught"—a word for which the denotation
is *all* and the connotation *very little*—"of the tragic."

In his struggle to balance the scales of justice, Vere's tragic heroism is
pinned to how he views Billy's ambiguous status. Vere, feeling the ineffable
ache of a dog owner when his best friend may no longer live in human society
and, so, must be "put down," goes to his own death accepting his decision without the "accents of remorse" (1432). By thus seeing Billy's limited but somehow transcendent nature, Vere accepts his own analogous—albeit higher than
Billy's—position in a moral chain of being. No wonder, then, that a critic like
Hunt all but throws up his hands to the "painful cognitive dissonance" (273)
represented in the case: "There are moments when *Billy Budd* resembles nothing
so much as a zen koan: a problem that one feels compelled to solve in spite of a
growing conviction that it has no solution" (293).

Precisely. For our part as teachers of the novella, this same unsolvable quality is its own lesson as we probe diverse readings of the novella.[9] And for our
students, that authority is only relative and that complex cases are not always
resolvable should come as some comfort when they, like Vere, struggle with
their own limitations.

END NOTES

1. Richard Posner neatly formulates these orientations in his *Law and Literature* as the "interpretive, methodological, classificatory, and evaluative" (220).

2. At the heart of genre studies is the distinction between "mode" and "genre." See John T. Shawcross's *Intentionality and the New Traditionalism: Some Liminal Means to Literary Revisionism* (1991). "Mode," Shawcross defines, "implies an authorial attitude toward the content" (16). In contrast, "Genre [. . .] implies the author's craft, not heartfelt emotions and believe [. . .]" (26); "Genre is a sign that makes explicit certain literary conventions, places a work within a literary context, and thus partakes of a semiotic system. It proves a limen into a novel in one area of genre meaning, and another limen into the same novel in such an area as 'tragedy' or comedy,' once we divorce those generic signs from only the play area of green meaning" (55). To be clear, mode is grounded in the author's interpretation of genre at the creative level; mode is a literary work's feeling—its spirit—within the boundaries of genre. In the confluence of genre and mode defining the *process* of the literary experience is the possibility of ambiguous effect. For instance, "tragicomedy" has a tragic mode within the overall genre of comedy. In contrast, genre preexists the author, different genres the summations of audience expectations in terms of narrative dimensions—character, action, setting, and conventions. Ultimately, genres are intellectual, deriving from overall philosophy and/or substantive principles (for example, justice, marriage, closure).

3. For the sake of convenience, references to *Billy Budd* are to the Harrison Hayford and Merton M. Sealts, Jr., edition, as reprinted by the Library of America. All other Melville references are from the *Northwestern-Newberry Edition of the Writings of Melville*, edited by Hayford, Hershel Parker, and G. Thomas Tanselle, as reprinted by the Library of America.

4. A pure hypothetical syllogism is in the form, if P then Q; if Q then R; therefore, if P then R. For a thorough view of logic, see David Kelley's *The Art of Reasoning: Expanded Edition (with Symbolic Logic)*.

5. Cast in these general terms, the case raises issues of law discussed by theorists like Pierre Schlag, who observes in a 1985 article for the *UCLA Law Review*, "Rules [also known as principles] are certain when they are appropriately flexible; standards are open-ended when they are appropriately stable. Once we introduce flexibility in order to achieve certainty, and stability in order to achieve open-endedness, it is hard to know where to stop" (411). In Schlag's estimation, then, valid legal dilemmas dissolve.

6. In her famous 1979 essay, "Melville's Fist: The Execution of *Billy Budd*," Barbara Johnson concludes, "The 'deadly space' or 'difference' that runs through *Billy Budd* is not located *between* knowledge and action, performance and cognition: it is that which, within cognition, functions as an act: it is that which, within action, prevents us from ever knowing whether what we hit coincides with what we understand" (599). Susan Weiner further comments in her 1992 study, *Law in Art: Melville's Major Fiction and Nineteenth-Century American Law*, "In *The Confidence-Man*, Melville reveals how the discourse of power works. In *Billy Budd* he attempts to prevent it from working by interrupting it, by self-consciously calling attention to the 'space between,' that space where decision-making habitually takes place in predetermined ways. By calling attention to that space, Melville tries to undermine the inevitability of the discourse of power" (160).

7. *Lochner v. New York* (1905), cited by Treusch (545). For a more recent critique of the syllogism in legal reasoning, see Richard A. Posner's *Problems in Jurisprudence* (1990). Posner argues that the syllogism, which he calls "the symbol of legal formalism" (107), is essentially interpretive because its premises often remain unconsidered.

8. It is worth noting that Melville's use of canine imagery did not start with *Billy Budd*. In Melville's world, dogs are delicately placed below human beings but above other animals in the order of nature. They are, then, closely allied with, but not equal to, human beings. In *Moby-Dick*, Queequeq, a figure of primitive instincts, awakens in the Spouter-Inn and shakes "himself all over like a Newfoundland dog just from the water [. . .]" (822); the manly Stubb retorts to Ahab that "'I will not tamely be called a dog, sir'" (113); and Ishmael ponders over the sight: "you can hardly regard any creatures of the deep with the same feelings that you do those of the shore. For though some old naturalists have maintained that all creatures of the land are of their kind in the sea; and though taking a broad general view of the thing, this may very well be, yet coming to specialties, where, for example, does the ocean furnish any fish that in disposition answers to the sagacious kindness of the dog?" (1085). In *Benito Cereno*, Melville again uses canine imagery in depicting the credulity of Amasa Delano. Delano shuttles aboard the *Rover*, and only in this small craft's presence does he feel safe. In fact, Melville carefully notes Delano's position in the chain of being: "Captain Delano took to Negroes, not philanthropically, but genially, just as other men to Newfoundland dogs" (716).

9. Dan McCall's Norton Critical Edition (*Melville's Short Novels*) includes fifteen excerpts of readings (thus perfect for classroom approaches), including a view about how homosexuality factors into the novel (Cooke "Homosexuality in *Billy Budd*" 359–61), a negative estimation of Vere (Martin "Is Vere a Hero?" 361–65), and a discussion about why the human law is inadequate to answer the moral absolutes represented in Billy and Claggart (Arendt "Compassion and Goodness" 396–97).

WORKS CITED

Hunt, Lester H. "*Billy Budd*: Melville's Dilemma." *Philosophy and Literature* 26 (2002): 273–95.

Johnson, Barbara. "Melville's Fist: The Execution of *Billy Budd*." *Studies in Romanticism* 18 (1979): 567–99.

Kelley, David. *The Art of Reasoning: Expanded Edition (with Symbolic Logic)*. New York: Norton, 1990.

McCall, Dan. *Melville's Short Novels*. New York: W. W. Norton, 2002.

Melville, Herman. *Pierre, or, The Ambiguities; Israel Potter, His Fifty Years of Exile; The Piazza Tales; The Confidence-Man, His Masquerade, Uncollected Prose, and Billy Budd, Sailor (An Inside Narrative)*. New York: Library of America, 1984.

————. *Redburn, His First Voyage; White Jacket, or the World in a Man-of-War; Moby-Dick, or, The Whale*. New York: Library of America, 1983.

Posner, Richard A. *Law and Literature: A Misunderstood Relation*. Cambridge, MA: Harvard University Press, 1988.

————. *The Problems of Jurisprudence*. Cambridge, MA: Harvard University Press, 1990.

Rosenberry, Edward H. "Melville's Comedy and Tragedy." In *A Companion to Melville Studies,* edited by John Bryant, 603–24. Westport, CT: Greenwood, 1986.

Sarat, Austin, and Thomas R. Kearns. "A Journey Through Forgetting: Toward a Jurisprudence of Violence." In *The Fate of Law*, edited by Austin Sarat and Thomas R. Kearns. Ann Arbor: University of Michigan Press, 1991.

Schlag, Pierre. "Rules and Standards." *UCLA Law Review* 33 (1985): 379–430.

Shawcross, John T. *Intentionality and the New Traditionalism: Some Liminal Means to Literary Revisionism*. University Park: Pennsylvania State University Press, 1991.

Stern, Milton R. "Introduction [and Notes to text]." In *Billy Budd, Sailor: An Inside Narrative*, by Herman Melville, vii–lx. Indianapolis: Bobbs-Merrill, 1975.

Treusch, Paul E. "The Syllogism." In *Readings in Jurisprudence*, edited by Jerome Hall, 539–60. Indianapolis: Bobbs-Merrill, 1938.

Vizinczey, Stephen. "Engineers of a Sham: How Literature Lies About Power." *Harpers* (June 1986): 69–73.

Weiner, Susan. *Law in Art: Melville's Major Fiction and Nineteenth-Century American Law*. New York: Lang, 1992.

USING THE NOVEL TO TEACH MULTICULTURALISM

Using the Novel to Teach Multiculturalism
Michelle Loris

INTRODUCTION

Multiculturalism, though not exclusively an American phenomenon, finds its roots in the Civil Rights Movement of the late 1950s and develops its agenda during the Student Movements of the Vietnam Era. Following the paths of these movements, multiculturalism sought tolerance, inclusivity, and justice for women and racial and ethnic groups in America's educational, business, religious, and political systems.

Within the schools and universities, multicultural education, by demanding representation of these marginalized groups in the curriculum and pedagogy, challenged the American canon and its primarily white, Western, and male authority. Some forty years later the impact of multicultural education is perhaps nowhere more evident than in literary studies, especially American literature, in which the inclusion of multicultural literatures has increased at an unprecedented rate. Another hallmark of change at colleges and universities within the last third of the twentieth century has been the development of women and gender studies and ethnic studies programs or departments and the inclusion of women, African American, and ethnic writers in literary anthologies, curriculum, as well as faculty syllabi and research.

For some educators, the impact of multicultural education in the schools and universities represents positive change and an impetus for continued development. For others, whose understanding of democracy emphasizes more what we have in common than in what makes us different, the aims and assumptions of multicultural education are not so easily celebrated. Yet ethnic and racial diversity is a fact of life in America and it is becoming more so if we consider the U.S. Census Bureau (2000), which reports that approximately 30 percent of the population identifies itself as coming from different racial and ethnic groups not to mention the increasing portion of the population which identifies itself as "mixed."

Despite the lamentations of those who cling to the notion of forming a harmonious "melting pot" in America, enough recent events—consider the post–September 11 rhetoric of patriotism, recent immigration debates, legal and religious debates about Constitutional Amendments to bar gay marriage, and proposed legislation in various states regarding school integration—point to the cultural gaps that continue to exist in America and present us with the challenges facing multicultural education today.

In her recent seminal essay "Multiculturalisms Past, Present, and Future," Marilyn Edelstein tells us that multicultural education "is faced with a number of challenges, many of which entail balancing or integrating two seemingly binary choices":

1. How to teach about multiple cultures without homogenizing them ... or essentializing them.
2. Whether or how to move beyond "the single group studies" model of multicultural education.
3. How to teach classes that achieve our desired outcomes for both white students and students of color.
4. How to explore whiteness as a racial identity without recentering whiteness.
5. How to teach about histories and current practices of racism, oppression ... without ignoring practices of resistance. (15)

I had read Edelstein's essay a few months after having taught a semester-long course titled *Recent Ethnic American Fictions* and I realized that, for better and worse, I had used novels as well as some short works of fiction and contemporary literary theory to engage students in critical thinking, discussing, and writing about some of these "binary choices" as well as literary theory, pedagogy, and the literary canon—all issues germane to multicultural education.

APPROACH TO THE NOVEL

I teach courses mainly in nineteenth- and twentieth-century American novels. When I teach these courses, my focus is to provide students with an understanding and appreciation of the form and aesthetic elements of the novel. My critical approach is mainly New Criticism, but I also give attention to the novel's relationship to its historical and cultural context. I want students to see that literature and social history are related, and so I make an effort to help students understand the historical and cultural context of the novels by presenting a general background of that context and by having students research historical events, social issues, or cultural phenomena referenced in the novels. My assumption is that the novel is both a literary work of art and a representation of human experience, including specific experiences of gender, race, ethnicity, and class. This approach—teaching students to read the novel both as literary art as well as a literary representation of social reality—lends itself to examining the historical, social, and political complexities inherent in any discussion of novels by multicultural writers.

In this course on *Recent Ethnic American Fictions*, I added to my repertoire by introducing students to several concepts from contemporary literary theory. It was my assumption that these different theoretical perspectives would give students the tools to become critical readers, which would then provide them with a deeper understanding of these multicultural novels and their particular cultural contexts. It was not my aim that students should acquire an in-depth expertise with any single theory but rather that they would have enough of an understanding of the general concepts or principles of the different perspectives that would allow them to "use" or "apply" these concepts to their reading of the novels. My work then was to translate sometimes dense and esoteric theoretical material into language that would be accessible to my students.

THEORETICAL APPROACHES

New Criticism

I had students purchase *A Handbook of Critical Approaches to Literature* to learn the theory. This text provides explanation, applications, and examples of the theories and concludes each section with a statement of the limitations of each theoretical approach. I began the theory section of the course with a discussion of New Criticism for three reasons: first, this is the critical approach with which students are most familiar; second, it is the approach they have been taught to use to examine the aesthetic form and style of a novel; and third, this is the main critical approach to which postmodern theories react. I explained to them that New Criticism posits that a great literary text is an objective, autonomous work possessing a central unity and integrity of form and theme and that it is the reader's responsibility to interpret this theme or themes through a close reading of the literary elements of the text. For the follower of New Criticism, theme in the text is paramount, and the more complex, ironic, or ambiguous the themes, the richer the text is in meaning. Meaning, according to a New Critic, is inherent in the text, not in the author's intention, or in the historical context, or in the reader's experience of the work. According to New Criticism, the more a text achieves a coherent unity of form and meaning, the greater the text is valued and the more probable the text will be included in the literary canon of great literature. At this point, I asked students to consider what makes New Criticism both a valuable and a limited critical tool and I asked them to consider what other criteria or ways of reading a novel might be valuable.

Deconstruction

I taught deconstruction next because somewhat like New Criticism, deconstructive theory focuses on a close reading of the literary elements of a text, but quite unlike New Criticism, deconstruction aims to de-center our assumptions about the Western tradition and its literary canon. Deconstruction is impossible to define satisfactorily, but I explained to my students that what is central to understand is deconstruction's skeptical examination of the binary and hierarchical thinking (for example male/female, white/black) that has formed the basis of Western culture and that is represented in language. Deconstruction posits that language is indeterminate and to deconstruct a text is to show how that text undermines binary and hierarchical claims, arguments, or concepts. It is not the intent of deconstruction to dismantle meaning per se in a text; but rather, by employing a careful rhetorical analysis of a text, a deconstructive reading strategy aims to tease apart the claim to unequivocal or dominant meaning and to propose multiple meanings in a text. Such a reading strategy teaches students to examine closely the inconsistencies between what a text may say and what it does, to look at ambiguity and obscurity in a text, or to observe incompatibilities between what may be prominent in a text against what may be more subtle. A deconstructive analysis engages students in an active and critical reading of a novel.

Reading multicultural novels deconstructively challenges and de-centers students' assumptions about gender, racial, or ethnic identity. This critical theory asks students to think about whether identity is a material, objective, essential entity or if it is a social and linguistic construction with many meanings. It engages students in considering how categories of identity are created, used, internalized, or changed. And it pushes them to examine the human consequences of binary and hierarchical modes of thought and language.

Cultural Studies

For students reading multicultural novels, cultural studies forms a good link to reading deconstructively. Like deconstruction, cultural studies is not easy to define. In fact, it is less a unified theory and more a diverse, interdisciplinary set of perspectives and approaches to a text. It combines literary theory, social theory, sociology, popular culture, film and media studies, feminist and gender studies, racial and ethnic studies, postcolonial studies, as well as postmodernism and poststructuralism to its loose federation of thought. But what it is, I tell the students, *is* politically engaged. So, for instance, if deconstruction asks students to examine the linguistic construction of say, "racial identity," cultural studies prods students to interrogate the power structures underlying the linguistic construction that would privilege one race over another. Cultural studies challenges students to investigate the practices of oppression that might prevail against a racial or ethnic group. Its emphasis on the present allows students to examine issues of race, class, gender, and ethnicity in a novel and to relate these issues to existing power structures and social inequities.

New Historicism

I introduced new historicism because it examines the relationship between a text and its social, political, and economic context and because somewhat like cultural studies, it aims to demonstrate how society maintains control or domination over a group through the interaction of power structures within the culture, or through the creation of language that posits what is "natural" or "universal." For new historicists, history and literature are both viewed as texts that tell us stories about a culture's problems, issues, struggles, and hopes. Thus, new historicist critics may interpret a novel within its historical contexts, just as they may understand the social history of a given time period through reading its novels. I also explained that new historicist critics emphasize the importance for self-awareness on the part of the critic so that he or she understands how their reading of a text is influenced by their own assumptions and values. I tell my students that they need to be critically aware of the social and cultural context from which they view the world as they read multicultural novels.

Feminist Theory

While its focus is on critiquing the marginalization and disempowerment of women, feminist theory has been in the vanguard of interrogating issues of power and social inequities related not only to gender and sexuality, but also to race, class, and ethnicity. Feminist literary theory emerges from this model. Feminist literary critics have unearthed, assessed, and promoted women's writing; they have examined the cultural, sexual, and psychological stereotyped roles and images of women in literature; and they have interrogated and expanded a literary canon that was dominated by male writers. Furthermore, in the past half century many approaches have evolved under the general category of feminist literary theory and it now includes such perspectives as Marxist, psychoanalytic, poststructuralist, cultural studies, gender studies, multiculturalisms, and others as well.

By introducing these different critical models, I was attempting to give students the tools they needed to help them analyze the issues of power, dominance, and social inequities embedded in the novels. I was attempting to give them pathways for thinking about the complex issues of racial and ethnic identities, and I was hoping that this critical material would enable students to better understand the historical and cultural contexts of multicultural novels. My aim was to provide my students with basic critical approaches and perspectives that would help move them (and me) beyond our traditional and canonical reading of literature and that would help create for us, as Helen Grice puts it, "a transformation of ourselves as readers and as people in the world beyond the classroom or lecture hall" (6).

PEDAGOGY

Student Background

This fourteen-week course, *Recent Ethnic American Fictions*, was an elective for English majors. Fifteen students enrolled in the course, and fortunate for me, they were top-notch students—Dean's List and members of Sigma Tau Delta, the International English Honor Society. They were typically a homogenized group—white, middle class, mostly (at least nominally) Catholic, approximately twenty years old, and residential students from the suburbs of New England, Long Island, and New Jersey. Before the first class I had e-mailed the students and asked them to prepare, for the first class, a brief introduction of themselves including their racial and ethnic origins and their family history and heritage (at the time I did not know they were all white). I also asked them to include in their presentation some explanation of how they thought their background may have influenced their attitudes, goals, and life perspectives.

At the first class, I found out that their parents and most all of their grandparents had been born in the United States. These students identified themselves as having Irish, Italian, German, or French Canadian or mixed ethnic backgrounds. A few students had one or both grandparents or great-grandparent who had emigrated from Italy, Ireland, Germany, or England. As a group, they seemed generally socially liberal (regarding attitudes about women's roles, gay marriage, immigration regulations, and school integration) and community minded (several had participated in one or more than one of the University's many social service learning opportunities). Some of them said that they had registered for the course because they wanted to learn more about multicultural issues and that the course seemed like it might be a good complement to their minor or second major. Three of them said they thought the course would be useful for graduate school. Two students enrolled because they had electives to fulfill.

Assignments

Blackboard Discussion

Students were required to read all the material and come to each class prepared for discussion. To help facilitate this requirement and to sustain discussion outside of and between class periods, each week I posted one or two questions on the Blackboard discussion board site. The questions were based on that week's reading. Students were asked to respond to a question by formulating and posting at least a five-paragraph essay and to cite the readings to support their responses. In addition, they were to respond briefly to one of their classmate's responses, thereby starting a discussion. This assignment worked well; sometimes a few students became quite engaged in the discussion and posted more than one response to a classmate or carried on an ongoing dialogue with a classmate. I often began the next class by referencing the Blackboard question to initiate discussion in class. One of the themes that began on Blackboard and that continued throughout the semester was the question of the social construction of racial identity.

Class Discussions

At the beginning of the semester I had randomly assigned the students to three-person groups. For weeks two to four of the semester, each student in the group had to be prepared to present and explain at least one of the critical approaches we were studying (this is when the Blackboard discussion on race began and spilled over into class). From weeks five to twelve, as we would discuss the fiction of different ethnic and racial groups, students were required to use a different critical approach, apply it to their reading of the novel or short fiction, and be prepared to discuss their reading and analysis.

As I have already indicated, the first and overriding issue was the question of the creation of racial identity. I had posted on the Blackboard the following quote from *A Handbook of Critical Approaches to Literature* and asked them to consider the implications of this quote and to discuss, too, that if "race" is a construction, then how is "white" not a construction among many other constructed races.

[E]volving identities of racial and ethnic groups have not only claimed a place in the mainstream of American life, but have challenged the very notion of "race," more and more seen by social scientists as a construct invented by whites to assign social status and privilege without scientific relevance. Unlike sex, for which there are x and y chromosomes, race has no genetic markers. (287)

Student responses ranged from Brendan's thoughtful "I had never considered this idea or its implications and what that might mean about me as a white male" to Jared's more defensive or incredulous response "but people have different skin color, types of hair; they even smell different" It was clear from both the Blackboard and the class discussions that the students were being challenged. They had grown up assuming that race was an unchanging biological and permanent fact, and they were further assuming that physical differences in skin color, hair texture, and facial features implied distinct genetic and biological differences. They had grown up assuming "white" to be a colorless, neutral, but "prior" human nature or standard by which other groups were measured.

But as we began to read the fiction of the Italian, Irish, and Jewish American writers, they became aware, from their reading and research, how many of these groups, who are considered "white" now in the twenty-first century, had not been considered "white" in the eighteenth and nineteenth centuries in America. Spurred by the terms "Black Irish" and "Black Wop" from the readings, some students brought in information attempting to explain the origin and use of these terms. The sources of the information were varied (a book, an Internet search, a photo journalism text, and even a clip of Scorcese's film *Gangs of New York*) but what they all were doing was attempting to use various critical concepts to interrogate the social construction of race and ethnicity. They wanted to know: How did the binary between black and white originate, with black assuming all of the negative? By this time we were reading Morrison's "Recitatif" and *Jazz*.

In "Recitatif," Morrison's masterful strategy of never identifying the race of either character but describing each one ambiguously enough so that at times either one might be black or white completely decentered my students' assumptions about race. The students had different opinions about which character was white and which was black, and they came to realize that their opinions were based upon their constructed assumptions about racial identity. They agreed that a deconstructive reading of this text had, as Lindsay put it, "opened them up to the fluidity of identity" and to the stereotyped lens through which they automatically viewed race.

This conversation segued pretty easily to our discussion of *Jazz*. We began with the epigraph. (We began discussion of each novel from a New Critical approach). I explained that epigraphs were often the writer's key to the themes of a novel and so, I asked, what did they make of this epigraph? Nadayne was quick to respond by quoting *Beginning Ethnic American Literatures*: "to signify on somebody or something is to use language in order to change the meanings by which somebody or something knows itself" (89). She explained that "the epigraph was the novel itself: the reader was kept from ever knowing anything definite or predictable and in this way the novel was signifying on the reader." Amy jumped in:

The epigraph suggests the multiple meanings of identity we've been discussing. The "I" can mean more than one thing about a person and those meanings are all tied up with language. For instance, Violet at the beginning of the novel is not the Violet she comes to be at the end of the novel. And we never really know who the narrator is.

Michael, who was a double major in religious studies, having done some research, asserted that the epigraph, taken from The Nag Hammadi poem, was referencing an early Christian gnostic group and he explained that the gnostics were thought of as heretical by the church because they rebelled against the "institutional" church. In this way, he reasoned, Morrison's novel was meant to undermine our stereotypical understanding of African Americans. The group presentations became an elaboration of these class discussions.

Group Presentations

Each group was required to give PowerPoint presentations of an assigned novel using more than one critical approach. Although different critical approaches were used, the groups seemed to focus on the theme of oppression and the resistance to oppression. So, for example, in the student group that was assigned *Jazz*, Jeff attempted a cultural studies approach and presented a clip from Spielberg's *The Amistad* to illustrate how the Middle Passage and slavery had eradicated the African person's sense of identity and humanity and how white people constructed a "slave" identity for Africans who eventually became African Americans and that this was fundamental to understanding the foundation of racism portrayed in Morrison's novel. But we also had to discuss that the film was a fiction, though one based on history, and how that issue should be incorporated into our discussion from a cultural studies perspective. This presentation was followed by Brendan's try at a new historicist approach. He wanted to show how the context of the novel was integral to its meaning about the effects of racism on the formation of relationships between black men and women. He presented a brief history of the Great Migration of blacks to the north, its impact on northern whites' attitudes toward blacks and the St. Louis race riots. He then explicated how these events, and the racism embedded in these events, formed the historical and cultural context that affected Joe, Violet, and Dorcas's lives going back to each of these character's parents.

Similar approaches were taken with the other novels: Chris presented on Louise Erdrich's *Love Medicine*. His discussion was about the consequences of contact with the white man's world on the Native American male. In one part of the presentation, he focused on "The Red Convertible," included a clip of Jimi Hendrix playing "The Star Spangled Banner," and provided a summary from the psychology literature on post-traumatic stress in Native American Vietnam vets. Mike took a different tack and offered an analysis of the Catholic imagery and references in *Love Medicine*. His analysis included a critical examination of Catholicism's contact with early Native Americans and concluded by deconstructing the story "Saint Marie" as a sadistic "allegory" to depict the dynamic of this contact.

Students gave similar presentations on *The House on Mango Street* and *The Woman Warrior*. Amy and Lindsay offered feminist critical approaches to discuss the themes of sexual oppression and abuse; the relation between the individual and her community; the triple oppression of race, gender, and class; and the use of writing for both these authors as a strategy for resistance. One of the most important issues these students brought up was a continuation of our discussion on whether race is essential or constructed. They asked: "What constitutes Chicano/a? Or Asian? Is there only one type? Are all Asian Americans or Chicano/a Americans or African Americans or Native Americans or white Americans the same? What about issues of class? Or mixed races and ethnicities? Or geographical origins? Or origins of tribes?" Their questions about essentializing a group had raised some of the most significant conversations we had had that semester about the multiplicity of identity within a single cultural group. Lauren then gave a New Critical approach analyzing the literary elements and their relation to theme in *The House on Mango Street* and concluded with a discussion of why this novel belongs in the literary canon, which brought us to a class discussion on canon formation.

Discussion of the Literary Canon

Students had not, in previous courses, been much engaged in thinking about the canon. Lindsay said,

This course was the first time I was made to think about the canon. I understand more now how marginalized authors may not be included in the canon because of issues of race and gender and how they may have less access to political and social power. But that means that who gets into the canon is a political issue and not an issue based on literary merit.

Chris added that he was "surprised that with all the advances in society since the 1960s that more changes had not been made in the literary canon." Amy brought up the fact that "by teaching a class on 'Ethnic Fiction' wasn't I in fact contributing to the marginalization of these authors and shouldn't I just include these works in my 'regular' courses?" Brendan said he thought that "reading the works by different multicultural authors by themselves in their own course would give students a chance to gain a deeper knowledge of each group and that he was interested in taking courses on just one group at a time." Jared said he thought that "the mix of groups was good because he had never before thought of 'white identity' as just one of many others, made up by society for different political reasons." But Aisling brought us back to important questions like, "Who decides on this canon? Who makes it up? I don't want to give up writers like Shakespeare but I definitely think Morrison belongs there." The students were dissatisfied that we never able to resolve the issues raised in this discussion.

Cocurricular Activities

Two events—one planned, one not planned—were included in the course. One event was part of the University Lecture Series and it was a talk given by Carrie Dann, Western Shoshone Elder. She spoke on the effects of mining on the land and on the livelihood of indigenous people. We followed up this lecture with a class discussion, to which Brendan brought a series of articles from the *New York Times,* which was covering the same topic. The second event was a planned "Friday Night Dinner and a Movie" at my home, which was held about three weeks before the end of the semester. The movie was *Crash* and had been recommended by Jared early in the semester. The discussion was open ended but covered the issues of power and domination, prejudice, and hate that we had discussed in class throughout the semester. During that evening's conversation, we talked about not only what was being taught in the course but also how it was being taught.

CONFERENCE PRESENTATION

Based on our conversation about pedagogy, three students—Mike, Amy, and Chris—wrote a proposal that was accepted as a panel presentation at the Sigma Tau Delta International Convention. The title of their panel was "Perception and Struggle: Exposing the Ideological and Pedagogical Issues in Ethnic American Fiction." A quote from their proposal states:

[S]tudents gave major group presentations examining the literary qualities, social and cultural context, and political issues embedded in a novel. Because the learning in the class was so equally dependent upon the students and the professor, the class was able to transcend traditional class hierarchies and this experience became a lesson about what we were studying.

CONCLUSION

At our end-of-semester assessment, the students agreed that the course had been demanding and had required them to work twice as hard as they had expected. A few students said that they could not keep up with the pace of the course and accomplish the quality of work they were accustomed to doing. Some students expressed that they had not had a class in which they were responsible to present and discuss the material as much as this class had required. Some students found this style of learning to be enlightening. As Chris described it: "The course never let up; but we never stopped learning something every time." We all agreed that because we covered so much material that we did not cover each topic, novel, or literary theory as much as we would have wanted to do. A few students felt dissatisfied about this aspect of the course. But they all acknowledged that the readings, discussions, and class presentations had "radically opened their thinking," "made them so much more aware," "challenged their way of thinking," and "made them learn much more by teaching it themselves." For these last comments, I was ever so grateful. Had this course "transformed" the way these students would live and work in the world as Grice had proposed? Impossible to know.

But for a semester, reading and thinking about these multicultural novels engaged and challenged the students' assumptions about themselves and the America in which they live. Through their reading, research, and discussion of these multicultural novels, students had been exposed to a course dealing with more than a single group; they had grappled with the questions of identity as an essential or as a constructed quality, as well as with the issue of "essentializing" a single group; they had interrogated the forces of power and domination, of prejudice, and of hate; and they had thought about pedagogy and canon formation. Most important, reading these novels developed in the students a realization of our common humanity with all people, as well as an understanding of and respect for our multicultural society. I like to believe that this course helped my students become more critical readers of the novel and more knowledgeable and empathic human beings.

WORKS CITED

Barreca, Regina, ed. *Don't Tell Mama! The Penguin Book of Italian American Writing.* New York: Penguin Books, 2002.

Bellow, Saul. "Looking For Mr. Green." In *The Norton Anthology of American Literature*, Vol. E, edited by Nina Baym. 6th ed. New York: W. W. Norton, 2003.

Casey, Daniel, and Robert E. Rhodes, eds. *Modern Irish-American Fiction: A Reader*. Syracuse, NY: Syracuse University Press, 1989.

Cisneros, Sandra. *The House on Mango Street*. New York: Vintage Books, 1984.

Edelstein, Marilyn. "Multiculturalisms Past, Present, and Future." *College English* 68 (2005): 14–41.

Erdrich, Louise. *Love Medicine*. New York: HarperCollins Books, 1984.

Grice, Helena, Candida Hepworth, Maria Lauret, and Martin Padget. *Beginning Ethnic American Literatures*. Manchester, United Kingdom: Manchester University Press, 2001.

Guerin, Wilfred, Earle Labor, Lee Morgan, Jeanne Reesman, and John Willingham, eds. *A Handbook of Critical Approaches to Literature*. 5th ed. New York: Oxford University Press, 2005.

Kingston, Maxine Hong. *The Woman Warrior: Memoirs of a Girlhood among Ghosts*. New York: Vintage International, 1975.

Malamud, Bernard. "The Magic Barrel." In *The Norton Anthology of American Literature,* Vol. E, edited by Nina Baym. 6th ed. New York: W. W. Norton, 2003.

Morrison, Toni. *Jazz*. New York: Plume, 1992.

———. "Recitatif." In *The Norton Anthology of American Literature,* Vol. E, edited by Nina Baym. 6th ed. New York: W. W. Norton, 2003.

Roth, Philip. "The Conversion of the Jews." In *The Norton Anthology of American Literature,* Vol. E, edited by Nina Baym. 6th ed. New York: W. W. Norton, 2003.

Teaching Chinua Achebe's Novel *Things Fall Apart* in Survey of English Literature II

Eric Sterling

I teach Chinua Achebe's thought-provoking and poignant Nigerian novel *Things Fall Apart* (first published in 1958) in my English Literature II survey, which covers literature from 1789 to the present. The only text for the course is the second volume of the *Norton Anthology of English Literature*, 7th edition, which contains Achebe's novel. *Things Fall Apart* is a novel about a headstrong and ambitious protagonist, Okonkwo, who strives to be more successful than his father. When an oracle declares that his adopted son, Ikemefuna, must die, he kills the boy himself. He then undergoes a change of fortune when he is exiled for accidentally shooting another man at a funeral and when European missionaries and colonists attempt to assume control of his village, Umuofia, in southeastern Nigeria. This is the only novel that I teach in the course, along with some short stories, poems, nonfiction essays, and plays. It is important for students to study an extensive narrative in any literature survey, particularly because the novel allows the writer to portray characters thoroughly and to manifest character development in a complex way that literature of other genres, such as short stories and poetry, cannot achieve. It would, furthermore, have been impossible for Achebe, in a short story, to manifest in detail the manifold changes in Okonkwo's village during the emergence and the development of the white man's settlement and hegemony. What follows are my thoughts and methodology on teaching Achebe's novel in a sophomore- and junior-level core literary survey designed primarily for non-English majors.

I want my students to know the reason why I choose to teach a novel in class. When introducing *Things Fall Apart* to the class, I ask my students to define the word "novel" so that I can begin discussing the significance of the genre and the inclusion of this genre in the course. Students tend to define a novel as a long story, with a singular, extended plot or several intertwined plots, that contains more depth than a short story and more characters. Students assume that, in a novel, ideas and dialogue will be spelled out more clearly and deliberately than in a condensed and minimalistic form, as in, say, a Raymond Carver short story such as "Cathedral." I also want students to read a novel in a literature survey—a core requirement for non-English majors—because it will be, for many students, the last English course they ever take and thus perhaps the last novel of literary substance they will read. If, however, students have a rewarding and enjoyable experience when reading and discussing *Things Fall Apart*, they probably will decide to read more novels on their own, whether it is another Achebe book such as *Anthills of the Savannah* (1987) or a novel by another author.

Novels are read and taught in stages, as opposed to short stories that are read in one sitting and taught in one class period. I teach *Things Fall Apart* in four class periods (over a two-week period), which allows students to reflect during reading, to anticipate future plot action so that they may understand connections that authors make between different sections of a text, and to analyze in a unique manner. Students can, for instance, stop during a break in Achebe's novel (as in part one, between chapters seven and eight) and question why Okonkwo chooses to accompany the other villagers during the killing of Ikemefuna and why he slays the boy himself.

Readers of a short story often read the literary piece in one sitting; because the works are brief, students do not pause at pivotal junctures within a text, but rather read straight through to the end. As the instructor, I can choose strategically where in the novel I want my students to pause and reflect. During such a break in the text, I can ask students to anticipate what they expect to happen, such as how Nwoye, Ikemefuna's friend and surrogate brother, will respond to his friend's death at the hands of his father, Okonkwo. Anticipation plays a significant role in critical-thinking skills and character analysis. As they read a novel, students can discern different stages of the book's development and thus see writing and reading as a process. Students see how Achebe divided his novel into different segments, such as Okonkwo's life before and after Ikemefuna's death, before and after his accidental killing of Ezeudu's son at Ezeudu's funeral, his life in exile, his return to Umuofia, and his life before and after the coming of the missionaries. These are clear stages of development in the novel. Similarly, when Mark Twain wrote about the life of Huckleberry Finn, he stopped halfway through the novel because he was stuck and was unable to figure out how to continue the book; only after he created the Duke and the Dauphin characters did the book manuscript continue. The book then embarked upon a new stage, one more picaresque than before. Similarly, in each of the aforementioned stages in *Things Fall Apart*, the reader can observe pivotal moments and situations in the life of Okonkwo.

Reading and discussing a novel over a two-week period enables students to comprehend the passing of time, such as the years in the novel in which Okonkwo is banished from Umuofia for committing a female *ochu*—accidentally killing Ezeudu's son; the slaying (*ochu*) is considered female because it is accidental. Students can anticipate the accident, for Achebe foreshadows the slaying in part one, chapter five, when Okonkwo misfires his rusty gun, manifesting that he cannot use it properly. The banishment of Okonkwo, I tell my students, seems real to readers in part because the large size of the novel (compared with a short story) causes students to read the book intermittently over two weeks, so they can imagine the passing of years that the protagonist spends in exile. A great deal of significant action, such as the coming of the first white missionaries to

Umuofia and the maturation of his daughter Ezinma, occurs during Okonkwo's exile in Mbanta as he awaits his return. I mention to my students, by way of contrast, how artificial the passing of time can be in a play. For example, audiences watching William Shakespeare's *The Winter's Tale* must suspend their disbelief as sixteen years pass in between Acts III and IV, while they sit in their seats. Today, those sixteen years occur during a fifteen-minute intermission. Shakespeare is forced to employ an artificial construct—the unconvincing character named Time, who functions as a Chorus; Time tells the audience:

> Impute it not a crime
> To me, or my swift passage, that I slide
> O'er sixteen years and leave the growth untried
> Of that wide gap, since it is in my pow'r
> To o'erthrow law, and in one self-born hour
> To plant and o'erwhelm custom. (IV.i.4–9)

Unable to fill in the passage of time that must consume sixteen years (for Perdita and Florizel to grow up) in a realistic manner while audience members sit in a theater seat in between Acts III and IV, Shakespeare resorts to inserting a character designed merely to explain the artificial and unnatural passing of sixteen years. In Shakespeare's drama—unlike in a novel—time cannot pass normally because of the constraint of theater, and thus the realistic effect is lost when a nonhuman character interrupts the plot to announce the passage of years. Achebe's novel, by virtue of its length and its use of a narrative, avoids such an unrealistic intrusion.

I show my students the value of the novel, how the extended and comprehensive form of the genre is essential and unique to Achebe's narrative. A short story or poem could never paint the picture of the Igbo society as comprehensively as Achebe's novel does. Dan Izevbaye claims that while Achebe's "novel is essentially an account of the Igbo past, it acts as a form of education through which the novelist as teacher might correct current misperceptions of African history and the contemporary status of African culture" (45). To show what has been lost through the terrible destruction of the autonomous, charming, and vibrant society of Umuofia, the reader must initially learn in detail the beauty and pride of the village and its inhabitants. To portray the depth and significance of Okonkwo's fall, the author must first show in detail the rise and success of the hero. As stated in Aristotle's *Poetics* and dramatized in classical Greek tragedy, the greater the status of the tragic hero initially, the greater his fall will be at the conclusion. All this information and detail about the culture, the protagonist, and supporting characters cannot be provided comprehensively in a fifteen-page short story. Only a full-length book can do justice to such a story and to such a worthy and complex protagonist. As the novel concludes, the narrator claims that the prejudiced white district commissioner contemplates the death of Okonkwo and the book he (the commissioner) is writing about his experiences with the Igbo people:

The story of this man [Okonkwo] who had killed a messenger and hanged himself would make interesting reading. One could almost write a whole chapter on him. Perhaps not a whole chapter but a reasonable paragraph, at any rate. There was so much else to include, and one must be firm in cutting out details. He had already chosen the title of the book, after much thought: *The Pacification of the Primitive Tribes of the Lower Niger*." (Achebe 2705–6)

Robert M. Wren correctly notes that "*pacification* and *primitive* are used with great irony at the end of the novel," indicating the district commissioner's dehumanization and misunderstanding of the natives and their rich culture (39, Wren's italics). Here Achebe makes the case for the novel as the appropriate genre for his work. While the prejudiced district commissioner, who fails to appreciate the culture and its people, believes that Okonkwo merits a mere paragraph, Achebe, in contrast, demonstrates via the novel that his heroic protagonist is worthy of an extended, developed narrative—a full-length novel. Thus, the novel as the medium for relating Okonkwo's life story correlates with an understanding and a respect for the Nigerian culture.

A sincere respect for the Nigerian culture is important because virtually all of my students are native Alabamians and thus possess little knowledge of villagers who live in another continent thousands of miles away. Few of my students have ever visited foreign cultures; many, in fact, have never left the South. Therefore, life in the American South is what they know. This absence of knowledge of Africa in American universities is by no means unique. Jeremy Hawthorn observes that "Europeans, Africans and Asians are today generally much more familiar with parts of the culture of the United States than Americans are familiar with European, African or Asian culture" (35). Franco Moretti suggests that the strong familiarity with cultures such the English society, and the lack of knowledge about other cultures such as African society, derives from the power of the novel. The huge success of British novels, for instance, has enabled inhabitants of other cultures to learn a great deal about English society (186–87). Hawthorn adds that "if the novel is significantly the *product* of social change on the national level and cultural influence on the international one, at the same time it becomes one of the most important and powerful *tools* of cultural influence both nationally and internationally" (36, Hawthorn's italics). That is another reason why it is important for American students to read a novel concerning a non-Western culture. I choose to teach Achebe's novel partly to expose my students to literature and culture outside of the Western hemisphere. I want my students to learn about African culture and to confront and challenge stereotypes of Africa and Africans. The questioning of such stereotypes, in fact, partly motivated Chinua Achebe to write *Things Fall Apart*. The introduction to Achebe's novel in the *Norton Anthology* claims that *Things Fall Apart* permanently transformed the landscape of African fiction, both in his own continent

and in the Western imagination. His novels, while steadfastly refusing to sentimentalize their Nigerian subjects, effectively challenged many of the West's entrenched impressions of African life and culture, replacing simplistic stereotypes with portrayals of a complex society still suffering from a legacy of Western colonial oppression. (Abrams 2616)

Disturbed by Western condescending attitudes and patronizing portrayals of African life, Achebe resolved to alter their attitudes about his culture, which constitutes one of the primary reasons why he chose to write his novel in English rather than in his native African language. *Things Fall Apart* serves in part as Achebe's response to British author Joyce Cary's novel *Mister Johnson*, which portrays the Nigerian native protagonist from an outsider's perspective—the view of a Westerner clearly lacking in the appreciation of the people and their customs. Cary's characterization of the protagonist can be considered simplistic, reductive, and condescending—failing to do justice to the complexity of the Nigerian people and the richness and beauty of the culture. *Things Fall Apart* is, unlike Cary's novel, "written with an insider's understanding of the African world and its history, [and] depicts the destruction of an individual, a family, and a culture at the moment of colonial incursion" (Abrams 2616). One way for students to acquire respect for this culture they consider alien is to imagine themselves in the culture, as part of the society. Lisa Zunshine claims,

The cognitive rewards of reading fiction might thus be aligned with the cognitive rewards of pretend play through a shared capacity to stimulate and develop the imagination. It may mean that our enjoyment of fiction is predicated—at least in part—upon our *awareness* of our "trying on" mental states *potentially available* to us but at a given moment *differing* from our own. (17, Zunshine's italics)

This ability to feel a part of the society rather than outside of it allows students to achieve a greater respect for the culture.

Students enjoy reading about foreign cultures, although they are taken aback initially by how alien the Nigerian culture and language seem to be in contrast with their own. They consider Igbo customs weird while taking American customs for granted. When the students express an air of superiority while talking about the Nigerian superstitions, I mention superstitions in our own culture, such as the fear of walking under a ladder, of black cats, of broken mirrors, and of walking on the foul lines during baseball games. I want my students to discern that this alien culture to which they feel superior is actually very much like their own, more so than my students realize or want to believe. When teaching Achebe's novel, I want my students to gain an appreciation of a foreign culture while also gaining insight into their own, seeing their own society through a different and objective lens. When students call the characters uncivilized because the villagers use bags of cowry shells for a bride price, I point out that Western cultures have employed dowries for centuries and that in some societies (perhaps even our own) there is an exchange value—a price—for women. Students express disdain for Uzowulu, the plaintiff in a marital dispute in Achebe's novel, when he tells the judges (the *egwugwu*), "I married her [his wife, Mgbafo] with my money and my yams" (Achebe 2657). When my students use this example to show the primitive nature of the society, I respond by discussing the exchange value of women in a patriarchal culture. I ask students if they know of anyone who has dated or married someone because that person was wealthy. Almost all hands go up. When I ask my students if Anna Nicole Smith truly loved eighty-six-year-old millionaire J. Howard Marshall or married him simply for his money, the connection becomes even more clear. Students agree unanimously that Smith possessed a body that the man found attractive, so she gave up her body to him in exchange for his millions; there was an exchange of a female's body for money or commerce, as in Achebe's novel. When Smith's collection of Marshall's millions upon his demise was contested in court, she protested that she did her wifely duties—in other words, she let him have sex with her, so she felt entitled to his millions. I provide my students with an example of this exchange value: at American weddings, even today, the father of the bride walks his daughter down the aisle and hands her to her new husband; the woman is symbolically being transferred from one man (her father) to another (her husband) in a ritual called "giving away the bride." Thus, my students realize that the exchange value of women between men can exist not only in the Igbo village, but also in the United States.

In addition to gaining an understanding of African culture, my students acquire from the novel a more insightful and objective comprehension of American culture. Deeply immersed in American culture, people take it for granted and assume a natural feeling of superiority about their own way of life, accepting cultural norms and values without question. When my students read about a foreign culture, such as the southeastern Nigerian Igbo, I want them to juxtapose it with their own, to reflect upon their own society freshly and objectively. Students who read about the *egwugwu* judicial council and the bride price of women should learn to respect these cultural practices and to compare them to similar American cultural conventions. I try to strip my students of condescending attitudes toward the Nigerian tribe members and to get them to appreciate this culture that is alien to them. Students initially argue that American culture is far more civilized than Nigerian society and that our culture does not follow such practices, but I incite my students to explore the connection between the two societies. By the end of the discussion, students tend to learn about their own culture and see it from a new and unique perspective.

When students express disgust that the natives eat locusts, saying that such behavior is uncivilized and unlike American customs, I point out that people in the United States eat frog's legs, squid, cows, ostrich, and rabbit—the consumption of which some people in other countries and our own find revolting. I ask my students to define the word "civilized" and ask them to ponder whether they can think of any American customs that the Nigerian tribesmen would consider "uncivilized." We discuss some possibilities. Students realize that some of our customs would, no doubt, seem uncivilized or strange to members of the Igbo villages, such as the husband and wife sharing a home together rather than living in separate abodes, monogamy, and the equality of the sexes. For instance, upon hearing that a married couple in his village has lived as equal partners, Okonkwo demasculates the man, saying, "I did not know that. . . . I thought he was a strong man in his youth" (Achebe 2647). We must respect other cultures if we want them to respect our own and if we want to truly understand them. I then discuss the concept of cultural relativism with my students, urging them to understand and appreciate the Igbo society, to evaluate it according to its own merits rather than judging it by Western standards. I urge my students to accept and respect the different cultural ethos of the Umuofia tribe and to refrain from judging the Igbo people with a condescending air of superiority.

My students comprehend my argument regarding cultural relativism but challenge it nonetheless, saying that cultural relativism is inapplicable in parts of the novel, such as when the natives decide to obey the oracle by murdering the innocent Ikemefuna and when Okonkwo's daughter Ezinma, while suffering from *iba* (a form of malaria), is carried for miles, while she is trying to sleep, because of the customs of the village. My students generally believe in a moral ethos that transcends culture, and they argue convincingly. They believe that despite the demand by the Umuofia oracle, whether it derives from a deity or a human surrogate masquerading as a god, innocent people such as Ikemefuna should not be murdered sacrificially in any culture. My students approve of Okonkwo's friend Obierika for questioning the oracle and refusing to take part in the ritual murder of Ikemefuna; Obierika's troubled thoughts suggest that some members of the tribe are beginning to challenge or reconsider such spiritual beliefs that lead to violence. My students also believe that Ezinma should not be carried around for miles because of the whim of Chielo, a priestess of the god Agbala. Furthermore, they are horrified that twins in Umuofia are murdered simply because of a superstition that claims that they are cursed and not deserving to live. Thus, my students effectively challenge cultural relativism while still learning to respect aspects of the society. Nonetheless, they still view American culture as superior to that of the Nigerian natives.

From *Things Fall Apart*, students here in the Bible Belt gain a new insight into Christianity and missionary work, one that makes them realize the complexity of religion and its potential uses as a means to help or to exploit people. Although most of my students have never lived outside of the Deep South, some have gone on missionary trips to African countries such as Malawi. They built churches and brought food and medicine to the impoverished inhabitants of the country they visited. They have enjoyed these trips, rewarding experiences that have strengthened their faith as they taught villagers about Christ. They consider their missionary trips a calling and God's work. Achebe's novel forces them to confront missionary work from a different perspective, for in the book they see a strong bond between the missionaries' role and British governmental imperialism in Africa. Such students are shocked by the behavior and attitude of Reverend James Smith and the actions of the British governmental officials. Their experiences differ markedly from those of the missionaries in the novel, and they never witnessed such aggressive and imperialistic tendencies. They learn that not all missionaries are as sincere and honest as they are. The class explores the possibility that, in Achebe's novel, the government works in conjunction with the missionaries to exploit the natives. Knowing that the Nigerian natives would act aggressively toward government officials coming in directly to create a white-controlled government with hegemonical authority over the Africans, the government officials might have instead sent over Christian missionaries. These missionaries in the novel, although sincere, perhaps, in their efforts to convert the natives, are being used by the government to allow the natives of Umuofia and other tribes to let their guard down and even donate some land in the Evil Forest (land designated for the tribes' undesirables) so that the government can abruptly seize control of the villages. The missionaries in Achebe's book attract Nigerian followers for their church, dividing the loyalty of the natives, turning the villagers against themselves, and allowing the governmental officials, who seemingly arrive merely to protect the missionaries, to garner complete authority over the villagers. Such a process is complex and takes many months, for the missionaries first need to gain the trust and loyalty of some natives (usually the tribe outcasts such as *osu*) before allowing the government to arrive and assume control. Such a complicated and extensive process could not be described in great deal in a condensed medium such as a short story; thus, Achebe sagaciously employs the novel.

The concept of British imperialism, with its rigid rules and codes of conduct, works well in class when I juxtapose the theme with the idea of freedom and liberty discussed earlier in the semester in the Romantic poetry of William Blake, William Wordsworth, Samuel Taylor Coleridge, and Percy Bysshe Shelley, which begins the course. In the beginning of the semester, we discuss the relationship between British romantic poetry and the French Revolution, emphasizing, in part, the freedom of the individual and the independence that exists within a society. These discussions are significant later in the semester when we contrast such ideas regarding liberty with the restrictions that permeate the British occupation of Umuofia in Achebe's novel.

In class, we break up into groups of five, with each group having a specific assigned task. The groups must discuss a certain theme in the novel; they do not, however, need to reach a consensus. Often the disagreements lead to insightful and provocative discussions. The students in each group must then report to the class, where an in-depth discussion subsequently opens for everyone. I list some discussion questions below:

- Discuss the role of religion in the novel. Is the Igbo religion compatible with Christianity? Please discuss the link between Christians and the British government apparatus. Does Achebe portray Christians favorably, unfavorably, or ambivalently?
- Compare and contrast the *egwugwu* trial and the justice system in the United States. Does the Nigerian judicial system seem fair? Is it as equitable or more equitable than the American system? Do the *egwugwu* make a sagacious and fair judgment in the trial involving Mgbafo and Uzowulu?
- Discuss and analyze the treatment of women in the Igbo society. How are the women treated? Do the women object to the way they are treated? Why or why not? Does the text suggest that there is any hope that females in this society will be treated as equals in the near future?
- Discuss the significance of farming, an occupation that in this Nigerian culture involves more than merely growing crops. Please correlate farming with gender, status, power, and marriage in the Igbo society.
- Discuss the themes of superstition and spirituality in the novel. What roles do superstition and religious faith play in the village in regard to the plot, power, and everyday life in the village?
- Discuss the theme of violence in the village. Does a correlation exist between violence and power? How does the wrestling match that begins the novel foreshadow the violence in the work? What impact does violence have on the Igbo society?

I have found that students perform well in their small groups. Quiet and shy students, who never make comments to the entire class, feel quite comfortable when expressing their opinions to other members of their small groups. Shortly thereafter, they feel more comfortable about speaking to the whole class. Thus, the small groups serve as a stepping stone as I encourage reserved students to participate actively in class.

The aforementioned teaching strategies are an integral part of my teaching of Chinua Achebe's poignant novel, *Things Fall Apart*, in my sophomore- and junior-level survey. Students learn about the novel as a genre. However, these methodologies are designed for more than merely teaching my students about one particular novel; instead, these strategies can be employed by instructors when they teach other works of literature and by students when they read subsequent texts. Critical-thinking skills can be strengthened through the reading of literature, and literature invites students to learn about new cultures. Furthermore, literature can teach students to learn more about themselves and about their own culture. Lisa Zunshine observes that "most narrative works of fiction, including Achebe's *Things Fall Apart*, center on the characters' *reweighing* the truth-value of various cultural and personal beliefs" (60–61, Zunshine's italics). Students are impressed by Obierika when he "reweighs," or questions, the oracle that demands the blood of Ikemefuna. They witness how the character's introspection enables him to think objectively and critically. In contrast, students witness the ramifications of Okonkwo's blind adherence to, and acceptance of, his cultural beliefs; his life moves steadily toward tragedy as soon as he fulfills the oracle's demand by murdering his surrogate son. From this juxtaposition, students see the importance of questioning and challenging aspects of one's own culture, the significance of questioning what they read, and the need to understand one's self, which are integral benefits of studying literature.

WORKS CITED

Achebe, Chinua. *Things Fall Apart*. In *The Norton Anthology of English Literature,* 2 vols., 2617–2706. 7th ed. New York: W. W. Norton, 2000. All quotations from the novel derive from this edition.

Hawthorn, Jeremy. *Studying the Novel*. 5th ed. London: Hodder Arnold, 2005.

"Introduction" to *Things Fall Apart*. In *The Norton Anthology of English Literature,* 2 vols., 2616–17. 7th ed. New York: W. W. Norton, 2000.

Izevbaye, Dan. "The Igbo as Exceptional Colonial Subjects: Fictionalizing an Abnormal Historical Situation." In *Approaches to Teaching Achebe's Things Fall Apart*, 45–51. New York: Modern Language Association of America, 1991.

Lindfors, Bernth, ed. *Approaches to Teaching Achebe's Things Fall Apart*. New York: Modern Language Association of America, 1991.

Moretti, Franco. *Atlas of the European Novel, 1800-1900*. New York: Verso, 1998.

Shakespeare, William. *The Winter's Tale*. In *The Riverside Shakespeare,* edited by G. Blakemore Evans and J. J. M. Tobin. 2nd ed. Boston: Houghton Mifflin, 1997.

Wren, Robert M. "*Things Fall Apart* in Its Time and Place." In *Approaches to Teaching Achebe's Things Fall Apart,* 38–44. New York: Modern Language Association of America, 1991.

Zunshine, Lisa. *Why We Read Fiction: Theory of Mind and the Novel*. Columbus: Ohio State University Press, 2006.

Implicating Knowledge with Practice, Intercultural Communication Education with the Novel

Yuko Kawai

I returned to Japan a few years ago after having experienced teaching intercultural communication in a culturally, ethnically, and racially heterogeneous southwestern university in the United States. In such an environment, it was not difficult to have students discuss their intercultural communication experiences or interview a person with a different cultural background as a class assignment. This, however, is not the case in a Japanese university where I currently teach. In my intercultural communication class, except for a few international students from China, it "appeared" that almost all students had Japanese names, spoke in Japanese, and were racially, ethnically, and culturally similar. When I asked their intercultural communication experiences, it was often the case that a couple of privileged students talked about their experience of traveling and studying abroad. To deal with the different teaching environment, I started to include the novel *Yuhee* written by Lee Yangi, a Korean Japanese author, as a teaching material in my intercultural communication course.[1]

The novel *Yuhee* is an autobiographical novel based on Lee Yangi's experience as a second-generation Korean Japanese who went to study at a university in Korea. It was published in 1988 and awarded in 1989 the 100th Acutagawa Award, one of the most prestigious literary awards in Japan. This is a story of the second-generation Korean Japanese Yuhee's struggle in her "return" to Korea that she has regarded as her "homeland." For Yuhee who was born and grew up in Japan, Korean culture (including the Korean language) is "foreign." She is torn between her desire to feel "at home" and her actual experience in Korea that she finds herself feeling upset, frustrated, and suffocated. She changes her lodging several times trying to find her "home" before she finally finds it in a boarding house run by a widow, *Ajumoni,* and her niece in her mid-thirties, *Onni.*[2] Eventually, however, Yuhee drops out of university and returns to Japan.

Yuhee is a site for practice in which students engage in intercultural communication employing knowledge that they gained in the classroom. By reading the novel, students indirectly experience living in a different cultural environment, which they often think as a "typical" intercultural communication. In addition, Japanese students experience a "direct" intercultural communication with a Korean Japanese author listening to her voice and knowing about what it means to be a person of Korean heritage in Japan. Simultaneously this experience creates an occasion to rethink the ideology of Japanese homogeneity and ultimately interrogate the notions of nation-state, nationality, and ethnicity, which are often seen as natural and self-evident.

Instead of using *Yuhee* in class sessions, I assign a final paper that asks students to read the novel, examine theoretical concepts that they find in the story, and discuss what is important for improved intercultural communication. I use the novel in this way for two reasons. First, to illustrate a certain concept in the classroom, shorter texts such as video clips, newspaper articles, and letters to the editor serve better than the novel that is longer and includes multiple concepts. Although it is possible to use a portion of the novel for explaining each concept, doing so would cut the novel as a whole into pieces and thereby can decontextualize the novel. Consequently, the purpose of listening to a Korean Japanese voice may not be attained. Second, the novel is used best at the end of the semester when students are furnished with a variety of lenses to view intercultural communication. The novel, which deals with a complex intercultural communication situation involving the diasporic, multicultural, and transnational protagonist, requires students to employ multiple concepts to grasp the complexity of intercultural communication. Also, I can assess students' levels of overall understanding of the course with this assignment.

At the end of the fall semester in 2005, I sought feedback from students about the use of a novel for understanding intercultural communication.[3] Incorporating their comments and a few student papers, I discuss the following four issues in this essay. First, the novel as narrative provides "real" communication in which students integrate knowledge and practice by applying theoretical concepts to specific communication situations depicted in the novel. Second, *Yuhee* unfolds in an intricate intercultural communication context, making it a useful material for students to recognize that a theoretical concept is not independent; it needs to be understood in relation to other concepts. Third, *Yuhee* is authored by an ethnic-minority writer, which provides an opportunity to experience an important intercultural communication for Japanese students who live in a seemingly homogenous environment and, consequently, to reexamine Japan and the Japanese. Last, the preceding three points leads to teaching "implicature," an ontological and epistemological principle that stresses the interrelatedness and interdependence in intercultural communication (Dace and McPhail 345–46).

THE NOVEL AS "REAL" COMMUNICATION

The novel is a mediated, imaginary form of communication and thus differs from face-to-face communication in everyday life. In the student comments, however, many students regarded the novel as "real [*ji'sai no*]" communication and claimed that abstract concepts became more understandable through reading the novel. For example, one student commented that "I was able to understand the concepts that I learned when they appear in people's *real* behaviors and thoughts" (14, emphasis added).[4] Another student pointed out that "knowing concepts does not mean that I can explain what is happening in real life situations using them. By reading the novel, which is closer to *real* communication, I learned to use concepts" (29, emphasis added). One student also posited that "I was able to understand concepts more by applying them to a *real* life situation described in the novel" (17, emphasis added).

"Real" means being concrete as opposed to being abstract as argued in the following student comment: "*Yuhee* was like a study guide that explains concepts and theories with concrete examples" (8). The novel is "real" because it provides a quasi experience in which students "feel" and "enact" concepts that they cognitively learned beforehand. In a student comment, it was posited that "the novel makes you feel as if you actually experienced the life in the story. The novel is a great material to enhance your understanding of what you learn in the class because it makes you go beyond thinking about concepts simply in your head" (16). One student also claimed that "I experienced what I could not in my life through reading the novel. Before reading the novel, I was only able to think about concepts in my limited life experience" (18).

Viewing the novel as "real" communication can be explained with the narrative paradigm developed by a communication scholar, Walter Fisher. Fisher defines humans as "*homo narrans*" (6) and the world as made of "a set of stories" (8). Narratives mean "symbolic actions—words and/or deeds—that have sequence and meaning for those who live, create, or interpret them" (2). Fisher's narrative paradigm assumes that humans as storytellers make sense of the world best through narratives. As humans try to understand who we are through telling stories about ourselves and constructing identities, we also make sense of ideas and events and ultimately what the world is through patching up and ordering pieces of our knowledge and experiences that are often fragmented, chaotic, and seem meaningless in isolation.

Referring to the narrative paradigm, it is possible to argue that the novel is "real" to students, because the novel—a form of narration—accords with their epistemological and ontological condition. The novel as narrative organizes a series of events into a meaningful whole using various methods. Abstract concepts become more accessible and comprehensible when they are presented in a narrative form through a stream of events. If the world is composed of stories, the world constructed in the novel is familiar to students. Knowledge that is often taught in nonnarrative forms becomes "alive" when it is practiced in the "real" world.

EXPLORING CONNECTIONS AMONG THEORETICAL CONCEPTS

Yuhee is filled with scenes that can be explained with intercultural communication concepts. Moreover, each concept cannot be discussed alone without referring to other concepts for analyzing intercultural communication in the novel sufficiently. Thus, students learn not only to apply theoretical concepts to communication phenomena in the novel but also to explore connections among concepts that they learn individually in the classroom. For example, one student commented that "reading the novel made me realize that I understood each concept in isolation. But I learned that in fact concepts are interrelated observing intercultural communication in the novel" (4). Another student stated that "I thought I understood the concepts that I learned in the class, but it was difficult when I tried to apply them to the novel.... Sometimes I found two or three concepts in one scene" (15).

The novel depicts Yuhee's culture shock, which is defined as "a relatively short-term feeling of disorientation, of discomfort due to the unfamiliarity of surroundings and the lack of familiar cues in the environment" (Martin and Nakayama 270–71). People attempt to deal with culture shock taking the subsequent three approaches: fight, flight, and cultural adaptation (Ikeda and Cramer 153–56). People who take a fight approach do not appreciate cultural differences: they negatively perceive people, values, and customs in a new cultural context compared with their own cultural values and customs. In the flight approach, they refuse to experience a different culture by avoiding contacts with local people and hesitating to speak the local language. The ultimate action of the flight approach is to take flight from the new, different cultural environment and return to the old, familiar one. While going back and forth from fight to flight approaches or vice versa, they go through cultural adaptation—"the long-term process of adjusting to and finally feeling comfortable in a new environment" (Martin and Nakayama 277)—so that they may come to terms with culture shock.

It is not difficult for students to point out culture shock and the fight and flight approaches in Yuhee's struggle in Korea. Yuhee, however, is a person of Korean descent who "returned" to Korea for the first time. Thus, examining her culture shock is not complete if not considering other concepts such as identity and diaspora. Identities, the meanings of who you are, are constructed through communication with others and influenced by historical, political, economic, and other sociocultural contexts (Martin and Nakayama 151–53). National, ethnic, and racial identities often play a critical role in understanding a diaspora, "a massive migration, often caused by war or famine or persecution, that results in the dispersal of a unified group" (131).

Yuhee's diasporic identity as a Korean in Japan often unsettles her. For example, *Onni* and *Ajumoni* refer to Yuhee as "*zainichi dōhō* [a fellow Korean in Japan]" (Lee 267) or "*kaigai dōhō* [a fellow Korean abroad] (289). Yet they concurrently call her "a foreigner" (338) and "a Japanese" (313). Yuhee's identity as both an "insider" and "outsider" of Korean culture puts her in an ambivalent situation when she deals with culture shock. Yuhee says to *Onni*:

Students in this country [Korea] spit on the floor of cafeteria and litter everywhere. They do not wash hands after using the restroom. They borrow your textbook and return it not feeling apologetic for notes and marks that they wrote with a ballpoint pen on the textbook. People in this country try to rip you off when they know you are a foreigner. They do not say "excuse me" when they step on your foot. They are too loud. They do not know how to be considerate to others. (312)

This statement is a typical example of the fight approach in which Yuhee totalizes Koreans and judges their behaviors only negatively not considering cultural differences. Yuhee's act of fight, however, is more complicated because Yuhee as a person of Korean heritage cannot release cultural stress simply by blaming Korean people and culture. Immediately after complaining about Koreans, "Yuhee was hurt by her own words and looked tormented" (314). The fight approach that Yuhee takes trying to relieve culture shock affects her adversely and increases her feelings of stress. The Koreans that she attacks are the people who she desires to identify herself with: she ends up fighting against "her" people.

Yuhee also flights to deal with her culture shock. Except for writing class papers and preparing for exams, Yuhee rarely studies Korean: her room is filled with Japanese books that were sent to her and she brought from Japan (Lee 296). *Onni* says:

Yuhee's Korean did not improve at all after she came to live in this house. Her Korean pronunciation was as bad as before, and her sentences were grammatically so incorrect that I could not believe that she was a Korean major. [...] I could not help thinking that she did not want to improve her Korean. [...] She did not read Korean novels at all and read Japanese novels all the time. (331)

Yuhee started learning Korean after she enrolled a university in Japan because her Korean father, who lost his business deceived by a Korean in Japan, would not speak Korean at home (288, 341–42). Yuhee studied Korean and came to Korea "to defend her country [*jibun no kuni*] to her father." (341). The language that Yuhee tried hard to master in Japan, however, "sounds just like the explosives of a tear gas bomb—bitter, painful, and exasperating" and turns into "the hateful Korean language" when she is in Korea (334).

Although Yuhee takes flight from the Korean language, the language that she flights to—Japanese—does not offer a shelter that protects her from the "harshness" of the Korean language. Japanese is her first language, but she cannot feel totally comfortable with the Japanese language. Recalling Yuhee, *Ajumoni* says:

Yuhee was a good girl. I came to think it is not good to keep having prejudice against the Japanese. So once I asked Yuhee to teach me Japanese but she said "no." I told her she could earn some money by teaching Japanese. But Yuhee said, "I am sorry but I cannot do that." [...] I did not understand why she felt so bad about teaching Japanese. (Lee 330)

Japanese is the language that *Ajumoni*'s late husband would not speak even though he was able to because he had to learn it under Japan's colonial rule; it is the language that *Ajumoni*'s daughter refused to learn as a foreign language at school because of her grudge against Japanese imperialism in the past (345). Yet Yuhee does not have a choice to reject the Japanese language; she has to keep using it because it is the language with which she can express herself most clearly. Yuhee is wandering between the two languages. Her diasporic identity as a Korean Japanese is almost like an oxymoron that consists of two incongruent and contradictory parts: Korean and Japanese, the colonized and the colonizer.

While examining Yuhee's culture shock, students are constantly reminded of her diasporic condition and identity. Reading the novel, students learn not only to see the concept culture shock in relation to other concepts, such as identity and diaspora, but also to rethink notions of nation, nationality, and ethnicity. Since she is a person of Korean descent, most Japanese students expect that Korean culture is not "foreign" to her. Yuhee, however, experiences a severe culture shock in Korea despite *and* because of her ethnic affiliation with Koreans.

EXPERIENCING INTERCULTURAL COMMUNICATION BEYOND THE NATION-STATE FRAMEWORK

Through reading *Yuhee*, Japanese students experience intercultural communication with a Korean Japanese, which is not easily available in their daily life. Japanese homogeneity has been an influential Japanese nationalist, ideological concept since Japan gave up its colonies after the defeat in World War II and removed its "multiethnic/racial identity" as an empire that colonized Korea, Taiwan, Manchuria, and other parts of Asia and the Pacific (Oguma 339–61). Due to the strong nationalist ideology and assimilation policies based on the ideology, ethnic-minority groups have been suppressed and made invisible in Japan (Ryang 2–7). For example, it was only in the late 1980s that the Japanese government officially recognized the Ainu, the indigenous people of Japan, as an ethnic-minority group (Uemura 11). The number of Japanese citizens of other ethnic descent is unknown because the Japanese government does not keep such official statistics insisting that once naturalized, they are all Japanese (Okamoto 41). Until a local court in Kobe ruled in favor of a naturalized Japanese citizen from Vietnam who tried to recover his/her ethnic name in 1983, people who attempted to naturalize were practically coerced to change ethnic names into Japanese names (Okamoto 86–87).[5]

Koreans are the largest ethnic minority group in Japan. According to the Japanese Immigration Bureau, as of 2005, the number of officially registered foreign residents in Japan was 2,011,555, which is about 1.5 percent of the total Japanese population.[6] The Korean population (598,687), which includes permanent residents and short-term residents who temporally stay in Japan on student or working visa, constitutes 30 percent of the official foreign population in Japan.[7] If naturalized Korean Japanese and children of Japanese and Korean parents are included, however, the number of people with Korean background is estimated to exceed 1 million (Okamoto 76). Koreans have suffered from various forms of prejudice and discrimination during *and* after Japan's colonial rule in employment, education, housing, and other areas (Fields 642–44; Kim). Thus people of Korean descent often use Japanese names in public to avert prejudice and discrimination from Japanese, and the issue of Koreans in Japan is "still considered taboo" in Japanese society (Brasor par. 10).[8] Consequently, not only Koreans but also ethnic-minority groups in general are often invisible in classrooms. I can never be sure whether there are students of Korean descent in my class as long as they use Japanese names; Japanese students are often unaware even when they are in fact interacting with Koreans in Japan.

Yuhee provides Japanese students with an opportunity to listen to a Korean Japanese voice, which is often silenced in face-to-face communication. Experiencing Yuhee's diasporic identity struggle helps students see nation, nationality, and ethnicity from an alternative perspective. One student wrote:

Yuhee is a diasporic Korean. Yuhee cannot call Japan her motherland. [...] Although she came to Korea that she had long regarded as her motherland, she realized that Korea was not her home. [...] I believe, however, that she actually found her homeland. Yuhee says, "I love the Korean language spoken by *Onni* and *Ajumoni*. It was worth staying in this country just to know that there are people who speak Korean like you two. I was in this house, not in this country, but in this house." [...] If you go beyond the notions of nation [*kuni*] and nationality/ethnicity [*minzoku*],[9] you can easily return to your "home." (Kudo 6)

Students need to transcend the nation-state framework and adopt a transnational point of view to fully capture Yuhee's intercultural communication situation. In this student paper, it is understood that motherland or homeland does not have to be a nation-state, because for diasporic people like Yuhee, "the homeland is no longer simply a nation-state" (Drewiecka and Halualani 361). At the same time, the novel describes the difficulty of shaking off the grip of the nation-state framework. While Yuhee says that "I was in this house, not in this country, but in this house" (Lee 323), she cannot completely shed the idea that Korea is "her country" (341). One day Yuhee, being drunk and crying, painfully confesses to *Onni*, "I am a hypocrite. I am a liar. [...] I cannot bring myself to love *uri nara* [my country]" (319–20). Yuhee is confused because she cannot come to terms with the situation in which she cannot fully embrace Korea, which she has long regarded as her country.

Questioning the nation-state framework leads to taking a second look at Japanese homogeneity and what the Japanese mean. Another student claims in his final paper:

As long as we live under the nation-state system, we share a national identity with so many other people in one nation. The differences of such shared identity create cultural differences and thus intercultural communication. [...] For example, if you compare Japanese with Americans, Japanese people share an identity as 'Japanese.' If Japanese people are carefully examined, however, we are so different. You never have a completely identical identity with other people. (Morikane 8)

In the paper, difference within an identity category is recognized: the category Japanese includes so many different Japanese. Debunking the concept of Japanese homogeneity is a first step to make ethnic-minority groups within Japanese society more visible and make the boundary between the Japanese and the "non-Japanese" less rigid. Recognizing ethnic-minority groups in Japan is critical to make intercultural communication more relevant for Japanese students as well as to build a better Japanese society in which difference is respected.

Furthermore, examining intercultural communication beyond the nation-state framework is important particularly in Japan. The framework is susceptible to homogenizing and totalizing people in a nation-state because it presumes that the world consists of nation-states and that national and ethnic identity is corresponding neatly to nation-state borders. Contesting the dominant paradigm of the 1980s in which culture was conceived mostly in terms of the nation-state (Moon 74), a new paradigm has emerged in intercultural communication studies (Collier ix–xi). The new paradigm challenges the assumption of the dominant paradigm based on the nation-state framework by incorporating critical perspectives for understanding culture and communication, problematizing the notion of the nation, and investigating more various cultures in terms of race, ethnicity, transnationality, gender, sexuality, class, and others. Incorporating the new paradigm and exploring a diasporic and transnational communication through *Yuhee* is necessary for teaching intercultural communication in Japan because the dominant paradigm of the 1980s reinforces the ideology of Japanese homogeneity.

CONCLUDING REMARKS: TEACHING "IMPLICATURE" THROUGH THE NOVEL

Experiencing "real" communication with a Korean Japanese and learning the interconnectedness among theoretical concepts, students learn a key concept for building an ethical intercultural relationship, that is, the "implicature" proposed by Dace and McPhail. Implicature refers to an ontological and epistemological principle that "human beings are linguistically, materially, psychologically, and spiritually interrelated and interdependent, or 'implicated' in each other" (345–46). The concept implicature extends the notion of empathy, which has been examined as an important aspect of intercultural communication competence (Broome 235). Traditionally, empathy was understood as a cognitive or affective skill that one uses to reproduce another person's thinking and feeling as accurately as possible (Arnett and Nakagawa 369–70; Broome 236–40). Broome argues that such conceptualization of empathy is not useful for intercultural communication because cultural difference makes it difficult for communicators to predict and replicate each other's thoughts and emotions (236–37). In addition, empathy defined as a "reproductive skill" is based on the assumption that self is completely independent of other (Arnett and Nakagawa 370). Contesting such assumption of the traditional notion of empathy, Dace and McPhail offer an alternative notion of implicature in which people from different racial, ethnic, and cultural background are assumed to be "always interdependent and interrelated" (350).

To create ethical intercultural relationships, it is crucial to view different cultural groups as interdependent and interrelated instead of seeing them as completely separated. Considering Japan's specific context that Koreans in Japan have suffered from assimilation policies, acknowledging their difference is equally important. Doing so based on dualism between Koreans and Japanese, however, obscures the fact that the presence of Koreans in Japan is a consequence or implication of Japan's colonial rule over the Korean Peninsula. Recognizing and respecting Koreans in Japan as an ethnic-minority group is indispensable but not sufficient. Without implicating Japanese with Koreans and vice versa, building an ethical relationship between the two people is unattainable. What is needed is to see Koreans in Japan both different from and interrelated with the Japanese historically, materially, politically, psychologically, and culturally. *Yuhee* is a valuable material to illustrate that Koreans in both Korea and Japan are implicated with the Japanese: Yuhee herself embodies implicature between the two people.

Dace and McPhail's notion of implicature is also applicable when thinking about theory. Theoretical concepts attempt to capture complex phenomena in succinct manners. Actual communication phenomena require multiple concepts to fully grasp its complexity. Condon argues that the novel, which is filled with "ambiguity, nuance, latent meanings, suggested or inferable symbolism" (160), is a good milieu for learning intercultural communication. The novel appears as "real" communication not only because it is narration but also because it represents an ambiguous, nuanced, latent, and suggested human world. In such world, students learn that a concept is connected or implicated with other concepts. By having an opportunity to apply concepts to "real" communication situations in the novel, students realize that knowledge is not separated from practice; the former is implicated with the latter.

Culture, the process of producing and exchanging shared meanings (Hall 2), cannot be detached from communication or "the process of producing new shared meaning out of the interaction of historically given shared meanings and individually created meanings" (Grossberg, Wartella, and Whitney 20). The novel is an entity that participates in the cultural and communicational process. The cultural is simultaneously the communicational, and the novel is both cultural and communicational. Thus, the novel provides rich and important teaching and learning materials for intercultural communication.

END NOTES

1. Koreans in Japan, including both Korean permanent residents and naturalized Japanese citizens of Korean descent, are usually referred to as *zainichi* ("residing-in-Japan"). Norma Fields argues that Koreans who have lived in Japan for decades or were born there do not become "Korean Japanese" because of Japanese society's unwillingness to accept them as Japanese (641). Sonia Ryang claims that under the circumstance, it is difficult to call them "Korean Japanese" (12). In this essay, however, I use the term Korean Japanese for the sake of illuminating the interdependence and interrelatedness of Koreans and Japanese in the protagonist Yuhee's identity, which is also a purpose of using the novel *Yuhee* in my course.

2. *Ajumoni* means "aunt" in Korean and is a polite reference to older women in general. The Korean word *Onni* means "older sister," which is used by a female for referring to an older female.

3. I collected comments from thirty out of thirty-one students who enrolled and attended class until the end of the semester. I translated the comments that were originally written in Japanese.

4. The number shown in parentheses (for example, 14) indicates a number that I randomly assigned for each student comment.

5. Instead of directly prohibiting ethnic names in laws, the Japanese government used various maneuvers to bar naturalization applicants from using ethnic names. Legally limiting *kanji* (Chinese characters) that can be used for name forced especially Koreans and Chinese applicants to change their names. For another example, it was stated in the naturalization application form until 1984 that "your name needs to be appropriate as Japanese" (Okamoto 86).

6. The foreign population only includes those who are documented and do not have Japanese citizenship.

7. The Japan's nationality law adopts the *jus sanguinis* principle in which citizenship is granted only to people who were born to a Japanese parent. Koreans in Japan do not obtain Japanese citizenship unless they do not go through naturalization. See Kashiwazaki for further information about the nationality issues of Koreans in Japan.

8. According to a survey, only 6.4 percent of respondents answered that they always use their real (that is, Korean) names (Okamoto 86).

9. In common Japanese use, the word *minzoku* refers to nation, nationality, ethnicity, and race (Yoshino 25).

WORKS CITED

Arnett, Ronald C., and Gordon Nakagawa. "The Assumptive Roots of Empathic Listening: A Critique." *Communication Education* 32 (1983): 368–78.

Brasor, Philip. "Korean Wave May Help Erode Discrimination." *Japan Times,* June 27, 2004. Lexis-Nexis. http://web.lexis-nexis.com/universe/ (accessed July 31, 2006).

Broome, Benjamin J. "Building Shared Meaning: Implications of a Relational Approach to Empathy for Teaching Intercultural Communication." *Communication Education* 40 (1991): 235–49.

Collier, Mary Jane. "An Introduction." In *Transforming Communication about Culture*, edited by M. J. Collier, xi–xix. Thousand Oaks: Sage, 2001.

Condon, John. "Exploring Intercultural Communication through Literature and Film." *World Englishes* 5 (1986): 153–61.

Dace, Karen Lynnette, and McPhail, Mark Lawrence. "Crossing the Color Line: From Empathy to Implicature in Intercultural Communication." In *Readings in Intercultural Communication*, edited by Judith N. Martin, Thomas K. Nakayama, and Lisa A. Flores, 344–51. 2nd ed. New York: McGraw-Hill, 2001.

Drzewiecka, Jolanta A., and Rona Tamiko Halualani. "The Structural-Cultural Dialectic of Diasporic Politics." *Communication Theory* 12, no. 3 (2002): 340–66.

Fields, Norma. "Beyond Envy, Boredom, and Suffering: Toward an Emancipatory Politics for Resident Koreans and Other Japanese." *Positions* 1, no. 3 (1993): 640–70.

Fisher, Walter R. "Narration as a Human Communication Paradigm: The Case of Public Moral Argument." *Communication Monographs* 51 (1984): 1–22.

Grossberg, Lawrence, Ellen Wartella, and Charles D. Whitney. *Media Making: Mass Media in a Popular Culture*. Thousand Oaks: Sage, 1998.

Hall, Stuart. "Introduction." In *Representation: Cultural Representations and Signifying Practices*, edited by Stuart Hall. London: Sage and Open University, 1997.

Ikeda, Richiko, and Eric. M. Cramer. *Ibunka komyunikēshon nyūmon [Introduction to Intercultural Communication]*. Tokyo: Yūhikaku, 2000.

Japanese Immigration Bureau. "Heisei 17 nen matsu ni okeru gaikokujin torokusha tokei ni tsuite [Registered Foreign Population in 2005]." The Ministry of Justice Web site, May 2006. http://www.moj.go.jp/PRESS/060530-1/060530-1.html (accessed August 12, 2006).

Kashiwazaki, Chikako. "The Politics of Legal Status: The Equation of Nationality with Ethnonational Identity." *Koreans in Japan: Critical Voices from the Margin*, edited by Sonia Ryang, 13–31. Oxon, UK: RoutledgeCurzon, 2000.

Kim, Chan Jong. *Zainichi: Gekidō no hyakunen [Resident Koreans: One Hundred Years of Struggle]*. Tokyo: Asahi Shimbun Sha, 2004.

Kudo, Satsuki. "Kokyō to aidentitī no yoridokoro: Bokoku karuchā sho'ku [A Place for Home and Identity: Culture Shock in 'Motherland']." Unpublished student paper. 2005.

Lee, Yangji. *Yuhee/Nabi Taryung*. Tokyo: Kōdansha, 1997.

Martin, Judith N., and Thomas K. Nakayama. *Intercultural Communication in Contexts*. 2nd ed. New York: McGraw-Hill, 2004.

Moon, Dreama G. "Concepts of 'Culture': Implications for Intercultural Communication Research." *Communication Quarterly* 44, no. 1 (1996): 70–84.

Morikane, Kenji. "Yuhee no naka ni miru aidentitī [Exploring Identity in Yuhee]." Unpublished student paper. 2005.

Oguma, Eiji. *Tan'istu minzoku sin'wa no kigen [The Myth of the Homogenous Nation]*. Tokyo: Sin'yōsha, 1995.

Okamoto, Masataka, ed. *Nihon no minzoku sabetsu [Ethnic/National/Racial Discriminations in Japan]*. Tokyo: Akashi Shoten, 2005.

Ryang, Sonia. "Introduction: Resident Koreans in Japan." *Koreans in Japan: Critical Voices from the Margin*, edited by Sonia Ryang, 1–12. Oxon, United Kingdom: RoutledgeCurzon, 2000.

Uemura, Hideaki. "Ainu." In *Encyclopedia of Contemporary Japanese Culture,* edited by Sandra Buckley, 10–11. London: Routledge, 2002.

Yoshino, Kosaku. *Cultural Nationalism in Contemporary Japan: A Sociological Inquiry*. London: Routledge, 1992.

Teaching Nora Okja Keller's *Comfort Woman* in a Comparative Literature Classroom

Lan Dong

This essay examines how the incorporation of Nora Okja Keller's novel *Comfort Woman* (1997) into a comparative literature class enabled the students to better comprehend the historical phenomenon of "comfort women" as well as its political and critical aftermath. Two issues are usually emphasized in my general education classes offered through the Comparative Literature Program at the University of Massachusetts at Amherst: comparative perspective and cross-cultural context. Keller's novel provides a good example to carry out these goals in teaching. First, the focus on a novel that is written by a contemporary American writer of Korean and German heritage and deals with such a historical and political topic as comfort women helps to facilitate classroom discussion within a comparative framework. We addressed some of the following key questions in class: How does the issue of comfort women become a feminist topic? How does the phenomenon affect Korean Americans' lives and writing? And how does it reflect the history, politics, and economy of Japan and Korea during World War II? What makes Keller's novel a powerful statement of the issue of comfort women when considered along with the testimonies of surviving women of this status? The act of viewing these topics from a comparative perspective aids the students in making connections between history and the present, and between East and West. Second, study of this novel, in which the main characters cross cultural borderlines (Akiko[1] by actual travel and Beccah by her bicultural heritage), cultivates ways of knowing that are germane to understanding issues and problems in a cross-cultural context.

I offered the comparative literature class, entitled "Good Evil, East West," at the University of Massachusetts at Amherst in the spring of 2006. It was a 100-level undergraduate course that fulfills the requirements for general education, diversity, and global education, as well as arts and literature. Among the twenty-five students enrolled (that is, at full capacity), more than half were freshmen without declared majors. The juniors, sophomores, and seniors had such diverse majors as psychology, journalism, political science, premed, communication, sociology, biology, biochemistry, history, and English. The class met twice a week, seventy-five minutes each time. The course was part of the Residential Academic Program (RAP) and was taught in a dormitory lounge on campus. Many of the students were neighbors and friends; they knew each other outside the classroom. This fact proved to be a positive aspect in enhancing students' active participation in discussion in class: they appeared to be comfortable and relaxed enough to speak up more with their pals around than I had witnessed in other classroom contexts. Such social associations seemed to encourage collaboration and teamwork when it came to assignments and research projects.

In this fourteen-week class, I assigned six books, two films, and a list of critical essays as their required reading and viewing. We read Nora Okja Keller's novel *Comfort Women* after discussing two other books: the first was Joy Kogawa's novel *Obasan* (1981), which reflects the Japanese Canadian internment through a young girl's eyes; and the second was Keiji Nakazawa's graphic novel, *Barefoot Gen: A Cartoon Story of Hiroshima* (2004), the first volume of his autobiographical series on the atomic bombing in Hiroshima, Japan, in 1945. Turning to Keller's work after reading two texts on World War II established from the outset the complexity of war as it is reflected in literature, portraying the nuances inherent in the notions of "good" and "evil." Contextualizing Keller's novel in terms of Kogawa's book, both of which reveal the experiences of people of Asian heritage in North America, led the students to reconsider their understanding of "East" and "West."

"Comfort women" is a euphemistic term used by the Japanese Imperial Army to refer to women who were forced to provide sexual services to Japanese officers and soldiers in "comfort houses" or "comfort stations" during World War II (Sancho iii). Even though the terminology of comfort women has been considered an ironic misnomer,[2] I use it in this essay to follow the conventional usage. The Japanese-enforced military sexual slavery during their occupation of Asia in World War II was not discussed publicly until the 1980s.[3] Before Keller published her debut novel *Comfort Woman* in 1997, the stories regarding the experiences of these victims of rape and military sexual slavery were for the most part survivors' testimonies.[4] In her interview with Robert Birnbaum, Keller reveals:

While I was working on the novel [*Comfort Woman*], I'd type in "comfort women" into search engine and come up with Martha Stewart articles about how to make the home more comfortable. When I came back from my book tour I could find actual articles about comfort women and my book ... as for me, it was incredible to be tied into that whole history and growing awareness. (Birnbaum)

In this sense, Keller's book holds a particular position not only in its representation of the experiences of comfort women in a different genre than "life story," but also in its education of people about that particular period of history through literature.

When I introduced *Comfort Woman* to the students, I emphasize that Keller's novel is not only a literary reflection of this little-known war crime against women in the form of fiction, but also a portrayal of the issues of survival, migration, and mother–daughter relationships. The story unfolds through the narrative of Akiko (a former comfort woman who later married a Caucasian

American missionary and migrated to the United States after the war) and her American-born daughter Beccah who grows up in Hawaii. For her part, Keller maintains that "it's not just a story about one woman's experience in the camps ... but it's also about how that woman goes on to live with it" (cited in Noguera). The chapters in the novel *Comfort Woman* are alternating narrations by the mother and the daughter, thus providing two perspectives that link their American life in the present with the mother's past in Korea. Because of its complex and comprehensive way of revisiting history through personal narratives, Keller's novel can be taught as a cultural vehicle for the class to explore such broad range of issues as the historical crime against comfort women; this crime's impact on those women and their families; the survivors' struggle to live with the trauma postwar; and their efforts since the 1980s to win justice and official apologies from the Japanese government.

To help the students to achieve a comprehensive view of the topic, I also assigned critical reading related to Keller's novel: Kandice Chuh's "Guest Editor's Introduction: On Korean 'Comfort Women'" (2003) and Laura Hyun Yi Kang's article "Conjuring 'Comfort Women': Mediated Affiliations and Disciplined Subjects in Korean/American Transnationality" (2003). In addition, I incorporated into my lectures excerpts from the collection edited by Clark Chilson and Peter Knecht—*Shamans in Asia* (2003) as well as Chunghee Sarah Soh's article "Women's Sexual Labor and State in Korean History" (2004), so that the students were exposed to a broader range of cultural contexts that were addressed in Keller's novel.

We spent two weeks (four class meetings) on *Comfort Woman*: the first two class meetings focused solely on the text itself and the second week concentrated on critical reading along with historical and political background on the phenomenon of comfort women. I started out by introducing the topic of comfort women as a historical event in the first class when the students finished reading about half of the novel. It is not clear when the first Japanese military-run comfort station was set up nor the exact number of comfort women involved. Nevertheless, it is known that such military brothels were established in Shanghai, China, no later than 1932. It is estimated that 100,000 to 200,000 women from Korea, China, the Philippines, Indonesia, and Malaysia were recruited or kidnapped to serve in comfort stations or comfort camps during the Pacific War. More than 80 percent of these women were Korean. It was not until the late 1980s that the topic of comfort women was brought to the public attention, mainly through survivors' testimonies and human right groups' activities. In the 1990s, some Korean and Filipina comfort women survivors sued the Japanese government, requesting official apologies and compensation for the war crimes against them.[5]

In the class, I then moved on to make connections between the author and the event: namely, what Keller's background is as a writer, how she came to the idea of writing this novel, what responses her book has received, and what position her novel holds among the growing awareness about the notion of comfort women in the United States. When introducing the author to the class, I emphasized her ethnicity—an American-born daughter of a German father and a Korean mother—as well as the environment in which she grew up, that of Hawaii. Like most of the readers of her novel, Keller was unaware of the existence of comfort women until 1993 when she heard a confession by a survivor. At the time, she was deeply moved by the appalling testimony of this former comfort woman. Keller was then inspired to write a short story about a mother who used to be a comfort woman and her daughter, which later became a chapter of her novel (Noguera). The novel *Comfort Woman* has been well received and widely taught in colleges after its publication. It has educated readers on the hidden aspect of World War II and the brutal crime against women.

After such informative reviews delivered by my lecture, we spent the rest of the class going around the classroom to share our reading experiences. A number of students reported that they were so touched by Keller's story that they could not put the book down until they finished reading it, even though the reading assignment for that class was only the first half of the book. Despite the diverse aspects that the students' remarks touched on, their responses to Keller's novel mostly addressed the following issues: the striking surprise they felt when being informed about comfort women, the unique structure of the narrative, the "dark" moments of the comfort women's lives in the entertainment camps described metaphorically and vividly in the book, and the confusion about Akiko's trance and the spirits to which she frequently refers. For the most part, I encouraged the students to respond to each other's questions and comments while I played the role of a monitor. When there were questions or matters that the students had difficulty in understanding, I stepped in and gave explanatory answers.

For example, for the questions regarding shamanism in Asian culture, I introduced some basic ideas regarding shamans and shamanism as well as read excerpts from the collection *Shamans in Asia* to help the students better understand Akiko's trance and fortunetelling business in the novel. In introducing this collection on Asian shamanism to the students, I emphasized two concepts. The first is that shamanism differs from a world religion, because it is not "an established system of ideas, beliefs, and rituals in its own right that can be found wherever shamanistic religion is found" (Knecht 4). Shamanism has no definite form and therefore can respond to various cultural and social circumstances (Knecht 24). Second, an innate connection exists between shamans and trances. A shaman usually has the ability to fall into "a controlled state of ecstatic trance and to visit during a trance state the worlds of spirits" (Knecht 3). In this sense, a shaman deals with spirits in various ways as a mediator between humans and spirits, and is instrumental in maintaining or restoring the order of a society's cosmos (Knecht 18). In Keller's novel, Akiko plays the role of a shaman when she enters states of trance. She is considered specially gifted because of her ability to go into trances and therefore to visit the world of spirits. That is why other people who believe in spirits turn to her to communicate with their deceased ancestors, relatives, and friends.

For the next class meeting, I prepared a list of topics for the students to discuss, first in small groups and then with the whole class. Now that all students presumably had finished reading the novel, there was a more detailed discussion regarding the book itself. The following is the question list that I used:[6]

• Do you think Akiko is "crazy?" Do you think she possesses special powers? Do you think there is a connection between the psychological trauma that Akiko suffered as a result of her experiences as a comfort woman and her ability to communicate with spirits?

- In the novel, there seems to be much tension between Akiko and Beccah. How is theirs a typical mother–daughter relationship? How are the normal conflicts that flare up between mothers and their, especially adolescent, daughters made more complicated in Akiko and Beccah's case? Why do you think that Akiko keeps the truth about her past a secret from Beccah? How did this secret affect their relationship? How might it have changed their relationship had Akiko revealed the secret to Beccah while she was alive?
- Why do you think that in America the mother uses the Japanese name that was assigned to her in the army camp—"Akiko"—instead of reclaiming her Korean name, "Soon Hyo?" What is significant about the fact that the reader does not learn of her Korean name until close to the end of the novel?
- Discuss the character of Auntie Reno. What role does she play in Akiko and Beccah's lives? Is she a real friend to Akiko and Beccah? Does she take advantage of Akiko's vulnerability? And, what does she teach Beccah about her mother?
- What's your understanding of the alternating narrative voices in the novel? Why do you think that Keller chose to structure her book this way? What are the advantages for the reader to know Akiko's story before Beccah learns it? After you finish reading the novel, whom do you feel you get to know better: Beccah or Akiko?

As the students pointed out in the discussion, "craziness" is a much more complicated matter than insanity in Keller's novel. Particularly through the characters of Induk and Akiko, craziness is shown to be associated with trauma, disorientation in another culture, shamanism, and misunderstanding or lack of understanding of the "other" culture. Induk is a comfort woman in the camp who is assigned the name "Akiko" and is executed brutally by the Japanese soldiers. After her death, teenaged Soon Hyo, who is a servant girl to the comfort women at the time, is forced to take her place: her stall, her clothes, and her name. The image of a crazy Induk, in various transformations, haunts Akiko throughout the story. One of the students remarked on the connection between Akiko's special capability to be a mediator between humans and spirits and her post-traumatic stress disorder. To support his argument, he quotes from the novel. Toward the end of the book, Aunt Reno explains to Beccah that her mother is gifted: "She would look into a person's heart and know 'em—their heartache, their weakness, whatevah. Because she knew suffahrin' like I no can even imagine" (Keller 203). Reno goes on: "Your maddah was one survivah. Das how come she can read other people. Das how come she can see their wishes and their fears. Das how come she can travel out of dis world into hell, cause she already been there and back and know the way" (Keller 203). In Reno's understanding, Akiko's special "gift" comes from her traumatic experiences.

Akiko does not reveal her past to Beccah when she is alive. After she passes away, Beccah finds out the truth from a tape of songs that Akiko leaves behind. Beccah, in mourning and solitude in her mother's apartment, hears her mother singing on the tape:

Our brothers and fathers conscripted. The women left to be picked over like fruit to be tasted, consumed, the pits spit out as Chongshindae, where we rotted under the body of orders from the Emperor of Japan. Under the Emperor's orders, we were beaten and starved. Under Emperor's orders, the holes of our bodies were used to bury their excrement. Under Emperor's orders, we were bled again and again until we were thrown into a pit and burned, the ash from our thrashing arms dusting the surface of the river in which we had sometimes been allowed to bathe. Under Emperor's orders, we could not prepare those in the river for the journey out of hell. (Keller 193)

Upon hearing the appalling truth of her mother's experience, Beccah tells the reader: "I could not view my mother, whom I had always seen as weak and vulnerable, as one of the 'comfort women' she described ... I could not imagine her surviving what she described, for I cannot imagine myself surviving" (Keller 194).

With her father passing away when she was five, Beccah is raised by her mother single-handedly. From Beccah's perspective, it is a bittersweet relationship. On the one hand, Beccah loves her mother dearly. Her habit from childhood days shows this affection clearly. Before eating, she usually sets aside a small mount of food as a sacrifice for the spirits or God and prays: "Please, God—please, spirits and Induk—please, Daddy and whoever is listening: Leave my mother alone" (Keller 3). She also loves her mother during the normal times: while Akiko sings, laughs, tells stories, plays with her, or simply watches her doing her homework with her loving motherly eyes. But "when the spirits called to her, my mother would leave me and slip inside herself, to somewhere I could not and did not want to follow. It was as if the mother I knew turned off, checked out, and someone else came to rent the space" (Keller 4). During her mother's spells, Beccah locks Akiko inside their apartment in fear that someone might know and lock her mother up on grounds of insanity until Reno finds out about it and turns it into a fortunetelling business. Conversely, as a teenager, Beccah sometimes wishes her mother dead or being taken away when Akiko is "in her spell." It is embarrassing to have a crazy mother who does bizarre things, especially in front of her peers. After losing her mother, Beccah realizes "it has taken me nearly thirty years, almost all of my life, but finally the wishes I flung out in childhood have come true ... My mother is dead" (Keller 13).

A female student pointed out that there is love yet also tension between the rebellious adolescent daughter and the overprotective mother. Since early childhood, Beccah has to learn how to care for herself and her mother when Akiko is "out" in the world of the spirits. Young as she is, Beccah sometimes has to shoulder the responsibility to run the household and to protect her mother from being taken away as a mentally ill patient. In this sense, most female students in my class, as readers and daughters, have a lot of sympathy for the daughter's character. One female student says she is disturbed by the fact that Akiko kept her past a secret from Beccah when she was alive. The student remarks that even though she understands Akiko's intention is probably out of shame and protection, she still feels sorry for Beccah. From a daughter's perspective, the student thought that if Akiko had revealed her trauma earlier, Beccah might have felt closer to her mother, there might have been more understanding between the two, and then Beccah possibly would have felt less guilty when her mother past away.

Among the other characters included in the novel *Comfort Woman*, Aunt Reno, a family friend, seems to be the closest to Akiko and Beccah. Reno is a successful businesswoman who has a shrewd vision for business opportunities. Her management turns Akiko's trances into a practical avenue by which Akiko and Beccah can make a living as well as a profitable business for Reno herself.

Most students agree that the character of Reno is not portrayed as a real friend to Akiko and Beccah in the novel, but still it is Reno who helps them out of poverty. Akiko works as fry cook and clean-up girl at Reno's Waikiki Bar-B-Q Hut after drifting in and out of odd jobs. She is allowed to bring home leftovers from the daily special. Beccah admits: "Auntie Reno, who isn't a blood relative, was good to us in that way: she always made sure we had enough to eat" (Keller 3). Maybe that is why Akiko seems to be aware of Reno's manipulations when she is in trance, but she never says anything against Reno being her agent.

In terms of the structure of the novel, there are differing opinions in the class. One group of students thought of the novel's organization as a highlight of Keller's work. In their view, the alternating narratives by the mother and daughter provide two distinct points of view that connect the past with the present, while unveiling a touching story and a tormented soul. The juxtaposition of the two narratives also shows Keller's talent as a young writer and the complexity in her writing technique. Nevertheless, another group of students acknowledged that they disliked the organization of Keller's novel. One student stated that she identified with some aspects of the daughter's life, but she was troubled by the fact that the narrative makes it impossible to construct a linear storyline. Another student said that since the narratives alternate between the mother and the daughter, the borderline between the past and the present is blurred. Consequentially, the structure sometimes made his reading experience confusing and frustrating.

For the third class on *Comfort Woman*, the students were required to read two essays: Kandice Chuh's "Guest Editor's Introduction" to the special issue of the *Journal of Asian American Studies* (vol. 6, no. 1) published in February 2003 as well as Laura Hyun Yi Kang's article, "Conjuring 'Comfort Women': Mediated Affiliations and Disciplined Subjects in Korean/American Transnationality," published in the same issue. Both pieces are related to Keller's novel; yet they address the issue of comfort women in a broader range than the literary representation. Chuh's introduction is helpful for the students to be aware of several concepts regarding the topic of comfort women. In introducing the articles in the special issue, Chuh contends that "these essays call critical attention to the signifying and material work of various representations of 'comfort women' in multiple discursive fields—the academic, the cultural, the literary, the judicial, and always, the political" (1). Short as it is, Chuh's introduction points out to students a few important guidelines in reading Keller's novel with a critical view. First, the issue of comfort women involves women from various regions besides Korea. Second, this particular phenomenon reflects not only history but also politics, colonialism, modernization, national identity, globalization, and others. Third, the existence of Korean comfort women, as a historical event, has profound influence on Korean American literature and media productions among which Keller's book is a perfect example. There is a potential advantage of this reading assignment for an undergraduate audience in a lower-level literature class: Chuh's introduction is brief while still being informative and thus accessible to students.

Kang's article provides useful insight in understanding Korean the phenomenon of comfort women as well as its contemporary representations in literature and media, although a number of students are bothered by its length as well as its critical jargon. Upon hearing the students' complaints, I tried to guide their discussion on Kang's article to focus on a few highlights. First, according to Kang, the issue of comfort women is interdisciplinary and transnational by nature. I encouraged the students to think about how Keller reflects such interdisciplinary and transnational features in her novel. Next, as Kang points out, there have been representations of comfort women in various genres in the United States, mostly by Korean American writers and artists. In those works, the subject, "we," has been used repeatedly. Kang emphasizes the question of identification—that is, how Korean Americans identify with such war victims as comfort women and how they show "an intimate connection" in representing these women's experiences. I asked the students to use Keller's book as one such example and to find examples that reveal such "intimate connection." Furthermore, Kang's article questions the problematic "silence": more often than not, Korean American literature and media productions portray surviving comfort women as voiceless (31). Consequently, Korean Americans present their works as an effort to "break the silence." Nonetheless, these works are usually inspired by the oral testimonies of the survivors. Keller's novel is one such example.

After spending the first half of the class addressing students' questions regarding the two essays and letting them share their comments, we moved on to discuss the two essays in detail and to revisit Keller's novel as a case study of comfort women. To lead the class discussion toward reading the novel more critically as well as comparatively, I gave the students the following list of questions:

- How much did you know about comfort women before reading Keller's novel? How much do you feel that you have learned from her book? What does Keller's novel let us know about the experiences of military comfort women during World War II?
- How much do you feel that you have learned about comfort women in terms of the related political and social issues that are discussed in Kandice Chuh's introduction and Lauren Hyun Yi Kang's article?
- How does the mother's life story reflect the history of Korea and Japan? Is she a victim because Korea was a country lower in economic and political status than Japan at the time?
- How does the issue of comfort women become used as a feminist issue?
- How does the issue of Korean comfort women become a Korean American issue?

For the last class meeting on the novel *Comfort Woman*, I assigned the following homework to my students: before class, find a creative or critical piece related to the topic of comfort women—an article, a film, a Web site, an excerpt from a book, an art work, or any other text—and review it and take notes; then discuss the piece and your review of it in class. At the beginning of the class, I asked the students to go around the classroom and use two or three sentences to describe briefly what they had researched and brought to the class for discussion. Then they split into groups according to the subjects. For example, students who searched for other literary or media representations of comfort women stayed in one group; another group focused on the historical information on the topic of comfort women; a third group shared an emphasis on the redress movement of survivors in the 1990s. After exchanging ideas, each group chose a student representative to report their discussion and findings to the whole class. In this way, every student had a chance to speak up and present his or her research; at the same time, the whole class was exposed to a broad range of aspects and information on this subject matter. This method introduced them to a wide-ranging context related to Keller's novel. Some students later told me that they enjoyed doing this assignment and felt encouraged and motivated to participate in such a learning experience.

Thus, in such an interdisciplinary course, in which the historical event comfort women is explored from a variety of perspectives—that is, literary, historical, sociological, political, humanistic, and others—Keller's novel enabled students to perceive why and how it is important to read novels with a critical view as well as from a comparative and cross-cultural perspective. Students in my class bring into the discussion such comparisons as the economic and political situations of Korea and Japan in the 1940s, Akiko's life in Korea and in America, the character of Akiko and the rape victim in contemporary American society, contextualization of Keller's novel and other works we read in class (for instance, *Obasan*, *Barefoot Gen*, and Art Spiegelman's *Maus A Survivor's Tale*), to name only a few. Through reading Keller's novel in a cross-cultural context, the students were inspired and encouraged to research the issue of comfort women in relation to such fields as history, international relations, politics, Asian shamanism, and the judicial process. Despite the sophistication it demands of readers, the novel helped to introduce important concepts and issues that are related to or revealed by the topic of comfort women. Moreover, I observed that the concurrence of a primary text (the novel) and criticism (the essays) enabled the students to learn to read and think more critically than I have witnessed in my other classes in which students read only a primary text.

END NOTES

1. The mother's Korean name is Soon Hyo. She is assigned the Japanese name of Akiko in the "comfort camp" that she continues to use in America. In this essay, I use "Akiko" to identify the mother character in Keller's novel, unless otherwise specified.

2. For example, Laura Hyun Yi Kang (2003) and Chunghee Sarah Soh (2004) have questioned the term of "comfort women" in their respective articles.

3. Chin-sung Chung's article, "An Overview of the Colonial and Socio-Economic Background of Japanese Military Sex Slavery in Korea" outlines the system of Japanese military sex slavery in Korea. Also see Stetz and Oh (2001), and the special issue (vol. 5, no. 1, 1997) of *Position: East Asia Cultures Critique*, focusing on "comfort women."

4. For such testimonial documents, see Howard 1995, Kim-Gibson 1999, and Henson 1999.

5. For more information on the redress movement of "comfort women," see Soh 1996, 12272–340.

6. I prepared this list based on the "questions for discussion" included in the Penguin Readers Guide in the 1997 Penguin edition of *Comfort Woman* (appendix 11–13).

WORKS CITED

Birnbaum, Robert. "Interview: Nora Okja Keller: Author of *Comfort Woman* and *Fox Girl* talks with Robert Birnbaum." April 29, 2002. http://www.identitytheory.com/people/birnbaum43.html (accessed June 7, 2006).

Chilson, Clark, and Peter Knecht, eds. *Shamans in Asia*. London and New York: RouledgeCurzon, 2003.

Chuh, Kandice. "Guest Editor's Introduction: On Korean 'Comfort Women.'" *Journal of Asian American Studies* 6, no. 1 (February 2003): 1–4.

Chung, Chin-sung. "An Overview of the Colonial and Socio-Economic Background of Japanese Military Sex Slavery in Korea." *Muae: A Journal of Transcultural Production* 1 (1995): 204–15.

Henson, Maria Rosa. *Comfort Woman: A Filipina's Story of Prostitution and Slavery under the Japanese Military*. Lanham, Boulder, New York, and Oxford: Rowman & Littlefield Publishers, Inc., 1999.

Howard, Keith, ed. *True Stories of the Korean Comfort Women*. London: Cassell, 1995.

Kang, Laura Hyun Yi. "Conjuring 'Comfort Women': Mediated Affiliations and Disciplined Subjects in Korean/American Transnationality." *Journal of Asian American Studies* 6, no. 1 (February 2003): 25–55.

Keller, Nora Okja. *Comfort Woman*. New York: Penguin Books, 1997.

Kim-Gibson, Dai Sil. *Silence Broken: Korean Comfort Women*. Parkersburg, Iowa: Mid-Prairie Books, 1999.

Knecht, Peter. "Aspects of Shamanism: An Introduction." In *Shamans in Asia,* edited by C. Clark and P. Knecht, 1–30. London and New York: RouledgeCurzon, 2003.

Noguera, Laura. "Sudden Comfort." March 10, 1998. http://www.dailybruin.ucla.edu/DB/issues/98/03.10/ae.keller.html (accessed June 7, 2006).

Roces, Mina. "Filipino Comfort Women." http://chnm.gmu.edu/wwh/d/198/wwh.html (accessed March 15, 2006).

Sancho, Nelia, ed. *War Crimes on Asian Women: Military Sexual Slavery by Japan During World War II: The Case of the Filipino Comfort Women*. Manila: Asian Women Human Rights Council, 1998.

Soh, Chunghee Sarah. "The Korean 'Comfort Women': Movement and Redress." *Asian Survey* 36, no. 12 (December 1996): 1226–40.

———. "Women's Sexual Labor and State in Korean History." *Journal of Women's History* 15, no. 4 (Winter 2004): 170–77.

Stetz, Margaret D., and Bonnie B. C. Oh, eds. *Legacies of the Comfort Women of World War II*. Armonk, NY: M. E. Sharpe, 2001.

"Who knows but that, on the lower frequencies, I speak for you?" The Polyphony of Ralph Ellison's *Invisible Man*

Stephanie Li

Over the past ten years, I have taught in a wide variety of settings, from overcrowded high school classrooms to the basement of a maximum security prison. However, while my students may be skeptical college seniors or anxious adult learners, I begin every class the same way: by telling the story of the elephant and the six blind men.

Once upon a time, there were six blind men sitting before an elephant. Each blind man touched a different part of the animal's body—the trunk, ear, tail, side, tusk, and leg—and then proceeded to describe the mysterious creature according to his unique encounter. The men independently declared the elephant to be a snake, a fan, a piece of rope, a wall, a spear, and a tree, causing much confusion among the group. How could a single object be so many different things? Looking at the amused but curious faces of my students, I then ask, are the men right or are they wrong? And most important, how are they going to determine that an elephant is not a snake or a spear or anything else but an elephant?

This story prompts students to explore and define the difference between subjective and objective approaches to reality. As they grapple with the limitations of individual perspective, some students contend that all of the blind men are misguided while others argue that they cannot be faulted for their pronouncements. The six men are somehow both wholly correct to draw their conclusions and grossly mistaken. Despite often vehement disagreements over this slippery paradox, students agree that the best and perhaps only way for the blind men to conceive of the elephant before them is through discussion.

I begin all of my classes with this story to emphasize my belief that dialogue is the key to successful learning and, when teaching the novel, to illustrating Mikhail Bakhtin's notion of polyphony. Just as the blind men are each limited to their individual encounter with the elephant, so we all approach texts or new information with personal biases derived from our distinct cultural experiences and identities. While our unique perspectives make us blind to certain realities, through discussion that recognizes individual difference, we may begin to perceive the elephant before us all. By recognizing one another as valuable sources of knowledge, students are better able to understand the rewards of a free exchange of ideas. This model of learning is especially appropriate when teaching *Invisible Man*, a novel that offers a rich example of literary polyphony. Ralph Ellison's masterpiece demonstrates how the study of a multivoiced narrative can provide a unique opportunity for the development of empathy and personal understanding, and consequently how it may enhance student appreciation of diverse perspectives.

BAKHTIN'S NOTION OF POLYPHONY

My opening classroom discussion on dialogue as a vehicle of truth highlights Bakhtin's conception of the polyphonic novel, which he defined as possessing a "plurality of independent and unmerged voices and consciousness" (4). I tell students that our conversation following the story of the blind men is an example of a polyphonic environment and I remind them that polyphony, or the articulation of multiple perspectives, is what would lead the blind men to comprehend the elephant before them. In explaining the concept of polyphony, I emphasize that, as a theorist, Bakhtin was especially concerned with understanding the formation of consciousness or how we become aware of ourselves in relation to others. For the blind men, their consciousness of the elephant was first derived from sense experiences, that is, they each touched a different part of the animal and drew conclusions based upon that initial impression. While the collection of empirical evidence through individual encounters is an important way to gain knowledge, polyphony represents another form of self-development and education as it highlights how we may learn from others.

According to Bakhtin, consciousness involves the process by which the individual establishes a distinct relationship to society. This relationship is derived from language that he understands as an essentially intersubjective phenomenon, that is, something generated through the exchange of separate subjects. It is impossible for language to exist solely within an individual because, as the foundation of human interaction, it is implicitly social. Consequently, the development of individual consciousness is a function by which the self formulates verbal and socially accepted terms of identification. He explains:

The motivation of our action, the attainment of self-consciousness (and self-consciousness is always verbal: it always leads to the search for a specific verbal complex), is always a way of putting oneself in relation to a given social norm: it is, so to speak, a socialization of the self and of its actions. Becoming conscious of myself, I attempt to see myself through the eyes of another person. (quoted in Todorov 30)

Consciousness does not exist in isolation, but rather it represents the culmination of the confrontation between the individual and society. From this formulation, Tzvetan Todorov has observed that "Meaning (communication) implies community" (30). The act of articulation immediately socializes the individual into a foundation of dialogue. And, as demonstrated by the story of the blind men and the elephant, dialogue creates an arena in which other subjects are presented and alternate perspectives are recognized.

The integration of multiple perspectives is the basis for the polyphonic novel as defined by Bakhtin in his critical work *Problems of Dostoevsky's Poetics*. The polyphonic novel is characterized by its discursive nature, which presents its characters as engaged in a continuous dialogue. Bakhtin described the narrative effect of Dostoevsky's innovative literary form with the following observation:

What matters to him most of all is the dialogical interaction of the discourses, whatever their linguistic particularities. The main object of the representation he constructs is discourse itself, and especially meaningful discourse. Dostoevsky's works are a discourse upon discourse, addressed to discourse. (quoted in Todorov 66)

The foundation of discourse in Dostoevsky's novels is derived from a constant affirmation of "someone else's 'I'" not as an object but as another subject—this is the principle governing Dostoevsky's worldview (quoted in Dentith 43). Within this construction of interacting and interfering subjectivities, dialogue is the primary objective because it establishes an arena for the relation of the self to others.

Rather than emphasizing absolute philosophical or social tenets, the polyphonic novel is focused on the recognition of multiple perspectives. According to Bakhtin, Dostoevsky achieved this effect by producing strong, distinct characters who express their philosophical and moral positions through extensive dialogues as well as through significant actions. The novel is the site of heteroglossia, in which a variety of individual narratives converge on a single thematic discourse mediated by the author. Polyphony produces an arena of layered dialogue that creates a necessary tension for the articulation of personal expression.

Although Bakhtin was the first to name polyphony as a literary phenomenon, it is a concept with application in a variety of settings. For example, Ralph Ellison notes that the jazz musician is confronted by a challenge of self-assertion similar to that experienced by an emerging voice within a polyphonic environment. The musician must create and define a unique style amid the sounds of previously established and often stronger melodies. This conflict is explained by Ellison, who poses the musician's struggle as an essential paradox of jazz:

There is a cruel contradiction implicit in the art form itself. For true jazz is an art of individual assertion within and against the group. Each true jazz moment (as distinct from the uninspired commercial performance) springs from a contest in which each artist challenges all the rest, each solo flight, or improvisation, represents (like the successive canvases of a painter) a definition of his identity: as individual, as member of the collectivity as a link in the chain of tradition. Thus, because jazz finds its very life in an endless improvisation upon traditional materials, the jazzman must lose his identity even as he finds it. (quoted in Gates vii)

The dialogic nature of the polyphonic novel and the challenge of the jazz musician demonstrate that consciousness can only exist and develop from the interaction and integration of multiple voices. To illustrate this concept in full, I have found it useful to play a jazz piece such as John Coltrane's "Blue Train" or Miles Davis's "Move" in which students can hear how individual sounds emerge from and respond to a polyphonic environment. Students may then perceive how art, both musical and literary, acts as a primary site of identity formation and as a vehicle for the development of consciousness.

Despite the similarity between literary polyphony and jazz music, however, there is an essential difference between the two. The latter lacks an overarching mediator who oversees the process of creating musical harmony. Within a novel, the author ultimately has the power to control and manipulate character voices, whereas in the "true jazz moment" each musician acts as an independent agent. While Ellison envisioned an "endless improvisation," every polyphonic novel arrives at a definitive end. The book at last closes and becomes a contained object. The ideal of such "endless improvisation" or eternal discourse in literature approaches fulfillment only through the activity of a community of readers who are the inheritors of literary dialogue.

THE POLYPHONIC LANGUAGE OF *INVISIBLE MAN*

Polyphony operates in multiple ways in Ralph Ellison's ground-breaking *Invisible Man*. Much like Dostoevsky, Ellison creates a number of strong, distinctive voices in the text that contribute to the novel's dynamic heteroglossia. However, he also stylizes polyphony through a deliberate refashioning of language. All of the varied narratives evident in *Invisible Man* are derived from Ellison's unique conception of American English, which he describes as having intrinsic polyphonic resonances:

It is a language that evolved from the king's English but, basing itself upon the realities of the American land and colonial institutions—or lack of institutions, began quite early as a vernacular against the signs, symbols, manners, and authority of the mother country. It is a language that began by merging the sounds of many tongues, brought together in the struggle of diverse regions. And whether it is admitted or not, much of the sound of that language is derived from the timbre of the African voice and the listening habits of the African ear. (*Going* 108–9)

The language of *Invisible Man* is itself polyphonic as it integrates a variety of distinct vernaculars and linguistic influences, and celebrates the implicitly rebellious nature of American English. While any language can be understood as the integration of multiple subjectivities, American English reflects a unique history of struggle—from colonial rebellion to the fight for civil rights to contemporary battles over immigration—translated into linguistic form. Consequently, it can be understood as a fundamentally heteroglossic phenomenon, which can both disorient and affirm the individual. I have found students to be especially receptive to this conception of American English, perhaps because youth and pop culture employs a language of slang and innuendo that is somewhat removed from the expectations and formality of a classroom. Moreover, students who come from bilingual households or from families that have not received university-level educations can readily identify how American English continues to evolve well beyond the confines of the classroom. Short in-class activities involving the newest words to be added to the dictionary each year help students appreciate how language can reflect the workings of a polyphonic community.[1]

As Ellison wrote *Invisible Man*, one of his primary concerns was to articulate a language that is not univocal, but rather inherently multifarious. His affirmation of black subjectivity includes the depiction of English as a discursive medium that is heavily influenced by African American cultural traditions:

Our speech I found resounding with an alive language whirling with over three hundred years of American living, a mixture of the folk, the Biblical, the scientific and political. Slangy in one instance, academic in another, loaded poetically with imagery at one moment, mathematically bare of imagery in the next. (Ellison, *Shadow* 103–4)

By presenting readers with a bold new, integrative language, Ellison created a narrative characterized by fluidity and freedom, qualities which also define much of the Invisible Man's experience. Ellison's novel draws on multiple sources, including musical and literary trends and European and black folk culture, to create an innovative language that is simultaneously polyphonic and individualized. To illustrate the power of this literary approach, I ask students to prepare short presentations on a number of *Invisible Man*'s vast array of allusions (such as T. S. Eliot, Dostoevsky, Booker T. Washington, Brer Rabbit and Brer Bear, and Biblical stories). These short reports help students appreciate how Ellison constructs his own literary tradition by drawing on multiple sources.

The factors influencing Ellison's linguistic confrontation and reformulation are also applicable to his evaluation of novelistic forms. Much like the Invisible Man who adopts and then disposes of external models, as a writer, Ellison sought to fashion his own literary voice:

After the usual apprenticeship of imitation and seeking with delight to examine my experience through the discipline of the novel, I became gradually aware that the forms of so many of the words which impressed me were too restricted to contain the experience which I knew. (103)

For Ellison, "the tight well-made Jamesian novel" was too confining and the understatement of the "hard boiled novel" was not a viable form because, as a black man, his assumptions were not those shared by most Americans. As a result, Ellison developed a new literary style that would convey the depths of the Invisible Man's experience:

I was to dream of a prose which was flexible, and swift as American change is swift, confronting the inequalities and brutalities of our society forthrightly, but yet thrusting forth its images of hope, human fraternity and individual self-realization. It would use the richness of our speech, the idiomatic expression and the rhetorical flourishes from past periods which are still alive among us. (105)

Ellison's language and style is marked by its departure from conventional forms. It is by turns imaginatively surreal and boldly realistic; it simultaneously resonates with jazz and black folk cultural influences and alludes to a variety of writers belonging to the Western tradition. Moreover, Ellison matches his literary voice to precise character developments and plot progressions. For example, he exchanges the realistic style of the opening chapters for a more impressionistic and surrealistic narrative as the Invisible Man is led from the familiar South to the wild streets of Harlem. The breadth of his literary style describes the broad spectrum of black experience in America and privileges diversity and exploration over a single, containing perspective. Although students will not be able to appreciate in full Ellison's stylistic innovations until they have completed the novel and thus experienced the full range of his narrative techniques, I begin my discussion of *Invisible Man* with the quotations I have excerpted here from *Shadow and Act* and *Going to the Territory*. By understanding Ellison's literary objectives from the onset of their study of the novel, students may read with greater attention to how changes in narrative style and voice point to a shift in the Invisible Man's perspective.

THE DANGERS OF POLYPHONY

Invisible Man is an ideal example of the polyphonic novel because of its emphasis on discourse and attention to multiple subjectivities. Ellison describes the difficulties of the Invisible Man's search for independence and identity amid a dynamic and heavily discursive environment. The words of the Invisible Man's grandfather, Dr. Bledsoe, Mr. Norton, Jim Trueblood, and Jack among many others resonate within Ellison's protagonist and greatly determine his life choices. The Invisible Man adopts many of the formulations and external projections concerning the nature of his own blackness and his subordinated place in society during his journey to consciousness and identity. Through his self-development, students are able to recognize the dangers as well as the benefits of validating multiple perspectives. He, like Ellison's jazz musician, must struggle to express his own melody and not become drowned out by the clamor of others, that is, by the social roles and stereotypes imposed upon him.

After introducing *Invisible Man* as a novel of discourse, I then ask the class to define the subject under discussion in Ellison's text. What, to return to the opening parable, is the elephant in the room? Students generally agree that Ellison's central concern is the nature of the Invisible Man's identity: who this narrator is and what values, beliefs, and ideas define him. We may then read the dialogue of such characters as the vet at the Golden Day, Homer Barbee, Dr. Bledsoe, and Jack as commentary on the Invisible Man, especially his status as a young black man and his place in society. What do these characters see in Ellison's protagonist? And perhaps, more important, what do they not see?

In our discussion of the opening chapters of the book, I have students examine in detail how the Invisible Man takes on ideas and even social positions that are not his own, and how he must learn to define himself on his own terms. As he explains at the start of the novel, "I was looking for myself and asking everyone except myself questions which I, and only I, could answer" (15). The difficulty of the Invisible Man is to determine his true self amid the changing projections that others place upon him.

When one is invisible he finds such problems as good and evil, honesty and dishonesty, of such shifting shapes that he confuses one with the other, depending upon who happens to be looking through him at the time.... Too often, in order to justify them, I had to take myself by the throat and choke myself until my eyes bulged and my tongue hung out and wagged like the door of an empty house in a wind. Oh yes, it made them happy and it made me sick.... So after years of trying to adopt the opinions of others I finally rebelled. I am an *invisible* man. (572–73)

The fundamental crisis of the Invisible Man is based on his internalization of social constructs, which cause self-alienation and the deterioration of his individuality. Ellison illustrates this destruction of self as the physical loss of voice that necessarily leads to the death of both self-expression and human communication. Students are asked to make note of instances in which the Invisible Man accepts various social projections external to him and to explain what motivates his actions. For example, we discuss the Invisible Man's graduation speech which extols "humility" as "the secret, indeed, the very essence of progress," although he parenthetically admits, "Not that I believed this—how could I, remembering my grandfather?—I only believed that it worked" (17). Having separated himself from his family, the Invisible Man embarks upon a quest for independence and success that is based on conventional models of American achievement. He admires men of wealth, power, and influence, and he believes that their success can be his own if he only shapes himself according to their commands. In one of the most powerful images of the novel, the Invisible Man chokes on his own blood to finish his graduation speech and act the part of the "good, smart boy" who will "lead his people in the proper paths" (32). The Invisible Man is far too overwhelmed by the scholarship he has received to consider what are the "proper paths" for "his people," much less for himself.

IN SEARCH OF A FATHER'S VOICE

I have found that students are best able to conceptualize the identity crisis of the Invisible Man through his search for an absent father. Significantly, Ellison's protagonist hardly describes his family, and the only relative who receives some individual description is his grandfather, whose death-bed advice haunts the Invisible Man throughout the novel:

I have been a traitor all my born days, a spy in enemy's country ever since I give up my gun back in the Reconstruction. Live with your head in the lion's mouth. I want you to overcome 'em with yeses, undermine 'em with grins, agree 'em to death and destruction, let 'em swoller you till they vomit or bust wide open. (16)

The Invisible Man is troubled by his grandfather's confession and unsure whether he should obey such a treasonous injunction. Though he feels guilty when he acts as "an example of desirable conduct" (17), he continues to do so to procure material success and social acclaim. The Invisible Man's inability to make sense of his grandfather's advice highlights the absence of a stable paternal figure in his life and suggests his need to formulate his own conception of self. The wise vet at the Golden Day expresses this very sentiment, thus establishing the terms of the Invisible Man's quest for identity:

"Now is the time for offering fatherly advice," he said, "but I'll have to spare you that—since I guess I'm nobody's father except my own. Perhaps that's the advice to give you: Be your own father, young man. And remember, the world is possibility if only you'll discover it." (156)

The vet's striking admonition personalizes the Invisible Man's search for guidance and suggests that ultimately he is responsible for his own fulfillment. Despite this early warning, Ellison's protagonist proceeds to emulate men like Mr. Norton, Dr. Bledsoe, and Jack, forging uneasy father–son relationships based on imitation and deluded admiration. However, as demonstrated by his encounters with these false father figures, the Invisible Man must be careful not to let the voices of others drown out his own emergent identity.

It would be possible to discuss in detail a number of failed father–son relationships presented in the novel, but I will limit my discussion here to the Invisible Man's encounter with Dr. Bledsoe. This relationship exemplifies the dangers of uncritical admiration of others and also points to the Invisible Man's destructive estrangement from his cultural heritage. Although the Invisible Man's respect for Dr. Bledsoe represents a marginal improvement from his solicitous behavior before the white men at his graduation speech, he once again falls into the trap of emulating the material trappings of American success. As he describes Dr. Bledsoe,

[H]e was the example of everything I hoped to be: Influential with wealthy men all over the country; consulted in matters concerning the race; a leader of his people; the possessor of not one, but two Cadillacs, a good salary and a soft, good-looking and creamy-complexioned wife. What was more, while black and bald and everything white folks poked fun at, he had achieved power and authority. (101)

Blinded by the material success and social influence of Dr. Bledsoe, the Invisible Man is unable to recognize the elder man's cunning and deception. Dr. Bledsoe derives his power from his duplicity as he projects humble deference to whites while instilling fear and respect among the black students. Dr. Bledsoe is fully aware of the social system that entraps both blacks and whites; but rather than working against it, he exploits racial and social differences for his own purposes. In a rare, candid moment, he explains to the Invisible Man:

It's a nasty deal and I don't always like it myself. But you listen to me: I didn't make it, and I know that I can't change it. But I've made my place in it and I'll have every Negro in the country hanging on tree limbs by morning if it means staying where I am. (143)

Dr. Bledsoe's power depends on acquiescence to a social system that operates through domination and hierarchy. His selfish focus on his own material comfort and success makes his every interaction a deceptive exploitation of the community he claims to support. He will even adopt the behavior of a white supremacist and kill others to preserve his individual power.

Dr. Bledsoe not only represents the dangers and consequences of masked duplicity, but also exemplifies a divorce from cultural consciousness, a key part of the Invisible Man's quest for identity. Dr. Bledsoe is content to ignore the poverty of men like Jim Trueblood, but will insist on his dedication to help poor blacks hustle money from white donors. At the start of his narrative, the Invisible Man is similarly dismissive of the black community. For example, he only makes cursory remarks about his past, as he is far more concerned with his ambitions and plans for the future than he is with his family. He also shares Dr. Bledsoe's disdain for Trueblood and he is embarrassed by the symbols of black folk traditions. However, through encounters with such characters as Mary Rambo and Tod Clifton, the Invisible Man eventually comes to realize the full value, meaning, and necessity of his cultural heritage.

This gradual awareness of the need to incorporate and embrace black traditions is highlighted by the scene with the yam seller, another key voice in the novel's polyphonic environment. Alone, unemployed, and disillusioned, the Invisible Man comes upon the yam seller at a crucial moment in his search for success and identity. He, like thousands of black men and women before him, has come North with great hopes for the future, but he has faced only disappointment and frustration. Alienated from his past and thwarted by his naïve hopes for the future, he exists in a precarious limbo that lacks a stable reference point for his already tenuous sense of self. The smell of yams, however, transports him to a time before his journey to Harlem, far before his failed experiences in college and the humiliation of the battle royal. "[A]s though struck by a shot" (262), the Invisible Man is suddenly inspired by memories of home and feelings of satisfaction. He employs the pronoun "we" rather than "I," suggesting a collectivity now lost in his individual aspirations and his lonely attempts at a success constructed on the value systems of others. For the first time in the novel, the Invisible Man does not need to subsume constructed images of himself to create a sense of personal identity; rather the memory of home comes to him easily and imbues him with comfort.

The guardian to this new awareness is the old yam seller whose make-shift clothes contrast with the tailored sophistication of Mr. Norton and Dr. Bledsoe. However, his most striking feature is his manner of speech. He drops syllables and ignores certain verbs; his clausal agreement is sometimes disordered. Although his speech is entirely removed from the elegance of the Invisible Man's narration, the yam seller communicates a generosity and wisdom that Ellison's protagonist struggles to attain. As the old man warns, "everything what looks good ain't necessarily good" (264). In expressing such insight through a character whose "low style" dialect suggests poverty and a lack of education, Ellison elevates the people that the Invisible Man left behind in his hasty desire for success. A few pages after this encounter, the Invisible Man proclaims, "I yam what I yam!" (266). This pun signals the awakening of a new orientation of his self as he rejects formal English and embraces a unifying sense of humor. The secret of his identity lies in this crucial moment. To understand himself, he must return to his past and honor the traditions of his culture, exemplified here by humor, food, and speech.

THE POLYPHONY OF READERS

As a chronicle of the relationships he establishes with false father figures, the Invisible Man's story appropriately ends with his interpretation of his grandfather's words. While such men as Dr. Bledsoe and Jack are revealed to be duplicitous manipulators, only the Invisible Man's grandfather and the various guardians of his cultural origins persist throughout his narrative and meld into the tones of his own voice. Ultimately, he learns the truth of the vet's original admonition as he discovers that he cannot embrace the power-hungry men he once emulated. The Invisible Man must instead create his own wisdom from his cultural legacy and his personal experiences. In the epilogue, he develops a dialogue between himself and the various interpretations of his grandfather's words, which enact Bakhtin's concept of polyphony within a single consciousness:

Could he have meant—hell, he *must* have meant the principle, that we were to affirm the principle on which the country was built and not the men.... Or did he mean that we had to take the responsibility for all of it, for the men as well as the principle because no other fitted our needs? Not for the power of for our vindication, but because we, with the given circumstances of our origin, could only thus find transcendence? ... Or was it, did he mean that we should affirm the principle because we, through no fault of our own, were linked to all the others in the loud, clamoring semi-visible world.... "Agree 'em to death and destruction," grandfather had advised. Hell, weren't they their own death and their own destruction except as the principle lived in them and in us? And here's the cream of the joke: Weren't we *part of them* as well as apart from them and subject to die when they died? I can't figure it out; it escapes me. (574–75)

Although the Invisible Man ends this passage with the declaration that he cannot understand his grandfather's words, it is clear that through the process of contemplation and reflection, he has learned to question the values and conventions of society. He finds his own voice by transforming and responding to the wisdom gathered by his predecessors and projecting this knowledge onto his own experiences and impressions. Self-realization is found in this dialogue between the past and the present, between the cultural with the individual, and the unity that results.

By leaving the advice of the Invisible Man's grandfather as an abiding enigma, Ellison suggests that concerns about race relations and identity require further exploration. The final line of the novel, "Who knows but that, on the lower frequencies, I speak for you?" (581), reaches toward such continuation by extending the novel's polyphony outside the confines of the text. The interrogative form of this sentence and its confrontational tone invite the reader to join the dialogue of the novel and reflect personal experiences upon Ellison's narrative. Moreover, the joined "who," "I," and "you" reveal the possibility and hope for a discourse infused with new perspectives and subjectivities. Ellison's text imagines a community of voices who will join in the Invisible Man's search for identity and find parts of themselves in his story.

END NOTE

1. The online version of the *Merriam-Webster Collegiate Dictionary* lists the forty most popular new words each year (www.macmillandictionary.com/2005/index.htm). I have used these words as journal prompts to get students to explore how and why a word like "infomania" has been included in the dictionary and what such a word tells us about the nature of our society. "Infomania" is defined as "a condition of reduced concentration caused by continually responding to electronic communications such as e-mail, text-messaging etc."

WORKS CITED

Bakhtin, Mikhail. *Problems of Dostoevsky's Poetics*, translated by R. W. Rotsel. Ann Arbor, MI: Ardis, 1973.

Dentith, Simon. *Bakhtinian Thought: An Introductory Reader*. London, Routledge, 1995.

Ellison, Ralph. *Going to the Territory*. New York: Vintage Books, 1986.

———. *Invisible Man*. New York: Vintage Books, 1947.

———. *Shadow and Act*. New York: Vintage Books, 1953.

Gates, Henry Louis. *The Signifying Monkey: A Theory of African-American Literary Criticism*. New York: Oxford University Press, 1988.

Todorov, Tzvetan. *Mikhail Bakhtin: The Dialogic Principle*, translated by Wlad Godzich. Minneapolis: University of Minnesota Press, 1984.

TEACHING THE NOVEL IN LITERATURE CLASSES

Written Images: Using Visual Literacy to Unravel the Novel

Ricia Anne Chansky

When I began teaching survey literature courses, I was dismayed to find that the great majority of my students had difficulty discerning the meaning of written symbolism. I soon realized that one of the great downfalls of the introductory literature course is that it typically is not populated by those possessing a great love of reading, more so by pupils needing to fulfill mandatory humanities or general education core credits, who often view the class as a necessary evil that they need to survive just to graduate. The presence of such disinterested students in these classes provides a unique opportunity to reach out to non-English majors in the hopes of creating a lifelong interest in reading, while presenting them with an opportunity to acquire critical-thinking skills that will serve them throughout their academic careers and lives.

My experience is not an uncommon one, as many literature teachers encounter non-English majors who feel lost in introductory courses because they find unraveling symbolic meaning and subtext from plot to be an overwhelming and daunting task. Separating story from significance can be accomplished by teaching critical analysis and image interpretation through visual media before engaging a written text. This article outlines a basic format for incorporating visual literacy into the initial literature courses as pedagogy designed specifically to meet the needs of the diverse student populations present in such classes.

As most American universities have obligatory core requirements in the humanities that undergraduates must pass to complete their degrees, there are going to be students in introductory literature classes who are unhappy to be there and only present to receive their mandated credit hours in the discipline. The pupil who enters the class viewing it simply as a requisite course will often times bring a hesitant attitude that questions the relevancy of this study to her or his major field and career goals. The challenge for instructors is then to develop creative methods of teaching prose that will excite and interest the beginning students, while still maintaining a high level of instruction that will serve the new

English majors present in the class who need a strong foundation of proficiency in analyzing literature.

Non-English majors in introductory-level courses often have distinct conflicts relating to the included materials. The instructor may have to overcome students' negative preconceived notions of what a language arts course consists of, an ignorance of the goals and objectives of such a class, or a deeply rooted insecurity about abilities to learn in this arena. There are frequently real and perceived elitist notions of written works and their intended audience. In addition to this, many beginning literature students become so caught up in the story of what they are reading that they lose sight of the greater meaning of the work, bypassing symbolism and subtext completely. It is then important for instructors to develop methods of working with these students that exemplify and explain the means of studying a text in a stimulating manner that inspires all of the students in the class to continue reading and reflect on what they have read.

Faculty members must also surmount their own preconceived notions of non-English major and introductory students. For many in the field, the truest pleasure imaginable is the graduate-level seminar consisting of students who are thrilled to be discussing works of great literature and bring new insight with their every comment. It can be daunting to rise to the occasion of inspiring students who drag themselves into class preparing for what they perceive to be tortuous hours spent talking about irrelevant matters. It is, of course, the faculty member's job to change their minds. Not necessarily to make them into fledgling English majors, but to demonstrate the importance of literature in their lives, as well as the benefits that critical reading brings to the study of other subject matters.

To successfully do this, the instructor must show the relevance of reading and critical engagement to her students while providing the basic skills necessary to read critically and analyze works. As the United States is a media society dependant on visual culture, students who may feel excluded from written text are well-versed in reading visuals, although they may not yet realize it. Students who feel isolated from the fundamental building blocks that create a written text, including symbolism, subtext, and composition, function quite capably when it comes to reading films, television programs, and advertisements. William Constanzo, reporting on a project he conducted for the National Endowment for the Humanities, states that

much of what once seemed revelatory about the role of visual media in our students' lives is now widely accepted, even taken for granted. Film and television continue to dominate a major portion of their formative years, creating expectations, shaping attitudes, influencing language patterns and providing a common frame of reference. (Constanzo, quoted in George 345)

George also believes that "it is crucial [for teachers] to understand how very complicated and sophisticated . . . visual communication [is] to students who have grown up in what is by all accounts is an aggressively visual culture" (337). This "aggressively visual culture" permeates all facets of life for Americans, but no where is it more forceful than in the life of a teenager who is willfully surrounded by visual media. Television and the Internet fill the free hours of students' lives, and the Internet has more visual advertisements present on each screen than most half-hour primetime programs. If students are comfortable and capable of critically reading the visuals that permeate their nonacademic lives, teachers should be utilizing these ingrained skills to educate within the classroom. Catherine L. Hobbs reminds teachers that they "are living through a revolution in literacy brought about by the capability of computers to combine blocks of text—or verbal *lexias*—with graphic images, sounds, video, and other multimedia" (27) and that "to condone and contribute to visual illiteracy contradicts our purpose of teaching" (28).

It would be helpful for faculty to recognize the ubiquitous nature of the multimodal Internet present in their students' lives and reference these modes of learning in which students are steeped. Furthermore, writing-across-the-curriculum specialist Mary E. Hocks discusses the "hybridity" of visual and verbal rhetoric that students bring to the contemporary classroom from their experiences with the multimodalities of the Internet, conferring that the online "hybridity" creates the need for instructors to think about the visual aspects of texts, as that is how the majority of students receive their information (358–82). Therefore, if teachers wish to fully communicate with students who take language arts classes as mandatory requirements with no interest in continuing on in the field, it behooves them to consider speaking about written texts through the common language of visuals.

Utilizing visual literacy with non-English majors in the language arts classroom succeeds for several reasons. Many students new to literary studies on the college level are insecure about the reading comprehension and critical-thinking aspects of literary analysis. This may be due to past instructor feedback being internalized as negative criticism or an ingrained sense that they are not comprehending the work on the same level as their peers. By demonstrating the tools of literary analysis through visual comprehension, a medium with which they are more comfortable, a great measure of concern and anxiety can be removed from the process, thus allowing for a higher level of understanding and retention of the materials covered.

The skills employed to critically read a visual text are the same as those utilized to discern the meaning of a written one, but often times students are stymied by the perceived threat of the language arts classroom and distracted by the entertainment value of the plot. By employing a comfortable visual text and constructing meaning through pictures before peeling away layers of story to get to significance, students can become oriented to both the ways of determining interpretations of texts and feel confident with their abilities. Guiding students toward recognizing the universal fundamentals that construct texts and explaining how to examine these texts using a medium with which they are conversant, offers them direct and immediate access to the analytical process and meets them on common ground while encouraging them to further their skills. Once students feel confident in their ability to evaluate a text, transitioning those abilities to a written work becomes easier than beginning primarily with the novel.

My own students were extremely superficial in their initial readings, not understanding that literature has both a literal and a figurative meaning. They had little perception of symbolism and were surprised to learn that to truly understand what they were reading they had to analyze the words and verbal constructions on many levels. At one point, I provided them with both a biography of the author we were reading and a statement on the historical context of the piece, and they were still unable to construct the message of the text. I received that age-old student question, "Are you sure *everything* means something?" Even looking at such contemporary texts as Chitra Divakaruni's *The Mistress of Spices* and Diana Abu-Jaber's *Arabian Jazz* frustrated them, the modern messages eluding them.

It was a challenging semester as the students wrestled with concepts of reading critically, which was an idea quite new to them. They had a hard time accepting that a story has another deeper, symbolic meaning that only becomes apparent through reflection on and engagement with the text. As they pressed further and I guided them through the historical and biographical context of the works we studied, the students became more and more astounded that so much thought went into the reading of every book. I desperately wanted them to see on their own that the explorations of American identity that Divakaruni and Abu-Jaber chronicle in their novels rely heavily on relating the physical features of the American world in contrast to their characters' countries of origin, but they just could not seem to get there.

I wanted my students to be able to recognize and engage with these verbal images that the authors so lovingly created and enter them with a firm recognition of the craft needed to construct them, in the hopes of then being capable of deconstructing them for investigation. Visual literacy scholar Kristie S. Fleckenstein feels as though incorporating visual literacy into the literature classroom is a natural connection, stating that teachers "cannot talk about ... literature without talking about symbolism, and symbols are invariably image based.... We cannot talk about either literature or writing without also talking about the power of verbal imagery to move ourselves and our readers" (8). With this statement in mind, the following semester I redesigned my survey courses to include an introductory section that would draw on visual literacy to introduce the fundamentals of symbolism and critical reading that would give students an opportunity to explore critical analysis, thereby giving them the tools to engage literature, as opposed to teaching them these skills as we were reading the works.

One of my primary concerns was that students seemed unable to grasp the basics that would act as a way into the works, especially because we were learning the pieces of literary analysis at the same time we were trying to critically engage the works. Part of this inability to connect to the works was certainly a perception some of the students had that they *couldn't* understand literature, but a greater problem was that they simply could not internalize the tools necessary to enter into the works. The concepts were too new and overwhelming for them to take hold of and, ultimately, there were too many new ideas to absorb all at once. They were at risk of becoming frustrated and disillusioned with the language arts. Of particular concern were the non-English majors, as the course might serve as their singular college experience with literary studies and the only opportunity to convey the importance and relevance of literature to their lives.

With these issues in mind, I designed a new opening unit independent of written text, instead favoring the visual arts as the demonstrative pieces with which to teach the concepts of text analysis. Of particular importance were the feelings of insecurity that many of the students experienced when faced with a "literary" text, which I hoped to eradicate by removing literature from the equation as we were learning the tools of critical analysis. It was essential to create a high level of excitement for the class at the start of the semester that would carry through working with denser texts. Furthermore, I wanted to present the relevance of textual analysis and engagement to their personal lives, even if they were not continuing on with their studies in English and had different academic and career goals in mind.

I selected photography as the primary genre to explain how to break down, analyze, and reconstruct the pieces of a novel because I felt that it was a visual medium with which most students would be eminently comfortable. The majority of people in contemporary Western society have grown up in front of the still or even moving cameras of their proud parents and, with the advent of digital technology, those numbers are only increasing. Younger and younger children are presented with cameras and given the opportunity to capture their surroundings in print, furthering the common experience with photography. This is on top of the hours spent pouring over family and public photography in albums, news and entertainment media sources, advertisements, and moving pictures in films and on television. Increasing numbers of children have access to computers in their homes and schools, and this also leads to more exposure to photography and opportunities for to express oneself visually.

As the instructor, I completed the visual assignments alongside my students. My desire with this series of exercises was to remove certain pressures that inhibit students' internalization of materials and to demonstrate the relevance of a specific skill set, not make them feel inadequate or trivialized by the assignment. I felt strongly that if I were only to observe their involvement with visual texts, I would be repeating some of the same patterns that had caused the timidity over their analytical abilities, and I did not want to reinforce insecurity by sending a message that there were specific answers I was expecting. I wanted to demonstrate that their responses were acceptable as long as they were supported and to make the lessons personal and therefore relevant. I felt firmly that I could only expect that my students to fulfill the letter and spirit of the lesson if I first, as their classroom role model, exhibited my willingness to do so.

After introducing the work of the semester, a survey of American literature from the Civil War to the Civil Rights Movement, I explained that before we began reading the verbal texts, we would have an opportunity to learn critical analysis from photography. I made it clear that while there was certainly an educational purpose to our endeavors that this project was to be looked upon as an exciting time, an experiment that the university was allowing us to participate in, and an unusual opportunity for creative expression in an otherwise rigid first year of college that placed many demands on them. My then-university's core requirements in the College of Arts and Sciences are certainly stringent, consisting of four humanities courses, as well as three social sciences, three natural sciences, and two mathematics classes, all of which should be completed within the first two years of school. I was hopeful that the students who were intimidated by the idea of literary analysis or unhappy to be in a required humanities class would be stimulated by the unusual approach and energized by the opportunity to work with a medium not typically considered part of the literature curriculum.

Students began by providing a definition of the word text and ultimately decided on a statement that included both two- and three-dimensional visual works, in addition to written pieces. Interestingly, many students initially felt that while a film was a text, two-dimensional images or three-dimensional objects were not. It was only through conversation that established the similarities and differences between the genres that they added two- and three-dimensional visual representations to their statement. They then copied this definition in the beginning of what became a personal text analysis journal, in which they would eventually explain in their own words how to work through complicated texts.

Their homework at the end of the first class period was to bring in two personal photographs that they felt comfortable sharing with the class. The next day the group began reading visuals through the most basic unit of photography in the United States, the snapshot. In pairs, small groups, and then as a class they analyzed one of everyone's two photos, discussing the characters present in the story and keeping lists in their analytical journals of some of the characters they should be on the lookout for in texts: parents, siblings, grandparents, friends, romantic interests, and so forth. Next to each type of character they found in the photos, they listed the visual clues available as to who each character was and what the relationships between characters were. For example, the mother may be the older-looking woman who bore a physical resemblance to the younger characters and put her hands on each of the younger character's shoulders. Or perhaps the two young men who resembled each other physically, but were scowling, were brothers who had recently disagreed. In this manner, they began to understand that stories are made up of characters and that storytellers provide us clues to their natures and relationships through physical descriptions or verbal image building.

At that point, students in pairs traded their second photographs and were asked to write the story of this new photograph based solely on the physical clues that they saw present. The depth of analysis and critical engagement was great, in no small part due to the level of excitement that students had in anticipation of hearing how their personal pictures would be read by a classmate. After fifteen minutes of writing in their analytical journals, students were asked to share their readings with the class. The lesson ended with a discussion of critical thinking on the premise that people are continually surrounded by objects that they read for information, but that most of them do not process the fact that their immediate, grand-scale absorption of meaning from visual texts is a form of reading critically.

Students were then asked to bring in completely nonverbal three-dimensional objects from home. The next class period, before discussing the objects they had brought, I introduced the concept of context and as a group we discussed what types of context we would need to have before we could fully read the grouping of objects. The students agreed that the primary means of necessary for a complete reading were biographical and cultural. After taking some time to write up discussion points that covered which aspects of biographical and cultural context would be important for a reading of their classmates' objects, they listed what they each felt were the five most important questions they would need answered before reading a work in context. They then broke into small groups to interview each other and determine the answers to their context questions before finally reading each other's objects to the class as a whole. That class meeting ended with the students free-writing in their journals about the importance of context to a critical reading.

At the end of this class, their homework assignment was to locate and research a photographer of public recognition, bring in a sample of her or his work, and read it in a cultural and biographical context. I suggested searching a museum's virtual collection for ideas of prominent photographers, and provided the Web addresses for the National Portrait Gallery, the National Gallery of Art, the Hirschhorn Museum and Sculpture Garden, and the National Museum of Women in the Arts as possibilities, as my university was in Washington, D.C., and I wanted to focus on local museums. This assignment works well with any museum that has a Web site, but as I am always interested in demonstrating the personal relevance of classroom materials, the community museum is usually the best resource because the students have the potential to visit it.

To fulfill the assignment, students brought in reprints of photographs, along with copies of the artists' biographies, written statements discussing the cultural context of the time and location where these artists were working, and an analysis of how they saw this information influencing the photographs. As a class, we spent a great deal of time discussing how sociopolitical and cultural events influence artists, whether they are visual or verbal, and the importance of investigating this framework to fully engage with texts. Each student wrote down an in-depth explanation of the relevance of cultural circumstances to works of art in their analytical journals so that they would have a ready outline for interpreting texts in their own words. Added to this task was the information on their individual photographers and their readings of the works, which were written in as examples of how to dissect texts in context. Additionally, they gave brief presentations to the class and received feedback from myself and their peers. The students were excited by this project, especially those who were the sole reporter on a particular photographer. They were eager to write about the photographs and were becoming increasingly comfortable with their abilities to critically engage with texts.

The next class period we returned to the students' selected works by professional photographers and used them to begin discussing composition. They listed all the details of the photographs that combined to create a story and then scrutinized the list, breaking it down into groups of like items such as colors, people, objects, landscape items, and buildings. For homework, the students referred to the *Penguin Dictionary of Symbolism* to start deciphering the different intricate pieces of the text. They wrote up their findings in their journals and discussed them in class the next day. A great deal of our conversation centered around linking symbols together to create complicated interpretations and, again, the photographs were quite useful here, because the students could clearly see how all the different parts of the picture worked together to create a unified, intricate statement.

Terri Pullen Guezzar implements a similar exercise in her classes, but she comes at the issue from an opposite vantage point, experimenting with student-made illustrations in the literature classroom. She has had a great measure of success with first-year students who practice writing-to-learn activities to internalize and process the images of a text for meaning and comprehension (52). Students note and comfortably analyze the complexities of the text they're reading in their drawings and in the written analysis accompanying them (54). Guezzar has found that asking her students to visualize the text in a concrete manner by sketching out certain scenes allows them to relate to the written words as tangible actualities, affording them the opportunity to evaluate them as verbal images and create greater meaning from them.

Similarly, I wanted my students to have the opportunity to create their own symbolic works so that they could have a fuller understanding of how artists create texts. Therefore, the final step of my new visual literacy unit was for students to craft their own projects. George worries that "only rarely do [instructors] encounter a suggestion that students might become producers as well as receivers or victims of mass media, especially visual media" (339). Brian Goldfarb echoes this sentiment when he recounts the successful use of video production, both shown and crafted by his students, to promote engagement and communication between his students and their language arts studies (57–83).

As a primary goal of this unit was to remove any sense of intimidation over studying the arts, it seemed imperative that my students become "producers" of media to eliminate any lingering sense of insecurity. Again, the majority of people in the United States have an ongoing relationship with the camera, both as subject and agent, which subsequently eradicates the typical uncertainty felt over engaging in an artistic process. Additionally, photography is an art form in which even a beginner can feel successful from the start of their pursuit, over perhaps drawing, which needs a certain level of study before one can feel comfortable. This approach allows for the further removal from the lesson of pressures relating to the fear of failure.

To create their own visual media, each student was provided with a keyword, such as greed or goodness, and asked to plan out and take a photograph that would embody the word. They were asked to rely on the analytical journals that they had compiled and were instructed to incorporate each of the elements of text reading that we had covered. Prior to taking the photograph, they had to sketch a mock up of what they intended the picture to look like and to write a plan of what they were trying to accomplish with their image selection, composition, and context, employing all that they had learned about how readers critically engage with texts. Students then traded keywords to create a second photograph that used both their original word and the new one, following the same guidelines.

By creating their own photographs constructed of symbolism, subtext, and composition, the students were able to actively process the fundamentals of text analysis by creating their own works. Through their original images that were rich with symbolism, metaphor, and subtext, the students were able to more fully grasp the depth of thought that goes into works of art, visual or written, and to process the fundamentals of text analysis on a cognitive level. According to Fleckenstein, what is common "to each kind of image is its apparent transparency and universality. Everyone knows what images are because everyone evokes them. An image is something we sense (see, feel, hear, taste, smell, etc.), either mentally in the absence of stimuli or physiologically in response to stimuli" (8). The trick was getting students to acknowledge this "universality" of visual images that they were continually reading and helping them to apply their ingrained skill set to a different medium, the written word. An important factor for this transition through visual literacy assignments is utilizing the visual as a two-way street. It is not enough for the class to study the elements of literary criticism through the visual; retention and internalization of these ideas requires students to create their own texts utilizing their new skills.

The final piece of this unit was to write an informal essay in their journals that documented what exactly they had learned about reading and engaging with texts in these visual literacy exercises. I asked them to view this last piece as a verbal map that would guide them through the literary texts we would be exploring over the course of the semester. Landmarks on this map would need to include the role of the biographical, sociopolitical, cultural, and historical contexts of a work of art, the artist's influences, symbolism, and the importance of linking symbols together in a composition. Students then had their own reference guide in their own words that they could utilize to understand these concepts and dissect the numerous written works they were going to read over the rest of the semester.

The evaluation for the entire unit was based on two criteria: the success of the final photograph and the depth of the critical journal. The photographs were rated as successful or not based on peer response to them. A majority of the target audience of student peers had to be able to successfully read the photos. To get an A, the students' classmates had to be able to analyze and interpret the work and have their reading correspond with the goals of the artist. Additionally, I read each student's journal with an eye to their internalization and comprehension of the concepts presented, no matter how these ideas were presented.

As we left the visual unit behind and concentrated on our main goal, reading and engaging with works of American literature, the students' rate of understanding and retention was impressive. We moved on to study several classic canonical works as a group, each of the students armed with tools to break down a text into manageable pieces and reassemble it as an understandable whole. The students were successful in separating the fundamentals of reading from a verbal text, learning them through visuals, and then reapplying them to written works. I was pleased and impressed with the majority of the literary criticism essays that I received that semester.

For example, one student in the class traced the physical details of Alexandra's clothing in Willa Cather's *O Pioneers!*, constructing a character analysis through what she wore (and didn't wear) in contrast to her brothers and the other men in the story. Another student studied the use of color as metaphor in Jack Kerouac's *On the Road*, while yet another looked at the physical descriptions of Hill House in Shirley Jackson's *The Haunting of Hill House* as a symbol for women's unengaged minds in the 1950s. I believe that the students were capable of and comfortable tracing written images throughout verbal texts not only because they had begun the course by studying imagery in a manner that allowed them to identify the facets that create symbolism and meaning, but also because they were able to do this through the nonthreatening medium of photography.

Using photography to visualize these key concepts allowed the students to find an easier entry point into textual analysis. Asking them to create their own symbols to critically engage an audience also made the concepts that we were discussing extremely tangible, better equipping students to be on alert for the artistic craft of others. The connectivity was forthcoming for each student and they found it much easier to bond with one aspect of a text at a time than to try to separate out each aspect when they were all presented simultaneously.

George presents an additional idea that rationalizes the use of visual literacy as a teaching tool across the curriculum. She argues that as our first mode of processing and identifying the world that surrounds us is a visual one, visual texts therefore become our first language. She reminds us that—

[S]eeing comes before words. The child looks and recognizes before it can speak. But there is also another sense in which seeing comes before words. It is seeing which establishes our place in the surrounding world with words, but words can never undo the fact that we are surrounded by it. (343)

Resting on that belief, she delineates how teaching our courses on the foundation of visual communication would be an extremely successful method for reaching our students. She suggests that the simultaneous study of language arts with visual texts promotes the progression of language arts comprehension (334–57) and further states that "writing is itself visual communication" (336). In fact, many of the earliest languages were pictograph languages, demonstrating that our connection with pictures is the way we first develop language. Fleckenstein refers to this fundamental idea of image reading proceeding verbal understanding, stating that "graphic and mental images serve as precursors to and mutual participants in the cultural development of humankind" (4).

As we are continually reminding our students to show and not tell in their writing, aren't we in fact asking them to create word pictures? When we teach students to analyze the writing of others, we ask them to identify and isolate the images to determine their meanings: again looking for the word picture. If we are continually asking our students to use words to visualize images, shouldn't we be teaching them with images?

Visual literacy serves to demonstrate to students that critical thinking and active engagement are continual presences in their lives whether they realize it or not. They understand how to read and break down texts, although they may not have the correct names for what they are doing readily available. A demonstrative visual exercise that shows students that they are already experts at reading texts, that they do have the tools to analyze literature, and that they can succeed in the language arts classroom is an excellent device to welcome both new English majors and non-English majors into the introductory literature course. In this role, visual literacy allows many beginning students to start analyzing and crafting texts with which they already feel comfortable and, to a great extent, has removed any sense of insecurity.

Incorporating the visual arts into the language arts class is an effective means of conveying information, but one that is not often explored. It would behoove instructors in the language arts, but especially teachers of introductory classes, to move toward pedagogies incorporating multiliteracies that utilize the visual arts as a teaching tool and model that is more accessible to students. As George explains,

[M]uch of what once seemed revelatory about the role of visual media in our students' lives is now widely accepted, even taken for granted. Film and television continue to dominate a major portion of their formative years, creating expectations, shaping attitudes, influencing language patterns and providing a common frame of reference. (345)

Len Unsworth supports this fear of underutilizing an arena in which students are already so comfortable. He instructs teachers to be aware of the fact that students "have already functionally and critically engaged with electronic and conventional format texts in ways which they do not encounter in their classrooms when they begin school" (7).

How can we as teachers do better than to instruct students using familiar terms and ideas to convey the knowledge we have to impart? It doesn't make sense to turn our backs on a means of educating our students that is so accessible. If students can apply themselves with such apparent ease to visuals and break down their components, the same as those in the language arts, it would serve us well to teach them these skills in a manner they are able to approach.

Even the National Council of Teachers of English (NCTE) agrees that teaching the language arts "occurs in different modalities and technologies." NCTE discusses the ever-increasing dependency of students and teachers on computers, especially the Internet, which allows for a new and intriguing combination of modalities to be present in the same work environment. This not only puts a great deal of information in the hands of students of all skill levels, but also allows for them to simultaneously create designs as they verbally express themselves (12). Their mission statement includes the mandate that students "be able to think about the physical design of text, about the appropriateness and thematic content of visual images, about the integration of sound with a reading experience, and about the medium that is most appropriate for a particular message, purpose, and audience." They further ask that "basic tools for communicating expand to include modes beyond print alone [and that] 'writing' comes to mean more than scratching words with pen and paper" (13).

Unfortunately, even with the endless possibilities that incorporating visual literacy into a language arts classroom can offer, there is a great deal of hesitation and resistance to the idea of doing so. One of the reasons for this may be that visual literacy is still a fairly underexplored field in this setting. Limited research is available on visual literacy as a teaching tool in the language arts classroom. Most scholars agree that there are similarities to the manner in which people read a written text and analyze a visual (identifying the message, the audience, the purpose, and so on), they seem to be at a loss for what to do with that information. This hesitation comes despite the great potential to use visual literacy across the curriculum as a way to express intricate theories to students and for them to practice what they have learned in the hopes of processing it on a deeper, more significant level.

Another problem impeding the incorporation of visual literacy into the language arts classroom is the overwhelming message that visual study belongs only in the fine art or art history classroom. Certain administrators, funding agents, and scholars see this inclusion as fun or break time without academic merit once it is removed from the boundaries of the arts class. George feels that instructors too often see "the visual figuring into the teaching of [language arts], something added, an anomaly, a 'new' way of composing, or, somewhat cynically, as a strategy for adding relevance or interest to a required course ... rarely does the call acknowledge the visual as much more than attendant to the verbal" (336). Fleckenstein picks up this thread by chastising the

traditional pedagogy in highly literate societies [which] has been based on a linguistic model of forming (as well as a linguistic model of assessment) in large part because intelligence has been defined in linguistic terms and determined through standardized testing since the work of Alfred Binet in the early 1900s. The underlying assumption has been that we represent and navigate the world through language. Acknowledging the power of imagery, in all its myriad forms, to connect, shape, and change us requires that we see all meaning as multimodal. (22)

Furthermore, there often seems to be a lack of trust on the part of teacher in the arena of the visual. The teacher trusts neither herself to lead the students through a visual literacy exercise nor does she trust the students' abilities to dissect and reconstruct the complexities of the visual. While teaching object-based learning and visual literacy to D.C. public school teachers, I observed a great deal of uncertainty on the teachers' part, stemming from their perceived lack of proficiency with visuals. Non-art teachers in general tend to feel that, if their own field of expertise is not the visual arts, than they cannot possibly teach it to their students.

This seems to be the biggest issue that scholars will need to address if they want to ultimately see this pedagogy incorporated into the English curriculum on any wide-scale manner. Teachers worry that they have to be art historians or mini-Picassos to integrate visual literacy into their classrooms, losing sight of the fact that they too live in a visual culture and therefore are also adept at reading visual texts. While age, education level, finances, and regional differences do play a role in our involvement with media, especially with new media, we cannot escape the fact that the Unites States depends on visuals for communication, a truth that will only become more encompassing as we continue to make technological progress. And if we, as teachers and scholars, want to go on reaching our students, we have to make an effort to learn their language—that is, a media-driven visual language.

WORKS CITED

"Composing Occurs in Different Modalities and Technologies." *National Council of Teachers of English Mission Statement*. National Council of Teachers of English. http://www.ncte.org/prog/writing/research/118876.htm (October 13, 2005).

Fleckenstein, Kristie S. "Inserting Imagery into Our Classrooms." In *Language and Image in the Reading Writing Classroom: Teaching Vision,* edited by Kristie S. Fleckenstein, Linda T. Calendrillo, and Demetrice A. Worley, 3–26. Mahwah, NJ: Lawrence Erlbaum Associates, 2002.

George, Diana. "From Analysis to Design: Visual Communication in the Teaching of Writing." In *Teaching Composition: Background Readings*, edited by T. R. Johnson, 334–58. Boston: Bedford/St. Martin's, 2005.

Goldfarb, Brian. *Visual Pedagogy: Media Cultures in and beyond the Classroom*. Durham, NC: Duke University Press, 2002.

Guezzar, Terri Pullen. "Mental Imagery and Literature: Centers and Vectors in Students' Visual and Verbal Responses." In *Language and Image in the Reading-Writing Classroom: Teaching Vision*, edited by Kristie S. Fleckenstein, Linda T. Calendrillo, and Demetrice A. Worley, 47–58. Mahwah, NJ: Lawrence Erlbaum Associates, 2002.

Hobbs, Catherine L. "Learning From the Past: Verbal and Visual Literacy in Early Modern Rhetoric and Writing Pedagogy." In *Language and Image in the Reading-Writing Classroom: Teaching Vision*, edited by Kristie S. Fleckenstein, Linda T. Calendrillo, and Demetrice A. Worley, 27–44. Mahwah, NJ: Lawrence Erlbaum Associates, 2002.

Hocks, Mary E. "Understanding Visual Rhetoric in Digital Writing Environments." In *Teaching Composition: Background Readings*, edited by T. R. Johnson, 358–82. Boston: Bedford/St. Martin's, 2005.

Unsworth, Len. *Teaching Multiliteracies across the Curriculum: Changing Contexts of Text and Image in Classroom Practice*. Buckingham, United Kingdom: Open University Press, 2001.

Reading Right to Left: How Defamiliarization Helps Students Read a Familiar Genre

Christine M. Doran

When I first bought *Tank Girl: The Odyssey*, my family asked me if there had been a mistake. They couldn't understand why there was a "comic book" in with my teaching books. My students told me they experienced a similar moment of puzzlement when they saw the book on the bookstore shelves. I had gone looking for something unusual to add to a new class and *Tank Girl: The Odyssey* seemed to fit the bill perfectly. It has now become somewhat common for me to include comic books, or graphic novels, in almost all of my classes. Teaching graphic novels allows me to foreground questions of genre, gender, and pedagogy in the lived daily experiences of my classroom in new ways. This essay explores how I have learned to teach graphic novels and the impact that has had on my "regular" teaching of novels, a genre my students sometimes seem all too familiar with. Throughout the essay, I examine how teaching graphic novels has worked for me in two different classes (Classical Heritage in Literature and Gender and Literature), with three different texts (*Fake*, *Blankets*, and *Tank Girl: The Odyssey*), over the course of two years.

Classical Heritage in Literature is a course designed to read Classical Greek texts and then trace allusions to those texts in more modern texts. Gender and Literature interrogated the ways in which literature both produces gender—that is, shapes the ways a culture understands what is acceptable behavior for males and females—and is gendered—that is, ways in which texts come to be considered "girls' books" or "boys' books," with romance novels, for example, being the most obvious example of books that girls read and boys do not. The texts under discussion in this essay include *Tank Girl: The Odyssey* by Milligan and Hewlett, a postmodern punk allegory that I have taught in two different versions of Classical Heritage in Literature; *Blankets* by Craig Thompson, which is a beautifully drawn personal history of first love; and *Fake* by Sanami Matoh, which is Japanese *shonen-ai manga*, in Gender and Literature. Each of these texts demands its own kind of retraining in the skills of reading as I will explicate more fully below.

The undergraduate population in my classes is primarily English majors, education majors, and gender studies majors. I often teach "difficult" novels[1] to them and have recently started to include graphic novels, both American texts and Japanese manga. Manga must be read from right to left, that is, "backward" for American students, and thus are often confusing for first-time readers of the genre. Most of my students read novels for pleasure and they often come to class imagining that this means they already know how to read novels critically. Therefore, for me, the key to teaching novels is defamiliarization—getting students to pay attention to what they are actually reading rather than what they assume they know about the texts. While defamiliarization is a common-enough technique in literature classes, I find it particularly suited to graphic novels because of the way these novels combine textual reading practices and visual reading practices, especially the practices of watching and reading films. Getting my students to see the filmic influences in the graphic novels, especially the manga, helps them to see and read in new ways.

An interesting side note to the question of visual reading practices is that I sometimes have students who note they prefer the purely textual novels, because they can then use their imagination with regard to characters' appearances, settings, and other details. For example, when we read *Confessions of a Shopaholic* in Gender and Literature, my students all had different ideas about what the heroine Rebecca Bloomwood looked like. We were able to consider reasons why an author might not describe a character fully—one reason, particularly with "romance" novels, is that imperfectly described characters allow for easier reader identification. This awareness of their own investment in what characters look like came after we spent time thinking through how we are influenced by artists' renditions of characters. Raina, in *Blankets*, is the most beautiful girl the narrator Craig has ever seen. My students, however, noticed that she is beautiful in a somewhat bland way and that we only know of her beauty through Craig's eyes, thus producing important critical distance in their reading.

It may help to begin with a discussion of what I mean by graphic novels. They are any of a category of novel that blends pictures and text. They are sometimes called "comic books," although for Americans that term carries stereotypes of geeky teenage boys reading about overly muscled superheroes in spandex. "Superheroes" should be taken as primarily male; by and large the characters who inhabit these books are male and any women are usually girlfriends in distress or villains in skimpy clothing. There are exceptions, such as the women in Marvel's *X-Men* universe and Joss Whedon's *Fray,* but the genre is still more often male than not.[2] Outside of the United States, comic books are not, and never have been, only for teenaged males, something which has become more true in the United States since the emergence of underground comic artists like Crumb, Clowes, and Pekar (all of whom have had movies made based on their works or their lives in the past ten years). This domination of male-centered action comics is partly market driven. In the United States, the two best-known comics companies are DC and Marvel, both of whom have their own particular style and both of whom are heavily dependent on their standard superhero titles. Underground comics, including feminist titles, gay titles, African American titles, and so on, have difficulty competing with the two major companies.

Comic book stores are still more likely to carry superhero titles from the mainstream companies. Perhaps best known in the category of "serious" comic books are Art Spiegelman's *Maus* books—in which Spiegelman retells the story of the Holocaust with Jewish "mice" and Nazi "cats"—and, more recently, Marjane Satrapi's *Persepolis*—which tells the story of a young girl growing up in Iran during the Islamic Revolution. But graphic can indicate more than "image," it also carries connotations of "explicit." The definitional layers of meaning remind us of the connection between "visual" and "transparency of meaning," and one of the first tasks of defamiliarization is to get students to rethink what they know about how images transmit meaning. *Tank Girl: The Odyssey* works these multiple levels of meaning nicely, because it contains scenes of nudity and violence that would give a film at least an R rating.[3]

Students are often well aware of other stereotypes about graphic novels, even those students who have never read one before. For defamiliarization to work, I must get them to acknowledge and begin to interrogate what they think they know about graphic novels. Before they read the graphic novels, I have a short introductory session in which I ask the students to think of any stereotypes they may have—we usually cover the expected ones, like those listed above about superheroes and geeks. I ask them, whether or not they have any experience with these kinds of texts, to treat them as unfamiliar and begin the following lessons by getting the students to tell me about the experience of reading something "new." Examples of "new" often include thinking about how text explicates, duplicates, and/or contradicts image. I have one student who told me it took her four or five hours to read *Tank Girl: The Odyssey*—a text of about 100 pages, something she noted would normally take her between one and two hours—because she kept deciphering the puns and visual jokes embedded in the images, in effect rereading as she was reading.

One thing that often comes up during our interrogation of stereotypes is the question of how suitable graphic novels are for classroom use. In fact, if I do not introduce this topic, my students are sure to bring it up. My education majors, in particular, are often well aware of the controversy around teaching comic books. During the 1940s and 1950s, comic books came under attack because their (often) violent and (sometimes) sexually provocative content was seen as unsuitable reading material for children.[4] Comic books in the United States began a long period of self-censorship geared toward making sure they were suitable for children—who were seen as their primary audience—thus entering a period during which they became the antithesis of material one would read in school.[5] The last few years, however, have seen increasing interest in using comic books to teach children and organizations like the National Association of Comics Art Educators (www.teachingcomics.org) offer advice for teachers who wish to use comic books in their classrooms. I like to think through this history with my students. It reminds them that what they learn in classrooms has a history and a politics. Defamiliarizing *what* they learn can often be as effective as defamiliarizing how they learn it.

Articulating assumptions about suitability often result in productive discussions. For example, in Classical Heritage in Literature, one of the assumptions is that the texts must be "old" to be "good," and I remind students that not all old texts are equally of interest to them. Sometimes, students assume that classroom-suitable texts must be boring, difficult, and unappealing. I like to ask students to tell the class things they like *and* things they dislike about texts as we read them. Students often find it interesting and useful to learn that their peers have different responses to texts; *The Odyssey* will be unexpectedly "cool" and griping for one student and "totally boring" for another. What ultimately matters, I tell them, is whether or not they can learn from the texts and use them to teach each other—this latter occurring most commonly during student presentations when they are asked to lead classroom discussion. I often ask the students who do the presentation on *Tank Girl: The Odyssey* to refer explicitly back to student presentations on Homer's *Odyssey*. Doing so works on a number of levels: it reinforces classroom collective memory, it often strengthens the current presentation, and it provides nice peer feedback to the students who did the earlier presentation.

With rare student exceptions, gender is the most common dividing line between those who have and have not read graphic novels. Male students have read comic books and are more likely to have read something other than super-hero books. Female students do not read comics, except those who self-identify as players of video games or viewers of Japanese anime (anime simply means "animated" and stories that appear in manga form often appear in anime versions as well). These categories are changing with the level of student engagement with various forms of fan culture (on the Internet and in other places) and are likely to continue to change. Furthermore, both male and female students are increasingly of the generation(s) that grew up on Pokemon and Power Rangers and are thus often well-versed in the techniques of Japanese media, whether or not they admit to having this knowledge.

One example of someone who crossed these gender categories was a female student in my Gender and Literature class who was outspoken about her reading preference for romance novels—making her stereotypically "girly." She, however, was also someone who had read and enjoyed manga before, particularly the subcategory of *yaoi* or *shonen-ai* manga. Both terms refer to manga with boys who love other boys.[6] The paradox of this student's investment in both kinds of texts, traditional heterosexual romance novels and *shonen-ai* manga, can be resolved if one notes that these texts emphasize the intensity of a relationship over almost all other narrative structures. Whether or not the boy gets the girl—or the other boy—is what matters most in heterosexual romance novels and in *shonen-ai* manga. The most useful aspect to me of these admittedly stereotypical gender divisions, however, comes when I foreground them for the students, defamiliarizing what they take as "natural." My romance-reading student became an example for the class of how surface differences may not bear up under close scrutiny. The class was initially unsure why she liked both genres, but through her example, they learned to see the more familiar genre of heterosexual romance in a new light.

Furthermore, the very question of subgenres such as heterosexual romance became a topic of debate for the Gender and Literature class. The "romance" novel we read, Amanda Quick's *Rendezvous*, is a historical Regency romance with a spy subplot and a women's education subplot. I had students who insisted it was not a romance because of these subplots. After reading the manga, however, they were able to rethink *Rendezvous* in terms of its foregrounding of the relationship between the male and female lead and compare it to the relationship between Dee and Ryo in *Fake*. Superficially quite different, *Rendezvous* and *Fake*, read together, produced new definitions of "romance" and pushed my students to think about the process of categorization.[7]

Teaching graphic novels involves teaching students how to read images. In *Understanding Comics*, Scott McCloud describes comics as "sequential art" (7). The text must be understood not as stand-alone images but as stories told combining words and images into panels, which are then arranged on the page. Students may not be aware that they are familiar with reading images or with reading sequentially—although they do both all the time. The most obvious example here is probably film, but I also like to use examples like advertisements and mystery novels. Advertisements tell stories, and thinking through how they do so can help students focus on how the images in graphic novels tell their stories. Mystery novels invite us to think sequentially and retrospectively—each new piece of information must be integrated into a complete pattern if the reader is to solve the mystery with, or even before, the detective. In integrated texts like graphic novels, images and words tell us the same thing—the story may be comprehensible reading only images or only text. The beauty and strength of the form, however, comes from the melding of the two, text explaining image and image replicating text.

The example of film viewing works well during discussions of manga, a genre that is strongly influenced by film technique. Images can move at different "speeds" across the page, just as it is possible to speed up or slow down a film image. A standard manga image of violence will include "slo-mo" depictions of the characters facing each other with weapons drawn, something my students were all able to read easily. Furthermore, film and manga can jump-cut, flashback, and so on, and getting my students to think about how film uses jump-cuts to connect disparate things or how flashbacks are used to fill in necessary backstory helped them read the manga.

Furthermore, texts are "difficult" or "easy" often in direct relation to how unfamiliar or familiar we are with their generic conventions. I often foreground students (unacknowledged) experience with generic conventions by focusing on the openings of texts. The first sentence or first paragraph of a novel tells us much of the information we need to understand to know how to read it. The cliché of "It was a dark and stormy night"[8] tells us we are about to read something dark and mysterious. "It is a truth universally acknowledged, that a single man in possession of a good fortune must be in want of a wife"[9] tells us we should expect to read about how money and marriage are connected. Finally, "Happy families are all alike; every unhappy family is unhappy in its own way"[10] tells us to expect a novel about unhappy families. I use all of these examples in my classes, reading the lines to students and asking them to tell me what the novels are about. Only after they have finished explaining what they think will happen, and thus articulating their knowledge of generic conventions, do I tell them the authors and titles.

Each graphic novel seemed to produce a particular epiphany for the class, usually coming after we as a class articulated the conventions at work in the text.

This key moment in reading *Fake* by Sanami Matoh came for the class when we discussed Dee and Ryo's first night together. Reading this manga text first involved learning to read right to left. The unfamiliar method of reading is the first level of defamiliarization I ask my students to think through. Another level of defamiliarization is often cultural, which is something my students also experienced when we read *Fake*. Ryo and Dee are New York City police[11] who have just been assigned as partners and Ryo invites Dee to his house for dinner to discuss Bikky, the eleven-year-old boy Ryo is planning on fostering. The three end up sleeping the night in Ryo's huge bed. While sharing the bed foreshadows the sexual relationship the two male cops will ultimately have, it also serves the purpose of family building in the world of the story. Realizing the importance of family and social grouping to Japanese culture helped my students understand this bed-sharing scene. We discussed how Japanese culture is based on many people sharing a small amount of space and how group identity is often more important than individual identity. To American students raised on the myths of rugged individualism and manifest destiny (whether or not they use those terms, my students are all familiar with the underlying assumptions), ideas of social harmony take some getting used to. In particular, duty and obligation to family and larger groups (school, club, team, company, and so on) run throughout Japanese culture, and maintaining social harmony is more important than individual happiness in many manga. Female characters, especially, are expected to display *yasashisa*, a gentle, compassionate quality that seeks to bring harmony to any group.[12] The absence of a central female character in *Fake* often leaves the role of maintaining yasashisa to Ryo. Doing so serves two functions: (1) it makes Ryo's connection to his Japanese heritage clearer and (2) it ties into his quandaries about his sexual identity. Ryo fears being the "girl" in his relationship with Dee; he resists their physical relationship because maintaining *yasashisa* already marks him as "female."

Many of my students were initially troubled by Bikky being in bed with the two men and by the fact that the bed is almost the only thing Ryo has left of his parents—a grown man sleeping in his parents' bed seems somehow perverse to them. The bed here must be understood not simply as a site of sexual activity but rather as a family home in embryo. If the bed were purely a foreshadowing of the erotic relationship between Dee and Ryo, Bikky's presence in the bed of Ryo's parents would have to be interpreted differently. Ryo, who has no other family, creates a new family through fostering Bikky. If Dee could not accept this fostering, there could be no hope for a romance between the two men. Dee and Bikky bicker throughout the seven-volume series, but this bed-sharing scene demonstrates that they can, and will, be part of Ryo's family. Lest one imagine the bed as completely nonsexual, however, it is important to remember that Bikky's presence in it foreshadows his role throughout the series as obstacle to the physical side of Dee and Ryo's relationship. Bikky almost always attempts to stop physical intimacy between the two men—something that works as a plot device as well as marking the necessity for a suitor to prove his intentions. If Dee just wanted Ryo as a sexual conquest, he would be unsuitable and Bikky's ham-handed interference to the physical relationship would put Dee off. But because Dee wants a long-lasting and serious relationship with Ryo, he persists despite the oftentimes obnoxious Bikky and ultimately is rewarded with Ryo's love.

Depicting emotions such as love involves an awareness of visual iconography, which was something we spent much of our class time discussing when we read *Blankets*, an American, twentieth-century, lush, lyrical text. It tells the story of Craig Thompson's strictly religious childhood and his first love. The illustrations evoke childhood with an emotional depth and honesty that is rare in any genre. The novel privileges the visual level of storytelling forcing my students to rethink their assumptions about the transparency of visual objects. They usually easily read the emotions a character displays (anger, joy, and so on), but I ask them to think about how they know when a character is mad, sad, glad, and so on, that is, what visual icons are they relying on and to think about the teaching and learning that goes into making, for example, an upside down semicircle a "frown."

There is a scene in *Blankets* in which Craig's brother Phil drags his hands down a door, after his father has locked him in a storage cupboard as punishment (17). The hands signal his childhood helplessness against his father's power and we see the marks his fingers leave on the door. Later, Craig is harassed by school bullies and when he washes his bloody nose in the school bathroom, we see the same kind of hand prints as he drags his bloody fingers down the bathroom mirror (25). Explaining to my students that the visual metaphors here operate the same as word metaphors do in purely textual novels was a breakthrough point for many of them. As English majors, they all have some experience with metaphors and making this connection actually transformed the unfamiliar back into the known. Each brother is experiencing anguished rage at the callous power of the world around them. The visual metaphor connects the brothers and draws in the readers. Craig's marks on the mirror make sense in relation to the earlier marks left by Phil on the storage cupboard door. Each set of marks could be understood on its own, perhaps, but the combination, the sequence, builds the story of the boys' world for the readers. Art and drawing are something else that connects the brothers. Craig explains that he and Phil would often draw together, not necessarily because Phil shared Craig's love for art but more as a way to spend time together (44).

Reading the visual does not start inside the graphic novels, and I encourage my students to start by reading the covers. *Tank Girl: The Odyssey* provides an excellent example of the benefits of reading the cover. The title tells us that the character we see is a girl, but I ask the class to pretend that the title words are not there. The only traditional marker of femininity we see is Tank Girl's bright red lipstick, and it is always interesting to see how long it takes the class to notice this. The other things they get from the cover include violence (there are phallic bombs all over the cover), humor (the girl is almost twice as large as the tank she rides on), sex (there is a condom taped to the large bomb at the bottom left of the image), and consumer culture (the Shell logo, other stickers on the tank). There are other words on the cover, notably the pennant flag on the back of the tank that reads "She Came 1st." Getting the class to work through all the layers of the phrase is always productive and often funny. The other thing to note about the front cover is that it does not say "The Odyssey." One has to open the book or turn to the back cover to get that piece of information, once more bringing up questions about generic conventions for my class.

When I last taught *Tank Girl: The Odyssey*, one student informed me that she was uncomfortable with the text. These novels may make students uncomfortable in ways purely textual novels do not, because the impact of the visual image is sometimes greater than the impact of words. Here, again, is a space in which questions of suitability may be raised, as this student did. Interestingly, this student did not come to me with complaints about Joyce's *Ulysses*, although we read the chapter that introduces Leopold Bloom going about his morning routine during which we are given access to his thoughts as he fantasizes about women, ponders the material world around him, and defecates. She had not read *Tank Girl: The Odyssey* but had looked through it briefly and was sure she did not want to read it fully or discuss it in class. Here, the visual trumped the textual.

In one scene, Tank Girl rises from the dead, naked and in a morgue. The scene parallels the journey to the Underworld that Odysseus undertakes with the help of Circe. Odysseus learns from this episode key information about the rest of his journey home and about the human condition. Tank Girl learns some of the same kind of information but does not treat it as seriously as Odysseus does. Rather, she blatantly seduces a scientist by the name of A. E. Olus who has invented a strain of fart that can reanimate the dead. She uses the farts to bring back her comrades and continue on her way home. Later, the group is shipwrecked at the Cyclops Hotel. Again, the parallel to the Cyclops section of the Odyssey encourages us to think Tank Girl will learn something from this experience. But rather than learning the importance of hospitality, Tank Girl uncovers a quasi-Christian religious cult that believes the sins of the world are caused by having two eyes, so each cult member has plucked out an eye, and guests at the hotel are subjected to the same cost. Without probing too deeply into her personal discomfort, it is scenes like these two that seemed most likely to be troubling to my student. Respecting her concerns, I gave her permission not to attend those classes and instead substituted individual meetings. The negative experience of this student was unusual but not without productive side-effects. The two things I learned from this student were patience and the reminder that one cannot manufacture paradigm shifts. It can never hurt to remember to be patient with our students, especially when one is involved in setting up conditions under which paradigm shifts might happen. I always consider student–teacher encounters that result in strengthened mutual respect a success, however, and so I was not displeased with the result of our individual meetings.

I often provide students with unfamiliar material and attempt to get them to negotiate and articulate their shock even if it means starting with emotional responses no more sophisticated than "yuck" or "gross." However, I also make it clear to them that someone's emotional response to a particular text is not a matter for laughter or scorn. Thinking of these classroom practices in terms of Brecht's alienation effect—that is, getting the students to give up their emotional responses and work toward critical distance—may help. Creating an atmosphere of respect allows my students to come to me with their concerns and students have told me how this open, respectful atmosphere has opened up critical, literary thinking for them. My students are often first-generation college students who sometimes struggle with the idea that there is not a single correct answer to a work of literature. Being encouraged to voice their own (sometimes emotional) responses to the texts and then hearing differing, sometimes dissenting, responses from other students is radically transformative for many of them.

Tank Girl: The Odyssey is, sometimes, lurid, as the two scenes I described above suggest. The protagonist is a postapocalyptic antiheroine who smokes and drinks too much; delights in violence, mayhem, and promiscuous sex; and resists all forms of authority. The text, however, also playfully and intelligently retells both Homer's *Odyssey* and Joyce's *Ulysses* and was wildly successful with the majority of my students each time I taught it. In fact, the book markets itself as tied to Homer. The back cover claims that it is "Tank Girl vs. Mythology! A twisted take on Homer's classical Greek epic . . . [the book] makes a few 'minor' changes to the original," thus challenging readers to notice those "minor" changes. We read it at the end of the semester, after we have read Homer and at least parts of Joyce and it serves as a metanarrative commentary on the aims of Classical Heritage in Literature. In particular, the ending of *Tank Girl: The Odyssey* explicitly asks the reader to think about retelling stories:

For those of you who've stuck with us all the way, you've probably noticed one or two allusions. . . . [Remember,] we've got to make our own books . . . find the historical structures and parallels that help us make sense out of our own world . . . and locate the epic in our everyday lives. (n.p.)

My at-this-point-in-the-semester familiar directive to the students about telling and retelling stories is thus rendered anew and, hopefully, productively unfamiliar.

What all these kinds of defamiliarization do for my students is help them think about the necessity of paying close attention to the details of whatever text they are reading. Reading purely textual novels after reading the graphic novels is a return to the familiar, but I hope a return with a difference. Once we have unpacked graphic images, students seem to have an easier time unpacking text. Because they have practiced how the attention to detail can help them read and interpret an image, the attention to detail a deconstructive textual close reading demands becomes something they do better. Where once they might have noted only that Michael Ondaatje's *The English Patient* mentions Herodotus's *Histories* repeatedly, now they will note how the *Histories*'s tales of stolen women[13] foreshadow what Ondaatje is doing in his novel. They are thus able to produce a more sophisticated analysis of the Ondaatje novel and can move beyond surface observation, a flaw that one finds in many undergraduate papers. I have also paired Herodotus with Geoff Ryman's *Was*, producing fruitful discussions about what counts as history under what conditions and according to whose definitions. Both times I taught Classical Heritage in Literature, I included this kind of pairing as a possible paper topic, that is, students were asked to find a definition of history in one text—usually from the Herodotus—and use it to analyze the paired text.

One student, an elementary education major, told me that the experience of reading the manga right to left was difficult. I told her to remember this experience when it comes time for her to teach children to read—if you know how things are supposed to be read, making sense of them is easy, before you have that knowledge, any text can seem impenetrable. Used in this way, reading with and against each other, novels and graphic novels have been successful in my classrooms. As we think about how to read, we also think about the whats and the whys of reading. We foreground individual emotional responses to art and transform them into critical group thinking about cultural textual practices. The graphic novels push boundaries my students sometimes do not even know that they have and, in the process, move us as a class to spaces of organic, collective learning. Graphic novels can make transparent how the narrative works through analysis of the relative power of image and text. The construction of the narrative is thus made more apparent and the dependence of meaning on form is more easily seen. Perhaps this particular lesson of defamiliarization has worked best, not for my students, but for myself. In teaching them to reread, I have been constantly reminded not to let my own expectations get in the way of their experiences.

END NOTES

1. For example, *Tristram Shandy* (1759–1769) is often considered difficult by undergraduates who encounter it for the first time. I have found it often helps those students to be reminded that novels were still new in English in the eighteenth century and that the things they struggle with in *Tristram Shandy*—constant narrator interruptions, digressions lasting pages, meandering plotlines, and so on—are the things that its first readers also struggled with.

2. Historically a genre drawn by men for men, comics books are changing and women are increasingly involved in this world. This view of comics as a male space is particularly true for action-oriented comics. There were a number of influential female artists in the United States throughout the twentieth century, but they tended to work in comedic or romance genres. In addition, their numbers were significantly affected by the return of women to the domestic sphere after World War II and by the slump in the comic industry during the 1950s when the genre came under attack (see note 4). For more on women's roles in comics, see Robbins—whose work includes texts like *A Century of Women Cartoonists* and *From Girls to Grrlz: A History of Women's Comics from Teens to Zines*—as well as Web sites like girlwonder.org and girlamatic.com. The first Web site deals with female characters in mainstream comics, the second is a site devoted to work by various female artists that ranges from superhero-type strips to "chick" strips concerned with issues facing contemporary women to strips that push the boundaries of art.

The women of the *X-Men* universe include Storm, Jean Grey, and Rogue, among others, all of whom have led teams at various points and all of whom have enough power to save/destroy the world, putting them on a level with the male characters.

Joss Whedon is perhaps best known as the creator of the television series *Buffy the Vampire Slayer*. *Fray* is a comic book he wrote that contains another strong female character; in fact, a slayer in a world that has forgotten the need for slayers. When asked why he creates such strong female characters, Whedon is well known for answering with a variety of reasons, ranging from the fact that they are characters he wished he had had available growing up, to the fact that such strong female characters echo what he knew in his mother, to the demand that he no longer be asked this question and that instead others be asked why they are not doing this.

3. An interesting note here is that one of the complaints about the 1995 *Tank Girl* movie is that it toned down the nudity and violence of its comic book source and thus lost much of the edgy social commentary that made the original so challenging and so beloved by its fans.

4. A key text here is Fredric Wertham's 1954 *Seduction of the Innocent,* which was the culmination of over ten years of controversy about comics. Wertham claimed that comics were a major cause of juvenile delinquents as well as being full of misinformation and questionable morality. Specifically, Superman was bad for children because the comic portrayed the Man of Steel flying, something which contradicted the laws of physics; Robin's bare legs were often shown wide spread, this and his devotion only to Batman encouraged homosexuality; and Wonder Woman gave girls false ideas about their place in society. Wertham was not the only voice in this discussion but he was one of most visible and influential.

5. Comic books still carry the Comics Code Authority (CCA) seal, although carrying the seal is voluntary and comics that do not meet the standards can still get published. Once, the CCA seal was prominently displayed on the front cover, now it is small and not always easy to find. The CCA was instituted in response to criticism such as those made by Wertham, and books that did not receive the seal of approval were often not carried in stores. Horror comics most often fell into this category—in fact, they still do. However, the efficacy of the seal was not universal and genres such as horror survived just fine without it.

6. "Boys" here usually means males in late adolescence; however, manga is so varied that one should not be surprised to find just about anything, including explicit heterosexual sex (*hentai*) and underage sex (*chan*). I find it best to remind students that American views of appropriate ages are not necessarily Japanese views on the subject and to send them to do research on Japanese history and culture. Furthermore, the American term "homosexual" is not quite accurate here, as sometimes the male characters do not self-identify as homosexual. They are more likely to call themselves bisexual or to think of themselves as straight except for the love they have for the other male. Indeed, many of these types of stories involve an acceptance of the person rather than the gender of the beloved. *Fake* is one such example because Dee repeatedly describes himself as bisexual and Ryo, throughout the course of the series, learns to look past the fact of Dee's biology to the person he loves.

7. With examples such as this, I like to ask my students to remember the Sesame Street game "One of these things is not like the others." I ask them to give me things as different as they can imagine and then I put them in the same category; I usually do the first one and then ask my students to provide other examples of how the different objects can go together. For example, I have been given "elephant" and "racing car"—animated and not animated, natural and manufactured, and so on. The list of ways the two things are not alike is long. However, if one imagines both things as children's toys, then they are "alike." My students thus practice thinking about how categories are constructed.

8. Opening line to Edward George Bulwer-Lytton's *Paul Clifford* (1830). It has since become a clichéd marker for bad writing and has inspired a bad writing contest.

9. Opening line to Austen's *Pride and Prejudice* (1813).

10. Opening line to Tolstoy's *Anna Karenina* (1873–1877).

11. Matoh makes it clear that realistic, procedural details of New York City police are not part of her story. The "New York" of her series is a setting as unreal as the "England" the two men visit in the second volume. Each setting is intended as background for the developing relationship between the two men and little else. The settings are conventions and not meant to be realistic. Manga is full of similar conventions, such as the one of drawing Asian characters who do not necessarily appear Asian. For more on these manga/anime conventions, see Drazen. Ryo fits this Asian/non-Asian appearance convention: he is blond but has dark eyes that cause his new partner Dee to ask him, almost immediately, "Hey, you got some Japanese in you or something? Your eyes are pitch black" (n.p.). Bikky is another such mixed-race character. In the black-and-white

drawings, his skin color is usually represented by a kind of shaded gray, but his white blond hair marks him as mixed race. Here again, Dee is the one who notices and asks Bikky, "Hey … was your mother white? … I'm just saying, your hair is an interesting shade of blonde. It's different … very cool" (n.p.). Dee's awareness of surface and depth here again mark him as suitable family material for Ryo. A lesser person would see only Bikky's mismatched skin and hair color or would not have noticed Ryo's Japanese heritage, Dee sees the "truth" of both people.

12. For more on *yasashisa* and other Japanese social conventions, see Drazen.

13. Herodotus attempts to explain the causes of war by retelling folktales about adulterous and/or stolen women. For him, war must ultimately have other causes. His rationale for why Helen cannot possibly have been in Troy during the Trojan War is persuasive: no one, he claims, would be stupid enough not to give back a single person rather than endure ten years of bloody conflict. Reading this other version of the better-known story in conjunction with Homer has always been productive for my classes, even if only for the ways in which it reminds students that point of view matters, that different authors have different agendas, and that the past is not one dimensional. Getting them to forego presentist mind-sets can be difficult but is always rewarding.

WORKS CITED

Austen, Jane. *Pride and Prejudice*, edited by Robert P. Irvine. Peterborough, Canada: Broadview, 2001.

Bulwer-Lytton, Edward George. *Paul Clifford*. 1830. London: Routledge. 1880.

Drazen, Patrick. *Anime Explosion: The What? Why? and Wow! of Japanese Animation*. Berkeley: Stone Bridge Press, 2003.

Herodotus. *Histories: New Translation, Selections, Backgrounds, Commentaries*, edited by Walter Blanco and Jennifer Tolbert Roberts. New York: Norton, 1992.

Kinsella, Sophie. *Confessions of a Shopaholic*. New York: Dial Press, 2001.

Matoh, Sanami. *Fake*. Vol 1. Los Angeles: Tokyopop, 1994.

McCloud, Scott. *Understanding Comics: The Invisible Art*. New York: Kitchen Sink Press, 1993. Harper Collins Rpt. 1994.

Milligan, Peter, and Jamie Hewlett. *Tank Girl: The Odyssey*. London: Titan Books, 1995.

Ondaatje, Michael. *The English Patient*. New York: Vintage, 1993.

Quick, Amanda. *Rendezvous*. New York: Bantam, 1991.

Robbins, Trina. *A Century of Women Cartoonists*. Northampton, MA: Kitchen Sink Press, 1993.

———. *From Girls to Grrlz: A History of Women's Comics from Teens to Zines*. New York: Chronicle Books, 1999.

Ryman, Geoff. *Was*. New York: Penguin, 1993.

Thompson, Craig. *Blankets*. Marietta, GA: Top Shelf Productions, 2004.

Tolstoy, Leo. *Anna Karenina*, edited by John Bayley, translated by Richard Pevear and Larissa Volokhonsky. New York: Penguin, 2003.

Wertham, Fredric. *Seduction of the Innocent*. New York: Rinehart, 1954.

Ford Madox Ford's *The Good Soldier*, Creative Writing, and Teaching the Modernist Novel in the Introductory-Level Literature Classroom

Stephen E. Severn

Writing in 1924 at the height of the artistic movement that eventually came to be called Modernism and still coming to grips with the impact of the Theory of Relativity and the fundamental shifts in human understanding that it wrought, Russian novelist Yevgeny Zamyatin recognized clearly that "Euclid's world is very simple and Einstein's world is very difficult—but it is no longer possible to return to Euclid" (112). Nearly a century later, that process has repeated itself, only now it is Einstein's world that is simple, while our post-9/11, String-Theory world is difficult. And, just as Zamyatin could not go back to Euclid, we cannot go back to Einstein. This parallel experience makes it crucial that the perspectives and insights offered by Modernist novels such as James Joyce's *Ulysses* and Virginia Woolf's *To the Lighthouse* find a place in our students' collegiate experiences. Deliberately abstract and fractured, replete with allusions, and lacking the conventions of traditional narratives, these texts challenge the hegemonic façade of realism that holds cultural dominance over our supposedly savvy, detached and ironized post-postmodern world and drives the majority of current television, movies and populist fiction. Students who grapple with a Modernist novel will no longer believe that all chronology must be linear; that all narrators are trustworthy, helpful, all-knowing guides; that all scenes transition smoothly from point A to point B and that all stories must draw to a logical and socially affirming resolution that usually involves or implies marriage. They will come to recognize that actual experience never tidies up as neatly as proto-Realist narratives would have us believe.

Successfully exposing students to this alternative worldview is no easy task, however. Indeed, of all genres, Modernist novels present perhaps the most formidable pedagogical challenge to teachers of English literature. Even in an upper-level English course composed exclusively of majors who are seasoned undergraduates and presumably possess advanced verbal, reading, and writing skills, these works require a great deal of effort, planning, and patience on the part of the teacher. In an introductory-level literature course like Introduction to

World Literature or British Literature from 1800 to the Present that challenge burgeons into an uphill battle of Sisyphean proportions, because such classes are populated primarily with students from a wide variety of academic backgrounds, who often have limited undergraduate experience, have done little literary analysis, and may be taking the class simply to fill a "core" requirement. The professor who places Gertrude Stein's *Three Lives* on the syllabus for introduction to the novel will first have to teach her students how to read the book—how to recognize its linguistic patterns, how to gauge its references, how to trace its storyline—before she can ever hope to promote anything resembling an appreciation for its incessant challenge to the fundamental character of language. For some teachers, that task simply seems too daunting. In the spring and summer of 2006, I surveyed English faculty from a wide variety of academic institutions in all fifty states. A full 35 percent of respondents who do not teach Modernist novels in survey courses admitted that they elect not to do so because they believe the texts are too difficult for their students to understand.[1]

To further complicate matters, the very process of disassembling a Modernist novel, of breaking it down into more easily approachable components in an effort to simply gain some level of comprehension, robs the text of the overwhelming power that defines its whole. In his groundbreaking essay "On The Teaching of Modern Literature," Lionel Trilling addresses this dilemma directly when he laments that his exam questions make such "good sense" and succeed so fully at stripping away the essence of their subject matter that "the young person who answers them can never again know the force and terror of what has been communicated to him by the works he is being examined on" (12).

So, when teaching Modernist novels, especially in literary survey courses, how do faculty promote comprehension and understanding in students without negating the ability of these texts to profoundly challenge and disturb their readers? Drawn from my own pedagogical experiences as well as relevant critical studies and survey data, the following essay addresses that provocative question. It proffers a specific, practical, and innovative response to the pedagogical challenge of the Modernist novel by establishing the clear pedagogical advantages that Ford Madox Ford's *The Good Soldier* holds for the introductory-level, literature classroom. It then offers a detailed strategy for teaching Ford's novel in conjunction with analytical assignments that feature creative writing components. My research suggests that, to date, neither *The Good Solider* nor the implementation of creative writing assignments as a pedagogical tool have enjoyed significant application in this particular teaching context. I believe faculty would do well to adopt both into their curricula.

STARTING POINTS

The construction of any pedagogical strategy focused upon Modernist literature—be it fiction, poetry, or drama—must begin with a two-part acknowledgement: These texts are difficult for students to understand, and that difficulty is the very reason that they should be taught. They offer students a chance to experience what Gail MacDonald calls the "deep educative value of being confused" (18). Ralph Ellison, author of *Invisible Man*, a crowning achievement of

American Modernist fiction, illustrated this point when he famously traced his own literary development back to the frustration caused by his first encounter with T. S. Eliot's *The Waste Land*:

The Waste Land seized my mind. I was intrigued by its power to move me while eluding my understanding. Somehow its rhythms were often closer to those of jazz than were those of the Negro poets, and even though I could not understand then, its range of allusion was as mixed and as varied as that of Louis Armstrong. Yet there were its discontinuities, its changes of pace and its hidden system of organization which escaped me.

There was nothing to do but look up the references in the footnotes to the poem, and thus began my conscious education in literature. (*Shadow and Act* 159–60)

His account speaks directly to the power of these works: "There was nothing to do but." Because they make no concessions to their audience, readers have no choice but to go after them as Ellison did by reading actively and consciously, by tracking down allusions, by deciphering abstract, decontextualized imagery, and—frankly—by frequently feeling deeply confused. Will a Modernist novel like *Invisible Man* frustrate students, especially those who are exposed to one for the first time? Without question. Will at least a few readers throw their texts angrily against dorm room walls during fits of aggravation? Highly likely. Might reading a Modernist novel produce a palpable sense of anomie? Possibly. Such moments, however, should be sought out, not avoided, for they are the points at which truly transformative learning—the kind of learning that started Ellison down the developmental path that eventually produced *Invisible Man*—can begin. They are why these texts belong in a literature survey course.[2]

Having said that, the difficulty of Modernist novels does produce an inescapable pedagogical reality. Due to the sheer abstraction and intellectual complexity of these texts, students must be engaged with them if they are to learn from them. Although engagement is obviously a broad term that can have a range of meanings and be influenced by a number of factors, for the purposes of this study, it will be defined simply as a commitment by the student to develop an understanding of the text and a recognition of its intellectual and aesthetic value. Ultimately, the degree of success that faculty experience when teaching a Modernist novel in an introductory-level literature class will be directly proportional to the level of student engagement that they promote. David Gugin, an expert in the teaching of English to foreign students in overseas universities, recognizes that a high level of motivation for his students is crucial because they are being asked to produce writing both in a foreign language and a foreign style (genre) and the latter requirement is particularly problematic. Compounding the difficulty is the fact that they are typically asked to write about texts and subjects that they often have no initial surface familiarity with or interest in. It is little wonder then that many students do not succeed at academic writing (2).

Although the context of Gugin's observations—overseas academic writing classrooms for nonnative English speakers—may seem radically different from an introductory-level literature classroom populated predominantly by native English speakers, a clear analogy exists. For many (if not most) undergraduates in an introduction to British literature course, both the form and content of a Modernist novel will appear (at least initially) to have come from a foreign, perhaps even extraterrestrial, land. If they approach the text with a lackadaisical, disinterested attitude, they will gain nothing from it. They will not experience the "deep educative value" of confusion, just confusion.

Although to some degree teachers can foster student engagement by consistently reminding them of the "point of the point" and by making it clear why these texts matter, the most lasting and effective way to generate interest is through the comprehensive construction of the course itself. To begin with, a work whose essential subject matter appeals to students' interests tends to produce greater learning results simply because the class will be naturally more attracted to it and more inclined to read it carefully. Sadly, the day-long planning for Clarissa's party that serves as the backdrop for Woolf's *Mrs. Dalloway* will probably not engender the same level of excitement as the espionage plot that underscores Joseph Conrad's *The Secret Agent*. Faculty are advised to select texts that strike a balance between abstraction and accessibility—texts that will expose students to the challenge of reading a Modernist novel but are not so abstract that only the most erudite and disciplined readers can approach them. This may sound like a justification for "dumbing down" a class. It is not. There are some Modernist novels that are so dauntingly complex that teaching them would be counterproductive. Given that many faculty would think twice before placing all of Joyce's *Finnegan's Wake* on the syllabus of a graduate-level seminar, excluding it from consideration for an undergraduate survey course is an exercise in pragmatic reasoning, not pedagogical cowardice.

A potential danger exists in focusing attention too closely on student engagement when designing a course and selecting its texts. Teachers must not be so concerned with the possible reaction of a class to the syllabus or the intellectual challenge presented by a novel that they shirk their fundamental role as leaders and instead become fatuous panderers. As Abram Van Engen cautions, "teaching is not necessarily about giving students what they want—that might amount to little more than free pizza" (9). For his part, Trilling takes that stance to its extreme conclusion:

As for students, I have never given assent to the modern saw about "teaching students, not subjects"—I have always thought it right to teach subjects, believing that if one gives his first loyalty to the subject, the student is best instructed. So I resolved to give the course with no considerations in mind except my own interests. (13)

Whether one reads that statement as a stubborn defense of pedagogical idealism or an unconscious revelation of a fundamental narcissism is largely beside the point. Although such a completely teacher-centered strategy may have proved efficacious when dealing with English majors at Columbia University in the 1950s and 1960s—and even that seems doubtful—it would most certainly lead to disaster in an introductory-level classroom today. Addressing the question of which factors faculty consider when adopting a Modernist text, one survey respondent commented that "Most important to me is whether I think the novel will interest students. Without their interest, the things you list above [factors such as length of the novel, availability of a critical edition, and so on] don't matter much." There is a balance to be struck here. Van Engen's warning is well-taken. But, to successfully incorporate a Modernist novel into an introductory-level literature course, teachers will have to give greater consideration to students' interests, reactions, and intellectual capabilities than they would when selecting other types of texts.

THE CASE FOR *THE GOOD SOLDIER*

Having set forth some general considerations to follow when choosing a Modernist novel for an introductory-level literature course, which specific text should faculty actually incorporate in their syllabi? I have taught *The Good Soldier* on multiple occasions in two different introductory-level literature courses and believe strongly that its specific subject matter, structure, style, degree of accessibility, and suitability for use with creative writing assignments combine to promote a remarkable level of student engagement. Apparently, however, few others share this opinion. Survey data suggests that Ford's saga of the adultery and lies that occur between two wealthy couples living in turn-of-the-century Europe is virtually untaught at the undergraduate level. Only 10 percent of respondents indicated that they had ever used the text in a survey course. Such avoidance is unfortunate because my professional experience has convinced me that *The Good Soldier* works extremely well in a literature survey course.

Told exclusively from the perspective of John Dowell, a wealthy American expatriate, Ford's novel details the long-term friendship that he and his wife, Florence, shared with Edward and Leonara Ashburnham, members of the British landed gentry. John[3] opens his narrative by claiming that "This is the saddest story I have ever heard" (11), and the source of his sorrow quickly becomes clear. Florence and Edward—the actual "Good Soldier" of the title—are both dead and John is now estranged from Leonara. The story itself is actually John's attempt to arrive at a greater understanding of the events that led to such dissolution, for as he tells the reader early on, "I know nothing" (14). It is also his attempt to regain some semblance of psychological health:

You may well ask why I write. And yet my reasons are quite many. For it is not unusual in human beings who have witnessed the sack of the city or the falling to pieces of a people to desire to set down what they have witnessed for the benefit of unknown heirs or of generations infinitely remote; or if you please, just to get the sight out of their heads. (13)

Over the course of an erratic and digression-filled narrative, a tale of deceit, betrayal, sex, and death emerges. Although Edward was a gifted officer and a generous landlord, he was also a serial philanderer. Several of his extramartial affairs resulted in public scandal, and the final one caused Edward to take his own life by slitting his throat. While recounting the story, John comes to realize that one of Edward's infidelities was with Florence, who used the pretence of a bad heart to hide a relationship with him that lasted for several years. Worse still, John determines that not only was Leonara aware of the affair, she promoted it as a way to keep her husband from directing his amorous attentions toward less socially acceptable partners. In perhaps the most emotionally damaging epiphany, John learns that Florence committed suicide and did not die of natural causes, as he had originally assumed.

Because both the Ashburnhams and Dowells are members of the upper class and the novel's action moves through a series of rarified European settings, Ford's novel might seem at first glance to be unsuited to the tastes of the predominantly middle- and working-class American audiences found in most introductory-level literature courses. And, indeed, a number of survey respondents pointed to this concern as the primary reason why they have elected not to teach it. But, once students strip away *The Good Soldier's* effete and delicate exterior, they find a sordid and sensational tale that proves anxiety over sexual misconduct is hardly a new phenomenon and that the impeccably dressed and well-mannered upper classes have their dirty little secrets, too. Invariably, they respond eagerly to these realizations.

Karen Hoffman has noted that Ford's work "particularly stands out [from other Modernist fiction] for its explicit commentary on the narrative process" (31). Accordingly, John opens the fourth section of *The Good Soldier* by offering his audience a guilt-driven justification of his narrative style:

I have, I am aware, told this story in a very rambling way so that it may be difficult for anyone to find their path through what may be a sort of a maze ... when one discusses an affair—a long, sad affair—one goes back, one goes forward. ... I console myself with thinking that this is a real story and that, after all, real stories are probably told best in the way a person telling a story would tell them. They will then seem most real. (167)

These comments, much like the previously cited question of "You may well ask why I write," find the novel undertaking the quintessentially Modernist practice of highlighting its own status as textual act. More important, however, they contain the key for recognizing how its style and structure strike the balance between accessibility and abstraction that is so critical to the successful teaching of a Modernist novel. This study accepts as a central premise that Modernist novels present distinct interpretive challenges and that those challenges are a primary reason why these texts should be taught in the introductory-level literature classroom. These works, however, are not homogeneous in their complexity. Different Modernist novels are difficult in different ways. Some, such as *Ulysses*, use incessant allusion and intricate structure to overwhelm the reader; others, such as the writings of Gertrude Stein or Ivy Compton-Burnette, feature an unmatched linguistic complexity; while still others, such as Henry James's *The Golden Bowl*, prove daunting by their sheer size and textual density.

In the case of *The Good Solider*, as John himself the suggests, the primary barrier to understanding lies in its disjointed temporality—he goes back, he goes forward, he goes back yet again. His discussion of the steps taken to preserve Florence's supposedly delicate heart illustrates this tendency perfectly:

For twelve years I had to watch every word that any person uttered in any conversation and I had to head off what the English call "things"—off love, poverty, crime, religion, and the rest of it. Yes, the first doctor that we had when she was carried off the ship at Havre assured me that this must be done. Good God, are all of these fellows monstrous idiots, or is there a freemasonry between all of them from end to end of the earth? ... That is what makes me think of Peire Vidal.

Because, of course, his story is culture and I had to head her towards culture and at the same time it's so funny and she hadn't got to laugh, and it's so full of love and she wasn't to think of love. Do you know the story? (22)

From there, he enters into a page-long digression on Vidal, a twelfth-century French troubadour. By the time he is finished, he turns to a three-page discussion of Florence's uncle instead of completing his thoughts about her supposed condition. Open the text to almost any page and a similar example will appear. Without question, students will initially find navigating such passages challenging, and they will experience the educative confusion that MacDonald identifies. Thankfully, however, a number of factors associated with John's narrative style combine to make *The Good Soldier* an intellectual obstacle course, which a class can conquer with a reasonable amount of instruction and guidance and which will sharpen significantly their critical-thinking and close-reading skills.

To begin with, as the above examples demonstrate clearly, John has a readily identifiable narrative voice. Indeed, his persona looms so large over the novel that numerous critical studies have focused primarily on its rhetorical and epistemological impact. As readers come to know John and become accustomed to his digressive style, their level of understanding will quickly increase. The experience is not unlike taking a class to see their first Shakespeare performance. At first, the students sit there fairly befuddled. But by the second act, the cadence of the blank verse starts to sink in, the Elizabethan diction seems less strange and they find themselves able to follow both the action and the dialogue. Every time that I teach *The Good Soldier*, on the first day that we discuss the text in class, upon entering the room, I am greeted with a sea of obviously frustrated faces. Each subsequent day, however, the atmosphere grows markedly more at ease. Because John demonstrates a complete inability to take action against the catastrophic events that surround him, many students soon find him exasperating. But, at least they know him, and that promotes comprehension.

Moreover, while the class will grow more at ease with the style of *The Good Soldier* as they read it, in one sense, they should be familiar with it from the very outset. As John suggests in his apology, his narrative is in fact "the way a person telling a story would tell [it]" (167). The novel violates the conventions of traditional Realist fiction and initially seems so strange because it is actually a one-sided conversation. John establishes this fact at the start of the second chapter: "I shall just imagine myself for a fortnight or so at one side of the fireplace of a country cottage, with a sympathetic soul opposite me. And I shall go on talking, in a low voice" (19). Faculty are advised to focus on this passage early in class discussions, because once students recognize the essential premise behind the text's form, they can relate it quite easily to their own experience. Seemingly everyone has a friend or family member who is known for telling long-winded, rambling stories that can only go from point A to point B by way of points D, Q, S, K, and back through Q. Ultimately, Michael Levenson's estimation that "[a]lthough one remembers Dowell's narrative for insistent formal dislocations—its inversions, postponements repetitions, reversals—it relies in significant measure on certain, highly traditional methods of characterization" is correct

(374). Students find such familiarity reassuring, which in turn boosts their confidence as readers.

The conversational structure of *The Good Soldier* produces another pedagogical advantage. It is a self-contained puzzle in ways that many other Modernist novels are not. Alan Judd refers to this as the "sphere effect, the impression it gives of coming from nowhere, leading nowhere, of being perfect in itself" (137). Whereas other highly allusive works force readers to consistently look outside of the text to arrive at understanding, here they must look primarily within, for thanks to Ford's tremendous attention to detail, all the scattered elements of the narrative actually do connect logically.

Consider, for instance, the following statement that John makes midway through the first section of part II about Jimmy, a man with whom Florence undertook a world tour two years before marrying him: "I understand that he had been slim and dark and very graceful at the time of her first disgrace" (84). Buried at it is in the middle of a nondescript paragraph, the sentence may seem insignificant, but in fact, it represents a major revelation. The offhand remark about Florence's "disgrace" is the first time that John explicitly speaks of her as having been sexually promiscuous. That knowledge brings into much sharper focus a cryptic statement that he makes several pages earlier in that same section when speaking of his wife's personal history:

To begin with, she was born on the 4th of August. Then, on that date, in the year 1899, she set out with her uncle for the tour round the world in company with a young man called Jimmy. But that was not merely a coincidence. Her kindly old uncle, with the supposedly damaged heart, was in his delicate way, offering her in this trip, a birthday present to celebrate her coming of age. Then, on the 4th of August 1900, she yielded to an action that certainly coloured her own life—as well as mine. She had no luck. She was probably offering herself a birthday present that morning. (75)

There can now be no question as to what the vague, innuendo-laden "action" might be. Clearly, Florence and Jimmy were lovers.

If *The Good Soldier* operated as a traditional, Realist narrative, the facts that lead to this conclusion would be presented in an easy-to-understand, sequential order. But, as the novel eschews that form, the inattentive reader is likely to overlook the disclosure of a crucial element. Similar cryptic implications abound throughout the text, and showing students how to put those disjointed pieces together is a powerful pedagogical strategy for developing their ability to read closely and actively. Passages like the ones just touched upon make it clear that the reader must be constantly aware of and engaged with this novel. Note, however, that the actual mysteries contained in such references are, generally speaking, not difficult to solve, once all of the relevant data have been identified through careful and continual attention to the text. Thus, *The Good Soldier* strikes a reasonable balance between accessibility and difficulty and provides teachers with an unmatched opportunity to demonstrate clearly the tremendous impact of even a seemingly negligible phrase, since every word in it truly is important.

Because the novel is so intricately plotted, it is possible to construct a linear timeline that renders its major events in chronological order. Having students undertake this exercise periodically as they progress through the text is an effective way to measure both their understanding of it and the extent of their close reading. It is particularly beneficial to have students do this as a small-group exercise, in which each group is asked to identify the major events that they have encountered to that point in the assigned readings and then place them in the temporal—not textual—order in which they occur. Once the timelines have been completed, they are placed on the board, and each group is asked to justify their ordering to the rest of the class. Thus, the exercise develops both analytical and rhetorical skills. It also provides the teacher with a chance to correct any misreadings of the objective information within the text—dates, places, and so on— and call attention to any elements or clues that might have been overlooked by the students.[4]

CREATIVE WRITING IN THE LITERATURE CLASSROOM

In constructing such timelines, students are making exactly the kind of "good sense" of the novel that Trilling warned against. To some degree, this normalizing is unavoidable, as a central goal of introductory-level literature courses is to develop the ability of students to read and analyze texts effectively. Lessons and writing assignments must be devised, however, that go beyond simply dissecting works in an attempt to build close-reading skills. Students must be encouraged to put these novels back together again, for reconstruction can lead to at least a partial restoration of the "force and terror" that Trilling finds so elemental in the Modernist text. The use of creative writing assignments provides one possible context for undertaking such a rebuilding process.

Unfortunately, the very notion of using creative writing as the basis for teaching literature may seem surprising to some. For many years, it was recognized as having pedagogical value in only a relatively small number of specific contexts. Having conducted a detailed examination of education reports published in the United States from the early twentieth century up through the 1970s, Alice Brand argues that teachers traditionally employed creative writing in just three ways: (1) as a therapeutic exercise designed to promote emotional and psychological health; (2) as means to identify and foster the development of those students who demonstrated potential talent as creative writers; and (3) to create interest for writing in general among all students, regardless of their talent levels (77). In his English as a Second Language (ESL) classes, Gugin has witnessed the pedagogical benefits of the third aspect: "perhaps the real value of creative writing, at least in an academic writing context, is that it can indeed generate student motivation—defined here as interest and involvement—for both academic (critical) reading and writing. If such motivation exists, writing improvement can occur" (2). Given that student engagement is so central to the successful teaching of Modernist novels, his example suggests that creative writing could prove a valuable tool in the introductory-level literature classroom as well.

Note, however, that none of the pedagogical contexts from Brand's study focus on developing students' analytical and critical capabilities. Phyllis Creme challenges this rather limiting assumption with the concept of "creative criticality." She argues that by fostering creativity among students, teachers can produce a "reflexive objectivity that evolves from engagement and connectedness, rather than alienation and fear" (276). Thus, creative writing can do more that merely get students excited; it can get them thinking as well. My own pedagogical strategy for *The Good Soldier* embodies Creme's fundamental ideas about creative criticality. I have found that allowing students to be creative when working with the text generates greater interest in it and pushes them to conceive of it in new ways. Although such an approach would likely produce positive results with any Modernist novel, the essential narrative structure of *The Good Soldier* makes it particularly conducive to creative writing assignments. Dominated as it is by John's subjective impressions and completely exclusive of any other voices, the text offers students the chance to create different versions of the same events that John has just described.

When teaching the text, I forego having students produce a traditional, expository essay, and instead assign a two-part, hybrid project. In the first part, students retell a scene of their choosing from the perspective of one of the other three main characters—Edward, Leonara, or Florence. Creativity is encouraged. Past submissions have included dialogues of conversations overheard in a bar, tear-stained (literally) love letters, suicide notes, transcripts from court cases, interviews given to local newspapers, and diary entries. These works were not merely typed on standard letter-size paper. One student actually dried flowers to include in a note from Florence to Edward; another placed pieces of parchment in her oven to simulate the weathering that would occur to a vituperative letter left by Leonara on Edward's grave. The level of effort required to produce such works echoes the impact of creative writing that Gugin has witnessed in his ESL class. Skeptics may argue that offering students the opportunity to produce a single creative writing assignment at the conclusion of reading a novel hardly seems enough to develop significant interest in it. My own experience, however, suggests otherwise. Indeed, my impetus for developing a hybrid assignment stemmed from initially having taught *The Good Soldier* in conjunction with a traditional analytical paper. That first time, the level of student interest in the text, as measured by end-of-semester evaluations, informal conferences, and my own observation of class discussions and group work, was markedly lower than in all subsequent offerings. I attribute the difference to the interest sparked by tapping into the students' creative instincts. Even so, when teaching *The Good Soldier* in the future, I do hope to promote an even greater level of excitement by offering students more creative opportunities than simply the preparation of a final project. In particular, I intend to have the class repeatedly render either visually or verbally a single scene, such as when the Ashburnhams and Dowells first meet, and trace how their impressions of it change as the narrative unfolds and more "facts" about it are revealed by John.

Returning briefly to the discussion of balance that began this section, it would be pedagogically ineffective to allow students to submit a creative writing sample and nothing more, as there would be no impetus for them to read the text carefully and no objective means by which to evaluate the quality of their work. Therefore, the creative component of the project is accompanied by a second rhetorical and analytical component in which students explain, using specific textual evidence for justification, what they have based their retellings upon. Doing so forces them to confront the central Modernist belief that form and content are inseparable, for they must justify both what the other character might say and how he or she might say it. Why, for instance, would Leonara choose a note for communicating with Edward and what particular aspect(s) of their disastrous marriage would she focus on? Assuming that students have made an effort to produce something for the first part, it receives no formal grade. The second component, however, is reviewed carefully to ensure that the student has produced a complete and thoughtful argument that supports and reflects the creative submission.

By reimagining *The Good Soldier*, students fulfill Ezra Pound's famous exhortation that provided Modernism with its rallying cry: "make it new." Having deconstructed the novel through directed close readings and class discussion, they now reassemble a portion of it. The creative writing project pushes them, however, to question the text and many of its assumptions, particularly John's narration itself, and in doing so, they undertake a fundamentally Modernist act. As Irving Howe notes in "The Idea of the Modern," one of the earliest attempts to codify the nature of Modernism, "the modern writer ... works with unfamiliar forms; he chooses subjects that disturb the audience and threaten its most cherished sentiments" (140). In the case of *The Good Soldier*, those "most cherished sentiments" are an overwhelming scholarly affinity for its narrator. John Reichert laments that "everyone who has heard Dowell out and shared his impressions of him with us in writing has staunchly defended him, making excuses for his shortcomings, finding other 'villains' lurking in the wings of his life ... deep down they believe in him and in his story" (161–62). Many of my students, however, have taken exactly the opposite stance. Some have come to the defense of Florence as a wronged wife who has been neglected by a husband who is incapable of action and is indeed "no better than a eunuch" (18). Others have cut through the admiration and forgiving sentimentality that John feels for Edward and instead cast "The Good Soldier" as a selfish degenerate bent only on satisfying his own pleasure to the detriment of others. Even Leonara, of whom John finally proclaims "I cannot conceal from myself the fact that I now dislike Leonara," has had her advocates (226). Doubtless, some of these contrary opinions stem from the fact that students' minds are not clouded by the years of accumulated intellectual baggage that tend to weigh on academics. But, some of these opinions also took root in the creative freedom offered by the project itself, for as Creme notes, "a different genre sometimes enables them [students] to get to the heart of an issue" (275). At the outset of novel, John suggests that his narrative is his attempt to write himself to an understanding of the terrible events that have befallen him. By creatively retelling John's story, students can write themselves to a new understanding of the text itself, a quintessentially Modernist proposition if ever there was one.

CONCLUSIONS

Every syllabus constitutes a negotiation that must balance lofty pedagogical goals against the reality that there are only a finite number of class meetings every semester and faculty have limited time and effort to spend on any given course. Choices must be made and certain desirable elements invariably must be excluded. If a teacher believes that *The Deerslayer* will offer greater learning opportunities to her class than *In Our Time* and chooses James Fenimore Cooper over Ernest Hemingway, so be it. But, the rationale behind such a decision should not rest primarily upon the pedagogical and interpretive difficulties that the novels of writers like Hemingway, Joyce, Compton-Burnette, and Ellison pose. These texts *are* hard. That is why they are important. Faculty should commit themselves to teaching a Modernist novel in survey courses whenever possible. Unfortunately, if a student does not encounter one in an introductory-level literature classroom, chances are he never will. Although the challenges that these works present are significant, they are not insurmountable. Utilizing overlooked texts like *The Good Soldier* and exploring innovative teaching strategies such as creative writing assignments make these works pedagogically viable and opens the door to a teaching experience that holds great rewards for students and faculty alike.

END NOTES

1. I surveyed 137 professors and instructors of English at accredited, four-year colleges and universities in each of the fifty states regarding their rationale for and experience with teaching or choosing not to teach Modernist novels generally and *The Good Soldier* specifically. The survey was built around two questions that involved simple yes/no answers:

- Do you (or have you) usually teach at least one Modernist novel in your introductory-level literature course(s) such as introduction to the novel or introduction to American literature?
- Have you ever taught (or are you likely to ever teach) Ford Madox Ford's *The Good Soldier* in an introductory-level literature course(s)?

The remaining four questions offered insight into the rationale behind the responses given above, such as the following:

- Please indicate the reason(s) that you do not teach *The Good Soldier* in your introductory-level literature course(s). (Please indicate all that apply.)
  a. The language of the novel is too difficult for my students.
  b. The form of the novel is too difficult for my students.
  c. The subject matter of the novel is not engaging to my students.
  d. The form of the novel is not engaging to my students.
  e. The novel's length does not work well with my syllabus.
  f. The novel does not correspond well to my own scholarly interests.
  g. The novel does not fit well with my pedagogical objectives. (Please elaborate below.)
  h. Other reasons. (Please describe below.)

To promote comparability of data, subjects were provided with a series of likely responses. Personalized feedback was encouraged, however, and all individual comments were recorded.

To reduce the possibility for the distortion of results, great care was taken to maximize the diversity of colleges and universities surveyed, both in terms of location and type. One school from each state was selected randomly from a state-by-state list of degree-granting institutions published by the University of Texas at http://www.utexas.edu/world/univ/state/. Once an institution was chosen, surveys were e-mailed to those faculty members who, based on information provided on their school's Web site, appeared most likely to teach introductory literature courses. The list of institutions from which data was collected reasonably reflects the wide variety of higher-education options currently available to undergraduates in the United States and includes both rural and urban campuses; large, public, land-grant universities; small private liberal arts colleges; historically black colleges and universities; technically focused institutions and religiously affiliated schools.

2. From a more practical perspective, these texts also justify their inclusion simply because they constitute what is arguably the most dominant and influential literary form of the first half of the twentieth century. By design, literary survey courses seek to provide a basic knowledge of the fundamental components of either the genre or time period on which they focus. Thus, the student who enrolls in introduction to poetry will likely learn the components of verse (for example, rhyme, meter, and line), poetic diction (for example, metaphor, allusion, symbolism, and imagery), and a number of the essential poetic forms (for example ballad, sonnet, and blank verse). Excluding Modernist novels from those introductory-level literature courses where one could reasonably expect their inclusion would prevent students from gaining exposure to a critical aspect of twentieth-century literary history.

3. Essentially, all critical commentary on *The Good Solider* refers to John Dowell as merely "Dowell" but uses the first names of the other three characters—Edward, Leonara, and Florence. As Florence can also lay claim to the "Dowell" epithet, this practice is sexist. Therefore, I refer to all four characters by their first names.

4. When preparing for these exercises, faculty are encouraged to consult Victor Cheng's "A Chronology of *The Good Soldier*" as it provides a ready-made, linear encapsulation of the novel's events.

WORKS CITED

Brand, Alice Garden. "Creative Writing in English Education: An Historical Perspective." *Journal of Education.* 162, no. 4: 63–82.

Cheng, Vincent J. "A Chronology of *The Good Soldier*." *English Language Notes* 24, no. 4 (1986–1987): 91–97.

Creme, Phyllis. "Why Can't We Allow Students to be More Creative." *Teaching in Higher Education* 8, no. 2 (2003): 273–77.

Ellison, Ralph. "Hidden and Name and Complex Fate—A Writer's Experience in the United States." In *Shadow and Act,* 144–66. New York: Random House, 1964.

Ford, Ford Madox. *The Good Soldier.* The Bodley Head, 1915; New York: Penguin, 1946.

Gugin, David. "The Creative and the Critical: George Orwell in the ESL Classroom." In *The Hwa Kwang Journal of the Teaching of English as a Foreign Language.* May 2005. http://www.hkjtefl.org/2005-Gugin-Orwell.html (June 28, 2006).

Hoffman, Karen. "'Am I No Better Than a Eunuch?' Narrating Masculinity and Empire in Ford Madox Ford's *The Good Soldier*." *Journal of Modern Literature* 27, no. 3 (Winter 2004): 30–46.

Howe, Irving. "The Idea of the Modern." In *Selected Writings: 1950—1990.* New York: Harcourt Brace, 1990.

Judd, Alan. *"Using Ford in Fiction." History and Representation in Ford Madox Ford's Writings,* edited by Joseph Wiesenfarth, 135–45. New York: Rodopi, 2004.

Levenson, Michael. "Character in The Good Soldier." *Twentieth Century Literature: A Scholarly and Critical Journal* 30, no. 4 (Winter 1984): 373–87.

MacDonald, Gail. "Hypertext and the Teaching of Modernist Difficulty." *Pedagogy: Critical Approaches to Teaching Literature, Language, Composition and Culture* 2, no. 1 (2002): 17–30.

Reichert, John. "Poor Florence Indeed! Or: The Good Soldier Retold." *Studies in the Novel* 14, no. 2 (Summer 1982): 161–79.

Trilling, Lionel. "On the Teaching of Modern Literature." *Beyond Culture: Essays on Literature and Learning.* New York: The Viking Press, 1965.

Van Engen, Abram. "Reclaiming Claims: What English Students Want From English Profs." *Pedagogy: Critical Approaches to Teaching Literature, Composition and Culture* 5, no. 1 (2005): 5–18.

Zamyatin, Yevgeny. "On Literature, Revolution, Entropy and Other Matters." *A Soviet Heretic: Essays by Yevgeny Zamyatin,* edited and translated by Mirra Ginsburg. Chicago: Chicago University Press, 1970.

A. S. Byatt's Finishing School: Literary Criticism as Simulation

Alan Ramón Clinton

In this article, I would like to discuss a particular novel's role in my experience of helping develop Northeastern University's reformed Advanced Writing in the Disciplines (AWD) courses, required of all junior-level students at the university. One of the major shifts in the program involved offering more "discipline specific" options, including one that, at first glance, might seem redundant—that is, Advanced Writing for English Majors. After all, English is one of the few disciplines that, even from the freshman year, requires students to write essays in almost every course. My goal, from the outset, became to design a course that English majors wouldn't view as "redundant" or "a waste of time," the kiss of death for both students and teachers. That is why I chose to center the course around A. S. Byatt's novel *Possession* which, in addition to its more obvious claims to relevance concerning its (arguably romanticized) subject matter of literary critics, in fact does what any AWD course *should* do—interrogate the possibilities of writing as a practice with respect to the boundaries of a discipline. More specifically, the novel's implicit argument for simulation as a form of literary understanding makes it the perfect work to test the boundaries of criticism as a discourse.

Byatt, a literary critic and college professor as well as a novelist, performs various types of simulated criticism in her novel, all of which provide for fruitful discussion and paper topics. My first assignment, which combined selections from Roland Barthes' *Mythologies* with the first several chapters of the novel, asked students to read Byatt's simulated critics as promoting various mythologies surrounding the profession of literary academia, thus allowing them a critical entry into their own current and future encounters with the profession. One of Barthes's favorite critical moves in *Mythologies*, which students picked up on, is to identify a particular cultural object or phenomenon and show how it is actually figured as something other than its ostensible content. Thus, the way to understand mythologies of literary criticism in *Possession* is to find out how critics are presented as something other than literary critics. Roland Michell, for instance, the novel's protagonist, is alternately figured by the narrator or other characters as an ascetic monk (a penniless postdoc), a fetishist (poring over any scrap his favorite poet Randolph Henry Ash had once touched), and even a necrophiliac (one of his most prized possessions is a photograph of the Victorian poet's death mask). These somewhat ambivalent mythologies presented students with the need to unlock the mystery of motivation. What is to be gained by such depictions? Is all study of the past somewhat perverse? Xan it be figured as a "love for the dead"? Is perversity actually a key to scholarly interest and innovation, where fetishism can take on the more postmodern form of following the unpredictable itinerary of a detail?

Interestingly, asceticism, fetishism, and necrophilia all come together in the figure of the detective, which Roland becomes the moment he discovers, in Ash's personal copy of Vico's *Principi di una Scienza Nuova*, some unfinished letters in Ash's script that seem to counter the prevailing notion of his unfailing fidelity to his wife. From this moment, Roland's quest (another mythology) becomes to find out the addressee of these unaddressed letters, which involves following unlikely clues and even taking on a "partner," Maud Bailey. In an especially insightful exploration of the detective mythology, one of my students, Jessica Juarez, compared Roland Michell with detective Robert Goren, played by Vincent D'Onofrio, from the popular television show *Law and Order: Criminal Intent*. For Juarez, the detective show's equivalent of asceticism is the absence of information about the personal life of its detectives. We are led to believe, particularly in the case of Goren, that his only interest is also his obsession, pursuing the strange clues (fetish objects) that, in helping to solve the case, seem to require the knowledge of an extremely well-read and widely versed scholar/fetishist. Necrophilia, the ultimate perversion, takes the form of Goren's ability to think like the murderers he pursues, even from their point of view, to "identify" with them to an extent that sometimes seems to only differ in the fact that Goren has not committed these crimes. Even so, he retains the mystery surrounding the criminal mind, clinging to him in fascinating, slightly unnerving ways.

Consequently, the first assignment reveals a major difference between Barthes's approach in *Mythologies* and Byatt's mythological work in *Possession*. Whereas Barthes tends to decode the ideological content of glamorous myths, Byatt's somewhat dubious characterization of scholars actually serves to endow them with a certain glamour, ultimately resulting in a mythology that can be mined for critical methodologies. This realization, which many students arrive at completely on their own, serves as the springboard for the second assignment of the course.

The most "glamorous" critical methodology of recent years—in terms of its critical esteem, its appearance in journals, and its general entrenchment within the academy—could be labeled as the variety of approaches that led to, stem from, and sustain the rubric often called "New Historicism." Historical approaches to literature, which result in their own genres of writing, are arguably the most difficult to teach students. Indeed, the "coverage principle" that dominates most literary courses and curricula at the undergraduate level would seem to prohibit the most important element of historicist writing, a wide-ranging reading of history from a given "period" or periods. Yet, in a course whose coverage principle is centered around genres of writing that literary scholars do, having students practice historical writing may be more feasible. *Possession*, by creating a "realistic" portrayal of literary scholars pursuing historicist criticism, provides students with an image-repertoire of detectives navigating the often open-ended "clues" associated with historical knowledge: unaddressed letters, incomplete correspondence, private journals, obscure allusions, and most important, the many gaps that lead to competing historical theories. Once students view themselves as detective figures, they may be more willing to encounter the difficulties presented by this kind of historical material. Furthermore, by placing themselves in role of the detective, who is always working with fragments of information, students tend to be less overwhelmed by the "comprehensiveness" associated with historical knowledge.

Thus, my second assignment (much of the novel has been read by this point) encouraged students to work historically, but with "clues" that were partially created by their own curiosity:

Looking over the syllabus, you should notice two preparatory assignments that will give you an idea as to how to write the historicist paper. The first assignment will ask you to write a two page analysis of a section/theme from *Possession* you would like to "historicize." This paper should focus on *Possession* and a (to use Louis Montrose's terminology) "radical and fascinating otherness" (407) you have discovered in the text. You should describe what attracted you to this particular theme/thing/practice/event and so on, why you think it is important, and what you hope to find out by investigating it. Thus, you are already embarking on an historical reading of the text by first marking the site(s) of investigation that will be further illuminated by some historical context. The second paper, also two pages, will require you to report on a source or sources you have found and speculate on their significance historically and to the related questions in *Possession*. Remember, however, you are not citing "facts" that will "explain" the elements of *Possession* you wish to discuss but, as Montrose might say, looking for points of mutual reflection and refraction that will illuminate both text and context. You should be willing to apply the same interpretive rigor to all the texts you use in this assignment (and that goes for the rest of the course as well).

As the assignment suggests, students were encouraged to focus on the fascinating yet unfamiliar, a combination of qualities with which *Possession*, in its simulation of literary scholarship, historical documents, and Victorian poetry, is plentifully supplied. A few of the researchable topics in this panoply of Victorian discourses include séances and spiritualism; letter and journal writing; gender relations; industrialism; scientific, archaeological, and historical practices; interiors and collecting practices; photography; death rituals and mythological allusions; literary styles; and so on.

The novel's Victorian poets themselves become models for such curiosity. Christabel LaMotte, the addressee of Randolph Ash's letters, writes insect poems of scientific detail and studies the Melusina myths to write an epic poem of female agency. Ash, for his part, not only studies Vico, but theories of evolution, the histories of his friend Michelet, and Norse myth. Byatt's poets, in effect, become indistinguishable from scholars, an imbrication suggesting that historicist critics become fascinating when they create new webs of meaning between fetish objects that are already saturated with semantic possibility.

Byatt encourages a historical approach to criticism not only by including extended documents that don't fit in the classical schema of "literature," but also by making them rival literature on the level of mystery, ambiguity, and density. Take, for instance, Roland's response to reading the complete set of letters Ash wrote to LaMotte:

Letters, Roland discovered, are a form of narrative that envisages no outcome, no closure.... Letters tell no story, because they do not know, from line to line, where they are going. Letters, finally, exclude not only the reader as co-writer, or predictor, or guesser, but they exclude the reader as reader; they are written, if they are true letters, for *a* reader. Roland had another thought; none of Randolph Henry Ash's other correspondence had this quality. All was urbane, considerate, often witty, sometimes wise— but written wholly without *urgent* interest in the recipients, whether they were his publisher, his literary allies and rivals, or even—in the notes that survived—his wife. (145)

In these letters, Roland discovers that an ephemeral, personal form of writing not meant for publication, not "real" literature, possesses the unpredictable openness that has come to be valued as *the* primary virtue of modernist and postmodernist writing. These letters, to paraphrase Derrida, have in this case *not* arrived at their destination, in fact were not sure of their destination from line to line, and yet are all the more alluring for this fact. Furthermore, Byatt emphasizes this open-ended quality of the genre by placing the poets' correspondence in a chapter unto itself, devoid of narrative commentary.

Similar complexity is expressed later in the novel in another "marginal" text, the journal of the young Sabine de Kercoz, LaMotte's cousin. The pregnant LaMotte, who has sought sanctuary in Brittany with Sabine and her father Raoul de Kercoz, has, upon hearing of Sabine's desire to become a writer, advised her to keep a journal because "[a] writer only becomes a true writer by practicing his craft" (364). This practice book, however, due to its uncertain nature and audience, soon becomes a thoughtful meditation on the nature and purpose of writing itself, as if the genre's lack of definition leads Sabine to these philosophical meanderings:

The last two sentences cause me to think of a problem. Am I writing this for Christabel to see, as a kind of *devoir*—a writer's exercises—or even as a kind of intimate letter, for her to read alone, in moments of contemplation and withdrawal? Or am I writing it privately to myself, in an attempt to be wholly truthful to myself, for the sake of truth alone? (365)

Like the personal letter, the personal journal lacks a clear destination, even from line to line. On some level, both forms begin to take on the paratactical qualities most often associated with postmodern poetry.

This brings us to the most officially recognized "literature" in the novel, Byatt's postmodern poems written in the Victorian style. The most obvious fact to students about these poems "by" Randolph Henry Ash and Christabel LaMotte was that Byatt must know Victorian poetry *intimately* to produce such

believable and virtuoso performances. Byatt's main sources of inspiration—
Robert Browning, Christina Rosetti, and Emily Dickinson—are duly apparent in
Byatt's poems even as the poems are inescapably other, that is, poems written
by mythical Victorians. This "realistic" effect begs the question, however, about
how best to understand or "know" literature. Assuming one is intimately
acquainted with a body of writing from a historical period, what would be the
best way of demonstrating, creating, or achieving a deeper knowledge of this literature? Traditionally, the answer to this question has been to write essays, like
this one, exploring nuances of history or literature from an analytical perspective,
but Byatt's poetry suggests to students how simulation may be another way of
understanding. In other words, if one really wants to understand Victorian poetry, how it works and means, perhaps one should, like Byatt, write Victorian
poems. Or, to pose a related question, can the novel *Possession* be considered a
form of literary criticism? To answer this question in the affirmative, one must
consider literature to be a legitimate, if unique, form of knowledge.

There is a significant, if marginalized, tradition of blending so-called literary
and analytic modes. In his essay "*Longtemps, je me suis couché de bonne
heure,*" Roland Barthes cites Proust's *In Search of Lost Time* as the paradigm of
a discourse, "a third form," that combines the novel with the essay (280). But,
what of a work like *Possession,* which combines even more modes of discourse,
particularly the one seemingly missing from Barthes's "third form," poetry?
Barthes's answer is that what is really at stake for Proust, and for us, is not so
much a matter of genre as it is a rhetorical dilemma:

I should point out that Proust's hesitation—to which, quite naturally, he gives a psychological form—corresponds to a structural alternation: the two "ways" he hesitates
between are the two terms of an opposition articulated by Jakobson: that of Metaphor
and Metonymy. Metaphor sustains any discourse which asks: "What is it? What does it
mean?—the real question of any Essay. Metonymy, on the contrary, asks another question: "What can follow what I say? What can be engendered by the episode I am telling?"; this is the Novel's question. (278)

Significantly, metaphor, the figure we most often associate with poetic discourse,
is here associated with the discourse of inquiry, of truth, of the essay. If we
accept Jakobson's categorizations, even provisionally, it begs the question of
poetry's relationship to the truth and, more specifically, to the essay. Can an alternative form of essay can maximize the potential energy in the alliance
between poetic and analytic discourse?

To help students consider this latter question and prepare them for the third
assignment, the one which, along with *Possession*, interrogates the boundaries
and thus the possibilities of literary criticism, I assign a chapter from Robert
Ray's experimental book of film criticism, *The Avant-Garde Finds Andy Hardy*.
As the book's title suggests, Ray finds the historical avant-garde to be not only a
literary and artistic tradition, but a disposition of inquiry that has influenced contemporary poststructural theorists (like Roland Barthes) inasmuch as the avant-
garde represents "that branch of the humanities which, since the nineteenth century,
has functioned as the equivalent of science's pure research" (10). Consequently,

avant-garde art can be described as "experimental" not only for its novelty, but also because it is a knowledge process modeled on scientific experimentation. One performs an experiment to see what will result, not to demonstrate something already known.

A successful critical experiment addressing poetry's potential with respect to critical discourse is Roland Barthes's autobiography simply titled *Roland Barthes*, which is the subject of Robert Ray's chapter entitled "The Alphabet." When they begin the chapter, students are presented with a provocative definition of poetry from *Roland Barthes*: "One might call 'poetic' (without value judgment) any discourse in which the word leads the idea" (quoted in Ray 120). According to this definition, Barthes's poetic discourse in *Roland Barthes* relates to how the autobiography was produced and organized. Barthes used all twenty-six letters of the alphabet at least once to generate words, "topics" relating to his life and life's work, his personal and critical interests and dispositions. The words came first, and the meditations or "ideas" came afterward. This mode of working seemed fruitful to Barthes for several reasons. First of all, writing in alphabetized fragments absolved him of the duty of schema—a "thesis" that would tie all of his life together. Although the alphabet may be read as an escape from the demands of organization, it also allows for the element of surprise to enter the writing process. One is not sure what word or words will enter into one's head when confronting a particular letter. Just looking over the titles of some of Barthes's fragments clues one in to the surprising things that can spur self-reflective critical discourse. What place do a rib chop, the game of prisoner's base, and a caboose have in a book devoted to literary theory? This is Barthes's provocation not only to others, but also to his own inventive procedures. Most important, Barthes's poetic method of invention actually allows for more kinds of discourse to enter the critical repertoire. In "The Alphabet," Ray gives examples of six kinds of discourse in the autobiography: epigrammatic, metaphorical, anecdotal, playful, lyrical, and analytical. Barthes's fragments allow for more *kinds* of language to enter criticism, thus granting his critical autobiography the property of linguistic "dialogism" in which Mikhail Bakhtin saw the virtue of embodied inclusiveness that is characteristic of the novel as a genre.

By requiring a poetic method of criticism that exhibits the dialogism of the novel, my third assignment prepared students to write about *Possession* in a way that simulates its poetic subject matter, its panoply of fragmentary discourses, and its own implicit argument for simulation as a form of literary criticism. For reasons I will more fully explain later, I entitled this assignment "Objects of Post-Criticism":

As you should have picked up from "The Alphabet" and class discussion, this essay will ask you to employ fetishism (preference for the part over the whole, seeking ideas from language rather than language for one's ideas) as a research strategy, where you are interested in discussing various facets of *Possession* and what you deem to be related topics. Since, as the first alphabet Ray "performs" reminds us, "constraints encourage invention" (123), here are the exact constraints under which your paper must operate.

You must write eight entries of around 250 words, each starting with consecutive letters from your first, last, and/or middle names. For instance, I might use "A. Clinton" if performing this assignment. At least one letter must deal with criticism on the novel.

At least one letter must address some historical research which, while it may be on the same topic of your previous essay, must cover new ground. The other six letters can address passages/issues from the novel, more criticism or historicism, or intertextualities you deem pertinent. None of your "letters" need necessarily relate to any of the other letters.

In fact, you should think more of producing an ensemble which could, perhaps, be titled nothing other than "Notes on *Possession*." The goals of the assignment are as follows: (1) acknowledge the many types of discourses contained in or inspired by a work of literature; (2) focus on issues of interest to you; (3) produce a work that doesn't say the same things as other essays you would write in more "traditional" formats; (4) use what Barthes in his autobiography refers to as the "glory of language" (147) to surprise yourself (and consequently me) with the entries you produce—for example, C for "Christabel" is a bad choice, whereas W for "White" would be a much better one. Of all the previous goals, numbers 2 and 4 are most crucial with respect to the entries you produce. It should be just as easy to surprise yourself and please me by using the six "floating" entries to address specific elements of the novel as it would be if you rely on other sources/connections, and of course hybrid entries are always a possibility. Use Ray's two demonstrations (but perhaps especially the one on the Andy Hardy series, which most resembles literary criticism) as models of the stylistic economy and variety of approaches available to you.

The title "Objects of Post-Criticism" refers to a characteristic and to a theorist I associate with this form of critical writing. It designates to the open-ended character of dialogic literature like *Possession*. Rather than embodying a formal or thematic whole, such writing may be viewed as a particular arrangement of discourses from which we can extract or, perhaps more truthfully, create objects for discussion. The number of such objects, given the intertextual capacities of literature, is potentially infinite. One way to navigate this infinity is, as I allude to in the assignment, to impose a formal constraint like the alphabet which, to use Ray's words, "encourages invention." By focusing on form and on language first, one allows ideas to come about through the associative logic of poetry rather than through the concept imposed from without. In other words, one is approaching the work of literature called *Possession* by producing knowledge in a literary fashion rather than in a way that suppresses the materiality of language and what Roland Barthes calls in his autobiography "ideas *on the level of language*" (85).

In his essay "The Object of Post-Criticism," Gregory Ulmer explores the aims and properties of criticism that may best simulate our understandings of language in the postmodern era. He comes up with the following touchstones that, he admits, are criticism's belated (and still marginalized) response to the "break with 'mimesis,' with the values and assumptions of 'realism,' which revolutionized the modernist arts"(93): collage/montage, grammatology, allegory, and parasite/saprophyte. In the remainder of the essay, I would like to explore how these terms relate to *Possession* and the concept of criticism as simulation.

With respect to collage, Ulmer comments, "By most accounts, collage is the single most revolutionary formal innovation in artistic representation to occur in [the twentieth] century" (94). Collage and montage are so important, at least on one level, because they deny the organic unity of an original context in favor of new combinatorial possibilities. Barthes's autobiography, utilizing collage/montage by piecing together alphabetized fragments, goes a long way toward deconstructing the idea of Roland Barthes as a unified subject. Likewise, my third assignment, on the level of practice, deconstructs both the idea of a unified work of literature called *Possession* and what Robert Ray deems to be the positivistic ideology of the expository essay (9). The collage effects of *Possession* itself seem to operate most vividly in the chapters that, dedicated to simulating particular Victorian documents, have a somewhat uncertain relation to the narrative itself. For instance, chapters ten and eleven, both devoid of narrative commentary, are respectively devoted to the Ash-Lamotte correspondence and to Ash's poem "Swammerdam." The correspondence chapter is easily defended on an exegetical level, but the "Swammerdam" chapter's reason for being is more mysterious. Do we read it to learn about the seventeenth-century scientist, as an "example" of Ash's poetic style, or in more biographical or psychoanalytic terms with respect to Ash and his relationship with LaMotte? Byatt's use of the collage form opens up the possibilities of reading even as it problematizes the grounds on which we base our various readings of texts.

Grammatology, the term coined by Jacques Derrida, could be viewed, according to Ulmer, as the linguistic theorization of collage in which "collage takes the form of citation, but citation carried to an extreme (in postcriticism), collage being the 'limit case' of citation, and grammatology being the theory of writing as citation" (100). Throughout his oeuvre, Derrida tends to characterize this citation/collage in terms of the ability of any mark or "gram" to be torn from its (present) context and placed anywhere else. It is more than anything else a theory of language's ability to get lost, be set adrift, disseminated. While traditional, "logocentric" thought tends to repress this "element of danger" in language, postcritics like Derrida exploit it for creative ends. One of my students, Erin Simmons, seemed to intuit this state of perpetual ventriloquism in *Possession* itself:

While Ash relies on the concept of ventriloquism as a metaphor, he relies on its action in the world to make his words have meaning beyond his own ruminations. For his words to have any sort of impact, they must speak to another without his physical recitation of them. Mrs. Cropper becomes that *other* in this particular case. But Maud and Roland seek to hear this voice as well as Cropper and many other scholars.

As Simmons points out, ventriloquism not only structures Ash's views of how his dramatic monologues operate, but the logic of writing and interpretation itself. Language, at its most basic level, requires a ventriloquistic citation to be communicated to another, and this citational effect ensures that there will never be an end to interpretation, for there is no "pure source" to begin with.

One of Derrida's most notorious uses of citation, antonomasia, becomes a fruitful source of discussion in *Possession*. In *Glas* Derrida announces his use of the figure and its potential effects on reading as a practice:

The rhetorical flower organizing this antitrope, this metonymy simulating autonymy, I baptize it anthonymy. One could also say anthonomasia. Antonomasia [according to Littré] is a "Kind of synechdoche that consists in taking a common noun for a proper name, or a proper name for a common noun." (181)

Derrida converts antonomasia to antonomasia not only because he is discussing Jean Genet's identification of his proper name with the French word for broomflower (genêt), but because the writing and reading strategies it provokes involve an awareness of the "antitrope's" floral (anthic) properties of dissemination. Once a proper name becomes common, it begins to appear in unlikely places, not only in its direct citations but also in its attendant metaphorical associations. Allusion becomes part of the more general strategy of citation. In *Possession*, Randolph Henry Ash is the most prolific perpetrator of this antitrope. In Ash scholar Mortimer Cropper's account of Ash's journey to North Yorkshire, he alludes to the extent of the poet's investment in antonomasia: "He carried also to be sure the sturdy *ash-plant* from which he was hardly to be parted, and which was, as I have already indicated, a part of his personal mythology, a solid metaphorical extension of his Self" (268). As a poet, Ash is naturally fascinated by the proliferation/citation of his name in a word, which can signify both life and death, and both types of "ash" appear throughout his poetry as a means of literary invention that has personal as well as public meanings.

While one applauds this sort of inventiveness in poetry, arbitrary poetic association—following the citations of words rather than "concepts"—has traditionally been banished from the practice of literary criticism, which is supposed to "objectively" explain literary techniques and their contribution to larger thematic concerns. Thinking of literary criticism as simulation, however, suggests using the literary devices one studies as a means of understanding their logic. In fact, the "Objects of Post-Criticism" assignment operates as a modified version of Derrida's anthonomasia by combining the letters of students' proper names with the "common" words generated from each letter. This poetic device often leads to an associative, poetic form of criticism. Again, I will cite a passage from Simmons, who used her middle initial "L" to trace the novel's citations of "Leaves":

Language allows for so many different word choices that translate what we see and experience into images on the page. I am fascinated by how Byatt [or is it Simmons?] weaves together [cites?] multiple uses [here lies the glory of the antitropic dissemination of poetic drift] of the leaf image. She creates illustrations of leaves as both dead and living, both hidden and exposed; she uses leaves in their traditional representations but also to connote the artifacts of Ash's life.

The leaves that adorn the wall near Christabel's grave site help to form the "lost village" (79) that characterizes her hidden grave. But Byatt also points to the newly cleared leaves as a clue that someone has recently been to this concealed place. The interaction of the hidden and the revealed makes for thought provoking images of these leaves. In that same scene, the leaves take on a human personification to mirror this grave site when Byatt writes of the "skeletal leaves of long-faded roses" (80). The image of a once-living relic—the skeleton—and the dead leaves mingling provides a sense of resurrection as Roland and Maud get closer to their discovery.

At another point in the novel, Lady Bailey is described as stacking "those dry leaves in her lap, ordering, squaring" (101). Now using the same image to represent the letters between Christabel and Ash, Byatt weaves the living and the dead even more closely together. These "leaves" are dead but also living in that they speak to the present and make a story heard. The attempt at ordering them parallels the attempt at ordering Christabel's grave site, sorting out where she lies and her place in that cemetery.

One final reference to the living and dead nature of both of these images comes when Cropper quotes Tennyson's words: "Those fallen leaves which keep their green / The noble letters of the dead" (115). Fallen leaves in fact do not keep their green, unless they come to represent something greater than a simple leaf. The coalescence of these images finds its way into clarity with this quote.

In this "analysis" of the novel, Simmons's following of leaves brings out one of the novel's many latent poetic structures, a structure that does produce concepts, but in an itinerary that moves like a leaf blowing in the wind. The conceptual virtue and pleasure of this grammatological method lies in its surprise value, as Ulmer describes in his discussion of "aleatory association" in *Teletheory*: "The surprise it produces in the writer [or reader] first of all is the academic equivalent of the uncanny, marking the place of the inmixing of self and other in the unconscious" (96).

Possession's most compelling representative of grammatological criticism's poetic possibilities takes the form of Maud Bailey's colleague Leonora Stern. Her book's title, *Motif and Matrix in the Poems of LaMotte*, alludes to the key Derridean concepts of what Ulmer has designated, as previously noted, "citation carried to the extreme," that is, citation without quotation marks (motif) and "writing beyond the line" (matrix). Stern flirts with both concepts in her poetic descriptions of female landscapes:

Women writers and painters are seen to have created their own significantly evasive landscapes, with features which deceive or elude the penetrating gaze, tactile landscapes which do not privilege the dominant stare. The heroine takes pleasure in a world which is both bare and not pushy, which has small hillocks and rises, with tufts of scrub and gently prominent rocky parts which disguise sloping declivities, hidden clefts, not one but a multitude of hidden holes and openings through which life-giving waters bubble and enter reciprocally. (Byatt 265)

This passage "quotes" from women artists without actually quoting them. Rather, it cites them by referring to their motifs in a description that simulates, in both verbal texture and syntax, the very matrices that, according to Stern, women like LaMotte embody in their landscapes. Although Stern's "theoretical" approach could be termed feminist-psychoanalysis, her critical style is grammatological in its adoption of a literary, concrete mode rather than a strictly abstract, "analytic" style of writing. In Leonora Stern, we have a simulated literary critic who simulates literature in her criticism. Consequently Stern, like Byatt, demonstrates how citation takes its most unruly and creative forms when it removes the quotation marks to become a more general (but not generalizable) practice of writing.

In writing a more "concrete" form of criticism, Stern also aligns herself with the postcritical definition of allegory which, Ulmer claims, differs from its earlier forms by becoming a means of invention rather than an embodiment of an already existing truth: "What the baroque or romantic allegorist conceived of as an emblem, the postcritic treats as a model.... a structural machine" (112). Thus, while the theory of grammatology could be seen as having poetic properties, postcritical allegory exploits the concrete objects of poetry for their theoretical possibilities. Although Ulmer discusses Derrida's use of an umbrella in *Spurs: Nietzsche's Styles* for this kind of structuring, Randolph Henry Ash employs an analogous form of allegorical theory with the microscope in his poem "Swammerdam." In this sense Ash, and by extension Robert Browning, could be viewed as prototypical of the critics Barthes envisions in "*Longtemps, je me suis couché de bonne heure*"—except, rather than combining the essay and the novel, they combine the essay and the poem even as the type of poetry resulting has the novelesque qualities characteristic of the dramatic monologue. In "Swammerdam," its eponymous seventeenth-century speaker (and thus Swammerdam's inventor, Ash, and Ash's inventor, Byatt) considers the philosophical significance of his "optic glass" in terms of its own structuring properties:

> That glass of water you hold to my lips,
> Had I my lenses, would reveal to us
> Not limpid clarity as we suppose—
> Pure water—but a seething, striving horde
> Of animalcules lashing dragon-tails
> Propelled by springs and coils and hairlike fronds
> Like whales athwart the oceans of the globe.
> The optic lens is like a slicing sword.
> It multiplies the world, or it divides—
> We see the many in the one, as here,
> We see the segments of what once seemed smooth,
> Rough pits and craters on a lady's skin,
> Or fur and scales along her gleaming hair. (226)

In these lines, in fact, we see how Swammerdam's microscope not only operates allegorically, but as a figure of the type of allegory postcriticism espouses. Rather than reconstructing an object mimetically, both the microscope and postmodern allegory create new objects of knowledge, resulting in proliferation rather than simplification.

In erasing the artificial boundaries between art and theory, where theory becomes invention rather than explanation, Randolph Henry Ash's poetry itself (and not just the research contributing to it) can be viewed as a form of criticism, thus paralleling the shift in postcriticism toward a saprophytic rather than parasitic mode/mood. In traditional criticism, Ulmer points out, the "critical" work is viewed as parasitic upon the "literary" work. What Byatt's novel and, as but one instance in the novel, Ash's historical poetry reveal, however, is that literary work is also dependent on research to the extent that the two become indistinguishable in intent and even, at times, method. Hence, literature and criticism depend on each other, just as living plants and trees depend on the saprophytes that survive by feeding off of their decaying matter. Furthermore, one can view literature and criticism not only as dependent on each other for survival, but as mutually benefiting one another to the extent that, as one simulates the other, there comes to be, as Barthes explains in "Theory of the Text," no definitive separation between text and commentary on a text (44). Rather, there is a new complexity of texts that, in their mutual citation, simulation, and dissimulation, are joined in the continual production of new knowledge-objects. In Advanced Writing for Literature Majors, *Possession* operates as a complex yet accessible model of this still emerging situation.

WORKS CITED

Barthes, Roland. "Longtemps, je me suis couche de bonne heure." In *The Rustle of Language,* translated by Richard Howard, 277–90. New York: Hill and Wang, 1986.

———. *Mythologies*, translated by Annette Lavers. New York: Hill and Wang, 1995.

———. *Roland Barthes*, translated by Richard Howard. Berkeley: University of California, 1994.

———. "Theory of the Text." In *Untying the Text*, edited by Robert Young, 31–44. Boston: Routledge, 1981.

Byatt, A. S. *Possession*. New York: Vintage, 1990.

Derrida, Jacques. *Glas,* translated by James Leavy and Richard Rand. Lincoln: University of Nebraska Press, 1986.

Juarez, Jessica. "Literary Critics as Detectives."

Montrose, Louis. "New Historicisms." In *Redrawing the Boundaries,* edited by Stephen Greenblatt, 393–418. New York: Modern Language Association, 1992.

Ray, Robert. *The Avant Garde Finds Andy Hardy*. Cambridge, MA: Harvard University Press, 1995.

Ulmer, Gregory. "The Object of Post-Criticism." In *The Anti-Aesthetic: Essays on Postmodern Culture*, edited by Hal Foster, 93–125. Seattle: Bay Press, 1983.

———. *Teletheory*. New York: Routledge, 1989.

TEACHING THE NOVEL IN THE HUMANITIES

Teach the Conflict: Using Critical Thinking to Evaluate Anthony Swofford's *Jarhead*

John Bruni

"[W]hat follows is neither true nor false but *what I know*" (2). So Anthony Swofford announces in *Jarhead: A Marine's Chronicle of the Gulf War and Other Battles* (2003), a graphic recounting of his experiences in Iraq. Swofford's rhetorical move illustrates the self-conscious tendency of novels to investigate the boundaries between truth and falsehood, between reality and illusion.[1] I want to suggest that the self-reflexive commentary of novels on the act of seeing connects with the concept of critical thinking (a kind of metacognition or thinking about thinking). As I will argue in this essay, novels are ideal for teaching critical thinking in freshman composition courses, for they dramatize theoretical concepts that students often find abstract and thus hard to understand. By focusing on my teaching in spring 2006 of *Jarhead*, I hope to shed light on how and why novels can be taught to beginning college students as part of promoting their intellectual development. First, I will explain in more detail the reasons for using *Jarhead*. Second, I will demonstrate how Swofford takes on the role of a critical thinker as he challenges what counts as objective historical knowledge. Third, I will show how students' interpretation of Swofford's novel can be informed by discussing his commentary on gender and race issues, screening the film of *Jarhead*, and writing essay-length responses to the questions that Swofford raises about U.S. politics and foreign policy.

GOALS AND OBJECTIVES FOR TEACHING *JARHEAD*

I thought *Jarhead* would be a good choice for the class reading list because it examined a recent political event from an ambivalent perspective. Students with varying political beliefs would all be able to identify with the complex character of Swofford. In addition, the author was close in age to the students; the discussion of his "initiation" into the Marine Corps would address the issue of becoming young adults that my students face. Last, the book is not aimed solely toward a male audience, for Swofford's critique of the male behaviors he describes sheds light on how war redefines gender relations. Overall, Swofford presents both a critical historical and personal account of human conflict told largely from the frontlines.

The novel, moreover, fit with the larger objectives for the course. As stated in the syllabus that students receive on the first day of class, "English 101 can best be described as a course in written communication, where learning how to ask questions, negotiate, and solve problems—what is called critical thinking—is essential for your success at Tech and your future career." Presenting *Jarhead* as a model for this approach, I asked the students to evaluate Swofford's critical-thinking skills. And examining the film of the book, directed by Sam Mendes in 2005, played to the strengths of visual learners and helped to clarify Swofford's at-times fragmented memories of war. It also allowed the class to investigate how the book's nonchronological plot and the film's more straightforward treatment of the subject matter differently represented the reality of armed conflict.

Thus, the novel and film complemented my efforts to have students not only understand critical thinking and how it might be defined but also apply it in their reading and writing assignments. The class schedule first emphasized defining critical thinking and then its applications, with assigned readings from *Thinking Critically*, a textbook written by John Chaffee. In unit one, students examine what Chaffee lists as characteristics of critical thinkers, such as being open-minded, self-aware, and curious (49–50). We proceed to discuss Chaffee's concept of "Stages of Knowing" and how a person progresses through these stages to "achieve an effective understanding of the world" (182).[2] "The Garden of Eden," the preliminary stage, is a belief in a black-and-white world with absolute and clear ideas of right and wrong (183–84). "Anything Goes," the intermediate stage, is a belief in a completely relativistic world, where all ideas are equally valid (184–85). The final stage, "Thinking Critically," calls for examining and evaluating evidence for opposing viewpoints to argue that one is more valid than the other (185–87). We look at the allegory of Plato's Cave as an example of this, arduous at times, progression to higher levels of knowledge. While students often feel that intellectual development seems a painful and anxiety-producing process that requires them to venture beyond their "comfort zones," I pledge that I will encourage and support their attempts to take risks that can result in greater insight and self-awareness. In unit two, students use critical-thinking concepts to investigate complex social and historical conflicts. Students consider the consequences of failing to think critically, as they read about Stanley Milgram's psychological experiment on destructive obedience that revealed a tendency for people to willingly carry out acts that would harm other individuals.[3]

Yet the problem with teaching critical thinking is how to determine whether students have truly learned to think for themselves or are merely faking it. Any type of "problem-posing" methodology has limits, and, like Richard E. Miller attests in his critique of the liberatory pedagogy of Paulo Freire (11), I find that students eager to do well in my class will mimic critical-thinking traits, such as having an open-minded and inquisitive attitude. Or, more conservative students (who account for the majority at Tech) will resist on the grounds that thinking for themselves and questioning where knowledge comes from are somehow wrong or irrelevant. To address these difficulties, I first have my students sign a mutually negotiated evaluation agreement that states they have responsibility for their own learning. Second, instead of black-and-white arguments that tend to polarize students, we look at more complex issues that lack easy answers. For instance, when teaching Milgram's experiment, I ask students to write about how they would have reacted as one of the subjects, while requiring that their response take into account the fact that 65 percent of those tested obeyed until the end of the experiment (Sabini and Silver 475).

Novels, I think, are particularly valuable for engaging political topics. That novelistic treatments of politics tend to have multiple interpretations help to remind students that political issues have more than one meaning or answer. Novels can depict in detail the historical and cultural contexts that shorter works, such as essays or articles, can only offer in an abbreviated version. While I believe political discussions offer students the chance to look at opposing points of view and negotiate among their own views and those of their classmates, often there is resistance to airing political opinions in class. To encourage students' input, I try to allow for the different rates that they process information. Political issues are addressed both through more immediate forms of expression, such as group work and class discussion, and more reflective forms, such as out-of-class written assignments. I seek to accommodate different learning styles by combining both written and visual representations of politics. In addition, I try to choose novels that dramatize political issues in interesting and unusual ways. As we will see, *Jarhead* goes to considerable lengths to depict politics in a manner that will capture the reader's attention.

SWOFFORD'S NONLINEAR STORY AND THE LIMITS OF OBJECTIVE KNOWLEDGE

To be sure, *Jarhead* upped the ante for my students. While the book is informed by a fragmented, journalistic style, the writing can at times be rather dense. Graphic language and images seem intended to shock readers and force them to confront what Swofford himself faces. He spares no details in describing his suicide attempt while in Iraq, his feelings of frustration, alienation, and loneliness, and his fear of being killed. The rhetorical effects are both hilarious and disturbing. To prepare students for this brutally honest narrative of a soldier's life, we watched during class the boot camp scene in Stanley Kubrick's *Full Metal Jacket* (1987), in which the drill instructor verbally and physically assaults the new Marine recruits. This scene is rather similar to an early chapter of the book, in which during boot camp the drill instructor shoves Swofford's head through a chalkboard. I told the students that the film's profanity-laced dialogue broke new ground for its realistic portrayal of war; it held nothing back. In the same way, I suggest, Swofford's book expresses a similar commitment to realism. Because profanity is the linguistic coin of the military realm, it would be inaccurate to sanitize the language. I assert, moreover, to the students that Swofford means to shock them; while they do have the right to be offended or outraged, they must realize that such a reaction marks a symbolic victory for the author. Hence, it is implied that those in the class who might dislike Swofford would do well to not overreact emotionally to his argument. As a result,

I presented students with a situation in which arguing against a writer's point of view must be done through logical reasoning, not emotional outrage.

I broke down the book into six assigned readings, spanning two weeks, and encouraged the students to read ahead. My teaching strategy focused on having students discuss in class their initial impressions of the day's assigned readings and investigate to what degree, over the course of discussion, their impressions changed. To ready students for the discussion, I asked students to write in their journals a brief paragraph on a question central to the assigned reading. For example, the first question was how Swofford's experiences in boot camp shaped his attitudes. In addition, I wanted to emphasize both close reading of the text and the larger thematic connections. For every one of the six classes devoted to the novel, I had a series of scenes that I wanted to cover and would allow the students to dictate how much time we spent discussing each scene. Usually, two or three scenes would be examined in depth. For instance, Swofford stated that, to get ready for their deployment to Iraq, the Marines would watch Vietnam films, such as Francis Ford Coppola's *Apocalypse Now* (1979) and *Full Metal Jacket*. After watching in class the specific scenes that Swofford mentions, for example, the helicopter attack set to the music of Wagner in Coppola's film, I asked students whether they agreed with Swofford's assessment of Vietnam films. Rather than being seen by soldiers as antiwar statements, he claims that the "magic brutality of the films celebrates the terrible and despicable beauty of their fighting skills ... Filmic images of death and carnage are pornography for the military man" (6–7). We came to a consensus that, for the soldiers, the poignant image of the Vietnam village, in its unspoiled beauty before the attack, would matter less than the excitement of watching its destruction. Thus it became all too easy to be caught up in the moment and forget some of the unpleasant truths about the cost of war that Coppola was trying to convey. Swofford's argument connects to the larger idea that how a war is represented shapes the meaning and value of death, destruction, and loss. I also pointed out how Swofford subtly undercuts the male bravado of the beer-fueled Vietnam film festival. The book can be a good test of close reading, because Swofford uses understatement to describe charged emotional moments, the full weight of which can elude students if they're not paying careful attention: "We watch our films and drink our beer and occasionally someone begins weeping and exits the room ... Once, this person is me" (7). In what is, overall, a graphic account of his experiences, his understated reporting makes certain scenes, such as the Vietnam war film festival, even more powerful. In discussing this scene, students discover that having to imagine, rather than being told completely, his reaction to the news of impending war can make for a more memorable reading experience.

When Swofford expresses his feelings about going to war, students begin to better understand his complex character. They realize that Swofford is committed to narrating his experiences as honestly as he can. In the introduction, he states that what he says is neither "true nor false" (2). His statement compels students to regard what he says as not received truth, but as a story that has to be critically examined. Since his argument is in part about the seductive powers of political propaganda, he does not want his rhetoric to overwhelm the reader. Rather, he draws attention to the seductiveness of his own rhetoric to caution the reader about accepting at face value what he has to say. Swofford forces students into having to actively decide whether to believe him. As part of his rhetorical strategy, he leaves himself open to the accusation that he is distorting what happened or, even, lying about it. By doing so, he distances students from his experiences, as if he doesn't want them to identify with him too closely or sympathize too much with him. Students are not slow to realize his ambivalence about the war, and some students will indeed accuse him of having an anti-American agenda. When these accusations surfaced during class discussion, several students who had been in the U.S. armed forces responded to charges that Swofford was slanting the truth to make an argument against war by testifying to the overall accuracy of Swofford's account of military life. This incident became an important teaching moment, for it allowed me to point out that Swofford's argument is fascinating precisely because it questions an objective picture of reality at the same time it conveys personal experience in a realistic way. Thus, the book eloquently details the contradictory feelings of the Marine. While Swofford may question why he is in Iraq, he nevertheless feels bound to his military obligations. By maintaining a stance of complete honesty, he can express both his feelings of love and hate about being in the Marines.

Swofford deglamorizes the Marine life, showing students the reality that lies underneath the traditional portrait of the soldier as national hero. Some students might see Swofford as an antihero whose experiences question notions of individualism. For being a Marine, rather than encouraging individual valor, makes one part of a group. As Swofford comments, "[T]he jarheads fighting and warring and cussing and killing in every filthy corner of the godforsaken globe, from 1775 until now, they are you" (120). He likens being in the Marines to being part of a family that transforms the individual, and not always in positive ways, "The simple domesticity of the Marine Corps is seductive and dangerous.... The Corps always waits up for you. The Corps forgives your drunkenness and stupidity. The Corps encourages your brutality" (145). As an example of how training to be a sniper dehumanizes a person, one chapter of the book is an outline for the "Care and Cleaning of the M40A1 Rifle System and Optics" (121–22). While the point is to emphasize how the sniper's identity is subsumed into his weapon, several of my students were fascinated by the inclusion of this technical data in Swofford's narrative. It thus created an effective way for students planning to major in the sciences or a technical field to connect with Swofford. They found that he thinks much like they do, in a logical chain of step-by-step routines and procedures. Of course, they may be blind to the terrible irony that all of these routines and procedures have but one end goal, to develop a killer. Here, it can be made evident to students how Swofford's understated tone makes the abnormal seem normal, the extraordinary appear commonplace.

In particular, *Jarhead* openly questions the idea of a completely objective account of history. Swofford's narrative (that, he says, is neither true nor false but *what he knows*), I argue, expresses a version of Donna Haraway's "situated knowledges," that is, partial and incomplete truths that are grounded in subjective experience (33). Many times, Swofford alludes to the physical and emotional limits of his vision, "blurred," he says, "by wind and sand and distance, by false signals, poor communication, and bad coordinates, by stupidity and fear and ignorance, by valor and false pride" (2). From his account, students discover that there are no easy answers for the question of how history should be portrayed. Not only then does *Jarhead* connect writing to history, the novel allows students to evaluate how truth claims are made about history.

Swofford's approach negotiates between what Dominic LaCapra, in his discussion of historiography, calls positivism and radical constructionism. In the former, truth claims are a mirror to reality; in the latter, truth claims "are of restricted, indeed marginal, significance" (1). Although Swofford argues that his account is necessarily incomplete, at the end of the book, he will claim that his being there at the scene of battle, as a historical witness, validates his story. On the whole, his book does work against a positivist model, as he frequently implicates himself in what he is observing (LaCapra 5). So, too, does Swofford's stylistic language disrupt the notion that writing should "be transparent to content or an open window on the past" (3). Thus the book fits what LaCapra has defined as "traumatic realism," a narrative that cannot "be understood in terms of positivism or essentialism but as a metaphor that signifies a referential relation (or truth claim) that is more or less direct or indirect" (14). Swofford admits that he must rely on his memory to reconstruct his traumatic experiences and reveals his confusion in the (re)telling of his story: "I remember being told I must remember and then for many years forgetting" (3). At almost every turn, Swofford reminds the students that his experiences cannot be received in a complete and uncontaminated form. Thus, the book depicts the limits of objective knowledge making.

Another factor that guides a larger understanding of the First Gulf War is censorship. Swofford is openly cynical about why he has been sent to Iraq. In his words,

[W]e laugh to obscure the tragedy of our cheap, squandered lives with the comedy of combat and being deployed to protect oil reserves and the rights and profits of certain American companies, many of which have direct ties to the White House and oblique financial entanglements with the secretary of defense, Dick Cheney, and the commander in chief, George Bush, and the commander's progeny. (11)

At the same time, he points out that freedom of speech is sharply restricted in Iraq. The staff sergeant announces, "You do as you're told. You signed the contract. You have no rights, you can't speak out against your country. We call that treason. You can be shot for it" (14). Given the heated political debate about past and present U.S. involvement in the Persian Gulf, the discussion of war invariably touches on questions about patriotism. By addressing these issues, I hoped that students might become more comfortable with different and opposing perspectives and learn how to express their beliefs in a reasoned and civil manner in the classroom. By doing so, they would acquire skills in negotiating the personal and the political. Hence, I tried not to overly emphasize or endorse Swofford's attitudes, rather I thought it best to let students deal with his politics on their own terms. From my experiences teaching political topics at Tech, students are reluctant to respond if they feel I am expecting a certain response from them. When students, regardless of their political leanings, do start to speak out, the rest of the class will not join in the discussion until they feel completely familiar with the topic. I waited until we had a roundtable discussion with several pilots from nearby Ellsworth Air Force base about the novel to bring up questions about to what degree dissent can be seen as patriotic. Nevertheless, the students largely evaded the topic, preferring instead to ask the pilots about their experiences flying. Yet the roundtable did have a positive outcome, for it helped students to better grasp the reality of military life. And the pilots' responses reinforced many of Swofford's points. For example, the pilots said that they were excited by some of the same films as Swofford.

Even if students are reluctant to directly engage with Swofford's political viewpoint, they will find the nonlinear narrative challenging because it refutes a positivist historical model by troubling the "identification of historical understanding with causal explanation" (LaCapra 4–5). Swofford's account personalizes history, while blurring the differences between free will and determinism. For instance, I asked students whether when Swofford, in Iraq and depressed, puts a rifle in his mouth, he really intends to kill himself. This question is left unanswered, for his friend, Troy, stops him, as Swofford remarks, "only half a second or many seconds, or even many years, from pulling the trigger, because who knows how many tries one is allowed until one gets it right" (71). Here, Swofford acts as the role of an unreliable narrator, compelling readers to figure out for themselves what may, or may not, have happened. The scene then shifts to Troy's funeral, after the war in Greenville, Michigan. Prevented from reenlisting in the Marines because of a failed drug test years before, Troy wrecked on an icy road en route to his civilian job. During class discussion, I focused on how Swofford's perspective guided our reading of the scene. Swofford writes, "Visiting Greenville, Michigan, helped me to understand Troy's love of the Marines. The town had obviously been the site of a gross failure of industry" (78). In such an economically depressed environment, Swofford implies, enlisting was one of the few opportunities for a better life. Because Troy became a local success story, his friends in Greenville want to claim him as their own, even though Swofford thinks, "I couldn't announce that Troy had not been one of them for many years; it would've been callous for me not to let them grieve with that fiction" (78). At the wake, a bar fight starts when one of the locals insults Troy's name and physically assaults a passed-out Marine. After the Marines beat up the locals, Swofford compares the attitudes of the locals to Troy's family and friends in Greenville. Swofford remarks that the local men

had actually shown Troy more respect than his family or his friends, because the family and the friends had loved Troy and with their selfishness and love had wanted him to again be a part of their world, but the men we'd fought were willing to tell Troy that he didn't belong. (81)

My students appeared to agree with this assessment, seeming to understand the rigid divisions of loyalty and the subtle and complex codes of group membership. In probability, they were going through the same situation, having left their hometowns, family, and friends to go to college; the book certainly shed light on their own feelings of belonging and alienation.

Months later, Swofford tries to find the reason for Troy's death. The Marines are to blame, for they didn't allow Troy to reenlist. The economic conditions in Greenville are to blame, because Troy had to drive to a job thirty miles away. Troy's fiancée is responsible, because if she hadn't delayed the marriage, he would be in San Diego, where there were no icy roads. Swofford concludes that "the cause of a death like Troy's is ineffable, everywhere and nowhere at once, unknowable, like the mirage" (83). By not offering a resolution to this scene, Swofford makes students aware of the difficulties in interpreting complex events. The confluence of political, personal, and social factors that cause Troy's death forces students to reject simplistic cause and effect explanations.

The scenes of military engagement in Iraq are spliced with earlier scenes of Swofford's life in the Marines to show the consequences of his decisions. This type of sequencing allows Swofford to critique, without appearing heavy-handed to students, the motivations of those who exploit the young men who wish to serve their country. Reinforcing his cynicism about the Iraq war, he is ordered to be part of a six-person scout team to report, from a hidden position and without support, on enemy troop movements. In Swofford's words, they are "completely dispensable.... If we get carved to oblivion out there, it doesn't matter, as long as we don't massacre surrendering Iraqis, and the current mission is to convince the Iraqis to surrender" (194). His team gets attacked by rockets; Swofford forgets how to take evasive action and standing in place completely loses control of his bladder. My students were amazed at his honesty in this scene, one of many that describes the brutal realities of surviving war. As if to point out the limits of his military "education," the scene shifts to his recruitment. Seventeen years old, he is seduced by the recruiter's pitch that describes the buying of prostitutes for cheap in the Philippines, Italy, Sweden, and Panama. Needing his parents' permission, Swofford takes the recruiter to talk to his father. His father, having the experience of having served in the military, sees through the recruiter's tactics and refuses to sign the contract. Swofford is downfallen, "I needed the Marine Corps to save me from the other life I'd fail at—the life of the college boy hoping to find a girlfriend and later a job" (207). Here, the theme of the Corps as a place to belong is taken up from the scene of Troy's funeral. Continuing to offer complex reasons for Swofford's decisions, the book demonstrates that many factors cause people to enlist, some idealistic, some personal, some base. A half a year later, he no longer needs his parents' approval and signs up. His dad drives him to boot camp. In this brief but powerful scene, we perceive a kind of transfer of familial obligations. On the one hand, Swofford now has a new "father," who will discipline him and train him to be a killer. On the other, Swofford has a duty to his old father, that is, not to get himself killed.

Another trait of Swofford's narrative is to return to prior scenes to offer further commentary from the perspective of the present. As a result, the theme of loss caused by war seems less blatant and more integrated into the overall storyline. Often students will tire of heavily thematic material; Swofford keeps them engaged by shifting his perspective, as if the novel were a movie filmed with many cameras rather than one. During the war, Swofford has a chance to do what he has been trained to do; he has two enemy soldiers in his gun sights. But he is refused permission. He is told that if he kills the two, the rest of the men won't surrender. Swofford believes otherwise; he says that his captains know if he takes the two out, the rest will indeed surrender, and the captains want to continue fighting (230). This moment informs the tripartite conclusion, articulated in brief chapters. In the first, Swofford argues that he has a right to be heard, "[B]ecause I signed the contract and fulfilled my obligation to fight one of America's wars, I am entitled to speak, to say, *I belonged to a fucked situation*" (254). The section ends with his cryptic warning, the meaning of which readers must decide for themselves, "More bombs are coming. Dig your holes with the hands God gave you" (254). The second is a brief apology, "Some wars are unavoidable and need well be fought, but this doesn't erase warfare's waste. Sorry, we must say to the mothers whose sons will die horribly. This will never end. Sorry" (255). The final chapter expresses his gratitude for not having killed the two soldiers, "I think that by taking my two kills the pompous captain handed me life, some extra moments of living for myself or that I can offer others, though I have no idea how to use or disburse these extra moments, or if I've wasted them already" (257). At the end of the book, he moves from despair to a moment of uneasy acceptance. The conclusion gives his story a sense of hard-earned truth; LaCapra posits that "narrativization is closest to fictionalization in the sense of a dubious departure from, or distortion of, historical reality when it conveys relatively unproblematic closure" (15–16). Far from a conventional resolution, the closing chapters hint at the trauma that is being worked through in Swofford's mind.

GOING BEYOND THE FRONTLINE

A discussion of Swofford's narrative need not be restricted to his experiences in battle. Students should be encouraged to look at his commentary on larger issues of gender and race as they shape the formation of national and personal identities. Watching the film of the novel, which is in chronological order, allows students to gain a better understanding of how Swofford connects life before, during, and after war. Finally, students can respond to his argument about the aftermath of war through written essay assignments.

To be sure, the issue of gender surfaces in the narrative. It is almost inevitable that, with the soldiers in Iraq apart from their wives and girlfriends, the book addresses the subject of cheating. Swofford at first takes a rather evenhanded view; he says everyone cheats. Yet we are reminded that, while earlier he admitted that both he and his girlfriend had mutual infidelities, the situation came close (although to what degree remains undetermined) to driving him to suicide. He also details the belief that Marines are inherently unfaithful, "Often, back at home, old grungy jarheads years out of the uniform, the woman's drunkard uncle or her father's poker buddy, will fan the flames of jealousy and mistrust with comments like 'I know when I was in the Corps, I never knew a faithful jarhead, other than myself'" (92). In addition, he implicates the military tradition with its emphasis on masculine dominance, "[W]e're carrying on our backs the overseas sins of generations of fighting American GIs" (92). In class discussion, I asked if there were a double standard at work when he describes the Wall of Shame, where soldiers post pictures of unfaithful women. One student replied to the effect that Swofford was being realistic, because it would have been impossible for him to present fairly a woman's perspective of wartime infidelities. In any case, it seems that this episode focuses on the masculinity of the soldiers. Swofford suggests that the Wall of Shame is a means, through creating a sense of male comradeship, for enduring the loneliness of Iraq: "It is not necessarily a bad thing to be able to tell the story of your woman's betrayal" (91).

Swofford exhibits a more critical understanding of racial relations in the desert. While on patrol, he encounters a group of Bedouins. Unsure whether they are friendly, he waits for their response. One man waves and approaches him. It turns out that the men think that Swofford and his comrade are responsible for shooting their camels. Swofford lets the man inspect his rifle to see if it has been fired and thus averts a possible conflict. Some of the soldiers make racist jokes about the Bedouins, and Swofford finds their "heartlessness particularly disturbing," saying that they "are afraid of the humanity of the Bedouin, unable to see through their desert garb into the human" (139). Swofford suggests that these soldiers have confused the Bedouins with the Iraqis, a result of Corps training that emphasizes that anyone different is the enemy. Even with regards to the Iraqis he is fighting, Swofford makes distinctions between those who are dead and those who have been captured:

When I'd considered my enemy in the past, I'd been able to imagine them as men similar to me, similarly caught in a trap of their own making, but now that I see these [captured] men breathing and within arm's reach ... I no longer care for the men or their safety or the cessation of combat. (227–28)

In other words, the dead pose no threat to him, while the captured men rouse his anger and hostility. I asked students how they felt about the distinctions that Swofford makes, and, as I recall, there was little response from the class. Perhaps, they felt the same way I did, that it is chilling to look into the mind of a trained killer and realize the simplistic distinctions between the living and the dead that are necessary for survival on the battlefield. Like so many important and pressing issues addressed in the book, the question of race thus remains open.

After finishing the book, we watched the film adaptation of *Jarhead*. Many of the students felt the film was somewhat disappointing in its treatment of Swofford's experiences, with which I agreed. We did discuss the ability of film to create arresting visual images. One scene in *Jarhead* that the class commented upon was the troops silhouetted against burning oil wells, ignited by the Iraqis. In the novel, Swofford writes, "The oil fires burn in the distance, the sky a smoke-filled landscape, a new dimension really, thick and billowing. A burning, fiery oil hell awaits us" (200). But his words can't equal their filmic counterpart, where the men are dwarfed by immense columns of orange flame and a bleak, desolate landscape, covered by roiling clouds of smoke, that seems to stretch to infinity. The last scene of the film is also surreal, as we see the character of Swofford seated in a gray room looking out through a window at the Iraqi desert. Such scenes help to convey the emptiness that Swofford feels, but the film overall does little to explore the psychological layers of his narrative. The film feels at times flat in its retelling of Swofford's story in chronological order. This arrangement reduces one of the most powerful aspects of the book, that is, the way the narrative assembles scenes out of sequence to convey mood and tone. For example, the funeral scene, so memorably described in the novel, appears only briefly at the end of the film.

Having read the novel and watched the film, the students are ready to express their thoughts in a formal essay. The research paper assigned on *Jarhead* revisits some of the more pressing questions that the book raises. Students investigate the disturbing power of Swofford's narrative or argue to what degree he is a critical thinker. Another option is to compare the film of *Jarhead* with one of its cinematic predecessors, *Full Metal Jacket* or *Apocalypse Now*. All of these options attempt to meet the goals and objectives for teaching critical thinking, which I earlier outlined. The questions for the paper allow students to engage with Swofford's viewpoint, address his ambivalent feelings about war, and gauge his criticisms of U.S. foreign policy. In particular, the option to compare films enables students to look at how the depiction of war changes over time, from the Vietnam era to the present, while investigating to what degree the U.S. objectives in Iraq and Vietnam are similar.

CONCLUSION: NOVELS AND "THE GLOBAL TURN"

Teaching novels in composition classes offers students a prolonged inquiry into global relationships. Novels comment on the conditions of their production; the larger economic, social, and political systems in which they are located influence the lived realities of people all over the world. They complement what Wendy S. Hesford calls the "global turn" that calls for "new collaborations and frameworks, broader notions of composing practices, critical literacies that are linked to global citizenship ... and the formation of new critical frameworks in the light of a changing world" (796). But, in attempting to expand students' global awareness, we should be wary of narratives of cultural diversity that promote universal "truths" about human behavior. Given the exigencies of this global turn, what makes *Jarhead* such a relevant text is that it reveals the power relations that shape U.S. foreign policy and the inequalities that result from national desires for imperial adventures. Swofford's allusions to *Apocalypse Now*, an imaginative reworking of Joseph Conrad's portrayal of modernist-era imperialism, *The Heart of Darkness* (1899), illustrate how desires for global expansionism have influenced literary writing over history. Not only does Swofford leave open the consequences of U.S. involvement in the Middle East, he also impresses on readers the need to take seriously how the nation should perform its global role. He reminds us that we all bear some responsibility, by virtue of our lifestyle choices, for the nation's current dependency on foreign oil. *Jarhead* exposes students to the political reality of their times, a vital part of their intellectual development. Students need to be able to discuss current events and speculate about a future yet to be determined, a future in which they will be dealing with the demands placed on them as global citizens. Moreover, for those of us teaching engineering students, we should remember that some of these students may be designing the future technological means for maintaining and extending U.S. influence over the globe. Hence, it is imperative that they should gain an understanding of the ethical consequences of their future actions. None too subtly does Swofford give such issues a sharper clarity.

END NOTES

1. Throughout this essay, I shall make the case for reading *Jarhead* as an autobiographical novel.

2. As Chaffee explains (183), his Stages of Knowing framework is based on the model of intellectual development proposed by William Perry. For a discussion of this model, refer to Felder and Brent (269–70).

3. In Milgram's experiment, subjects think they are participating in a study about memory. They are instructed to give a shock to a person whenever he gives a wrong answer. But the person is an actor who deliberately gives wrong answers and simulates being in pain (while the shocks are false, the "demonstration" shock given to each subject is real). Refer to Sabini and Silver (473–75).

WORKS CITED

Apocalypse Now. Dir. Francis Ford Coppola. Perf. Martin Sheen, Marlin Brando. United Artists, 1979.

Chaffee, John, ed. *Thinking Critically*. 8th ed. Boston: Houghton Mifflin, 2006.

Conrad, Joseph. *The Heart of Darkness*. London: Everyman, 1995.

Felder, Richard M., and Rebecca Brent. "The Intellectual Development of Science and Engineering Students. Part 1: Models and Challenges." *Journal of Engineering Education* (October 2004): 269–77.

Full Metal Jacket. Dir. Stanley Kubrick. Perf. Matthew Modine, Vincent D'Onofrio. Warner Bros, 1987.

Haraway, Donna J. *Modest_Witness@Second_Millenium. Female Man_Meets_OncoMouse*. New York: Routledge, 1997.

Hesford, Wendy S. "Global Turns and Cautions in Rhetoric and Composition Studies." *PMLA* 121, no. 3 (2006): 787–801.

Jarhead. Dir. Sam Mendes. Perf. Jake Gyllenhaal, Jamie Foxx. Universal, 2005.

LaCapra, Dominick. *Writing History, Writing Trauma*. Baltimore: Johns Hopkins University Press, 2001.

Miller, Richard E. "The Arts of Complicity: Pragmatism and the Culture of Schooling." *College English* 61, no. 1 (1998): 10–28.

Sabini, John, and Maury Silver. "Critical Thinking and Obedience to Authority." In *Thinking Critically*, 7th ed., 473–82. Boston: Houghton Mifflin, 2002.

Swofford, Anthony. *Jarhead: A Marine's Chronicle of the Gulf War and Other Battles*. New York: Scribner, 2003.

Novel Truths: *The Things They Carried* and Student Narratives about History

John Lennon

INTRODUCTION

Although this is an article about teaching Tim O'Brien's *The Things They Carried*, a powerful and haunting novel about the Vietnam War, I will not be discussing pedagogical ideas or teaching techniques that center on the Vietnam War itself. In fact, after reading this article, I may be accused by some as being, at best, ahistorical and, at worst, insensitive to the "meaning" of the war. To me, though, this novel—which I used in many different types of classes, but most specifically composition classes—is a perfect conduit for students to discuss the ways in which they, and not the author, construct personalized narratives of large, national events. In my classes, then, I have my students think of Vietnam as background to the more central goal of uncovering the arbitrational ways that historical narratives are formed. By allowing them to use their own postmodern sensibilities, I am asking my students to create their own stories of historical events while at the same time, and just as important, I am using this novel to acknowledge that this process of creating these narratives have consequential ramifications that affect the way that we experience our national histories.

This article, I hope, will accomplish two things. First, it will give the reader who wishes to teach this novel a practical guide to create lessons that will accentuate the way that *The Things They Carried* examines historical constructs. Second, I use this space to discuss my pedagogical rationale for using this novel and its debunking (or spinning) of "truth" in an effort to continue the perpetual conversation of how best to serve our students in a humanities classroom. To do this, though, I must reach back into my own memories and tell you the story of the first (and almost last) class I ever taught.

SO A NEWBIE TEACHER WALKS INTO A CLASSROOM ...

The first time I ever read Tim O'Brien, I was a nervous first-year graduate student who, in between trying to figure out where the free lunches were being offered and registering for my own classes, was handed a copy of *The Things*

They Carried by the chair of the writing program. The first time I ever taught Tim O'Brien was two days later when I found myself in front of my very own composition and literature class, politely coughing while attempting to hand out papers with semi-still hands, all the while questioning the logic of entering graduate school in the first place. Teach a book about Vietnam? I knew nothing about the war, or, really, any war at all. The only war "experience" I had was walking around my high school with a Sony Walkman tuned to the news when the initial "smart" bombs began dropping on Iraq (the first time). But Vietnam? That war was "history"; I was still a month from being born when the last ten Marines were helicoptered out of Saigon in 1975. My father was too old to be drafted into the armed forces and, if any of my friends father's fought, no one ever brought it up over lunch at the cafeteria. Even more telling, I never thought to ask. In fact, the only class period I ever had that dealt specifically with the Vietnam War in my entire academic career was one hot June day when I was in the seventh grade and Mrs. Swanski, frustrated that we were all talking and not paying attention to her, told us to take out our textbooks and start reading chapter twelve ("The Vietnam War") silently to ourselves. I didn't, and standing in front of a group of students who were, at most, five years younger than me, I suddenly found myself wishing that I had.

As all new young teachers feel the first time they are in front of a classroom, I wanted to be prepared. I had stayed up the night before concocting a witty and inspiring story about how we would work together that semester to become better thinkers and writers and that through hard work we were going to surmount obstacles and reach our goals. I saw myself as a benevolent although tough taskmaster and, while we were going to have fun, I was going to teach my students how to become scholars and academics. I am not sure if I thought that the eighteen-year-old students staring blankly at me were going to jump up on their chairs and yell "Captain, my Captain!" but after five minutes, my speech was done and thirty pairs of eyes were staring at me carefully holding a pristine copy of the novel in my hands. Apparently, in all my hours of preparing the night before, I had forgotten to think about what I would do *after* my introduction.

How would I introduce this novel to my class? And, even more important, why should I teach this novel? Shouldn't we be writing something easier like "what I did on my summer vacation?" instead of reading a novel about a war that happened decades ago? Shouldn't first-year composition deal with the personal and the concrete instead of the political and abstract? The night before, while preparing my awe-inspiring speech, I had fit in the time to actually read *The Things They Carried*. And I found it to be an incredibly frustrating book to read. But I was frustrated not only with the novel itself (its unreliable author, the seeming plot contradictions, its experimental style) but also with the prospect of teaching a novel about a historical event. I was pretty confident that I "got" the book: The Vietnam War was a complex and harrowing war fought by young men who many times were afraid to look and created stories to fill in the spaces when their eyes were closed. But like many new instructors teaching a novel about history, I felt my job as their professor would be to enlighten them by giving to them information that would contextualize the text. Regardless of the fact that I understood the book without knowing the history of the Vietnam conflict, I was sure that the students in my class, who would have even less contact with the war, would at least need a cursory lecture on the background of Vietnam. Maybe they wouldn't need a discussion on the geopolitical forces that were swirling around this country in the 1960s and 1970s but, at the very least, a balanced overview of the various players in the war was surely needed.

But since I had spent the evening before on my introduction and not my lecture, standing in front of the class, I did the next best thing: I tried to buy time. Slowly and carefully I wrote the words THE VIETNAM WAR in large, neat block letters on the blackboard. The clock inched forward two minutes. Thinking about the prep session I had with twelve other new composition teachers the day before, I decided that I would allow the students to become "active participants" in their "learning initiative." I cleared my throat and asked the most logical question I could think of, "Does anyone know anything about Vietnam?" Complete silence. Don't panic, I thought and then fell back on the only other thing that I remembered from our prep session: wait time. So I stood there, pedagogically waiting for someone to save me, sure that tumbleweeds would blow through the classroom. Finally, a student, evidently feeling sorry for me, called out: "I've watched *Platoon* twelve times." A few students smiled thinking that he was making a joke. And quite possibly he was, but it was a response, wait time was officially over, and, not knowing what else to do, I wrote PLATOON on the blackboard just to the side of THE VIETNAM WAR. Seeing that the first student was successful, another student ventured: *Full Metal Jacket*. Another: *Rambo*. Another: *Forest Gump*. I wrote those titles down as well. I could feel the momentum building (to where I didn't know) but as I was writing, I kept thinking to myself: "Okay, this is good but what happens when they run out of movie titles?" They did run out of movies, but then they quickly began naming songs: *Fortunate Son*. Another: *Give Peace a Chance*. Then a student said: *The Unknown Soldier*. This led to a discussion about how Jim Morrison died, which led to another student talking about drug use, which led to another student talking about hippies, which led another student talking about miniskirts. Soon they were off talking about clothing and discussing the rationale for bell-bottoms and jungle fatigues. I wrote down all of this, trying at first to order the words but eventually just placing them on the blackboard arbitrarily next to each other like this:

Agent Orange. Canada. Draft Dodging. Spitting. We lost the war. It was against communism. Hippies. Killing on Campus. Nixon. Flower Power. Disabled veterans. Never again will happen. Guilt. Free Love. Only poor people fought. Media coverage. Napalm. Apocalypse Now. Peace sign. The Wall. Dogtags. China Beach. Hot. Missing in Action. Flag burning. 18 year old soldiers. Mud. Marijuana. M-16's. Jungle. Death.

Blackboard after blackboard, I wrote list after list. Students quickly forgot the syllabus that was in front of them ("students will be respectful of each other and talk only when called upon") and started shouting out answers so quickly that I couldn't keep up. Finally, looking at the clock on the wall and realizing that we had gone over the allotted class time by five minutes, I turned to them and said succinctly: "So I guess that's Vietnam. Read the first five chapters of *The Things They Carried* for Wednesday."

The students looked obviously confused as they walked out the door. And, standing in front of the blackboard, I was too. Something had happened there in the classroom, but I didn't know what it was. It was only later that night, telling this story to my colleagues, did I realize that what happened was actually good. Both my students and I—without really being conscious of it—knew things about Vietnam. But while we knew nothing of the official history of the war (when asked later on in the semester, only one student had discussed the war in their high school classrooms), these students, by being their culturally alive selves, had already formed a narrative about the war that resonated with them personally. The narrative was loose and somewhat inarticulate, but they did have stories to tell as evidenced by our classroom discussion.

In *The Things They Carried*, O'Brien plays with the idea that soldiers tell stories to discover the truth of what happened to them. In my classroom, the students formed their own narratives (Spitting. Flower Power. Dog Tags. Mud. The Flag.) to tell a version of history that was happening during the 1960s and 1970s. And while both soldiers and students know that this is not the whole truth of Vietnam, it is a truth nonetheless.

THE "TRUTH" ABOUT COLLEGE EDUCATION

It has been a few years since I was standing in front of my first class. And in my career so far, I have been lucky to teach a range of classes in various departments, including American literature, composition, American studies, and film. But as many interdisciplinary professors find, even though the particular subjects that they teach may be drastically different, a few key ideas inevitably reappear in every course. It is one of my goals as a professor to have my students become resistive readers who are aware of multiple readings (and their ramifications) when encountering a text. Simply, I want them to understand the ways in which they construct meaning. In all of my classes, therefore, I place the idea of "truth" under the microscope.

What I accidentally found out on that first day of class, and which we discussed in subsequent classes, is that students are for the most part able to realize that the "truth" about Vietnam is the relationship between all of these words that I placed on the blackboard. This truth, in other words, is constructed by linking these words (that is, ideas) together. Looking at them on the board, it was exciting to see how the idea of Vietnam changed as the number of words grew. The Vietnam War was just too complex and no one idea or word (or person writing a novel about the war) could contain it. Standing side by side, the individual words, therefore, entered into a dialogue with each other (Agent Orange. Canada) and part of the truth of Vietnam became the story of this relationship between these two words. Just as one has to understand the meaning of the zoot suit to understand the riots in Los Angeles during the 1940s, according to my class, one has to understand the role of bell-bottoms on college campuses to understand the "truth" of Vietnam.

What I discovered worked really well with this exercise was that the words on the blackboard were not given to the students but instead came from them. These words and ideas are a part of their cultural selves simply because they listen to the radio, or go to the movies, or shop in the mall. While they might be short on "facts" about the war, this small example made them realize that they, in fact, can and do create a rich and complicated truth narrative about the Vietnam War by using their postmodern sensibilities to navigate among all of these varied cultural input. It is the way that we discuss these words in conjunction with each other that will have a direct effect on the narrative they are creating. But before I enter into a discussion about how this construction happens, let me first take a step back and explain briefly what I mean by postmodern sensibilities and the construction of truth.

Unlike some cultural theorists who believe that the current generation of students who were brought up on reality television and X-Box are no more than naive "cultural dopes" who are unable to distinguish subtleties in the pastiche-infested postmodern world, it is my experience that students, who have been navigating their ways through this terrain all their lives, are judicious consumers who understand that they are being exploited and, for the most part, are happy to "play" along with these forms of manipulation to create their own personalized spaces of freedom. In other words, current-day students are not dumb or brainwashed. Instead, they are skilled at continuously creating and recreating themselves. While we are all influenced by what we see and hear, the overt commercialization of everyday life has forced youth cultures to be more discerning when it comes to those vying for their attention (and money). This discernment is a type of play, and in most cases, they embrace it. Growing up in the twenty-first century allows and privileges reflexivity and self-conscious behavior. Students know they are performing and will play various roles, slipping on different skins as the mood or the role changes. Far from being passive consumers (whether in a sneaker store or a classroom), they are in more control than many pessimistic theorists will allow. Unwilling to take most things at face value, there is agency on the student's part as they sift through the information and products presented, using their lifetime of skill to weed out the mistruths that do not interest them particularly, and finally concentrating on personalized accepted truths that resonate within them. Far from wholly swallowing everything that is placed in front of them, they, in fact, have a more delicate palate that is able to discover hints of their "truth" that speak to them. And while a discussion of whether or not these skills are harmful or beneficial for youth cultures is still being made, and rightfully so, it doesn't change the fact that these are skills that they must learn in order to survive.

In the everyday realm, therefore, their truth is always in the act of becoming. To accept a static and unchanging truth would be social suicide, and so they are always willing to change their understandings of truth. Always in the process of being formed, the rigidity of accepted truths that are given to them has large fault lines that they dance over. This play is a skill that the students possess, and I, as a college professor of the humanities, want to use this skill as a foundation as they grow as intellectuals. I want them to continue to develop their ability to construct truths as we read a Toni Morrison novel or watch a John Cassavetes film or write essays on the meanings of graffiti for urban gangs in Brooklyn, New York. But here's the problem: while students are willing to dance outside of the classroom, inside, they become wallflowers. As tuition's rise and the importance placed on grade averages becomes more central to a university education, the ambiguity of "truth" can be disturbing to some students. Speaking about multiple meanings of truth to a student who wants to know how exactly she will be graded on an essay can be frustrating to both parties involved. And when a grade is at stake, most wish to be given simple, straightforward truths that they can point to and rely on. They want to know what *Beloved* is about, or what they should say about *Faces,* or what is the right answer about the meaning of graffiti. Many students feel that the less ambiguity, the better. But by bringing in *The Things They Carried* as the first book that we read as a class, I have found it extremely helpful in bridging this gap between their cultural selves that are willing to experiment and play and their academic selves that are more rigid and serious. But this task certainly isn't easy.

Although a student who watches a rerun of *Friends* is easily able to distinguish and accept the Brad Pitt character on the episode as different from Brad Pitt star of *Fight Club*, as separate from Brad Pitt, ex-husband of Jennifer Aniston (who plays the character Rachel on *Friends* who, on an episode, was in high school with Brad Pitt, the character), they are suddenly confused, frustrated, and even angry when they are forced to attempt to untangle the writer Tim O'Brien, from the soldier Tim O'Brien, from Tim O'Brien, the character in the book *The Things They Carried*. While we are ready to suspend our belief when watching a popular television show, or are old hats at negotiating the truth of statements from a friend talking about what she did over the weekend, novels about wars are supposed to be serious. And seriousness implies a binding and stable "truth," which, in turn, implies an almost naive trust in the author to present that "truth" to her readers. As much as we can "play" in our everyday life, we feel that there must be sobriety when dealing with a novel about Vietnam. Experts at discerning truth values in our experiences in postmodern culture, we turn off the questioning function in our brains when it comes to important historical events and believe, or at least accept, what we are told. What O'Brien does specifically in this novel is force us to turn this function back on to question the validity of the factual truth (and its overall usefulness), and instead he brings us to the realm of the more ambiguous—and in O'Brien's view, the more authentic—story truth. In other words, O'Brien allows us to use our postmodern sensibility and shows us that all truth—including serious truths about the Vietnam War—are narratives that must be formed and reformed through stories that are constantly changing.

When it comes to the Vietnam War, then, while we might want to fall back on the easy and straightforward "truth" that, for example, "war is hell," O'Brien will not allow it. Instead, he alters that truth and writes that war can be, in fact, beautiful. His stories, he therefore insists, are not war stories per se, but they are actually love stories. By making these statements in this novel, the historic simplicity of that truth value of "war is hell" is shattered. The reader is forced to rethink and reform their truths of the war by relying on their own abilities to pick up the pieces and create narratives and thus must meet O'Brien, who refuses to give any stable truths, halfway.

CONFLICTING TRUTHS IN *THE THINGS THEY CARRIED*

Nominated for the National Book Critics Circle Award, The Pulitzer Prize, and winner of the Prix du Meilleur Livre Etranger in 1990, *The Things They*

Carried has, in the last twenty-five or so years, become a popular novel to teach at the college and high school level. A truly gripping and powerful read with bold, direct sentences, the book defies easy categorization. In the end, though, it really doesn't matter how you do it—whether you label this book "metafiction," "creative nonfiction," "magical realism," or a "war novel," in essence, this is a novel about the meaning and creation of stories.

"Stories are for joining the past to the future ... Stories are for eternity, when memory is erased, when there is nothing to remember except the story" (O'Brien 40). From the absence of memory is born *The Things They Carried*, the story of Tim O'Brien's experience in Vietnam. But, as every reader soon finds out after she has bent the spine of this book, these are not necessarily the memories of Tim O'Brien, the novelist—although the author does make guest appearances—but, rather, Tim O'Brien, the invented character that the author created to tell a "truth" about Vietnam. The author, therefore, puts a particular spin on the truth describing this spin as akin to the spin put on a ping-pong when returning a serve—both are used to make their object "dance" in a particular way (35). But because *The Things They Carried* is about a soldier's experience with the Vietnam War, we as readers are not expecting the spin and, when reading, are apt to miss the truth completely.

O'Brien explains that truth is what takes place in the world when we are afraid to look. The result is that we are left with "faceless responsibility and faceless grief" (203). And so we invent. We create. We tell a story. And this story becomes, to use Jean Baudrillard's famous phrase, "more real than real." The actual event becomes lost in the memory's print of the event. And each time the story is told, the memory breathes and, in its breathing, new stories are formed. Or to use O'Brien's words, "The thing about a story is that you dream it as you tell it, hoping that others might then dream along with you, and in this way memory and imagination and language combine to make the spirits in the head" (260). This is the story truth, and it is this type of truth telling in which we all participate. The story truth is therefore in a constant reformation and each addition and subtraction recreates this truth. Memories are not stable, and so each time we remember an event, we use our imagination to make it (more) real and alive. We do this to make our own truths dance.

But this isn't a free-form dance, and the way we spin the truth has direct consequences on our views of the world. It is this part that I find of utmost importance to discuss with my students. The way that we construct our narratives lead us—and if we are persuasive when we tell our stories, others—to see the world in a particular way. Our stories and the way we tell them, have consequences. And that is why using *The Things They Carried* is so helpful. This is a novel about a very real event in history; the truths that we tell about the war have plotlines that contain much bloodshed and death. This is why I do not have my students construct their "own war stories" or have units in which the focus is directly on themselves. I want them to move away from just using their own lives for stories but rather see how their stories are a part of a larger national narrative. Their stories, then, are not just explanations about summer vacations, but about a history that changed the way the country has viewed itself.

In an interview with the online magazine, *GadFly*, O'Brien explains the consequences of forming story truths, "The idea of truth is dependent on a kind of declaration we make about the world ... *Ultimately, the truth of things is what we say about things; what we say about things determines the way we think about truth*" (Lindbloom, italics mine). Even though in this novel, O'Brien tells "his" stories about the war, if we take his words at face value, then we need to realize that these spins of truth force upon our shoulders a large responsibility. Each one of us is a storyteller. Or to put it another way, each one of us is a truth makers. And so, even though we are many years removed from the Vietnam War, we as a class are speaking and writing truths about this war.

THE SECOND DAY OF CLASS, OR WHEN A NEWBIE TEACHER GETS A LITTLE SMARTER

If the truth of Vietnam becomes the relationship between the two words on the blackboard, then the particular words that we choose will alter or spin the truth in a certain way. The narratives that we create hold a power, and the more persuasive we are, the more effect our story truth has on those around us. In the sequential class of that first semester of teaching, then, I wanted to walk with my students through the particular ways that we spin truth. I wrote some of the words that they had said in the previous class back on the board. As we talked about the words that we saw, we focused our discussion on how our stories create truths. We decided, therefore, to tell our own truths about the war, and we did this by connecting certain words that were on the board together. But while this seemed easy at first, the results were a bit distressing for all of us. Every act of choosing words resulted in an act of denial, of slimming down the idea of the truth of Vietnam into smaller and smaller ideas. The flip side was also true: every word we did choose felt as if it gained in importance and therefore we wanted to make sure we chose the "right" word to tell our stories. We wanted words that created a dialogue between each other, and the narrative that was formed had to resonate within us. If stories are all we have, as O'Brien suggests, then we wanted to make sure that our stories were worth telling. For example, if we return to the first two words that I have already mentioned:

Agent Orange. Canada.

We looked at these two words sitting side by side and a narrative began to form as we talked about them and how they connect. If it is true, Joe asked, that the U.S. government did use this gas on their own troops, then why wouldn't a potential soldier run away to Canada? Doesn't this make sense? In fact, couldn't this be considered courageous? Another student then interjected by bringing in something that O'Brien, the character, refers to in the chapter "On Rainy River"—that is, that by going to Vietnam, and not "running away" to Canada, he had been a coward. But another student, Anne, was convinced that "Agent Orange" was just made up by "liberal media." A discussion (fight?) broke out between them about this controversial subject with many others joining in. So both Joe and Anne were set: their job that night was to look into this controversy and write about/report back what they found out. But other students in the class were not so excited about this topic and they added new words to the mix. We began discussing:

Agent Orange. Miniskirts. Canada.

Students stretched themselves trying to find links that could connect these three words. Melissa brought into the discussion the chapter, "The Sweetheart of the Song Tra Bong" and how Mary Anne showed up in the jungle with "white culottes and [a] sexy pink sweater" (102). After about ten minutes, though, we felt that the stories that we were creating weren't leading anywhere. They didn't dance, and we knew it. So we changed the words and started over:

Media Coverage. Napalm.

Immediately, Sam brought up the famous scene in *Apocalypse Now* in which Lieutenant Colonel Kilgore (Robert Duvall) stands up straight, nose high in the air and states, "I love the smell of Napalm in the morning." A discussion followed (with some tangential discussions about the scene and other movies that had similar lines) on the nature and role of capturing the war on film. During this discussion, Olivia interjected with the word "Guilt" that she remembered seeing on the board and linked it to the other two words explaining that the media representations of both American soldiers dying (as well as the deaths of the Vietnamese) might cause some vets to feel guilt as they watched these films. So we placed these words together:

Media Coverage. Napalm. *Apocalypse Now.* Guilt.

Sam then remembered the chapter on Norman Baker, and how he had killed himself because he couldn't help Kiowa out of the shit field in "Speaking of Courage," and thought that this would work really well when telling the story about these words. Others argued that it wouldn't work, because although there was certainly guilt and the need to tell the story in the media (Baker had asked O'Brien to write his story), there was no napalm. But Sam didn't care, and he went on to write a paper in which he didn't mention napalm or *Apocalypse Now* but instead focused on the need for Vets to keep retelling their stories. He found a great Web site that is dedicated to the chronicling of veterans' war stories, and he focused on how technology has been a vital force in allowing soldiers to tell their stories to a wider and wider audience.

STUDENTS AS STORYTELLERS, STUDENTS AS NATIONAL TRUTH MAKERS

I have used *The Things They Carried* as the opening novel in many of my classes, although differently depending on the course. In my introduction to American studies courses, for example, I usually only spend about one week with the novel. Even though we don't spend a great amount of time with the text, I have found that reading this novel coupled with the classroom activities mentioned above keys my students into the ways that we will strive to become resistive readers as we create our own historical stories and understandings when encountering future texts in our course. In my composition classes, however, we spend much more time with this text—usually five or six weeks. Focusing on a process-oriented approach to writing a paper, we work slowly through the process of creating a story. Using these two exercises, we talk about the ways that stories are created. We then read through the novel slowly and carefully, examining the places in the text where O'Brien explores the meaning and purpose of stories. We attempt to work through our frustrations about the lack of stable truths and instead try to explore the possibilities that open up when truth is acknowledged as a construct. In other words, we learn to play in an academic setting. We then spend time bringing the word/ideas together that we placed on the blackboard and, through multiple assignments and peer review sessions, the students slowly create their stories. Almost organically, these stories become research papers as they must find other texts besides *The Things They Carried* to couple and flesh out their ideas. But what is truly wonderful about using this text is that students become aware quite quickly of the bias in the reporting of history and become adept at questioning the sources that they use. Almost intuitively, they move away from generalized statements in their writing and hone their stories to sharp points that they can express and call their own.

In the classroom, then, one of our jobs as professors is to create a space in which students can become good storytellers. This is essentially what we are asking our students to do when entering a class discussion or writing a paper. But by using *The Things We Carried*, we are upping the ante. We are moving away from the more comfortable ground of the student's life in which she may feel at ease performing and analyzing truth narratives, and instead we are asking them to enter into a national discussion about the truth of the Vietnam War. With the stakes this high, we are showing them that there is a responsibility in the act of telling and writing stories. These two exercises that I have outlined above are ways for students to become self-aware of the histories that they are creating. And while O'Brien writes that he tells stories to save his own life, students are telling stories to understand how truths of our national history are continually recreated.

WORKS CITED

Lindbloom, Jim. "The Heart Under Stress: Interview with author Tim O'Brien," *GadFly Online.* March 1999. http://www.gadflyonline.com/back-issues/march99.html (accessed May 22, 2007).

O'Brien, Tim. *The Things They Carried*. New York: Penguin Books, 1990.

Questioning Ethics: Incorporating the Novel into Ethics Courses

Rachel McCoppin

Choosing to kill someone to save a friend and giving up personal freedom to "be there" for the unemployed masses of California, defending the murderer of a young girl because the social injustice of poverty and prejudice done to the murderer is hard to ignore, or deciding to embrace the self over one's children, even to the point of suicide, are all ethical dilemmas that arise in Steinbeck's *The Grapes of Wrath,* Wright's *Native Son,* or Chopin's *The Awakening.* As an assistant professor of literature, I am familiar with teaching the novel as part of a literature course. Ethical issues often naturally arise in these class discussions. Ethical criticism of literature arguably has been connected to the study of ethics in literature since ancient times, so the study of ethical issues in the novel is nothing new, but there is not an abundant amount of research that discusses the use of the novel in college ethics courses.

When I teach ethics courses, it feels natural to include novels as part of the curriculum. We teach novels as part of a humanities curriculum because they offer a detailed insight into human nature; through reading students become familiar with the ethical complications of life because of social background, race, religion, simple bad luck, and so on, and a character's motives behind an ethical dilemma becomes intensified more than a terse case study can reveal. Therefore, incorporating novels into an ethics course can strengthen understanding and discussion of important ethical theories. Novels develop "moral capacities without which citizens will not succeed in making reality out of the normative conclusions of any moral or political theory, however excellent" (Nussbaum "The Literary" 364). Also, incorporating literature into an ethics course can strengthen a college's use of interdisciplinary teaching methods. Simply incorporating a novel into an ethics course is not enough, however; instructors need to integrate open dialogue and possibly class debate as part of a process toward an understanding and acceptance of the "other," which is vital to an ethics course.

In my ethics course, I teach Dostoevsky's *Crime and Punishment* and Vonnegut's *Mother Night.* The incorporation of these novels to an ethics course allows students to obtain an intimacy with the characters that adds a human element and blurs the boundaries of right and wrong, creating a valuable, engaged discussion of ethics. These are definitely not, however, the only two choices of novels that lead to powerful class discussion in an ethics course. Later in this paper, I will include a detailed discussion of some of the assignments focused around these two choices, but I will also provide some other suggestions of effective novels.

THE PEDAGOGY OF LITERATURE

First and foremost, students of literature are usually expected to gain an awareness of the scope and variety of works found in ancient to contemporary literature. But literature, as part of a humanities curriculum, is meant to offer students more than a task in the memorization of various texts, literary eras, and author backgrounds. Most literature instructors strive to provide their students with an understanding of these various literary works as expressions of their human values, struggles, fears, and triumphs within a historical and social context. Literature allows students to gain a perspective on the human condition as it pertains to differing individuals; diverse social and economic backgrounds; conflicting political, religious, and social views; and various cultures and races in historical and contemporary dimensions. The study of literature encourages students to apply a comparative perspective to cross-cultural, social, economic, and political experiences. Through study in the discipline of literature, students will form their own personal critical judgments on the specific works, but they may, and often do, develop a connection between literature and ethics, because students have spent a semester immersed in an intimate study of humanity with all its intricacies, differences, and similarities.

James Meffan and Kim L. Worthington, in their "Ethics before Politics: J. M Coetzee's *Disgrace*," state the philosopher Levinas's theory of alterity as it pertains to the study of literature:

Significantly, then, for Levinas alterity is to be understood as an experience rather than as a realizable quality. It is an experience that is entirely subject- and context-specific: alterity is that which exceed the terms and bounds of the (individual) thinker's cognition, and hence varies with the limits of understanding for each percipient subject.... The experience of alterity, in Levinas's terms, is nothing more than a subjective acknowledgment of the limits of the percipient's knowledge, of his or her inability to contain all that is perceivable within the ambit of understanding. (135)

Levinas is often credited in discussions of the beginnings of ethical criticism in literature.

This form of alterity is close to Kant's theory of the sublime; if one tries to imagine a concept that cannot ever be fully understood by the human mind, like someone else's subjectivity, then the thinker is led to believe in the sublime. This theory of the sublime directly correlates with Levinas's later argument that his theory of alterity will eventually lead to ethics: "ethics is the ongoing process of self-critique, in particular, of putting the knowing ego into question through the process of the exposure to and recognition of alterity, absolute Otherness" (Meffan and Worthington 136). A consciousness of the "other" leads one to gain a sense of humility with the acknowledgment of a constant "other" putting the self in perspective, and literature offers complex glimpses of the lives and dilemmas of other human beings.

THE PEDAGOGY OF ETHICS

Most ethics courses strive to increase students' understanding of concepts, such as subjectivism, objectivism, Kantianism, utilitarianism, virtue ethics, care ethics, and so on. Students are often expected to become familiar with the literature pertaining to various ethical philosophers and theorists and apply critical-thinking and problem-solving skills to various ethical situations. But again, as with the study of literature, ethics is taught as part of the humanities curriculum because the field of ethics allows students to gain a perspective on the "other." An effective ethics course must introduce issues that pertain to discordant social, economical, religious, and political views within various cultures and subcultures in historical and contemporary society. Again, as with literature courses, students will form their own ethical conclusions on any given dilemma, but they will be consistently encouraged to view ethics in terms outside of themselves.

Levinas and Kant grasped an important part of ethics, perhaps the central component of ethics—the acceptance of the "other." Ethics must be about respect for "others" as individuals who are just as important as oneself: "Empathy, in essence, is an ideal of differentiated union with another, and that paradox should remind us that in literature, as in life, there are shared borders of identity that we are compelled to recognize but cannot cross" (Lundeen 92).

This position extends to Kenneth Burke's four rungs of learning in "Linguistic Approach to Problems of Education:" rung 1 seeks to defeat an opponent; rung 2 seeks to gain knowledge of other positions to defeat those other positions; rung 3 seeks to appreciate, accept, and understand other positions; and most important, rung 4 contends that an individual becomes willing to be revised by the "other." This is why ethics courses are essential to a liberal and multicultural education. "Being revised by the other" allows student to grow beyond their comfort zones and become active, healthy members of society. Literature, specifically the reading of novels followed by discussion and debate, can be used as a means toward achieving this end.

THE USE OF LITERATURE IN ETHICS

In ancient Greece and Rome, literature, recited orally in earlier times, was often used to teach ethics; "Reading [was] a foundation for moral instruction; the teaching of ethics in the ancient world almost always took place through the study of texts" (Stock 3, 6). In late antiquity,

Jews, Christians, and (in some cases) pagan students of theology held the view that truth could be revealed through a combination of philosophical reasoning and the close scrutiny of sacred writings. These "scriptures" ... could not be understood or interpreted unless they were read, whence the increased emphasis on reading as a means of gaining knowledge in ethical matters. (Stock "Reading" 3)

Seneca's *Moral Epistles* and Augustine's *Confessions* had a "belief in the reader's ethical responsibility for the postreading experience.... Reading [led] to a study of the self that [was] intended to achieve selflessness" (Stock 11–12). Augustine showed readers how "to engage in self-examination, step-by-step, by means of their personal memories"; he used stories of his personal life to teach others how to live an ethical life (Stock "Reading" 9).

In the Middle Ages and the Renaissance,

the literate culture was largely elitist. Books were scarce, expensive and not widely distributed. The major change in the size of the readership took place during the eighteenth century, when the large scale printing of books ... made it possible for persons of limited means to own private libraries for the first time ... During the nineteenth century ... book culture reached ... communities in the countryside. The expansion of literacy had political, and therefore ethical, implications. (Stock 3–4)

Books were often used to teach religious views of morality to the general public. Reading literature

was then, as it is now, a way of acquiring information that could be useful in reaching ethical decisions, but it was also an ... exercise through which readers focused their attention ... and attempted to achieve inner tranquility. It was in this state of mind, it was believed that ethical questions could be taken up in a balanced, impartial, and detached manner. (Stock 14–15)

In contemporary ethical studies, reading is still the most popular means for examining ethical theories and dilemmas, but the material read tends to be mostly nonfiction. Contemporary ethics students tend to learn about the historical predecessors' theories in the field; most ethics textbooks provide ethical situations or case studies for the students to ponder and apply these separate ethical theories. But, the study of ethics in many college classrooms today does not include fictionalized literature, unless it is a short, fictional case study. Therefore, it is important for ethics instructors to consider utilizing more fiction novels to teach their concepts.

ETHICAL CRITICISM IN LITERATURE

As stated earlier, there is not significant research on the inclusion of novels within ethics courses in the contemporary classroom, but the study of ethics in literature is a much-accepted form of scholarly criticism today, as it has been part of scholarly literary discussion for centuries; "Ethical critics [of literature], like cartographers, do not necessarily discover or make a territory, but, instead, describe and give shape to what has always existed" (Newton 631).

In looking at ethical criticism in literature, a sense of the "other" is paramount to ethics; "literature is an other-maker. It is to this activity that literary theory must attend. That is why it is natural for it to turn to ethics" (Sanders 4). Because the importance of the "other" is often recognized as essential to ethical criticism, Levinas is recognized as crucial to the creation of modern ethical criticism:

In a time after the demise of modern secular dogmas of reason, autonomy, and enlightenment, in a time after the Holocaust and communist depredations, when many thinkers have lost faith in Western ethics as well, Levinas' philosophy models what may seem to many to be one last hope for humanist dignity: an exorbitant responsibility to the Other. To teach the responsibility—in that sense, to teach it globally—Levinas offers a stunning reformation of modern ... theory. (Newton 606)

Wayne Booth is an avid supporter of ethical criticism in literature and has written many articles in its defense. He contends that "[s]tories do change us" (370). He believes that

[w]henever we fully engage with any story, we engage not with abstract concepts or moral codes but with *persons,* both with characters in the story and the implied person who has chosen to portray them in this precise way ... the characters ... always exhibit ... complex values—conflicts among the virtues. When we join such characters, loving them or hating them, in the virtual world of story, we are inescapably caught up in ethical activity. (375)

Booth continues to support ethical criticism of literature with his comment "it is ... 'literary' works, that make the most irresistible demands for ethical talk" (380).

Martha Nussbaum, in "Exactly and Responsibly: A Defense of Ethical Criticism," states what is basic to the study of literature and why, at its essential level, it is natural to connect literature to ethics:

In my childhood, the novels of Dickens provided ... a joyful sense of escape, from a world in which rich people ignored the claims of the poor, into a world where those claims were acknowledged ... it felt like a release from a ... confinement into a space of human possibility.... I do think that all citizens ought to think about justice, and it seems to me that reading certain novels offers assistance in that task. (363)

Richard Posner maintains that "Nussbaum thinks moral philosophy incomplete without literature" (3).

Gayatri Chakravorty Spivak also supports the use of literature in ethics:

[F]iction offers us an experience of the discontinuities that remain in place "in real life." That would be a description of fiction as an event—an indeterminate "sharing" between writer and reader, where the effort of reading is to taste the impossible status of being figured as object in the web of the other. Reading, in this special sense, is sacred. (18)

Spivak even applies literary ethical theory to contemporary society; "As I have watched [Paul Wolfowitz, the former Deputy Secretary of Defense] on television lately, I have often thought that if he had had serious training in literary reading and/or the imagining of the enemy as human, his position on Iraq would not be so inflexible" (22). Stock also connects the ethical study of literature to contemporary issues:

We now need to remind readers of their traditional obligations, as we have in other ethical issues in the media, for example concerning the right to print child pornography or to expose audiences to violence on television. Bringing this type of engagement to the humanities would help to ground ethical instruction in the personal experience of the individual, where it had a legitimate place in the ancient, medieval, and Renaissance periods. (16)

Ethical criticism of literature reveals a relationship between ethics and literature, and it seems evident that literature has always needed ethics. I contend that ethics also needs literature, particularly the novel.

THE EFFECTIVENESS OF THE NOVEL IN ETHICS COURSES

Ethics is inherently tied to what-if scenarios. Most ethics courses teach the various ethical theories as they progressed throughout time and try to connect these theories to concrete ethical dilemmas. The novel is an exceptional tool to become familiar with one or more complex, concrete ethical situation(s).

The novel rose into being mainly with the era of Realism. It became a form of literary expression that reached a broader audience and depicted "realistically the activities and experiences of ordinary life" (Posner 6). Lionel Trilling states,

For our time the most effective agent of the moral imagination has been the novel of the last two hundred years ... its greatness and its practical usefulness lay in its unremitting work of involving the reader himself in the moral life, inviting him to put his own motives under examination.... It taught us, as no other genre ever did, the extent of human variety and the value of this variety ... there never was a time when its particular activity was so much needed, was of so much practical, political, and social use. (90–91)

The novel is an especially valuable tool for an ethics class because of its format. Many novels are short enough for a class to be able to get through it in a week or a two, yet they are long enough to create an intricate set of real-world circumstances.

The novel allows readers to become close with a character or characters, revealing the necessary complexity of the characters' decisions on any given ethical scenario: [N]ovels present persistent forms of human need and desire realized in specific social situations. These situations frequently, indeed usually, differ a good deal from the reader's own" (Nussbaum "The Literary" 360). Nussbaum points out that the intricacy of the novel allows students to put themselves in the place of the literary characters: "Live the life of another person who might, given changes in circumstance, be oneself or one of one's loved ones.... Literature focuses on the possible, inviting its readers to wonder about themselves" (Nussbaum "The Literary" 359). Students of ethics need to be able to imagine the complicated life of another person choosing their actions in a complex world, and novels allow this depth to surface more than an abrupt case study can.

Novels allow one to become intimately aware of the "other": "In reading literature we are also learning about the values and experiences of cultures, epochs, and sensibilities remote from our own, yet not so remote as to be unintelligible. We are acquiring experience vicariously by dwelling in the imaginary worlds that literature creates" (Posner 19). Robin West states that even law student should use literary novels to become better lawyers: "Literature helps us understand others.... It makes us more moral.... Lawyers can learn how to represent lesbian clients better by studying books with lesbian characters'" (quoted in Posner 4). Many of James Boyd White's essays also encourages the use of "a certain kind of literary education to lawyers and judges so that they will be better lawyers and judges. *Morally* better, as well as professionally abler" (Posner 4).

Nussbaum discusses another important factor apparent in novels that helps to achieve distance from students' comfort zones:

[G]ood literature is disturbing in a way that history and social science writing frequently are not. Because it summons powerful emotions, it disconcerts and puzzles. It inspires distrust of conventional pieties and exacts a frequently painful confrontation with one's own thoughts and intentions. One may be told many things about people in one's own society and yet keep that knowledge at a distance. Literary works that promote identification and emotional reaction cut through those self-protective stratagems, requiring us to see and to respond to many things that may be difficult to confront. (Nussbaum "The Literary" 359)

This factor of confrontation with the "other" is a highly significant tool to incite open debate in the ethics classroom.

Booth argues for the vital importance of ethical dialogue as part of a process for using literature to aid in a realization of the "other":

"[T]he act of reading and assessing what one has read is ethically valuable precisely because it is constructed in a manner that demands both immersion and critical conversation, comparison of what one has read both with one's own unfolding experience and with the responses and arguments of other readers. If we think of reading in this way, as combining one's own imagining with periods of more detached (and interactive) critical scrutiny, we can already begin to see why we find in it an activity well suited to public reasoning in a democratic society." (quoted in Nussbaum "The Literary" 362)

The opponents of using novels to teach ethics might state that literature doesn't make people better:

The chief problem with the ... method of ethical instruction through literature ... is that it leads to productions of forms of thought rather than forms of behavior. There is nothing within this scheme that teaches the student how to relate what has been learned from texts to the ethical challenges encountered in everyday life. (Stock 5–6)

Posner states that "'Despite their familiarity with the classics, professors of literature do not appear to lead better lives than other people'.... Cultured people are not on the whole morally superior to philistines. Immersion in literature and art can breed rancorous and destructive feelings of personal superiority, alienation, and resentment" (5). It is true that there is no way to prove whether literature directly makes a person better; there seems no way to definitively prove that ethics courses make someone better, yet an education void of the thought encapsulated in the creation and discussion of literature and ethics does not seem beneficial to the character of today's students. Time spent considering the treatment of others cannot be wasted time.

Booth cites Posner as saying,

"Literature can expand our emotional as well as our intellectual horizons." Once more: "... literature continues to be an important component of high school and college education because of its effects in stretching the student's imagination, multiplying his cultural perspectives, . . . offering him a range of vicarious experience, and assisting him to read difficult texts, express complex thoughts, and write and speak persuasively." (quoted in Booth 372)

Booth continues, "If he thinks this list of effects is not about ethical qualities, he depends on a curiously narrow definition of ethics, contradicting grand parts of the philosophical tradition" (372).

Also, academia stresses the importance of interdisciplinarity. Susan H. Frost and Paul M. Jean in "Bridging the Disciplines" state such positive attributes of cross-disciplinary teaching as "more frequent and valuable contact with faculty," an increased "understanding of the nature of their disciplines" (134), "a deeper respect for the subtleties and complexities of other disciplines" (135), and an "increased level of confidence for reaching out to faculty members outside their own disciplines" (137). Mark Sanders in "Ethics in Interdisciplinarity in Philosophy and Literary Theory" discusses how Levinas's theory of alterity also applies to interdisciplinarity. He states that one's "responsibility before the other" makes the blending of literature and ethics also a matter of ethics. Many ethical critics of literature state the effectiveness of discerning ethical issues in literature; therefore, it is only plausible that the novel is a beneficial tool for ethics courses.

APPLIED PRACTICE FOR USING NOVELS IN ETHICS COURSES

As has been stated, many ethics courses teach the different ethical theories that are in place: divinity ethics, Kantianism, utilitarianism, care ethics, pragmatism, and so on, but they often include essays and case studies on contemporary ethical issues. Peter Singer's textbook *Applied Ethics* is a good example of a standard introductory ethics textbook. It includes various essay from contradictory perspective on such topics as abortion, euthanasia, suicide, capital punishment, gender inequality, and animal rights. His text deals with multiculturalism and human rights issues. Although his included nonfiction essays are beneficial, and students respond well to an open discussion and debate on the contradictory positions he includes on such topics, there is still something missing.

Students have a difficult time connecting to the intricate details of another person deciding whether to get an abortion, unplug the respirator of a loved one, or support hiring someone according to the laws of affirmative action, without the medium they have been continually indoctrinated to respond to—the narrative, fictional story. Without the detailed story found in novels, longer than a three- to ten-page short story, students do not tend to get emotionally involved with the ethical scenario presented. But when they have invested hours reading and pondering over the complex saga of the characters within a novel, they tend to want to discuss, sometime quite passionately, their feelings on the characters' ethical decisions.

Novels give concrete, expanded scenarios that allow ethical theories to come alive; once the students have to debate or apply theory/theories to the studied novel, they tend to understand the theory better than when their mode of connecting to a philosophical theory is a removed and brief case study or essay. Yet, simply assigning a novel to a class is not enough. Open dialogue and class debates are imperative to ensuring that the students get, first, what the ethical scenarios are, and second, a variety of interpretations on any ethical situation from their classmates. This part of the process is vital because it is what leads to an essential component of ethics courses—the effort to understand, accept, and possibly be changed by the "other." Booth argues that one person is not necessarily "qualified to judge the full ethical value of a work.... No one is qualified to 'extract' the full value of any great story if working utterly alone.... It is in the exchange among readers about their ethical responses that they learn to improve their own judgments" (372–73). Dialogue and debate on a topic they are invested in aids the learning process of a given theory, but more important, it helps them to listen and consider the position of the other students in the classroom.

Novels and dialogue assist each other. Novels introduce dynamic characters and elaborate scenarios involving the "other," but the voices of the fellow classmates in an atmosphere of open discourse help achieve a greater sense of ethical compassion and understanding.

If a novel has a controversial topic to discuss, and usually the good ones will, then because of discussion and debate, it is difficult for a student to overlook an unethical act within a story. It is often just as difficult for a student to hold a position that may be ethically questionable, unless they have proven that they have looked at other positions on the issue and still believe their initial interpretation. This helps not to ensure that all students come to the same interpretation of the ethical situations found in the novel, but that they have thought through many different viewpoints on the ethical situations, as well as listened to many of their classmates' varying opinions.

In almost every ethical situation that is raised in my classroom, whether it is a nonfiction case study or a fictional situation found in the novel they are reading, my students partake in an activity dealing with the opposition. In any given discussion or debate, once a student has stated his or her position, I repeatedly, at unexpected moments will ask the student to now become his or her opposition. The student will have to state to the class the main points of their oppositions' argument, as if he or she is the opposition. If the student cannot do this one the spot, then the student is asked to research the opposition's side as homework and present his or her new argument to the class the next class session.

The class, debating alternative views, critiques each student's oppositional argument; the classmates are encouraged to find every weakness in this oppositional argument, encouraging the student to truly support his or her oppositional stance (to truly treat the opposition fairly). For this assignment, the student becomes the "other."

During this debate, I will repeatedly ask the students if they think that they can modify their initial positions by incorporating the oppositional arguments they had presented. I ask them whether the activity was difficult for them, and why. I then ask what benefit they received from becoming the "other." This study of the "other" is beneficial, because it allows the student to assess his or her initial position, and sometimes results in the student refining his or her opinion based on the consideration of an oppositional position.

Posner contends that many novels include questionable themes that are hardly ethical, such as "adultery and manliness (for example Lawrence, Hemingway, and Joyce)," or "novels that presuppose an organization of society in which a leisured, titled, or educated upper crust lives off the sweat of the brow of a mass of toilers at whose existence the novel barely hints (for example, Austen, James, Wharton, . . . Fitzgerald)," or "novels preoccupied with issues more metaphysical than social (Beckett, Hesse, and much of Melville, Tolstoy)" (6). Even Posner points out that some of the works of these novelists do not fit his classifications, which would be my first point of disagreement on this issue. But what is revealing, and useful for an ethics course, is that each student may get a different interpretation of a novel. And that is exactly what makes novels so effective for discerning individual ethics.

Many students may read Lawrence's *Lady Chatterley's Lover* as a novel that at least attempts to capture feminist notions for the post–World War I era, or Fitzgerald's *The Great Gatsby* as a stirring social commentary about the ill, desolate world of the very rich, or all of Melville's works as extreme social activist novels. The students' individual interpretations of novels, especially controversial novels with intricate ethical scenarios, engage them in an environment of open, often-heated dialogue that allows students to come face to face with other viewpoints; and again, many times, students will alter their initial positions when they reconsider the ethical dilemma from someone else's interpretation.

Even if a novel deals with offensive topics, or the author has had disconcerting shortcomings in his or her personal life, this is not to say that an ethics instructor cannot use this information to incite a beneficial discussion. For instance, Conrad's *Heart of Darkness* could start insightful ethical discussions based on finding the unethical remarks on the native population found in his novel, as well as a discussion of the ethical flaws of the characters, or even the author, leading to a discussion of contemporary racism.

Some might argue that reading novels will reveal who students really are to begin with: "The characters and situations that interest us in literature are for the most part characters and situations that capture aspects of ourselves and our situation" (Posner 20). Students may be drawn only to what their background has made them interested in; readers may identify with "egomaniacs, scamps, seducers, conquerors, psychopaths, tricksters, and immoralists" (Posner 20). Although this is true to a certain extent, a course in ethics, ideally, is meant to broaden the comfort zones a student may hold. This is why, again, dialogue and open debate is imperative to an ethics course, so that students have the opportunity to be changed by the perspectives of other students. Booth points out that if a novel or character is despicable, most students, especially through dialogue, will look at "how the judged actions have been *placed* within the work itself" (369).

Posner suggests that there is no evidence that novels

provide a straighter path to knowledge about man and society than other sources of such knowledge, including writings in other fields, such as history and science, and interactions with real people. Some people *prefer* to get their knowledge of human nature from novels, but it doesn't follow that novels are a superior source of such knowledge to life and the various genres of nonfiction. (9)

This is true; novels are not the only method one should use to teach or learn about ethics, but this does not refute the fact that in teaching one needs to make use of many different kinds of mediums. Many students may be positively affected by the intimacy a novel can achieve; other students may respond better to a visual a nonfiction case study. This is why it is important to offer a lot of different ethical materials to get students thinking and discussing.

It should be said that the novels that I have discussed, and will discuss, are not at all the only options that should be considered for students to reach the course goals and outcomes of an ethics course. The only true stipulation that a novel needs to have to be effective in an ethics course is an ethical scenario, and most novels have this. Any novel that the instructor feels worthwhile probably is. As long as an instructor feels that the novel fits nicely with the ethical theories he or she is trying to teach, it is probably a good choice. The length of the novel should be considered, as time constraints are always a consideration. Instructors should also consider their audience; some novels are naturally more interesting to younger audiences. Some novels deal with themes that are not centrally focused on ethical issues, and these may be ineffective choices. The best choices tend to be the novels that leave readers stumped and confused on how they would respond to the ethical issues. Complex moral situations in a novel with intricate characters lead to active discourse.

Some critics feel that only contemporary novels should be used to study ethics, so that students can apply the book to contemporary political or social issues, but I disagree with this assumption. Many ethical theories are quite dated with ancient and medieval roots, so a dated novel often serves well to connect and understand older theories, such as Homer's *Iliad.*

The *Iliad* is an exceptional novel to use for its ethical content. Students can study both Plato's and Aristotle's ethical philosophies with this timely piece, but also they can apply contemporary ethical theories to the moral dilemmas found in the book. Students not only get a philosophical discussion on the nature of war in the ancient world and can possibly draw similarities to modern warfare, but also, and perhaps more worthy of discussion, students can debate the internal struggle of Achilles. One sees the cost of revenge, first because of Helen and Paris's actions, and second because of Achilles' graphic revenge toward Hector for the death of Patroclus.

In my ethics course, I teach Dostoevsky's *Crime and Punishment,* which is quite dated but undeniably an ethical classic, and Vonnegut's *Mother Night*, a contemporary novel. I find the mixture of two different time periods leads to more dynamic discussions because the altering field of ethics throughout history can be explored.

My students read each novel at separate times in the semester when they are learning a specific ethical theory. For *Crime and Punishment,* the class is asked to apply Raskolnikov's justification for the two murders he committed to utilitarian ethics. First, I ask them to write their thoughts in a short paper on whether they feel Raskolnikov is guilty according to utilitarian ethics; he even states that he is not guilty for the first murder of the old woman, but is guilty for his second murder of the kind young woman. Raskolnikov's justification for the first murder reveals an interesting argument for one interpretation of utilitarian ethics. Then I allow class time for open discussion of the students' interpretations, which can get invigoratingly heated. Next, the students need to debate in groups on whether Raskolnikov deserved the death penalty, as well as debate for or against the death penalty according to utilitarian ethics. One group tends to be for the death penalty and one against, both according to utilitarian ethics, but I also allow other groups to form who argue for or against the death penalty according to different ethical theories that we have covered as a class, so that students can begin to discover which ethical theory feels most like their own. At any given time, groups will be asked to take part in my oppositional activity—becoming their own opposition—which definitely aids in an acceptance and understanding of the "other."

Later in the semester, I have my students read *Mother Night*. They again are asked to write a short essay independently looking at the character of the protagonist, Howard W. Campbell, Jr., according to virtue ethics. Again, we have an open discussion that tends to get even more heated and dynamic than the open discussion of *Crime and Punishment*. The class then debates whether Howard was to blame for his choice to serve as an American spy while appearing as a Nazi. Throughout the book, Howard even struggles himself with his own virtue. Everyone knows him to be a Nazi, but only he and his Blue Fairy Godmother know he is secretly serving as an American spy. So, the ethical quandary of the novel is—if he lives his life as a Nazi, does that truly make him a Nazi? Students tend to be able to defend his character according to virtue ethics from both sides quite easily. Once again other groups will be debating from the stance of any given earlier ethical theory, and quite often students are asked to switch their initial stance and defend their opposition.

Although I do not use Twain's *Huckleberry Finn* in my ethics course, I do teach it in one of my literature courses, and it offers countless ethical dilemmas for students to consider, most of which deal with Huck's endless ethical decisions. But what is especially appealing about this novel is the relationship of the reader with the implied author:

[H]e has made a vast range of choices, deliberately or unconsciously: *these* characters and their conflicts rather than a host of tempting other possibilities ... which virtues and vices to grant them ... when to interrupt with commentary revealing the author's judgment of events. It is that chooser who constitutes the full ethos of any work. (Booth 378)

Students initially have trouble with the timeliness of this novel; some also tend to judge Twain's prejudice, but when they learn that Twain actually served the abolitionist cause, they begin to view the novel as an ethical masterpiece. Each scene has hidden meaning for its readers, so that not only the situations within the novel become the content for debate, but also Twain's persuasive technique can be discussed.

Ethics courses are concerned with teaching an acceptance for the "other," opposite sex or sexual orientation, various cultures and subcultures, races, and so on. Many novelists can provide this necessary intimate portrayal, including Joyce Carol Oates, Toni Morrison, Margaret Atwood, Ralph Ellison, Amy Tan, John

Steinbeck, Truman Capote, Louise Erdrich, and of course others, who have all written excellent novels that deal with controversial moral issues often concerning the "other."

Kate Chopin's *The Awakening* is undoubtedly a controversial novel even today. It offers a unique perspective from a woman's perspective. Edna Pontellier is not content with the traditional female role in the late nineteenth century, so she rebels from this role. She presumably has an affair on her husband, she leaves "his" home to move into her own, and she is not close to her kids. In the end, to save her identity, she chooses to commit suicide seemingly because she realizes that her current world will never allow her to find happiness. Students either embrace Edna, or they absolutely hate her. Debates over her ethical choices are easily had in this novel, and it definitely makes students face the choices of another head on.

Spivak points to J. M. Coetzee's novel *Disgrace* as an exceptional work for the study of the "other" in ethics. *Disgrace* brings together two cultures and focuses on the difficulty of accepting and possibly even being changed by another culture, as seen through the protagonist's, David Lurie's, relationship with his daughter, Lucy. Spivak states,

Disgrace is relentless in keeping the focalization to David Lurie.... When Lucy is resolutely denied focalization, the reader is provoked, for he or she does not want to share in Lurie-the-chief-focalizer's inability to "read" Lucy as patient and agent.... He is staged as unable to touch either the racial or the gendered other. (22)

After Lucy is raped and thus impregnated by some South African local men, she wished to remain on her land, knowing that it could easily happen again. Her father, Lurie, who was set on fire, rendering him incapable of saving his daughter during the attack, cannot understand her decision. The wonderful lesson in this book is that one person is not necessarily always able to understand the decisions of other. This novel has sparked many critics to write about its ethical consideration of the "other," which makes it a good choice for an ethics course.

I also teach a section on personal responsibility in my ethics course. Novels can help with this by giving a fictional scenario of a historical event to judge how characters respond to these events. The novel also allows students to analyze their own willingness to act in certain instances.

Posner claims that novels are not significant to ethics unless they directly apply to the social concerns of today; he cites Stowe's *Uncle Tom's Cabin* as only significant as a piece of history. A study of how characters react during significant historical events reveals some of the best ethical scenarios on personal responsibility; one is able to see a more in-depth picture of what certain individuals were up against in these times of crisis. It could also be argued, though, that Stowe's novel would be effective for an ethics course because again, as with *Heart of Darkness,* this novel may offer a good experience of finding the character flaws, and possibly the author's flaws, that actually make the novel racist in today's terms.

In addition, novels that record important historical atrocities define contemporary culture, which is essential to a study of true ethical world dilemmas. As

Joseph Alkana discusses of Cynthia Ozick's *The Shawl,* "The task of telling Holocaust stories has involved a recognition that beyond the fundamental value of presenting witness and survivor accounts, whether in non-fictional or fictional forms, there is value in telling more stories" (963). Ozick's work is advantageous to teaching ethics because this novel and others like it (Elie Wiesel's *Night,* for example) teach not only the moral choices of characters in times of impossible cruelty and godlessness, but also the importance of teaching students their responsibility to never allow such atrocities to occur again.

Wright's *Native Son* is an extremely valuable novel to use in an ethics course because "it has a timely theme—interracial violence" (Posner 15). After Bigger Thomas kills Mary Dalton, then his own girlfriend, and is sentenced to death, Bigger's lawyer makes an argument that Bigger was only acting as his prejudiced environment demanded. This novel still remains controversial today, and many interpretations on Bigger's culpability can be found, as Bloom states, "'Either Bigger Thomas is a responsible consciousness, and so profoundly culpable, or else only the white world is responsible" (quoted in Posner 15). Novels that actually produced social change, like Orwell's *Animal Farm* and *Nineteen Eighty-Four,* Thoreau's *Walden,* Stowe's *Uncle Tom's Cabin,* and Sinclair's *The Jungle* can be constructive choices to discuss the possible benefits of accepting personal responsibility for social causes.

Finally, the introduction of novels to a course of ethics allows students to obtain an intimacy with the characters that adds a human element and blurs the boundaries of right and wrong, creating a valuable, engaged discussion of ethics. Arguably, all ethics, and humanities, courses must consider the role of the "other." An education of the "other" that leads to acceptance, understanding, and possible change is the essential consideration of ethics. Novels are a valuable tool to achieve this end.

WORKS CITED

Alkana, Joseph. "'Do We Not Know the Meaning of Aesthetic Gratification?' Cynthia Ozick's *The Shawl,* the Akedah, and the Ethics of Holocaust Literary Aesthetics." *Modern Fiction Studies* 43, no. 4 (1997): 963–90.

Booth, Wayne C. "Why Banning Ethical Criticism is a Serious Mistake." *Philosophy and Literature* 22, no. 2 (1998): 366–93.

Burke, Kenneth. "Linguistic Approach to Problems of Education:" *The Yearbook for the National Study of Education.* University of Chicago Press, 1955.

Frost, Susan H., and Paul M. Jean. "Bridging the Disciplines: Interdisciplinary Discourse and Faculty Scholarship." *The Journal of Higher Education* 74, no. 2 (2003): 119–149.

Lundeen, Kathleen. "Who Has the Right to Feel? The Ethics of Literary Empathy."In *Mapping the Ethical Turn*, edited by Todd F. Davis and Kenneth Womack. Charlottesville: University Press of Virginia, 2001.

Meffan, James, and Kim L. Worthington. "Ethics before Politics: J. M. Coetzee's *Disgrace.*" In *Mapping the Ethical Turn*, edited by Todd F. Davis and Kenneth Womack, 131–50. Charlottesville: University Press of Virginia, 2001.

Newton, Adam Zachary. "Version of Ethics; Or, The *SARL* of Criticism: Sonority, Arrogation, Letting-Be." *American Literary History* 13, no. 3 (2001): 603–37.

Nussbaum, Martha C. "Exactly and Responsibly: A Defense of Ethical Criticism." *Philosophy and Literature* 22, no. 2 (1998): 343–65.

―――. "The Literary Imagination." *Falling into Theory: Conflicting Views on Reading Literature*, edited by David H. Richter, 355–65. 2nd ed. New York: Bedford/St. Martin's, 2000.

Posner, Richard A. "Against Ethical Criticism." *Philosophy and Literature* 21, no. 1 (1997): 1–27.

Sanders, Mark. "Ethics and Interdisciplinarity in Philosophy and Literary Theory." *Diacritics* 32, no. 3–4 (2002): 3–16.

Spivak, Gayatri Chakravorty. "Ethics and Politics in Tagore, Coetzee, and Certain Scenes of Teaching." *Diacritics* 32, no. 3–4 (2002): 17–31.

Stock, Brian. "Ethics and the Humanities: Some Lessons of Historical Experience." *New Literary History* 36, no. 1 (2005): 1–17.

―――. "Reading, Ethics, and the Literary Imagination." *New Literary History* 34, no. 1 (2003): 1–17.

Trilling, Lionel. "Manners, Morals, and the Novel." In *Essentials of the Theory of Fiction,* edited by Micheal J. Hoffman and Patrick D. Murphy, 77–91. 2nd ed. Durham, NC: Duke University Press, 1996.

Wehrs, Donald R. "Moral Physiology, Ethical Prototypes, and the Denaturing of Sense in Shakespearean Tragedy." *College Literature* 33, no. 1 (2006): 67–92.

Teaching Dickens's *Hard Times* in a General Education Humanities Course

Marshall Toman

Teaching Charles Dickens's *Hard Times* in a humanities course seems a short remove from teaching a novel in an English course. The humanities includes literature after all, whereas the present volume focuses on the use of novels across the curriculum. Even within departments of English, however, novels can be deployed in ways beyond traditional concerns of theme, style, and form, and how *Hard Times* is put to use in the Interdisciplinary Capstone Course: Humanities is similar to how fiction could be used by a variety of social science and professional disciplines—that is, to embody abstract concepts so that students may approach an idea both deductively as a statement to be applied to the world and inductively as a case study in search of an organizing principle.

In our general education curriculum, students in their senior year must take a two-credit interdisciplinary course in the humanities, the social sciences, or the sciences. Students who take this humanities course do so because they enjoy the humanities or because they do not—a provision allows students to double count the senior-level course as both the Capstone requirement and as substitute for a three-credit course in whichever division the Capstone is taken, thus reducing the nine credits required in each division to eight. When the distaste for the disciplines in one of the three divisions is strong enough, the reduction of one credit plays a significant role in a student's course selection. And because students in the humanities are correspondingly concerned with reducing their credits in the sciences or social sciences, the humanities Capstone I teach is mostly subscribed to by those who resist the humanities. Consequently, as with introductory courses in any field, students need continual reinforcement of important concepts, even though, as a capstone to general education, the course is intended to put to use already developed skills (critical thinking, writing) and values (such as citizenship).

Teachers of humanities courses can speculate on whether, within the practice, one or more novels are ever taught in their entirety. Humanities textbooks, which encompass along with images and written texts the history, literature, art, architecture, music, philosophy, film, and theater of various periods, certainly include, at most, excerpts. Postmodern culture in general discourages the lengthy and concentrated analysis that this genre demands. And the students who take my course are already predisposed against reading a novel that is excessively "lengthy," to them, by definition. So the decision to employ *Hard Times* is one I confront with ambivalence each time I create the Capstone syllabus; so far I have not be able to justify leaving it out of the course as the one full-length novel that we read.

Students read Dickens's novel at the conceptual midpoint of the course. Core values of three preceding historical periods have been examined: "faith" of the Medieval period; "reason" of the Enlightenment; and for the Romantic period, "feeling" or "sympathy" (because "feeling" is problematic as a value, although nevertheless it is a necessary generality to include the contradictory empathy of Daumier's *Third-Class Carriage* or Wordsworth's "Tintern Abbey" and the self-ishness of Byron's Childe Harold or Shelley's Dr. Frankenstein). The course asks what a human being's relationship to the physical world, to some notion of the divine, and to one's self and others each historical period emphasizes. We uncover the differing historical answers to this same set of questions in texts that relate those answers to the periods' core values. Thomas Aquinas's goal for humans is to know the divinity in the afterlife; John Locke seeks to integrate individuals into a rational society; Wolfgang Goethe suggests that fulfillment lies in developing the potential powers of the individual in the here and now, possibly in disregard for social consequences—to suggest three differing historical paths to satisfaction. After students have had an opportunity to write about the differing approaches to one or more of these enduring questions and to produce detailed textual examples in support of their generalizations in a midterm examination, we turn to the course's final three units, "The Industrial Age," "Modernism," and "Postmodernism," collectively viewed as a period of extensions, modifications, or mixtures of the preceding periods' values. If the values of reason and sympathy play so important a role in the first part of the historical presentation and continue through the nineteenth century to the present, reinforcing them and seeing how they mix in *Hard Times* is valuable. I use the following assignment for this purpose:

The goal of this paper is to see the nineteenth century as heir to both the Enlightenment and the Romantic thought that preceded it. I would like you to trace the elements of Enlightenment thought in the novel and the elements of Romantic thought in the novel. Does the author favor one side over the other?

You will need five to seven pages of double-spaced prose for this assignment. I suggest that you note down passages that would be relevant for talking about Enlightenment thought in the novel and passages that relate to Romantic thought. You often get ideas as you read and if you note the places, you will have an easier time supporting your ideas in your paper. Once you have gathered this material, you can present it in a coherent fashion.

Coherency comes about through a paper's having a clear thesis. Is Dickens on the side of the Enlightenment? the Romantics? is he divided in some way?

Once you decide on this basic answer, how can you organize your material further? Does Dickens's style put him in either camp? What about his imagery and metaphors?

Are certain characters more like the philosophers and poets you know from the Enlightenment or those from the Romantic period? Do these characters remain the same or change. If some change, are the changes in a consistent direction that favors Enlightenment ideals over Romantic ones or vice versa?

Your thesis should be defended throughout the paper with supporting paragraphs that are clearly organized and use transitions.

Because I hope that students will employ material from the first half of the course to assist both their thinking about the assignment and creating their arguments, the connections they make are more important than perfect command of cultural concepts, which they are just beginning to employ, or perfect fidelity to Dickens's apparent intentions.

Accordingly, when I first encountered the idea in a student paper that James Harthouse was a Romantic Hero, I was surprised. After weeks of study, did the student think "Romanticism" as we were using it meant a "romantic" or "love" interest? We had studied Prometheus in Byron's poem and in our textbook's discussion of him (Fiero 5: 31–35) as an archetypal Romantic figure who brought fire to suffering human beings out of sympathy for their "wretchedness" and at great personal risk defying the (divine) authorities. Harthouse is manipulative and kind to no one. While he does not respect Louisa and Bounderby's marriage, he is no rebel. He works, to the extent that he condescends to "work"— "occupying his time" might be a more apt description—for a group, "the hard Fact fellows," of wealthy and powerful illiberal Liberals, just as his brother, a member of Parliament and also "born with each talent and each art to please," defends large corporations against the legitimate claims of their victims on the floor of the House of Commons (95). And Dickens intends Harthouse as a portrait of the callous, irresponsible aristocrat. But a sympathetic reaction to the student's response was to see some of the parallels that the student saw. Harthouse's disregard for Louisa's finer qualities in pursuit of his sexual conquest is as selfish as Dr. Frankenstein's rejection of his creature in the wake of his quest for scientific fulfillment. And while Harthouse moves from one form of experience to another out of boredom, "[he] had tried life as a Cornet of Dragoons, and found it a bore; and had afterwards tried it in the train of an English minister abroad, and found it a bore; and had then strolled to Jerusalem, and got bored there" (95) rather than any Romantic principle of self-actualization, the student was recalling lines from *Childe Harold's Pilgrimage* that we had read, about a similar broad range of experience made possible by a protagonist's extraordinary talents:

> Few earthly things found favour in his sight
> Save concubines and carnal companie ...
> For he through sin's long labyrinth had run. . . . (16–17, 37)

Of course, the connection of Harthouse with Romantic Hero remains a case of matching too few categories (wide experience, "sinner") and ignoring disjunctions (experience received because of a lack of imagination and boredom versus experience achieved to stretch personal potential). And were the connection to be made, how would it play out in the larger argument? If Dickens sees

Harthouse as a Romantic Hero and Harthouse is a manifestly unpleasant character, is Dickens rejecting Romantic values?

Many students, however, are able to see Dickens as a Romantic figure, making a fictional argument for the importance, if not primacy, of the imagination and of sympathy, despite some legitimate uncertainty over Enlightenment elements in the book.

The lack of certainty comes partly from lack of skill in novel reading. Through readings by Locke, Bentham, Shenstone, and, sometimes, Hume, students know the Enlightenment as a period of reason and social reform. Gradgrind and Bounderby, by his association with and early near indistinguishability from Gradgrind, are reformers. Bounderby financially supports the hard Fact fellows, and Gradgrind both employs his wealth and his talents in retirement from his hardware business as a Member of Parliament promoting reform. Reform is furthered by education, and again it is Gradgrind who has used his resources to establish an experimental and model school for the cause of reform. What needs reforming in the view of the hard Fact fellows is an indulgence in unreality, in the imagination. The means reform is to "[t]each these boys and girls nothing but Facts" (1). Humanities Capstone students equate the "Facts" in the novel with reason. Thus, in students' eyes, at least initially, the book's protagonists, even "heroes" (Gradgrind and Bounderby are, at least, the first characters a reader encounters) are promoting a reform curriculum of reason. Ergo, Dickens is all about promoting Enlightenment values. Students are guaranteed to get this far in the book because I've taken to using class time to play a portion of the first CD of Martin Jarvis's reading of *Hard Times* (a set of eight CDs for this unabridged version).

To shift the thinking from this too-easy association (the Enlightenment is present; it must be approved), the easiest grounds are the characters: "But do you like Gradgrind and Bounderby?" Early in the novel, the clues to likeability, and, as mentioned, even distinguishability, are slim. But they can be drawn out. "How does Gradgrind/Bounderby treat the children at the inspection of the school?" "How does Bounderby treat the people at the Pegasus's Arms? How do they react to him?" The Gradgrind/Bounderby monolith begins to separate itself when determining what to do with Sissy. It is discovered that she has been abandoned by her only remaining parent. Gradgrind proposes to take Sissy under his care, as an experiment in providing an unsentimental education. Bounderby opposes it, partly we can assume for selfish reasons if he fears any unsatisfactory affect on Louisa. But Gradgrind not only proposed it; his initial motivation was not an intellectual experiment. When Gradgrind is asked if he had come to offer Sissy assistance, his reply is "'On the contrary. . . . Still, if her father really has left her. . . .'" (26). Gradgrind's hesitancy suggests that he is motivated by pity, though he immediately turns the situation into a rational one as well by suggesting the educational experiment with Sissy. His moment of sympathy can be returned to at the end of the discussion of the novel. It proves to be the key to all the salvageable happiness for the Gradgrind family. Sissy's presence, though she is uneducatable as far as "facts" are concerned, banishes Harthouse, restores Louisa, protects Tom, makes the younger Gradgrind children far happier and better adjusted than their older siblings, and, by these outcomes, creates the most consolation available to Mr. Gradgrind after his disastrous myopia.

As students progress through the novel, this approach through character can be continued. "Who represents the Enlightenment [or Romantic] period?" and "Who do you like?" Dickens really creates a table that is quite consistent.

	Values?	Likable?
Gradgrind		
Bounderby	"Enlightenment"	NO
M'Choakumchild	"Enlightenment"	NO
Louisa		YES
Tom	"Enlightenment"	NO
Bitzer	"Enlightenment"	NO
Sissy	Romantic	YES
Sleary	Romantic	YES
Rachael	Romantic	YES

To foster review of the texts and the concepts, it is necessary to ask why a student would put any particular character in a given "values" category. Even better as preparation for their writing assignment would be to encourage students in the discussion to make a connection between their reasons and particular passages that prompted their thinking. For example, by asking a student why he or she would place Gradgrind in the "Enlightenment" category, I might—hypothetically and rather ideally—elicit the response "Because he measures the world mathematically just the way Bentham tried to create a formula for making choices based on pleasure and pain factors." The student or I could then point to the beginning of chapter two:

Thomas Gradgrind, sir. A man of realities. A man of facts and calculations. A man who proceeds upon the principle that two and two are four, and nothing over, and who is not to be talked into allowing for anything over. Thomas Gradgrind, sir—peremptorily Thomas—Thomas Gradgrind. With a rule and a pair of scales, and the multiplication table always in his pocket, sir, ready to weigh and measure any parcel of human nature, and tell you exactly what it comes to. (2)

I can ask how much this sounds like Bentham in his *Introduction to the Principles of Morals and Legislation*, where the formula for determining an action is outlined simply as the mathematical summation of pleasurable factors versus painful factors: each one's "intensity," "duration," "certainty," "propinquity," "fecundity," "purity," and "extent."

Of course, there can be debate on likableness as well as on category. Some students don't like Louisa. Some excuse Tom because of his upbringing. When a student doesn't like a character, it can be illuminating to ask him or her to locate a reason within the narrative chronology. The "when" applies particularly to Gradgrind and Louisa, because they are quite different at the end than they were at the start, and far more likable. "And why more likable at the end?" an instructor can prompt. As we read in the epilogue, Gradgrind makes "his facts and figures subservient to Faith, Hope, and Charity" (225), that is, to human sympathy. If Louisa is like Tom at the start in the molding of her education, she has resisted that education in a more acceptable way than her brother has. And if students see Sissy as a positive character, one can ask whether Louisa is increasingly like Sissy as the novel moves along. (Louisa is seen to be generous, for example, both to her brother and to Stephen Blackpool. She also learns to "mother" children, especially Sissy's, as we are told in the epilogue (226), through her sympathy [of "trying hard to know her humbler fellow creatures"] and her imagination [in her "thinking no innocent and pretty fancy ever to be despised"].) These changes are unidirectional, from an overemphasis on "reason" toward a more Romantic, sympathetic attitude.

A character approach correlates well with insights into historically Enlightenment and Romantic attitudes in the novel, but one doesn't have to rely on it solely, especially in the early reading stages when a reader knows little of upcoming development. "What do the narrator's word choices indicate?" as in the title of the second chapter ["Murdering the Innocents"] or in Mr. Bounderby's epithet ["The Bully of Humility"]" (11). In this novel, readers can rely on the narrator to inform them of how to think of a character: "Mr. Gradgrind, though hard enough, was by no means so rough a man as Mr. Bounderby. His character was not unkind, all things considered. . . ." (20). That is, readers can rely on the narrator when they can distinguish his "trust-me" voice from the parody, irony, understatement, and exaggeration that characterize the novel and make it difficult.

Just as Dickens's many dialects individualize and bring his characters to life, such language—the many different tones of Dickens—transforms the mechanistic, mathematic, monochromatic world of the Enlightenment and Coketown's factories into the organic world of Wordsworth's "something far more deeply interfused" ("Tintern Abbey" 98). Dickens's play with language animates the novel just as Coleridge's "intellectual breeze" enlivens the universe in "The Eolian Harp":

Coketown "was a town of machinery and tall chimneys, out of which interminable serpents of smoke trailed themselves for ever and ever, and never got uncoiled." (5)

    Coketown was a town "where the piston of the steam-engine worked monotonously up and down like the head of an elephant in a state of melancholy madness." (5)

    "A clattering of clogs upon the pavement; a rapid ringing of bells; and all the melancholy mad elephants, polished and oiled up for the day's monotony, were at their heavy exercise again." (11)

Here, in addition to events relevant to the plot, we encounter snakes in smoke and elephants in pistons. The class has understood the Romantics's perception of the aliveness of all nature in "The Eolian Harp," "Tintern Abbey," Ralph Waldo Emerson's *Nature*, and Constable's *Wivenhoe Park*. Students have associated "the good" in the Romantic values with nature and rural settings through Wordsworth's "Michael" or Jean-François Millet's *The Gleaners*: Dickens's book titles within the novel are "Sowing," "Reaping" (whose last scene presents Louisa, in whom facts were sown, fainting), and "Garnering"—each a rural, agricultural metaphor that ironically emphasizes the unnatural destruction sown by the bad seeds of "facts" alone.

Readers are introduced to the novel's humor and exaggeration from the beginning, and while these stylistic features can point to a way of interpreting the novel within the guidelines of the assignment, they also, as two of the recognizable techniques of satire, confuse. Satire we have studied through Voltaire's *Candide*, Pope's *Dunciad*, and Hogarth's *Marriage à la Mode* and *Gin Lane* and *Beer Street*. Just as lyric poetry and the diary were fitting expressions of Romantic preoccupations, students understand that the genre of satire flourished in an era in which an appeal to reason was supposedly simple; satirists could refer to norms that were agreed on by reasonable people (their audience) but violated by the objects of satire. Students understand Dickens's satire as an Enlightenment element of the novel. The judicious conclusion many are able to reach is that Dickens favors Romantic values, as is evident in his characters and style, and even uses an Enlightenment genre in the service of reforming an Enlightenment-like overreliance on a narrow-minded sense of "reason." Because Dickens exaggerates the worst tendency of the Enlightenment, I have often, as in the table above, enclosed the word Enlightenment in quotations. What is satirical in Dickens's work is his version of the Enlightenment. The rigorous quantification and narrow-minded reform from the Age of Reason are appropriately called into question.

As Karl Marx said, the rise of capitalism "has left remaining no other nexus between man and man than naked self-interest, than callous 'cash payment'" and drowned all "in the icy water of egotistical calculation" (Fiero 5: 80). Bitzer represents this thinking. When appealed to by Gradgrind, the man to whom he owes the most gratitude, he simply calculates, having put his education into one (paid-for) category and ignoring any other (human) bonds with his benefactor.

"Bitzer," said Mr. Gradgrind, broken down, and miserably submissive to him, "have you a heart?"

"The circulation, Sir," returned Bitzer, smiling at the oddity of the question, "couldn't be carried on without one. . . ."

"Is it accessible," cried Mr. Gradgrind, "to any compassionate influence?"

"It is accessible to Reason, Sir. . . . And to nothing else."

"What motive—even what motive in reason—can you have for preventing the escape of this wretched youth," said Mr. Gradgrind, "and crushing his miserable father? See his sister here. Pity us!"

"Sir," returned Bitzer, in a very business-like and logical manner, "since you ask me what motive I have in reason, for taking young Mr. Tom back to Coketown, it is only reasonable to let you know. I have suspected young Mr. Tom of this bank-robbery from the first. I had had my eye upon him before that time, for I knew his ways. . . . I am going to take young Mr. Tom back to Coketown, in order to deliver him over to Mr. Bounderby. Sir, I have no doubt whatever that Mr. Bounderby will then promote me to young Mr. Tom's situation. And I wish to have his situation, Sir, for it will be a rise to me, and will do me good."

"If this is solely a question of self-interest with you—" Mr. Gradgrind began.

"I beg pardon for interrupting you, Sir," returned Bitzer; "but I am sure you know that the whole social system is a question of self-interest. . . . I was brought up in that catechism when I was very young, Sir, as you are aware."

"What sum of money," said Mr. Gradgrind, "will you set against your expected promotion?"

"Thank you, Sir," returned Bitzer, "for hinting at the proposal; but I will not set any sum against it. Knowing that your clear head would propose that alternative, I have gone over the calculations in my mind; and I find that to compound a felony, even on very high terms indeed, would not be as safe and good for me as my improved prospects in the Bank." (218)

Bitzer can parse a horse—"Quadruped. Graminivorous." and so on (3)—but has no sense of the full range of a live horse's capabilities. He earns respect in M'Choakumchild's classroom for his abstract definition, while Sissy, who lives with horses in the circus riding, is treated as incompetent. But it is the totalizing, integrating imagination—which the Romantics touted and which could have thought to teach a horse to dance on command—that saves Tom from Bitzer's clutch (220). Sleary and the circus people can succeed because they are wrapped in Pegasus's arms, the imaginative approach of the Romantics.

Capstone students study Hogarth's pairing of evil *Gin Lane* and convivial *Beer Street*. Beer doesn't ruin but mildly stimulates imagination and fellow feeling. Tom, a product of his father's teaching until his repentance near his deathbed, is symbolically washed in beer near the end of the novel. (In terms of the plot, the beer shower removes Tom's blackface disguise.)

Pedagogically immersing themselves in this imaginative fiction allows students a better insight into two historical periods whose core values are still influential.

A like reinforcement of the Enlightenment and the Romantic values could be obtained if a similar assignment were used with John Stuart Mill's writing. In a different humanities course, one taught to honors students, I have assigned chapter one of *The Subjection of Women* and chapter five from his autobiography, in which Mill discusses his training in reason and debate, his work for reform, his crisis in his mental life, and, at his time of crisis, the saving effects of Wordsworth's poetry. I ask, "Is Mill more a product of the Enlightenment or of the Romantic period?" as an alternative paper for these students. But the imaginative world of Dickens works better for students resistant to reading Victorian prose, and *Hard Times* also embodies many perspectives of Marx, to whom we devote at least half a week. A use of *Hard Times* for the honors students is to ask them to answer at paper length, "How are Marx in The Communist Manifesto and Dickens in *Hard Times* addressing similar social concerns?" These honor students read a greater portion of the Manifesto than the Capstone students. But the Capstone's students' knowledge of *Hard Times* allows me to suggest concrete meanings to many of Marx's statements that are included in our Fiero humanities textbook. Bitzer's confrontation with Gradgind, reproduced above, is an example of human bonds being replaced by Marx and Engels's cash nexus. The working lives of Stephen Blackpool, his wife, and Rachael give concrete substance to this statement as well:

"Owing to the extensive use of machinery and to division of labor, the work of the proletarians has lost all individual character and, consequently, all charm for the workman" (Marx and Engels 80). The marriage of Louisa to Bounderby is relevant here: "The bourgeoisie has torn away from the family its sentimental veil, and has reduced the family relation to a mere money relation" (Marx and

Engels 80). The actions of Harthouse's brother in Parliament, mentioned above, are a concrete instance of the government "of the modern State [being] but a committee for managing the common affairs of the whole bourgeoisie" (Marx and Engels 79).

My use of *Hard Times* to explore the influence of the Enlightenment and Romanticism and to embody aspects of Marx and Engels's argument in the humanities Capstone course is not a traditional literary use of the novel and may not even be approved of from a traditional literary perspective. Such uses, however, are an aspect of my teaching. As a coordinator of my university's Ethnic Studies Program and thus responsible for its introductory course, which is largely presented through the social sciences, I found myself often attempting to better communicate with my students by reinforcing concepts through fiction. After taking up psychological mechanisms that influence ethnic prejudice, I asked students to find examples of displacement and projection in William Faulkner's story about vigilante "justice" called "Dry September." After working through Edna Bonacich's "A Theory of Ethnic Antagonism: The Split Labor Market," we watched Louis Malle's *Alamo Bay*, which centers around the economic conflict between Texas Gulf shrimpers and Vietnamese immigrants. Good fiction is representative and truthful. For concrete thinkers like many of our students, fictions are an often-productive means of understanding important generalities through representative specifics. As both Walter Fisher's narrative paradigm and politicians' actions show, we tend to think of ourselves as argumentative, as citizens in the Greek rationalist tradition, when we are, at heart, storytellers, persuaded by the coherent, engaging, sympathetic narrative.

WORKS CITED

Alamo Bay. Dir. Louis Malle. Perf. Amy Madigan, Ed Harris, Ho Nguyen, Donald Moffat. TriStar, 1985.

Baker, Carlos, ed. *William Wordsworth: The Prelude, Selected Poems and Sonnets*. Rev. ed. New York: Holt, 1952.

Bentham, Jeremy. *Introduction to the Principles of Morals and Legislation*. 1789. Oxford: Oxford University Press, 1907. A Bentham Hypertext. http://www.la.utexas. edu/labyrinth/ipml/ipml.toc.html (accessed August 1, 2006). Link from Paul Lyon. CUWS: Classical Utilitarianism Web Site. February 20, 2002. http://www.la.utexas. edu/labyrinth/ipml/ (accessed August 1, 2006).

Bonacich, Edna. "A Theory of Ethnic Antagonism: The Split Labor Market." In *From Different Shores: Perspectives on Race and Ethnicity in America*, edited by Ronald Takaki, 139–48. New York: Oxford University Press, 1987.

Byron, George Gordon. *Childe Harold's Pilgrimage*, Vol. 2, edited by G. B. Harrison, 166–74. New York: Harcourt, 1954.

———. "Prometheus." 1816. Fiero 5: 34–35.

Coleridge, Samuel Taylor. "The Eolian Harp." 1795. In *Selected Poetry and Prose of Coleridge*, edited by Donald A. Stauffer, 57–58. N.p.: Random, 1951.

Constable, John. *Wivenhoe Park, Essex*. 1816. National Gallery of Art, Washington. Fiero 5: 13.

Cowley, Robert L. S. *Hogarth's Marriage à-la-Mode*. Ithaca, NY: Cornell University Press, 1983.

Daumier, Honoré. *The Third-Class Carriage*. Ca. 1862. Metropolitan Museum of Art, New York. Fiero 5: 96.

Dickens, Charles. *Hard Times*. 1854. Ed. George Ford and Sylvère Monod. New York, Norton, 1966.

Emerson, Ralph Waldo. *Nature*. 1836. Fiero 5: 17.

Faulkner, William. "Dry September." 1931. In *Fiction 100: An Anthology of Short Stories*, edited by James H. Pickering, 360–66. 4th ed. New York: Macmillan, 1985.

Fiero, Gloria K. *The Humanistic Tradition*. 3rd ed. 6 vols. New York: McGraw-Hill, 1998.

Fournier, Stephen M. *A Brief History and Theory of Speaking*. http://stevefournier01.tripod.com/hist/hist-4.html (accessed July 31, 2006).

Hogarth, William. *Beer Street*. 1750. British Museum, London. The Artchive: William Hogarth. http://www.artchive.com/artchive/H/hogarth.html (accessed July 31, 2006).

———. *Gin Lane*. 1751. British Museum, London. Fiero 4: 133.

———. *Marriage à la Mode*. 1751. British Museum, London. Cowley 26, 56, 82, 100, 122, 146.

Hume, David. "Of Miracles." 1736. Tillotson, Fussell, and Waingrow 893–903.

Jarvis, Martin, perf. *Hard Times*. Charles Dickens. Chivers, n.d.

Langbaum, Robert. *The Poetry of Experience: The Dramatic Monologue in the Modern Literary Tradition*. Chicago: University of Chicago Press, 1985.

Locke, John. "An Essay Concerning Human Understanding." 1690. Fiero 4: 49–50.

———. "Of Civil Government." 1690. Fiero 4: 101–2.

Marx, Karl, and Friedrich Engels. *The Communist Manifesto*. 1848. Fiero 79–81.

Mill, John Stuart. *Autobiography*. 1873. Tennyson and Gray 578–93.

———. *The Subjection of Women*. 1869. 564–78.

Millet, Jean-François. *The Gleaners*. Ca. 1857. Fiero 93.

Pope, Alexander. *The Dunciad*. 1728–1743. Wimsatt 443–512.

———. "Epistle to Dr. Arbuthnot." 1735. Wimsatt 281–96.

Shelley, Mary. *Frankenstein; or, The Modern Prometheus*. 1818. Fiero 5: 32–32.

Shenstone, William. "On Religion." Tillotson, Fussell, and Waingrow 912–13.

Tennyson, G. B., and Donald J. Gray. *Victorian Literature: Prose*. New York: Macmillan, 1976.

Tillotson, Geoffrey, Paul Fussell, Jr., and Marshall Waingrow, eds. *Eighteenth-Century English Literature*. New York: Harcourt, 1969.

Voltaire [François-Marie Arouet]. *Candide*. Fiero 4: 121–29.

Wimsatt, William K., ed. *Alexander Pope: Selected Poetry and Prose*. 2nd ed. New York: Holt, 1972.

Wordsworth, William. "Lines Composed a Few Miles above Tintern Abbey." 1798. *Fiero* 5: 5–6.

———. "Michael." 1800. *Baker* 121–35.

Novels in History Classes: Teaching the Historical Context

Gregory F. Schroeder

INTRODUCTION

This essay offers several strategies and approaches for teaching novels in history courses and reflects practical, in-class experiences gained over the course of nine years of teaching college-level history.[1] Perhaps it is best to begin with one personal experience that speaks directly to the question of teaching and learning history through novels.

As a first-year history professor, I expected Milan Kundera's *The Joke* to be a relatively simple reading for the students in my Cold War Europe course, so I was surprised to learn they had trouble with the text. They were baffled by the multiple narrators, confused by the nonlinear flow of the story, and in many cases, unable to make connections to the history content of the course. Upon reflection, it became clear that they had so much difficulty in large part because I had not adequately prepared them to read the book, either as "merely a novel" or as a novel with "historical" aspects. I had assigned *The Joke* but not really taught it.

Since that first year as a history professor, I have continued to assign novels in my courses and, more important, have worked to teach them more effectively through an ongoing process of experimentation and revision. I should state at the outset, therefore, that the following presentation of the novels represents my approach to them now, after having taught them more than once and in some cases many times. I was not able to approach them so confidently the first time, and my understanding of both the novels and how they fit into my courses has developed with each iteration. In some cases, colleagues in other disciplines, such as philosophy and English, have helped me develop my approach.

This essay outlines various steps that historians might consider if they wish to teach novels, from the initial selection of a novel to the preparation of the students and finally to the actual incorporation of the novel into class discussions and assignments. It discusses approaches to five different novels: Voltaire's *Candide*, Theodor Fontane's *Effi Briest*, Alexander Solzhenitsyn's *One Day in the*

Life of Ivan Denisovich, Simone de Beauvoir's *The Mandarins*, and Milan Kundera's *The Joke*. These novels are relevant for modern European history, but the principles and approaches can be applied to other courses.

WHY TEACH NOVELS IN HISTORY COURSES?

Novels pose an important question for historians: why should a course devoted to understanding and interpreting what actually happened in the past incorporate a work of fiction? Although novels are not "real" with respect to their characters and events, they can contain much of value for history students. So what should historians look for in a novel? They should seek novels that were written by contemporaries of the society under study and can function as anthropological observations. Useful in this regard are novels that provide insights into such aspects as political questions, cultural mores, and social relations in the past. Some novels may be useful because they reflect a social movement, a political ideology, a response to social change, or even the fears of a given society. Novels can also offer "human stories" that relate everyday experiences and allow students to develop an emotional connection to the lives of people in the past. These various characteristics can help students imagine and reconstruct the past, and this is of primary concern for historians. Not all novels are appropriate for history courses, however, and history courses are not literature courses. I would avoid novels that focus so tightly on character development that they provide insufficient insight into the historical context of the story. Likewise problematic are novels that tell "timeless" stories lacking the specifics of time and place. I would also not select novels whose narratives are too subtle, too esoteric, or too fantastic for student readers to interpret historically.

Beyond these general considerations, history professors must ask themselves why they would teach a given novel in a given course—what would the novel contribute to the students' understanding of the past? To illustrate these considerations in specific cases, I will briefly explain why I teach each of the five books under discussion here. These explanations will both give the reader a sense of the novels themselves and illustrate the significance of fiction for history classes.

Introductory European History: Voltaire, *Candide* (1759)

Certain authors and novels have come to symbolize their era. Such is the case with Voltaire and his *Candide*, a satirical story of a young man, Candide, who travels through Europe and parts of the New World seeking his true love, confronting human suffering, and engaging the question of whether this is the "best of all possible worlds." This novel is well-suited for introductory courses because it is short, entertaining, and accessible for first-year students. From the historian's perspective, it presents important ideas of the Enlightenment and offers critiques of European society under the Old Regime. I use *Candide* to help students understand the transition from the Old Regime to the Revolutionary Era beginning in 1789. The novel is Voltaire's challenge to the ideas of the philosopher Gottfried Wilhelm Leibniz and the poet Alexander Pope, who addressed questions of God, the creation, and human understanding, arguing that this is the "best of all possible worlds" and "whatever is, is right." *Candide* therefore introduces students to a debate of the eighteenth century that remains valid today. Its cultural and intellectual influence has been so broad that students should have some knowledge of it.

Modern Germany (upper level): Theodor Fontane, *Effi Briest* (1895)

Effi Briest is a powerful story of a young woman who runs afoul of the prevailing mores of her society. At the heart of the narrative is a duel resulting from Effi's infidelity, and Fontane's portrayal of the circumstances leading to the duel and its consequences offers remarkable insights into the values and character of German society in the late nineteenth century. Fontane was a careful observer, and *Effi Briest* reflects many aspects of his society: the world of women and young girls in the middle and upper reaches of German society, the importance of social status and honor, class relations, religious tensions between Protestants and Catholics, military values, and regional and national identity. I use this novel as a nexus point to tie together other course materials; it offers the students a chance to see how the themes we have been studying in our course came together in the eyes of a contemporary observer.

Modern Russia (upper level): Alexander Solzhenitsyn, *One Day in the Life of Ivan Denisovich* (1962)

Some novels have themselves become part of the history under study, as in the case of Solzhenitsyn's *One Day in the Life of Ivan Denisovich*. This brief, stylistically simple novel describes life in the Stalinist gulag and provides insights into the political system that created the camps. It is an effective, powerfully human complement to the scholarly readings on Stalinism that are part of my course on Modern Russia, but the novel is also important for its role in Khrushchev's post-Stalinist "thaw." I stress the larger context of the novel, including the political calculations that allowed its publication in the first place, the novel's place in the emerging Soviet dissident movement, and the response of Soviet/Russian readers to the simplicity and honesty of the account. In this case, the story surrounding the novel is almost as interesting as the story within the novel. *One Day in the Life of Ivan Denisovich* helps upper-level students understand both the Stalinist and post-Stalinist eras in Russian and Soviet history; the novel could also be read in introductory courses, in which case the emphasis might fall simply on the novel's insights into life under Stalin.

Cold War Europe (upper level): Simone de Beauvoir, *The Mandarins* (1954)

Beauvoir's *The Mandarins* presents France in the immediate post–World War II years, when Europeans worked to rebuild even as the new Cold War began to define their world. Beauvoir portrays the tense political atmosphere, including the continuing conflicts between members of the resistance and collaborators after the war, the European situation between the superpowers, and the debates over communism in postwar society. As a French leftist sympathetic to the communists, Beauvoir was highly critical of United States policies, and many of her fictional characters take a similar stance; this perspective is valuable for American students, even if they disagree with it. Beauvoir was also an exponent of existentialism, one of the most important intellectual responses to the horrors and destruction of the war. Existentialism permeates the novel, and its presentation is reasonably accessible. Closely connected to Beauvoir's existentialism was her influential analysis of gender and society, *The Second Sex*, in which she describes the subjugation of women in society. *The Second Sex*, of great significance for Western women's movements, repeatedly finds expression in the portrayal of the novel's characters. Teaching *The Mandarins* thus means teaching several fundamentally important ideas and events for Cold War Europe.

Cold War Europe (upper level): Milan Kundera, *The Joke* (1967)

The Joke takes place in postwar Czechoslovakia, a society defined by the Communist Party. Milan Kundera has asserted that the book is a love story, a work of art, and "*merely* a novel," dismissing the notion that it is a political attack against or commentary on Stalinism. *The Joke* tells the story of several interwoven lives, and, indeed, the search for love and the frustrations inherent in this search are central to the novel. Also important are the topics of cultural authenticity, especially with respect to folk culture, and the power of revenge in the lives of individuals. Regardless of Kundera's protestations, however, the novel can be read for its political content, and it does offer insights into communist society, even if that society serves merely as the backdrop for the love story. He was an outspoken defender of cultural freedom and autonomy before the "Prague Spring" of 1968, and Communist authorities apparently thought the novel was a threat: after the Soviet invasion in 1968, *The Joke* and Kundera's other works were banned. The debate over whether the novel is "merely" a story or a political work presents students with an important intellectual and interpretive exercise. I teach this novel because it exhibits very well, as do his other works, Kundera's profound sense of history and the connections between the past and the present.

SELECTING A NOVEL

Novels as Primary Sources

If historians decide to teach novels, then they must first select novels appropriate for their courses. I always select novels that I can present and teach as primary sources, that is to say, as cultural products of the era and society under study created by someone who lived then and there. The authors discussed here wrote about their own societies, and they incorporated observations, first-hand experiences, and ideas and values of their respective societies into their fictional stories. If historians view novels as primary sources, they can then subject the novels to analysis: comparison with other primary sources and interpretation in the light of appropriate secondary sources. Novels cannot be cited as objective records regarding events, but they can be used as evidence of how contemporaries viewed their world and commented on it. For example, the duel in *Effi Briest* cannot be used as an example for a case study on duels in the German Empire—the duel never happened—but it can be used to explain the cultural and social mores that determined duels in German society, because it is a contemporary articulation (but not endorsement!) of those mores. In many cases, authors were public figures who critiqued and commented on their societies through nonfiction vehicles such as letters, speeches, treatises, and books. Those other writings and sources can be used to corroborate the ideas presented in the authors' fiction. Voltaire's writings on tolerance, for example, find their expression in *Candide* just as Kundera's 1967 speech to Czechoslovakian writers finds its counterpart in *The Joke*. (See section below on supporting readings.)

Seeking Specific Novels

If historians know the belletristic literature of the era of their history courses, they can rely on their own passions and experience to guide their selection of novels. For example, I read *Effi Briest* as a student and appreciated its literary qualities. As a historian of Germany, I realized that Fontane's fiction reflected much of what I knew about the era from my historical studies. It was easy to select this novel, and I did so naturally, without employing the strategies articulated below.

If historians are unfamiliar with the literature of a given era, they may consult general textbooks that devote reasonable attention to cultural and intellectual history. Upper-division or country-specific texts are more likely to provide guidance than the introductory Western civilization surveys, but the latter can be helpful. I learned of Beauvoir's *The Mandarins* while designing an upper-level course on twentieth-century Europe: one of my survey texts, Walter Laqueur's *Europe in Our Time*, discusses the novel in connection with existentialism and the emerging Cold War, and this prompted me to examine and then choose the novel. I used it for that course and continue to use it my Cold War Europe course. A more recent book, Tony Judt's *Postwar: A History of Europe since 1945*, offers another detailed and enticing discussion that could guide instructors to the novel. Walter Moss's *A History of Russia*, which I use for my course on Modern Russia, is an example of a country-specific text that can help instructors find appropriate novels. It contains several chapters on culture, including useful overviews of authors, movements, and specific literary works. For example, the chapter "Religion and Culture, 1953–1991" discusses Solzhenitsyn, his role as both author and political figure, and several of his works, including *One Day in the Life of Ivan Denisovich*. Textbook discussions of culture and literature, whether in Laqueur, Judt, Moss, or others, can help instructors select and contextualize novels.

Finally, historians may consult colleagues and resources in disciplines such as language and literature, philosophy, and English. Colleagues can make suggestions for novels and specific editions and even offer pedagogical tips. Literary reference works and studies of the literature of specific movements, languages, or countries can also be helpful. For example, I once sought an East German novel for my Modern Germany course and turned to a survey of post–1945 German literature; it helped me select Christa Wolf's *The Quest for Christ T.*

Selecting Editions and Specific Translations

If possible, instructors should select editions that provide solid introductions to the novel (including information about the author, themes, and the historical and social context of the novel). Even better are editions that provide glossaries and explanatory notes as well. The latter are especially valuable when the novels present now-archaic concepts, untranslatable ideas, or references that contemporaries would have understood but that mean little or nothing to modern undergraduates. For European history courses, using novels often means using translations. When novels are available in more than one translation, instructors should take the time to compare editions.

Voltaire's *Candide* is an excellent example of a novel that has been translated, annotated, and introduced many times. Here I will discuss three translations, those by the literary scholar John Butt (1947), historian Daniel Gordon (1999), and historian David Wootton (2000). My comments pertain specifically to *Candide*, but the considerations are valid for other novels as well.

I have taught the Butt edition several times and found it quite good. The translation is very readable and funny in the right spots. The introduction is relatively brief, but it does provide the essential, minimum commentary on the significance of Leibniz and Pope (see discussion above). When teaching this edition, I also assign primary source readings from Pope and provide lecture material on Leibniz to supplement the introduction. This edition provides no notes on translations or words or historical background, however, and after teaching it for several semesters, I decided to look for different one.

The first alternative was the Gordon edition, which includes not only his translation of the novel but also explanatory footnotes; excellent background discussions of the Old Regime, Leibniz, and Pope, and Voltaire's use of irony; and a brief selection of Voltaire's letters. The strength of this edition is the manner in which Gordon places *Candide* in the context of the Enlightenment and the "Age of Voltaire." He not only introduces the novel, he also offers a useful interpretive framework and clear cultural–political context for the novel.

The other option was Wootton's edition, including his translation, explanatory footnotes, and an extensive introduction covering topics such as "optimism," Leibniz and Pope, "happiness," forbidden books, and Voltaire's biography. Wootton compares various interpretations of *Candide* and its connection to Voltaire's own life. Furthermore, the Wootton edition contains many valuable and supporting primary sources, including excerpts from Leibniz and Pope, excerpts of other works by Voltaire, and several of Voltaire's letters that speak directly to the topic of "the best of all possible worlds."

Gordon and Wootton are both historians, and this is apparent in the way they introduce *Candide*: they devote much space to explaining the historical, cultural, and biographical context in which the novel was created. For my purposes, this is more important than an introduction which emphasizes literary theory. In the end, I selected Wootton over Gordon because of the quality and breadth of the related primary source texts.

TEACHING STUDENTS TO READ NOVELS AS NOVELS

Historians who wish to teach novels in their courses should probably not assume that their students are skilled readers of novels. It is better to assume that students need help in this regard and to prepare them to read the novel as a novel. If students do not understand the novel itself, they will not be able to interpret it as historians.

In the case of *Candide*, especially at the introductory level, the primary challenge is enabling the students to understand irony. If they do not, then much of the work, especially its Enlightenment critique, will be lost on them. I did not realize this problem the first time I assigned the book and was disappointed with the results; too many students simply read the book superficially. I abandoned the book for several years until I realized that I needed to teach the students to read with an eye for irony, specifically the way Voltaire employs it in the novel. In fact, it was Gordon's edition, discussed above, that brought me to this realization. In my revised approach, I address Voltaire's irony directly. Before students begin to read *Candide*, I comment briefly about irony as a literary device. For the reading assignment, I instruct students to seek specific scenes in which Voltaire employs irony and to offer interpretations of those scenes. The solution was not earthshaking, but it was a response, based on experience and further consideration, to the troubles my students had reading this particular novel, and the revised approach has helped a good deal.

For Kundera's *The Joke*, I found it necessary to provide a structural overview of the novel to avoid confusion. My study guide includes the following comments:

The Joke is told by four narrators: Ludvik, Helena, Jaroslav, and Kostka. Each narrator was or is a member of the Communist Party, and all of them joined in the period 1945–1949. Each speaks in the first person, has his/her own voice, relates his/her own experiences, perceptions, and perspectives.

None is omniscient. Please note that each of the parts I–VI represents the viewpoint of one of the narrators, whereas Part VII is a composite of the perspectives of three characters: Ludvik, Helena, and Jaroslav. You the reader must integrate the four perspectives to gain an overview of the novel, the characters, and their society.

The narrative present of the novel (mid-1960s) is the two days during which Ludvik, Helena, Kostka, Jaroslav, and others are in Ludvik's home town. Much of the action takes place during these two days, but essential parts of the story are told through flashbacks to past events. The narrative progression of the novel is, therefore, nonlinear.

The preceding comments address the specific issues regarding two different novels, but each novel will likely present some aspect that requires clarification. It is a good idea for instructors to read novels carefully before the course to identify potential problems for the student readers. In many cases, however, student difficulties with "simply reading the story" will not be apparent until the class is in the middle of the book. When that happens, instructors should help the students as much as possible and take notes for presenting the novel the next time. Professors of literature might prefer a different approach, but in a history course, where fiction represents an "exception" or "change of pace" in the readings, it is important to address these stumbling blocks directly, lest the reading of the novel hinder the history objectives of the course.

CONTEXTUALIZING NOVELS: THE HISTORIAN'S PERSPECTIVE

Selecting a novel and helping students understand its structure are really only preliminary to the task of teaching the novel from the historian's perspective, and this begins with its contextualization for the students. If novels are to be interpreted as primary sources, then they must be submitted to the sort of checking and cross-checking that other primary sources undergo to establish their relevance and reliability. Other readings, both primary and secondary, provide points of comparison and reference. In the case of a realistic novel such as *Effi Briest*, the supporting readings establish the verisimilitude of the novel's portrayal of German society in the late nineteenth century. In the case of an ironic, satirical novel such as *Candide*, the supporting readings help students understand what the author is attacking and why the novel is both funny and critical. Supporting readings for a complex intellectual work such as *The Mandarins* present students with philosophical arguments and historical background knowledge before they seek fictional parallels in the novel itself. Above all, however, the supporting readings demonstrate to the student that the novel is a product of the time and place they are studying.

Using Edition Introductions and Accompanying Materials

The simplest way to provide context for the novel is to draw on the introduction (if there is one). Students typically do not read the introduction unless required to do so, so instructors should consider making it part of the assignment, drawing the students' attention to it in the class period before they start the novel, and incorporating it into class discussions. Some instructors may hesitate to have the students read the introduction, fearing that this interpretation will overshadow the students' own readings, but instructors can make the introduction's interpretation part of the general discussion of the novel, offering students the opportunity to challenge the introduction and offer other interpretations. If the edition of the novel includes other supporting materials such as primary sources, instructors should consider assigning some of these and incorporating them explicitly into the interpretation of the novel. For introductory courses, the materials included in a given edition of the novel might provide sufficient background information.

Using Supporting Readings

Beyond utilizing the materials available in the edition itself, instructors may wish to assign and integrate selected readings from articles, books, and primary source collections, especially if they are teaching the novel in an upper-level course. Upper-level courses require not only more reading but also more demanding reading and higher levels of critical thinking. In this section, I will provide detailed comments for each book to demonstrate how one might put various materials together, and I should note that finding a given supporting reading has often been as much the result of serendipity as of a specific search.

For *Candide*, I assign a small set of primary sources by Voltaire, Leibniz, and Pope; the latter two are essential, because they present the ideas that Voltaire satirizes in the novel. Summaries or excerpts from Leibniz's metaphysics (*Theodicy*) provide necessary ideas about reason, cause, and the best of all possible worlds, and excerpts from Pope's *Essay on Man*, Epistle I, provide the idea of limitations of human understanding and the key phrase "whatever is, is right." Finally, I assign passages from Voltaire's *Treatise on Toleration*. One might also include his "Poem on the Lisbon Disaster" about the earthquake of 1755, which is portrayed in chapter five of *Candide*. This may seem like a lot, but the selections are excerpts of the sort found in many source readers and even in certain editions of the novel, and they need not be very long. Furthermore, the introductions to the various translations explain how these parts fit together. The novel and the supporting sources provide excellent materials for a discussion of the Enlightenment and the Old Regime in my introductory course.

In my course on Modern Germany, *Effi Briest* is one in a set of interrelated readings that analyze the society of Bismarck's empire, and I schedule the novel after students have completed the other readings. Alon Confino's *The Nation as a Local Metaphor* discusses the politics of local and regional identity in the newly formed German Empire, and its findings are reflected in the expressions of Prussian and Pomeranian "nationalism" portrayed in *Effi Briest*. David Blackbourn's article "Apparitions of the Virgin Mary in Bismarckian Germany" examines the *Kulturkampf* (campaign against the Catholic church) and provides a basis for understanding the novel's subtle commentary on the relations between Protestants and Catholics in Germany. I would include Confino and Blackbourn even if the novel were not part of the course, so they do not represent an extra "burden." I do, however, assign a chapter from Kevin McAleer's *Dueling: The Cult of Honor in Fin-de-Siècle Germany* specifically in support of the novel. McAleer investigates the social and gender implications of dueling and addresses Fontane's novel directly. Without this reading, most students would fail to understand both the significance of the duel and Fontane's social commentary. The course text, Frank Tipton's *A History of Modern Germany since 1815*, also provides context for both Fontane and the novel. Reading and discussing *Effi Briest* offers students an opportunity to interpret a primary source in light of secondary readings.

In my course on Modern Russia, we read Solzhenitsyn's *One Day in the Life of Ivan Denisovich* for the post-Stalinist/Khrushchev era. Students have already studied Stalinism, so preparing them to read the novel simply entails making them aware of the political context of its publication and its impact on Soviet society. I teach the Signet edition, which includes both a foreword by Alexander Tvardovsky and an introduction by the Russian poet Yevgeny Yevtuschenko. Tvardovsky was the publisher of the journal *Novy Mir* (New World) in which the novel first appeared, and he was instrumental in convincing Khrushchev to allow the publication of the book. His foreword conveys a sense of political immediacy. Yevtuschenko writes after the fact and offers a commentary on Khrushchev, Solzhenitsyn, and the significance of the novel from the Russian/Soviet perspective. Other supporting readings, useful even in the absence of the novel, are excerpts from Khrushchev's "secret speech" of 1956 (a key event in the "thaw" after Stalin) and H. Stuart Hughes's discussion of Solzhenitsyn and other Soviet dissidents in *Sophisticated Rebels*. Finally, the survey text, Walter Moss's *A History of Russia*, addresses Solzhenitsyn and his work, and I draw explicitly upon this when preparing the students to read. Class discussion focuses on the novel as a reflection of Soviet experience under Stalin and the novel as part of the post-Stalinist Soviet Union.

Beauvoir's *The Mandarins* is a wonderful fit for my Cold War course because of the contemporary frame of mind it presents. Students read this novel after studying the genesis of the Cold War in Europe, so preparing them for the novel means emphasizing the intellectual and philosophical themes it presents. Tony Judt's examination of French anti-Americanism in *Past Imperfect* provides background for understanding the suspicious stance of Beauvoir and her characters toward the United States. Additionally, I assign excerpts from two important primary sources: Jean-Paul Sartre's *Existentialism* and Beauvoir's *The Second Sex*; excerpts of these works can be found in various source readers, and the selected passages need not be all that long. The class reads and discusses these materials to become familiar with concepts such as existence/essence and immanence/contingence, and they use this knowledge to read and interpret the lives and actions of the fictional characters. *The Mandarins* is without a doubt the longest and most complex novel I teach, and it took me several iterations to arrive at the approach described here. It gives me a chance, however, to delve more deeply into intellectual history and to introduce my students to a challenging text that they most certainly would not encounter otherwise.

Teaching Kundera's *The Joke* offers an opportunity to address the experience of eastern Europe under communist rule, and if placed in the broader context of developments from the rise of the Communist Party to power in 1948 to the Soviet invasion of Czechoslovakia in 1968, it is especially effective. I schedule this novel after the class has already learned about the Stalinization of eastern Europe. We read the "definitive version," the last of several translations. To prepare the students, I assign the Author's Note to this edition and two other introductions. The first is Kundera's own author's preface to the 1982 Penguin edition of *The Joke*, in which Kundera asserts: "Spare me your Stalinism, please. *The Joke* is a love story!" The second is Philip Roth's "Introducing Milan Kundera," published with the 1974 Knopf edition of Kundera's *Laughable Loves*, in which Roth openly characterizes *The Joke* as a "political novel." The latter two, brief readings set up the interpretive question: is the novel merely a novel, or is it a political commentary? The final and most important supporting reading is Kundera's speech "A Nation which Cannot Take Itself for Granted," delivered in June 1967 to the Fourth Congress of the Union of Czechoslovak Writers. This speech directly presents Kundera's stance on national culture, intellectual freedom, and cultural "vandalism," and it serves as an interpretive key for much of the novel. Out of respect for Kundera's demand that the novel be read as a love story, the class always considers his position thoroughly, but we also consider *The Joke* as a statement of Czechoslovak cultural autonomy under threatening conditions.

Using Documentaries as Supporting Materials

When appropriate and possible, instructors may use documentaries to support novels. These can be showed in class in shorter segments or assigned as viewing assignments outside of class. One especially valuable documentary series for the post–1945 era is CNN's 24-episode *Cold War*, which offers a companion Web site. I have used episode 3, "Marshall Plan, 1947–1952" in support of *The Mandarins,* because it includes materials that illuminate the European frame of mind in the early postwar years, specifically with reference to the influence of the Soviet Union and the United States. Episode 14, "Red Spring, 1960s" includes an interview with Soviet poet Yevgeny Yevtuschenko and a discussion of Soviet cultural and political life in the 1960s as well as excellent materials about the "Prague Spring" and its suppression. This episode is therefore useful in support of both *One Day in the Life of Ivan Denisovich* and *The Joke*. In these cases, I do not assign the documentaries simply because they support the novels; rather I use the documentaries regardless to take advantage of their connections to the novels mentioned. Instructors can use documentaries specifically and primarily in support of novels.

Whatever supporting materials one selects, it is important, if not essential, to provide the students with something outside the novel itself, against which the students can compare the novel. Absent such points of reference, students will have little reason to consider the novel as anything but "mere fiction."

STUDY GUIDES AND SCHEDULING

I have developed and continue to refine study guides for each novel, and they reflect much of the preceding discussion. Study guides for the introductory course tend to be simpler than those for upper-division courses, but each typically contains the following parts:

- A brief introduction to the novel and why it is important to the course
- Tips on reading and note taking
- Comments on the structure or character of the novel
- Tips on topics/issues to look for in the novel
- Connections to other course materials and supporting readings, as appropriate
- Study and discussion questions

The study guides were initially designed to help the students, but I have found that they help me, too, by focusing my attention on the novels and the pedagogical strategies necessary to teach them effectively.

Instructors should carefully consider how much class time to devote to a novel. I can offer no formula here because courses vary significantly in length and frequency of class periods, and novels vary in length and complexity. I can suggest, however, that the discussion span at least two class periods, even if they are not full periods, because students often have questions simply about the story (structure, characters, plot). The instructor may wish to plan some time for those topics in addition to the historical analysis discussed in this essay, and one way to do this is to begin discussion of the novel (or part of it) in one meeting and continue in the next. As with other topics discussed here, instructors should modify their approach on the basis of experience.

ASSIGNMENTS

If instructors assign novels in history courses, then they should also incorporate the novels directly into the course assignments. Whether for discussions or essays, students should be required not only to address the novel itself but also to make explicit connections between the novel and the supporting readings. For example, when discussing *The Mandarins*, I pose several discussion questions that students must answer with reference to the supporting readings. Here are two examples:

- Are Tony Judt's arguments and ideas reflected in *The Mandarins*? What are the characters' stances on America? Explain and give examples (scenes, page references).
- Which characters take part in existentialist discussions or self-analysis? What are the subjects of these discussions? Explain and give examples (scenes, page references).

Likewise for written work, instructors should require students to discuss the novels with respect to the supporting readings and interpret the novel as a primary source. The following are examples of essay questions I have used in my courses, with expectations appropriate to the course level:

- *Candide* contains many scenes of suffering and pessimism. Is its categorization as an "Enlightenment" text justified? If so, explain. If not, explain. Provide examples.
- Compose an essay in which you analyze Fontane's *Effi Briest* as a cultural product of the German Empire—what insights into German society does the novel offer? The essay must discuss the novel explicitly and draw on at least two (2) of the supporting secondary sources.
- Discuss and interpret *One Day in the Life of Ivan Denisovich* and its place in Soviet history. Craft your essay for an audience that has not taken our class and likely would read over the nuances and complexities we have discussed.

None of the questions can be satisfactorily addressed by reading the novel as merely a work of fiction. Rather, each requires students to read the novel, read the supporting materials, and interpret the novel as a primary source with reference to other sources. That is to say, the questions require students to approach the novels as historians.

A note of caution is in order concerning films. Many novels been made into movies, so some students may decide to watch the movie rather than read the novel. (This happened once when I taught Erich Maria Remarque's *All Quiet on the Western Front*, which is available in two film versions.) To avoid this problem, instructors should structure assignments to require the use of the text itself, and this is often achieved simply by demanding page references for both discussions and papers.

CONCLUSION

Novels are neither extraneous to nor a distraction from the teaching of history. On the contrary, if they are well selected and properly contextualized, novels can be valuable sources that give students another way of thinking about the past. As this essay has demonstrated, historians can use novels for various purposes: to demonstrate an idea (existentialism in *The Mandarins*), to introduce important figures and debates from the past (Voltaire and *Candide*), to present a contemporary assessment of individuals in relation to their society (*Effi Briest*), to convey individual experiences from the past (Solzhenitsyn's highly autobiographical *One Day in the Life of Ivan Denisovich*), or to investigate the relation between culture and politics (*The Joke*). The task, of course, is to teach them appropriately for a history course, and this essay hopes to offer some insights into how historians might do just that.

END NOTE

1. I thank several of my colleagues at St. John's University and the College of St. Benedict, including Ken Jones, Scott Richardson, Steve Wagner, and Christina Shouse Tourino, who gave me advice on teaching the novels discussed here, visited my classes, team-taught a session on one of the novels, and commented on this essay.

WORKS CITED

Voltaire, *Candide* (1759)

Translations discussed: Translated and introduction by John Butt. New York: Penguin, 1947. Translated and introduction by Daniel Gordon. Boston: Bedford/St. Martin's, 1999. Translated and introduction by David Wootton. Indianapolis: Hackett, 2000.

Supporting Readings

Leibniz, Gottfried Wilhelm. *Theodicy* (excerpts or summary).
Pope, Alexander. *Essay on Man* (excerpts).
Voltaire. "Poem on the Lisbon Disaster."
———. *Treatise on Toleration* (excerpts).

These readings are available in various source readers and editions of the novel. For example, excerpts from Leibniz and Pope and Voltaire's poem are reprinted in David Wootton's edition. Pope is also excerpted in various collections, including *Discovering the Western Past: A Look at the Evidence*, vol. 2, edited by Merry E. Wiesner et al. 5th ed. Boston: Houghton Mifflin, 2004. Voltaire's *Treatise* is excerpted in *Aspects of Western Civilization: Problems and Sources in History*, vol. 2, edited by Perry M. Rogers, 4th ed. Upper Saddle River, NJ: Prentice Hall, 2000.

Theodor Fontane, *Effi Briest* (1895)

Translated by Hugh Rorrison and Helen Chambers, introduction and notes by Helen Chambers. New York: Penguin, 2000.

Supporting Readings

Blackbourn, David. "Apparitions of the Virgin Mary in Bismarckian Germany." In *Society, Culture, and the State in Germany, 1870–1930*, edited by Geoff Eley, 189–219. Ann Arbor: University of Michigan Press, 1996.
Confino, Alon. *The Nation as a Local Metaphor: Württemberg, Imperial Germany, and National Memory, 1871–1918*. Chapel Hill: University of North Carolina Press,

1997. See chapter 1, "Thinking about German Nationhood, 1871–1918"; chapter 3, "Sedan Day: A Memory for All Germans?"; and chapter 4, "An Unfulfilled National Community."

McAleer, Kevin. *Dueling: The Cult of Honor in Fin-de-Siècle Germany*. Princeton, NJ: Princeton University Press, 1994. See chapter 5, "Les Belles Dames Sans Merci."

Tipton, Frank B. *A History of Modern Germany since 1815*. Berkeley: University of California Press, See chapter 5, "An Anxious Generation, 1871–1890"; and chapter 6, "Neoclassical Façade and a Modernist Revolt, 1890-1914," especially 205–9.

Alexander Solzhenitsyn, *One Day in the Life of Ivan Denisovich* (1962)

Translated by Ralph Parker. Foreword by Alexander Tvardovsky. Introduction by Yevgeny Yevtushenko. 2nd rev. exp. ed. New York: Signet, 1993.

Supporting Readings

Hughes, H. Stuart. *Sophisticated Rebels: The Political Culture of European Dissent, 1968-1987*. Cambridge, MA: Harvard University Press, 1990. See chapter 5, "The Frustration of Soviet Dissent."

Khrushchev, Nikita. Speech to the Twentieth Congress (1956 "secret speech"). Excerpts of this speech are available in many source readers, for example in *Aspects of Western Civilization: Problems and Sources in History*, vol. 2, edited by Perry M. Rogers. 4th ed. Upper Saddle River, NJ: Prentice Hall, 2000.

Moss, Walter G. *A History of Russia*. Vol. 2, *Since 1855*. New York: McGraw-Hill, 1997. See chapter 21, "Religion and Culture, 1953–1991," especially 467–70.

Tvardovsky, Alexander. "Foreword." In *One Day in the Life of Ivan Denisovich*, v–vii, edition cited above.

Yevtuschenko, Yevgeny, "Introduction." In *One Day in the Life of Ivan Denisovich*, ix–xviii, edition cited above.

Simone de Beauvoir, *The Mandarins* (1954)

Translated by Leonard M. Friedman. New York: Norton, 1991.

Supporting Readings

Beauvoir, Simone de. *The Second Sex*. Relevant excerpts can be found in various source readers, for example in *Sources of the West: Readings in Western Civilization*, vol. 2, edited by Mark A. Kishlansky. 4th ed. New York: Longman, 2001.

Judt, Tony. *Past Imperfect: French Intellectuals, 1944-1956*. Berkeley: University of California Press, 1992. See chapter 10, "America Has Gone Mad: Anti-Americanism in Historical Perspective."

Sartre, Jean-Paul. *Existentialism*. Relevant excerpts can be found in various source readers, for example in *Sources of the West: Readings in Western Civilization*, vol. 2, edited by Mark A. Kishlansky. 4th ed. New York: Longman, 2001.

General Texts as Guides to Selection

Judt, Tony. *Postwar: A History of Europe since 1945*. New York: Penguin, 2005. See chapter 7, "Culture Wars," especially 209–17.

Laqueur, Walter. *Europe in Our Time: A History, 1945–1992*. New York: Viking, 1992. See the chapter titled "Postwar Blues."

Milan Kundera, *The Joke* (1967)

Definitive version, fully revised by the author. New York: HarperCollins, 1992.

Supporting Readings

Kundera, Milan. "Author's Note." *The Joke*, vii–xi, edition cited above.
———. "Author's Preface." *The Joke*, xi–xvi. New York: Penguin, 1982.
———. "A Nation Which Cannot Take Itself for Granted." In *From Stalinism to Pluralism: A Documentary History of Eastern Europe since 1945*, edited by Gale Stokes, 151–55. 2nd ed. New York: Oxford University Press, 1996.
Roth, Philip. "Introducing Milan Kundera." In Milan Kundera, *Laughable Loves*, vii–xvi. New York: Knopf, 1974.

TEACHING THE NOVEL IN THE SOCIAL, BEHAVIORAL, AND POLITICAL SCIENCES

Reading Our Social Worlds: Utilizing Novels in Introduction to Sociology Courses

Kristina B. Wolff

Similar to many lower-level undergraduate courses, most introduction to sociology courses present a survey of the main areas that the discipline covers, relying heavily on empirical studies and theories to provide students with a glimpse into the science. Many students quite easily relate to microlevel components but have difficulty fully comprehending the macrolevel and the relationships that exist between and within these levels. Often students use anecdotal experiences as examples in class, which is helpful but can also lead to a tendency to individualize most concepts, resulting in incorrect analysis as well as too much personal information being revealed in class. This can make conversation more challenging to negotiate as students may be afraid to offend other students who have divulged personal information when participating in class discussion. The practice of relying on individual anecdotes easily translates into examples in written assignments, which obviously may complicate assessment.

In an attempt to bridge the learning gap between macro- and microsociology and to reduce the use of personal stories as primary "evidence" in support or negation of a sociological concept, I introduced the use of novels into my introduction to sociology course. One of the main motivations in using these novels is to allow students to approach these texts as representative of a society, while reducing their fear of saying something that is potentially offensive to others or simply, uncomfortable. Memoirs and autobiographies can accomplish similar things, but my experience has been some hesitancy on the part of students to take risks in their applications or draw strong conclusions out of fear of critiquing someone's personal experiences.

This paper discusses the assignments used to analyze the novel using sociological concepts as well as the general outcomes. In the six semesters this exercise has been used, it has proven to be successful. Students report enjoying the book and they are less hesitant to dig into difficult issues such as alcoholism, violence, sexuality, racism, and other forms of inequality. The ability to examine events on both macro- and microlevels improves over the course of the semester and students often integrate examples from the novels into class discussion and other assignments. This technique has been used at a medium-sized urban private university and a small rural public university with similar success, thus showing its applicability to a variety of students.

The use of cultural artifacts such as film, poetry, music, or novels in sociology courses is certainly not a new phenomenon. As with other instructors, one of my main goals of using these types of materials, including novels, is to encourage active learning by students, as they are often comfortable working with these materials and can relate them to their own lives (Holtzman; Malcolm; Ross and Hurlbert). Students are able to use their creativity and enhance their critical-thinking skills when using cultural artifacts as tools of understanding sociological concepts (Cosbey; Gordy and Peary; Laz; Moran; Sullivan). Novels in particular, offer a unique means to cover a wider range of social issues than can often be addressed in an introduction to sociology course. Another challenge of the course itself is to explore the complexities of diversity in society. Through having students read a novel over the span of the semester, issues related to human diversity are integrated into the course from the beginning, rather then being treated as add-ons at some point in the semester. Due to the pace of the course, students often maintain some sort of emotional or intellectual distance from the issues we examine, often discussing social issues as being outside of or disconnected from their own reality. Novels help to humanize the topics we cover as students often feel a connection with one or more main characters, which then helps them to apply the characters' experiences to their own lives.

GOALS AND NOVEL ASSIGNMENTS

The key to success with this exercise is choosing novels that are accessible to a wide range of students. Most of the books used are popular in the mainstream U.S. book market and have received critical acclaim. The novels are primarily written for a general audience and students are told to read them for pleasure, to focus on the story and characters without attempting any sort of literary analysis. The intention behind this is for them to get the richness of the social worlds these characters negotiate and to ease them into a sociological analysis of the novel, which is often more difficult then many anticipate. These stories illustrate complex issues that are culturally relevant and, for many students, offer a glimpse into lives, albeit fictionalized, that are often distinctly different then their own.

Each book used lends itself well to an intersectional analysis (Collins; hooks) because strong themes focus on race/ethnicity, gender, sexuality, ability, age, and social as well as economic class. Many of these novels also address issues connected to the environment, politics, education, and law, illustrating different types of tensions between macro- and microlevels. Many of the characters are struggling with issues connected to their own identities particularly in relationship to society's expectations of "who" they are versus their own concepts of their sense of self. Some of the books I have used include *My Year of Meats* by Ozeki, *The Secret Life of Bees* by Kidd, *Push* by Sapphire, *How the Garcia Girls Lost Their Accents* by Alvarez and *Caucasia* by Senna. Students receive a list of four or five books and are required to read one book over the course of the semester. During the first day of class, I describe each of the books and the intent of the assignment to help them decide which book to choose and to begin to view the story as their own society to study.

For assessment purposes, students write papers about their novel. The overarching goal of the papers is to have students apply sociological concepts to their novel. From the beginning of the course, they learn to examine society using Mills's theory of the sociological imagination. This concept requires that one examines society and therefore, societal issues, on both a macro- and microlevel. Mills describes this as the combination of "personal troubles" and "public issues" (8). Students use this theory as one of the foundational components of the course and ideally, integrate this way of viewing society into their lives as a means to see connections between their own experiences in relationship to larger social structures and historical events. Other goals of this assignment include strengthening writing skills, practicing problem solving, developing critical-thinking skills, exploring issues related to inequality, and ideally, taking risks in their analysis, to move beyond what is comfortable for them (Malcom; Ross and Hurlbert; Sullivan).

APPLYING SOCIOLOGICAL CONCEPTS

Students begin to read their novel the first week of class. At four different points in the semester, approximately every four weeks, students write a short paper (five to six pages), applying recently discussed course materials and concepts to their novel as a means of understanding and analyzing the social structures, situations, and characters experiences (see Appendix). They are required to write only three of the four papers, but everyone must write the first paper. While students can read the entire book right away, and often many do, they are expected to focus on certain parts of the novel for each paper. I have found that this helps them to concentrate their analysis and work on their critical-thinking skills, because they are limited in scope; instead of discussing a wider range, they are forced to dig deeper. Many often end up rereading part of or their entire novel, which results in a greater understanding of the book and often a stronger analysis as they look at it differently with each rereading.

For the first assignment, students focus on a topic of their choice that they think is central to the story and occurs within the beginning chapters of the book. They examine it from both a micro- and macro-approach and utilize the sociological imagination as the foundation for their analysis (see Appendix). This paper is most difficult due to the amount of new tasks they are required to do, such as applying sociological theory and methods, using a new writing style, and creating a strong analysis based on evidence from their novel and materials from class readings. Issues related to inequality are quite prominent, so students are not allowed to discuss these with the first assignment. This is partially because they have not learned how sociology studies inequality and also because it directs students' attention to the assignment, back to discussing topics that may be less interesting for them such as social theory or methods of research. Hints at how to format the paper, provide support for their ideas, and reference their examples are provided with the first assignment. The format of their paper parallels the format of studies they read in the course as well as the way in which we discuss and analyze topics in class.

Students are expected to define the concepts they use, to only use class materials, to provide appropriate citation, and to clearly apply the concepts to analyze and explain what they are discussing. For example, if a student decided that the topic she wanted to discuss was how the main character felt alienated in the school he attended, she would be required to clearly explain and provide the definition of alienation as posited by Marx. She would be expected to show examples from the novel, usually involving some direct dialogue or text, that illustrate her points and also to discuss how Marx's theory helps her to understand what is happening in the novel. Students also read studies that use the concepts we are covering in class. These serve as another source of discussion and support for their novel papers and a means to illustrate similarities and differences between reality and fiction.

WRITING SKILLS

For many, this first paper is challenging for a wide array of reasons, including learning a new style of writing. One of students' biggest challenges is to not provide a summary of the story but rather an analysis of events and conditions utilizing concepts they have recently learned. I have found that requiring all students to write the first paper (it used to be optional), and allowing them to drop the lowest grade if they write all four papers, reduces some of the pressure that many feel when approaching this assignment. I discuss the parameters of the exercise when I hand it out, and at various times early on in the semester, I point out moments in class when we are analyzing materials in the same manner that I expect from the novel paper. This reinforces the format and skill building I am looking for in the paper. While it seems like an obvious technique, I did not do this when first using this assignment, and students had more difficulty making connections between course readings, class discussion, and their novel assignments.

Another technique used to improve their writing and to illustrate how this is a process is the use of a writing workshop for the first paper. Right after they receive their first assignment back and get the second novel paper assignment, a class period is set aside for students to meet in groups and work through their papers. They divide according to novel and I give them a list of steps, usually three or four points to address to guide them through their discussion. This includes compiling a list of questions for me. I leave for approximately thirty-five minutes (or about half of the class time) and then return to review what they have discussed and to answer questions they have about the next paper.

Students have the option to rewrite the first paper. This is done to support the work they have done during the workshop and to reinforce writing as a process. As a class, we discuss the positive and negative points to doing a rewrite. For many students, they choose to write a new paper primarily because, for most, their grade would not dramatically change and the focus of the first paper is more challenging. Students who have rewritten the paper have shown strong improvement in their second draft. Students have commented that the workshop helped them to feel more comfortable talking about their work with others and reinforced the point that first drafts of papers are not as strong as they believe them to be. Many report spending more time and effort on the remaining papers. The second paper usually reflects strong improvement for all students. The third paper has mixed results as some students believe they "got it" with the second paper and fall back into the habit of writing it at the last minute. Approximately one-half to two-thirds of the students will write the fourth paper and at least half write all four papers.

PROBLEM SOLVING AND CRITICAL THINKING

Each novel paper requires that students use a variety of materials and concepts to analyze their novel, rather then focus on one specific area of sociology. They need to integrate concepts and view issues from multiple perspectives, thus building problem-solving and critical-thinking skills. Every point made or concept used must be supported with evidence from their novel and studies from class materials. This increases their skills at sociological writing and ability to make an argument. In both the second and third paper assignments (see Appendix), students continue applying theoretical concepts to a theme in their novel and explore the connections of culture and identity or deviance, identity, and socialization. They examine how these things operate independently in society as well as relate and interrelate on micro- and macrolevels.

For example, one of the elements of culture is language. In addition to using different kinds of U.S. dialects, many of the novels chosen for the class use languages other then English, such as Spanish or Japanese, to illustrate how characters exist in multiple social worlds and often struggle to find ways to negotiate their daily lives as well as their identities in relationship with these cultures. A student's microanalysis might focus on discussing the experiences of a character attempting to find a job and being unable to do so because Spanish is his primary language and his English is not "good enough." The student could also examine this situation from a macroperspective discussing the types of jobs available in the United States for people with limited English skills and the impact this has on the Spanish-speaking population, particularly immigrants. She could also discuss other ways in which a different language is a benefit by illustrating how it is used to maintain the character's family and traditions. Another possibility would be to apply theories about deviance to how the character behaves, feels, and is treated like an outsider in various contexts of the novel. By exploring the same issue from different angles, students are able to strengthen their skills of critical analysis while also exploring the complexities of society through a sociological lens.

The fourth paper asks students to identify two different systems of inequality, discuss how these operate in the novel, and then propose a specific solution to address and possibly remedy the situation. Often students will develop a solution that deals with their issue on both a micro- and macrolevel, although many continue to have difficulties proposing changes in large social systems. The purpose of the final paper is to specifically discuss issues related to race/ethnicity, class, gender, and sexuality that they have been exploring throughout the semester and reading about in their novels. At this point in the semester, they have worked with foundational concepts enough that they are comfortable applying them to their argument, thus making stronger sociological analyses than they could accomplish midway through the course. Asking them to develop a solution assists students in recognizing that they are "creators and holders of knowledge" (Ross and Hurlbert 81) as they are able to develop and support their ideas for societal change in their novel. Students often connect their solution to existing issues in society both in this paper and other class assignments.

TAKING "RISKS"

My initial interest in using novels was to see whether these would be a useful means to help students take more chances in their writing and analysis, while also helping them to work beyond surface examinations of the topics we discuss in the course. I wanted to have the students read about issues related to people and cultures that were probably different from their own and to have this occur over the course of the semester rather then in a couple of short instances in the course. Issues connected to diversity typically get placed in their own section within introduction to sociology texts or are handled according to topic, such as having a section on race and ethnicity followed by one on gender. Due to the nature of the structure of the course and what students need to be exposed to before they deal with these often-challenging subjects, addressing these topics at the end of the course makes sense. I have found that by the time we reach these subjects, however, we have little time to spend on them, and once discussion starts around these issues, students want to spend quality time on them. The introduction of the use of novels has given them an opportunity to read about these topics and become more comfortable with them, and the students gain a better sense of the ways inequality and diversity are imbedded throughout our society.

The use of novels has helped many students expand their depth and breadth of analysis, particularly concerning explorations of race, gender, sexuality, and class. These stories provide a means for students to take chances with their scholarship. For example, before I used novels, when students wrote about race and racism, it was usually framed as an "us" versus "them" situation. They would present the definitions and theories we covered about race, but the application tended to focus on conflict—for example, on a discussion of how they knew of a white person who was discriminated against because of their race, or how people of color manipulate our social systems for personal gain, as if whites did not do the same thing. For many, applying a macrolevel analysis got lost in these discussions.

After novels were introduced, students would bring in short comments about race in their papers or class discussion, often in the context of the story, early on in the term. This allows them to think through the complexities of the topic for a longer period of time. When they write about race toward the end of the semester, they are better able to make connections to how racism affects everyone on micro- and macrolevels. Instead of the tendency to make proclamations in connection to their use of sociological concepts, students have become more willing to present an argument and to take a chance on what they write, rather than write what they think I want them to say. They may still talk about the white person who was discriminated against, but they are better able to support their point with materials from the class reading and the novel as well as bring in some discussion on a macrolevel. Their interpretation of events in the novel may still reflect their bias or frustrations, but their argument is stronger, more in-depth, and less of a knee-jerk reaction. Before novels were introduced, students were less willing to write about what they thought and were more likely to write about what the course readings covered as if they were in complete agreement with the studies or what I presented in class.

The use of novels was a risk for me. I initially decided to use them as a sort of an experiment, to simply see what would happen. I was surprised that the assignments were well received by the students and that there was a visible improvement in students' use and understanding of course concepts. One of the challenges for me is to ensure that students fully understand the rationale behind using the books—that is, that they are to serve as mini-societies for them to study but that they do not replace existing social phenomenon or serve as a sub-stitute for sociological research. DeVault address the complexity of this situation, noting that while sociologists understand that we must pay attention to the social context in which novels and all cultural works are created in, many readers eas-ily forget this and believe that the social issues presented in novels can be taken as fact (DeVault). The four novel papers are designed to help students remember that their book is a work of fiction and that only by using course readings, partic-ularly the studies we explore, can they examine and understand the social condi-tion(s) they are addressing.

SUCCESSES AND CHALLENGES

The use of novels has proven to be an effective teaching tool. There has been strong improvement in use and understanding of course concepts as well as a better integration of sociological materials overall. This is partially due to the fact that students are spending more time with the material, because they find the novels accessible and interesting and therefore are more comfortable examin-ing them. There has been a reduction of the hesitancy that students have when talking about sociological studies or concepts. In class discussion, students will often give qualifying comments before speaking about a concept or study, noting that they realize they may be wrong in their assessment or acknowledging that researchers know more then they do about the subject. When analyzing the nov-els, however, students don't question the intent of the author but instead focus on the issues at hand. This translates into a reduction of qualifying statements during class discussions.

Many students learn the concepts a bit more quickly and therefore are able to concentrate on honing their critical-thinking skills, which also increases their willingness to analyze course topics, including studies, more closely. When examining issues that may be personally challenging for students in class, some have resorted to using situations in their novels as examples, which enables many to more easily enter into tough discussions. Since four or five books are chosen for the course, this creates another means by which to divide students when doing group exercises in class. It also adds another way for students to connect with one another during class discussions and when they are in the process of writing their novel papers; many students have talked about their novels outside of class.

There are limits to this exercise. As with any subject, improvement is connected to the amount of time spent studying or reading class materials; students who skim the novel or wait until the last minute to write their paper do not perform well nor do they learn with as much depth. This assignment can be seen as a barrier to students who are uncomfortable with their reading or writing skills as well as to those who prefer taking tests. This assignment has only been used in smaller classes with forty or fewer students. I believe it would do well in a larger class, but it is grading intensive and sometimes requires a fair amount of meeting time with students outside of class. Although I have only used this approach in the introduction to sociology course, I believe that using novels would work well in a variety of classes, particularly including courses on social problems, race and ethnicity, and sex and gender, as well as courses on globalization or women in developing nations.

Progress in writing and analysis are difficult to track when courses are large, because some of the improvements are small and unless you know the student's work well, these shifts can easily be missed. Moving students into creating an analysis rather than a summary of the novel is a constant struggle with a few students every semester. Plagiarism, particularly the recycling of papers, may be difficult to catch in larger classes. To help counter this, novels are rotated at least once every two or three semesters (see Appendix). This also helps to keep the assignment fresh and interesting when grading. Students will often chose books based on price and size. Many of the titles used are current but a bit older and therefore available in libraries and as used copies. The novels that are used vary in style and content, but I try to pick ones of similar length in the hope that each student will chose a book that looks interesting.

CONCLUSION

As noted at the beginning, the main objective of using novels in Introductory to Sociology concepts was to provide an alternative way of learning and applying sociological concepts as a means of understanding society. Through the combination of the accessibility of the novels and requirement to analyze these books on a micro- and macrolevel, students more quickly grasp the sociological imagination, thus becoming successful in their ability to analyze society. This change in perspective helps them to make connections between course materials and their own lives. Use of the novels moves students beyond seeing the course as consisting of simply memorizing terms and repeating them back to their instructor. It provides one example of an interdisciplinary approach to examining our social worlds. Students are more successful in practicing problem solving, applying course concepts, developing their critical-thinking skills, and connecting sociological concepts and techniques to their lives.

APPENDIX

Assignments: Basic Parameters

Each paper provides a list of things that students are to address and the directions are vague enough that they can approach the paper with some flexibility, which allows them to bring more of their own ideas into the assignment. The mechanics for the paper are provided each time. Students are required to remain within the five- to six-page limit primarily to assist them in providing a strong, focused argument. Longer papers often end up being filled with extra information or background material from the novel, which turns the paper into more of a summary piece than an analysis.

When grading, students receive a short rubric with comments addressing areas for which they lost points. They receive points for organization and flow (5 or 10 percent), mechanics (15 or 20 percent), and then content (75 percent). The percents change for the first two areas as the class progresses to serve as a means to reinforce proper grammar, spelling, and citation, which sometimes becomes sloppier the nearer we get to the end of the semester. The content area replicates the list of things they are to address from the assignment sheet. I usually assign different point values for each of these areas to help with assessment. For example, items such as focusing on one topic would receive five of the seventy-five points, whereas using class materials for support is twenty-five or thirty points.

Novel Paper One: Applying Sociological Theories

Since the beginning of the semester, each of you has been required to read one of four novels. The purpose of these papers is to see how you understand course concepts, using the novel as your own "mini-society" to examine. Each assignment is designed for you to focus on applying specific concepts from the course material to your novel. Each paper will be a bit different in nature. If you have questions, it is best to meet with me rather then e-mailing or calling.

For this paper, I want you to do the following:

Find one or two emerging themes or topics that interest you in your novel so far. These topics should be tied to one or two main characters and her/his/their relationship to society in some way. For this first paper *do not* focus on an -ism (racism, sexism, classism, and so on). We are just beginning to understand these from a sociological perspective and you will be addressing isms in a later novel paper.

Once you pick your theme(s)/topic(s), use Mills's sociological imagination as a tool to discuss and analyze them. For example, if your main character murdered someone, how would you explain that using Mills's concept? Think about how we talked about the "Hernado Washington" article in class.

Remember to discuss your theme(s) on both a macro- and microlevel.

Utilizing one of the main bodies of theory we've discussed and McIntyre has outlined (structural functionalism, conflict theory, Marxism, or symbolic interaction), explain your topic/theme(s). How does the theory you choose help you to understand your topic/theme(s)? *Be sure to use material from the readings and/or class to support your points.* For example, if you decide to give me a definition of the theory you're using, provide a reference as to where you obtained/learned the definition. *This definition must come from class materials, DO NOT use* materials from the Internet or other sources. When discussing a concept, be sure to define it *using the original source* (that is, Mills's words).

Novel Paper Two: Culture, Social Structures, and Identity

For this paper, I want you to do the following:

Choose one or two different things that are important to the culture of your main character. Discuss/analyze this/these utilizing concepts from the class and readings in *Core Concepts*. Pay particular attention to different *elements* of culture.

Discuss different roles and statuses your main character or other characters have in their society. How do these work in relationship to various social structures and social institutions in their lives?

Use Goffman's theory of "The Presentation of Self" as a tool to understand and analyze one or more of your characters. Hint: You should be able to combine this with your discussion of one or both of the two areas above.

OR

You can rewrite the first novel paper. This can focus on the same material *but* you need to also integrate in Goffman's theory of "The Presentation of Self." For example, if you wrote on Mills and functionalism then you'd need to also add Goffman as well.

Novel Paper Three: Deviance and Social Control

This paper is a continuation of what we've been exploring in terms of identity and socialization on individual and group levels. Remember that you are showing me you've read and understood the texts we're using as well as applying material from class discussion to support your points.

For this paper, I want you to do the following:

Discuss one or two things about your main character(s) that could be considered "deviant." This includes a deviant act but even more so, something about their identity that can be considered "deviant." How does (or doesn't) this deviant status affect your character(s) identity?

Analyze your choice of deviant behavior/status in relationship to socialization and how people "learn" how to behave or misbehave in society. Bring in society's viewpoint here (macro), what exactly makes your choice deviant? Discuss this in relationship to the role that deviance plays in terms of maintaining the status quo. Obviously, you can tie in previous concepts here particularly socialization and resocialization.

Apply the McIntyre readings from both *Core Concepts in Sociology* and the *Readings in Sociology* text to support your points and analyze deviance. For example, how does Durkheim's idea of crime support or counter your view? What has Merton theorized that might help explain your points? Think about what we've read and the ways in which "who" is held accountable for deviance differs, and the types of excuses people use to justify their deviant behavior in relationship to what you are examining in your novel.

Novel Paper Four: Stratification and Inequality

This paper is a continuation of what we've been exploring all semester. Remember this paper is to show me that you've read and understand the readings in both *Core Concepts* and *Readings in Sociology* texts and that you can apply concepts from these to your analysis of your novel. Some things that we've discussed in class are not in McIntyre's texts. Feel free to use material from class discussion throughout your paper but remember that if there's a "solid" definition of a concept in our readings, then you should be using those first. *Do not use materials that are not directly related to the class.*

For this paper, I want you to do the following:

Discuss two -isms that appear throughout the book. These can include but are not limited to racism, sexism, classism, ageism, and heterosexism.

What are some of the ways that the -isms affect your character(s) on both a micro- and macrolevel?

If you could change something, one thing that you believe perpetuates one of the -isms you've addressed, what would you change? Be specific.

Apply any other concepts we've learned to your discussion. Strong papers should have some integration of other ideas from throughout the course—all of these things are related and interrelated. Remember, if you've addressed a concept before (that is, dramaturgy, socialization, identity, and so on) then you don't need to define it.

Assigned Novels

Alvarez, Julia. *How the Garcia Girls Lost Their Accents*. New York: Plume Books, 1998.
Cisneros, Sandra. *The House on Mango Street*. New York: Vintage Books, 1991.
Erdrich, Louise. *Love Medicine*. New York: Bantam, 1984.
Kidd, Sue Monk. *The Secret Life of Bees*. New York: Penguin, 2002.
Ozeki, Ruth L. *My Year of Meats*. New York: Penguin Books, 1998.
Roth, Philip. *The Plot Against America*. New York: Vintage International, 2004.
Sapphire. *Push*. New York: Alfred A. Knopf, 1996.
Senna, Danzy. *Caucasia*. New York: Riverhead Books, 1998.

WORKS CITED

Collins, Patricia Hill. *Black Feminist Thought: Knowledge, Consciousness, and the Politics of Empowerment*. New York: Routledge, 1991.
Cosbey, Janet. "Using Contemporary Fiction to Teach Family Issues." *Teaching Sociology* 25, no. 3 (1997): 227–33.
DeVault, Marjorie L. "Novel Readings: The Social Organization of Interpretation." In *Liberating Method,* by Marjorie L. DeVault, 109–38. Philadelphia: Temple University Press, 1999.
Gordy, Laurle L., and Alexandria Peary. "Bringing Creativity Into the Classroom: Using Sociology to Write First-Person Fiction." *Teaching Sociology* 335, no. 4 (October 2005): 396–402.
Holtzman, Mellisa. "Teaching Sociological Theory Through Active Learning: The Irrigation Exercise." *Teaching Sociology* 33, no. 2 (April 2006): 206–12.

hooks, bell. *Talking Back: Thinking Feminist Thinking Black*. Boston: South End Press, 1989.

Laz, Cheryl. "Science Fiction and Introduction to Sociology." *Teaching Sociology* 24, no. 1 (1996): 54–63.

Malcolm, Nancy L. "Analyzing the News: Teaching Critical Thinking Skills in a Writing Intensive Social Problems Course." *Teaching Sociology* 34, no. 2 (April 2006): 143–49.

McIntyre, Lisa J. *The Practical Skeptic: Core Concepts in Sociology*. 3rd ed. Boston: McGraw-Hill, 2006.

Mills, C. Wright. *The Sociological Imagination*. London: Oxford University Press, 1959.

Moran, Timothy Patrick. "Versifying Your Reading List: Using Poetry to Teach Inequality." *Teaching Sociology* 27, no. 2 (1999): 110–25.

Ross, Susan M., and Janet McNeil Hurlbert. "Problem-Based Learning: An Exercise on Vermont's Legalization of Civil Unions." *Teaching Sociology* 32 (January 2004): 79–93.

Sullivan, Theresa A. "Introductory Sociology Through Literature." *Teaching Sociology* 10, no. 1 (1982): 109–16.

Science Fiction as Social Fact: Review and Evaluation of the Use of Fiction in an Introductory Sociology Class

Peter P. Nieckarz, Jr.

This article is a review and evaluation of the use of fiction as required reading in an introductory sociology class at two schools: a private liberal arts university and a regional state university. The use of fiction is employed as a means to make the experience of an introductory-level class more engaging and long lasting. Kurt Vonnegut's *Player Piano* (1952) is used, although other works may also be appropriate. The issues and lessons from the book that are applied to the class are outlined. The article concludes with an analysis of survey data collected from students on their experience with the use of this teaching method. The data indicate that students rate this method somewhat favorably, but that they were not sure whether it made a distinct difference in what they learned. The fact that the liberal arts students rated the method more favorably is also examined.

THE CHALLENGE OF TEACHING "INTRO"

Teaching an introductory-level sociology class presents special challenges for the instructor. While most of the courses taught in a sociology program are geared toward the sociology major, this course is largely designed with the non-major in mind. As sociologists, we have a duty to present the material in our introductory classes in a manner that will have a lasting impact on these nonmajors (Sobal, Hinrichs, Emmons, and Hook). This is, after all, the intent of general education requirements. The instructor must be aware of the potential for students to memorize terms and concepts only to be forgotten a short time after completion of the class. Students should be encouraged to not only learn these concepts, but also be able to recognize their relevance in situations beyond the classroom, to be able to apply the sociological imagination (Mills). In addition to this, the goal of introductory classes is to recruit new sociology majors. The material needs to be presented in such a way as to make a major in sociology seem desirable to these students (Corbett; Sobal et al.).

Sullivan (1982) suggests that part of the problem with getting students to develop a lasting appreciation for the relevance of sociology emanates from sociology texts that are usually based solely on "deductive learning," which builds knowledge and comprehension, but does not foster the development of "cognitive skills." She says that cognitive skills are developed through "inductive learning." This means being able to look at specific social events and apply them to broad sociological concepts. Sullivan asserts that one way to incorporate inductive learning in the classroom is to use fiction as part of the required course reading. Fiction is an effective means of getting students to engage the concepts presented in the course on a deeper and more meaningful level. This notion has been recognized, supported, and described by several other instructors and scholars and is well represented in the literature (Cosbey; Coser; Sullivan; Laz; Lena and London; Lindstrom).

With this in mind, Kurt Vonnegut's first novel, *Player Piano* (1952) was used as a required text in introductory sociology sections. This article examines the use of this novel in an introduction to sociology class by illuminating its sociological relevance and how it may be applied to the subject matter of introductory classes with the intent of aiding students' understanding of the basic concepts covered in the course. The final part of the article reviews and evaluates students' reactions to this teaching technique.

THE SOCIOLOGY OF LITERATURE

To understand the use of literature as a work of sociology, one must consider the subdiscipline of the "Sociology of Literature." There are three basic approaches to the sociology of literature: the external structural approach, literary ethnography, and the internal approach (also known as Sociology *Through* Literature). The external structural approach deals with the production and consumption of literature (Hegvedt). In this perspective, scholars are concerned with the structure and social context surrounding the writing and publication of literature and the context surrounding how literature affects those who are actually reading it. Brenda Wineapple (1981) presents an apt example of this approach in her critical analysis of Kurt Vonnegut's novel *God Bless You, Mr. Rosewater* (1965). Griswold (1981) displays this approach by illustrating how copyright laws and the emergence of mass production in the nineteenth century affected the content of novels. The literary ethnography approach has emerged more recently. It looks to literature as a data source for ethnographic research. Frederique Van De Poel-Knottnerus and David J. Knottnerus (1994) develop a template for a literary ethnographic method. They suggest that thorough and deliberate analyses of both fictional and nonfictional works from a given historical time or geographical place will give the researcher a rich and detailed view into their given topic of research. What is suggested is that works of realism can't help but present an accurate depiction of social life in that particular setting.

SOCIOLOGY THROUGH LITERATURE

The use of fictional or literary texts in a sociology class represents the sociology through literature approach, which is the focus of the teaching method addressed here. This approach views the text as a reflection or commentary on societal dynamics (Hegvedt). Literature often gives detailed (albeit fictional) accounts of social life. Within this medium, the author, who is the creator of the social realm, is not bound by the limits of empirical reality. They often reflect reality, but have the ability to take social phenomenon and accentuate, enhance, or even exaggerate them to illustrate and make salient an observation about the empirical reality in which we all reside (Cosbey; Laz). Though it may not be factual, the "induced salience" of sociological phenomena within the text allows the reader to extend current reality to conceptual or hypothetical conclusions, thus affording us a better understanding of the implications of our more subtle and taken for granted "real" social world.

Perhaps the first notable proponent of this teaching technique for sociology was Lewis Coser (1963) who edited a fictional reader compiled with the intent of being used in an introduction to sociology class. He supported the idea that sociological knowledge can be gleaned from fiction:

The literary creator has the ability to identify with the wide ranges of experience, and he has the trained capacity to articulate through his fantasy the existential problems of his contemporaries. Why then should not sociology harness to its use, for the understanding of man and his society, those untapped resources in the rich accumulation of literature? (3)

The author has the ability to accentuate social issues found in real life. As instructors, we often try to accentuate things for students to instill a sense of importance or significance to them. Many works of fiction are able to accomplish that with greater eloquence. With this in mind, one can see how such texts allow a "deeper" understanding that Hegvedt (1991) alluded to.

Using literary texts in class is also useful in that it provides a common denominator among the students (Cosbey; Sullivan). The instructor is able to use examples from the assigned fictional reading that all students should be able to relate (assuming they have read it). Many times, when an instructor attempts to develop examples to illuminate abstract ideas and concepts, not all students are able to identify with it. Having read the same story establishes an implicit shared experience among the students.

Sobal, Hinrichs, Emmons, and Hooks (1981) included literature as part of a larger study on the effectiveness of experiential learning in introductory-level classes. In a quasi-experimental design they team taught one section of an introductory course using various experiential techniques and compared them to two control sections with the traditional lecture and text format. In addition to the use of fiction, the techniques used in the experimental class included films, guest lecturers, learning simulations, data analysis, and participant observation. They analyzed student evaluations and performance as a means to gauge the effectiveness of their model. The results were largely inconclusive, indicating that their teaching technique may not have made a significant difference in learning. However, the data did indicate that students in the experimental section showed a higher level of mastery of some difficult concepts and also were more likely to take additional sociology course, suggesting a positive experience in their first course.

Cosbey (1997) used fiction in her family issues class. She says that contemporary novels often reflect changing demographics and recent issues related to families. Citing the fact that most traditional undergraduate students may have limited life experience she says such novels are particularly useful in helping students get a glimpse of family patterns and issues that they have not been exposed to in their personal lives. Cosbey does not assign one particular title, but offers a list of books, many of which students may already be familiar with thanks to existing movie adaptations. She suggests that the familiarity will make the prospect of reading the book seem less daunting to students who have limited experience reading and analyzing fiction. Students have the choice of writing a traditional research a paper or writing a "novel analysis" paper.

Corbett (1994) finds fiction as a valid means of understanding of issues of crime and criminal justice. Pointing to the prevalence of novels with crime or "cops and robbers" as subject matter, he asserts that there is much to be learned from a well-written story. Corbett acknowledges that some sociologists may be skeptical of the sociological value of these works but responds by alluding to the fact that many novelists devote themselves to countless hours of research before they even begin writing, lending the story a measure of ethnographic validity. While Corbett warns that many more sensationalistic crime-based novels may not be valid representations of real life and thus not suited to a sociology though literature, he finds Peter Blauner's *Slow Motion Riot* to be a particularly detailed and accurate account of the life and experience of a probation officer. With this in mind, Corbett suggests that a "social novel" such at *Slow Motion Riot* can be assigned in conjunction with more traditional texts in a criminology or corrections course. Such texts can provide a totality of understanding and even foster a sense of empathy in the student, something not easily established through traditional texts.

Lena and London (1979) also wrote about the use of fiction in a sociology class. They employed Ken Kesey's *One Flew Over the Cuckoos Nest* as a class text, using it as a catalyst for class discussion and a means to help students understand sociological concepts more clearly. In their article, they addressed sociological relevance of *One Flew Over the Cuckoos Nest* and how it provided a common denominator among the students. Their intent was to make the sociology class a more meaningful experience, giving the students a better grasp of the material.

Since *Player Piano* is a work of *science* fiction, one issue to be addressed here is that of the appropriateness of the science fiction (sci-fi) genre. In the introduction to his reader, Coser (1963) asserts that only works of realism provide meaningful sociological analyses. Van De Poel-Knottnerus and Knottnerus also suggest that works of realism are the only place to find valid sociological knowledge. As addressed above, other published examples of sociology through literature employ books more of the Realist genre. What this implies is that works not ostensibly based in reality, such as science fiction or fantasy, present little scholarly value. Additionally, sci-fi in general sometimes is stigmatized as not being "real" literature.

These reservations toward science fiction should be examined. In her article addressing her use of *The Handmaid's Tale*, Cheryl Laz (1996) illustrates the aptness and even superiority of science fiction in the realm of sociology though literature. Though once overlooked by academia, Laz asserts that sci-fi is becoming more "credible" today; however, its value as a pedagogical tool has yet to be fully recognized. She states that sci-fi is a very "truthful" and "real" genre, thus making it useful in the classroom: It is not "real" in the sense of being actual, concrete, and verifiable, but it is "true" because it corresponds or conforms to that which *is* real, actual, and verifiable" (54). According to Laz, what makes some works in the sci-fi genre so useful to a sociology class is that sociology and sci-fi seem to have things common to them; both tend to estrange the audience, asking them to reach beyond their commonsense assumptions about the world. Another is the fact that the sci-fi authors are sometimes conscious of their present social structure and modify or exaggerate certain aspects of it to make a comment or observation about current society. In this aspect, it encourages students to think about society on different levels, to imagine what it is and how it can be, fostering "their sociological imaginations" (Laz). Much of how instructors approach sociology in classes has a future orientation. The material is often presented with a mind toward where society is headed or where it should be:

Sociology often has an eye to the future, in terms of either social change, preserving the status quo, or . . . simple prediction. SF (science fiction), aside from the future setting of its stories, likewise looks ahead. But science fiction . . . [I]s *not* about the future or about prediction. Rather it's descriptive or speculative. Le Guin describes science fiction as a "thought experiment." (Laz 1996, 56)

So, the true value of sci-fi is not about the future, but about an understanding of the present and its ramifications. The created setting of the story is a means to establish a sense of induced salience from which one can more meaningfully employ sociological analyses.

PLAYER PIANO AND ITS RELEVANCE

Many literary works are sociologically relevant for one reason or another, but few books seem to be as broadly relevant to sociology as Kurt Vonnegut's *Player Piano* (1952). My impression of this book is strongly supported by Thomas Hoffman (1994) who writes in a review of the novel, "*Player Piano* might also be classified as a work of sociology expressed in fictional form because in this book Vonnegut writes more like a social scientist than a novelist" (5). In addition to being sociologically relevant, *Player Piano* follows the progression and logic of many intro courses and introductory texts rather well (Henslin; Kendall; Lindsey and Beech; Sullivan). This novel is attractive in the fact that most students have never been exposed to it. Lena and London (1979) recognize potential problems that may arise when students may already be familiar with a book, either through previous class experiences or viewing a movie that may be vastly different from the original book. There is no screen adaptation, and this particular title is not one of Vonnegut's more popular works. It is a new story to nearly all students.

In the novel, Vonnegut offers several sociological observations. Many of these are clearly made as commentary on real life, but they are depicted at proportions that go beyond what most people agree to be presently true or realistic.

This was one of the initial reactions of many of the students when asked to respond to certain aspects of the story: at first, some were tempted to dismiss Vonnegut's portrayal as false or unrealistic. After some consideration, however, many were able to see the connection to their own personal experiences as well as a deeper sociological understanding that goes beyond their own lives.

Player Piano is a story of life in the United States at a nonspecified point in the future. Vonnegut makes allusions to a large war, perhaps World War III, in the recent past. The United States won this war largely by the use of automated machines and technology rather than human labor and participation. This technology of automation, developed and perfected during the war, found a large and lasting place in the postwar United States. Nearly all human labor had been replaced by some sort of machine. Resulting from this automation is a United States with a population that is largely divided into two classes. The first class is the highly educated managers and engineers, most of whom hold doctorates in those fields. This group is a numerical minority. The second group, which makes up the bulk of the population, has been relegated to a career of unskilled menial labor in the "Reconstruction and Reclamation Corps" (dubbed "The Wreeks and Recks"), or they enlisted in the military. The chance to get into college and be trained for a life in the managerial elite is based solely on the score one earns on a nationally administered standardized test. The specific career one is prepared for once in college is then determined by other standardized aptitude tests. Those who do not make it into college are well provided for by this system; they all have places to live and are guaranteed a minimum standard of living.

All manufacturing and business is still privately held and seek profit (characters in the story point out that it is not "socialism" or "communism"); these corporations have grown exceedingly monolithic and have developed monopolies over their given sector of the market. A central planning board (developed by the corporations) governs all production, consumption, and distribution. Behind all these decisions made by various committees and boards is a super computer named EPICAC. This computer is used to calculate and weigh all things pertaining to the workings of the United States. It decides what is to be done, and who is to do it. The motive behind all this automation is efficiency and accuracy, something that human beings are believed to be incapable of on their own.

The protagonist of the story, Dr. Paul Proteus, is a high-ranking engineer who is in charge of the manufacturing facility in his hometown of Illium, New York ("The Illium Works"). He is a well-respected figure who is likely to climb up the corporate ladder in the near future. When he is introduced, the reader learns he is currently under consideration for an opening as manager of the "Pittsburgh Works," a big promotion. At the same time, we learn that Paul has some reservations about his current position and the state of life in the completely automated United States. We meet others who, like Paul, are growing increasingly dissatisfied with the status quo, the result being an attempted revolution in the climax of the story. In the course of the story, the reader learns about all aspects of culture and social structure in a society dominated by automation.

TEACHING METHODS: FITTING IT INTO THE COURSE

I used *Player Piano* over three school years at two significantly different institutions. The book was first used in three sections of an introduction to sociology class at a private liberal arts university (referred to as the *Liberal Arts School*). I also used the book in three sections of introductory sociology at a regional state university (referred to as *Regional State University*). All five sections had enrollments of twenty-one to twenty-eight students.

The story had to be directly connected to the material covered in the class. This proved to be easy at times and more challenging at others. I connected the book to the class in two ways, first with lecture and discussion and second by having the students write a series of directed essays based on the story. The format of the essays was to look for examples of given sociological concepts within the story and illustrate how and why it was a good example. They then took this same concept and discussed how it was relevant to their own personal experience. The intent was to force them to draw comparisons between *Player Piano* and real life. This is congruent with Sullivan (1982) who says the student should be able to apply what they have learned to nonfiction examples. Students were able to develop some insightful and relevant observations based on the novel.

In this section, I provide a detailed account of themes and occurrences in the book that relate to the concepts addressed in an introductory class as indicated by a what is commonly covered in introductory-level textbooks. I illustrate some ways in which I used the material in lecture and discussion and assignments. Finally, I provide a brief discussion and analysis of students' reactions and evaluation of the book as it pertains to the course.

FORMAL RATIONALITY

What I find most useful to a sociology class is not so much the proliferation of automated technology, but the motives underlying its prominence. Above all else, Vonnegut's United States is governed by formal rationality. As one progresses through the story, we find that the machinery is just a facet of a world that has become completely rational and administered. When social theory was covered in class, the book was invoked to clarify Weber's formal rationality (Henslin). I found it useful to use the book as an example of this because the emphasis on rationality and efficiency is taken to such extremes by Vonnegut.

In the story, standardized tests are used to determine one's mental ability. The amount of people needed (if any) to perform a given task is completely calculated. Production and consumption of all manufactured products is strictly determined by a formula. What people spend on food, housing, and other goods is predetermined, and is taken directly out of their paychecks. No need for bank tellers, sales clerks, and no bad checks are written. All of this is decided by the inflexible, unemotional, supercomputer EPICAC:

EPICAC XIV ... was already deciding how many refrigerators, how many lamps, how many turbine generators, how many hub caps, how many dinner plates, how many doorknobs, how many rubber heels, how many television sets, how many pinochle decks— how many of everything America and her customers could have and how much they would cost.... It was EPICAC XIV who would decide ... how many engineers and managers and research men and civil servants, and of what skills, would be needed in order to deliver the goods; and what IQ and aptitude levels would separate the useful men from the useless ones, and how many Reconstruction and Reclamation Corps men and how many soldiers could be supported at what pay level and where ... (118)

This passage is a good example of the extent of the rationalization in this society, what is also apparent is how this has all been firmly imbedded into the character's values.

Along with formal rationality comes discussions of the "Iron Cage" (Ritzer) and all its inflexibility. Vonnegut illustrates this eloquently in several instances. In one case, Paul Proteus's coworker Bud Calhoun invents a machine that performs his tasks and duties as a "lubrication engineer." Once this new information is plugged into the administrative machines, Bud is laid off without hope of finding a new place in the company:

Now, personnel machines all over the country would be reset so as to no longer recognize the job as suited for men. The combinations of holes and nicks that Bud had been to personnel machines would no longer be acceptable. If it were to be slipped into a machine it would come popping right back out....

Bud was in a baffling mess and Paul didn't see how he could help him. If Bud were recorded as a lubrication engineer and introduced into the machines, they'd throw him right out again. (73)

Some examples from *Player Piano* are exceedingly effective when discussing the concepts of rationality, division of labor, and bureaucracy in class. The book not only illustrates its intent, but also its consequences (both intended and unintended), quite well. Students may have difficulty gaining a true understanding of the abstract concepts of social theory. Seeing how it may work in a realistic social setting may aid in their gaining a lasting impression of some of the ideas.

CULTURE

The values and ideology of efficiency and rationality are expressed in all aspects of the culture in Vonnegut's United States. Many characters express the desirability and support of such a system. It is a widely shared and accepted value and ideology. Many times we see characters expressing animosity toward anything that might be deemed to be inefficient or imperfect. At one point in the story, we learn how even the expressive forms of culture had succumbed to the dominance of the world's rationality through the comment of a U.S. diplomat escorting a foreign dignitary on tour of the country:

"Well a fully automatic setup like that makes culture very cheap. Books cost less than seven packs of chewing gum. And there are picture clubs too—pictures for your walls at amazingly cheap prices.... A lot of research goes into what's run off, believe me. Survey's of public reading tastes, readability and appeal tests on books being considered. Heavens, running off an unpopular book would put a book club out of business like that!" ... "The way they get culture so cheap is by knowing in advance what and how

much of it people want. They get it right, right down to the color of the jacket. Gutten-
berg would be amazed." (243)

What is so interesting about this particular example is that it fits well with the
concept of George Ritzer's *McDonaldization of Society* (2000), which is
addressed in many introductory-level texts. Parallels can be drawn from these
passages with students' own experience of the real world.

DRAMATURGICAL ANALYSIS

What initially lead me to consider using Vonnegut in the classroom was the
unmistakable similarities between his writing and the ideas of Erving Goffman.
Vonnegut portrays humans as not only acting out roles, but doing so to the point
of routine and ritual:

Anita had the mechanics of marriage down pat, even to the subtlest conventions. If her
approach was disturbingly rational, systematic, she was thorough enough to turn out a
credible counterfeit of warmth. (17)

The relationship between Paul and (his wife) Anita are particularly Goffman-
esque in that so much of what they say to each other amounts to little more than
a script repeated over time. The many phone conversations they have during the
story are always ended with "I love you Paul," "I love *you* Anita." Paul's emphasis suggesting perhaps he was trying to convince himself as well as Anita.

The presentation of self and the use of props are illustrated by a minor character, Luke Lubbock, who is the member of several uniformed fraternal organizations. While in a bar in Homestead, Paul witnesses a parade of these
organizations of which Luke is marching with several different groups so Luke
needed to return to the bar periodically to change costumes:

The man was in his underwear now, ragged and drab, and none-too-clean. And Luke had
somehow shrunk and saddened and was knobbed and scarred and scrawny. He was sub-
dued now, not talking at all, and meeting no ones eyes. Almost desperately, hungrily, he
ripped open the brown parcel and took from it a pale blue uniform, encrusted with gold
embroidery and piped in scarlet. He pulled on the trousers and black boots ... Luke was
growing again, getting his color back, and as he strapped on his saber, he was talkative
again, important and strong. (95)

The reader also encounters a demonstration of face-saving behavior (Henslin) when Paul's rival, Lawson Shepherd is mistakenly exposed at a company
dinner party as attempting to undermine Paul's promotion and career hopes by
telling their bosses that he is under extreme mental stress and anxiety, on the
verge of a breakdown. At this point, Shepherd runs outside in embarrassment as
Paul follows. Paul acknowledged and even justifies Shepherd's actions a bit and
the two return inside to the dinner table:

"Under the weather?" Kroner said to Shepherd kindly.
"Yessir, scallops for lunch did it, I think."

Kroner nodded sympathetically and turned to the waiter, "Could the boy have milk toast do you suppose?" Kroner was willing to go to any lengths to preserve harmony in his family, to give a man in a tight spot a way out. For the rest of the evening, Paul supposed, Kroner would be keeping alive—as with the milk toast now—the polite fiction of Shepherd's illness. (51)

These dramaturgical examples are just a few of the countless relevant passages in the book. A separate a paper could be written on this similarity alone.

DEVIANCE AND SOCIAL CONTROL

Chapters on deviance and social control in most intro textbooks include a discussion of Merton's *Deviant Career Paths*, which categorizes people based on whether they accept or reject the goals of society and means of obtaining those goals (Lindsey and Beach). Similarly, a major theme of *Player Piano* is whether people accept or question the current social order. Beginning with Paul Proteus and continuing throughout the novel, we meet many people who have grown dissatisfied or at least have doubts about the social system. One can clearly place many of these characters into Merton's classifications of conformist, innovator, ritualist, retreatist, or rebel. Kroner, who is one of Paul's bosses and believes wholeheartedly in the system, is the obvious conformist. Paul Proteus who longs for a simpler time and wishes to go off and live in the woods without machines is the retreatist. Lasher who we find wants to overthrow the current technocracy is the rebel. Alfy, a minor character we meet in the bar in Homestead is a good innovator. Though not a member of the elite, he refuses to join the Reeks and Wrecks. He makes his living by running betting games in the bars. We find a ritualist in George Baer, Paul's other boss and Kroner's counterpart. When Paul confronts him with question regarding any possible shortcomings of their social system he replies:

"Is progress bad ... Maybe progress is bad, eh?"
    Kroner looked at him with surprise, "Look, you know darned good and well history's answered the question a thousand times."
    "It Has? Has it? You know; I wouldn't. Answered it a thousand times, has it? That's good, good. All I know is you've got to act like it has, or you might as well throw in the towel. Don't know, my boy. Guess I should, but I don't. Just do my job. Maybe that's wrong." (132)

Some characters in the book may arguably fit into one category or another (Henslin). This usually provides for lively class discussion.
    Building on the same theme of dissatisfaction, Vonnegut demonstrates how people who do not follow prescribed norms are subject to attempts at social control via the use of both positive and negative sanctions. There are many examples of blatant and subtle, formal and informal attempts at social control throughout the story. One good example surrounds Paul Proteus. It had become apparent to his superiors in the engineering community that Paul may have had reservations about sticking with the status quo. They offered him a large promotion to not only bring him back in line, but to get him to become an informer on his revolutionary friends.

STRATIFICATION

Vonnegut's United States provides a good point of discussion about stratification. Many texts address how and why societies are stratified. In *Player Piano,* we find a society that has an extremely polarized and distinct class system. The mangers and engineers and the Reeks and Wrecks are the only two significant classes. These groups are extremely segregated, living on opposite sides of a river and have little face-to-face interaction. This aspect of the story is useful in discussions on how (in real life) people are segregated in much the same way, with our own neighborhoods, places to shop, workplaces, and eating establishments. Though unequal, Vonnegut's world has striven to achieve the fairest way of allocating wealth, power, and prestige. All people are required to pass standardized exams to get into college and take aptitude tests to determine what specific jobs they can perform. Family ties or wealth have nothing to do with determining who makes it into the educated elite. It is based entirely on intelligence and capabilities. Many texts discuss the concept of meritocracy with respect to the Davis-Moore explanation of stratification (Henslin; Kendall). Based on the concept of meritocracy and the novel, students were asked in class to determine the extent to which that stratification in the United States is really based on such standards.

The concept of social mobility (or lack thereof) can also be gleaned from the novel. This society is based on the ultimate meritocracy, but the reader finds that once people are placed in a track after their examination, there is no room for upward mobility. No matter how hard one works, they will not receive the chance to improve their social standing. Additionally, higher education has become increasingly important. Having a doctorate has become a requirement for success in *Player Piano.* This is particularly useful when coupled with a discussion on the increasing prominence of a college education and an emerging importance placed on earning some sort of advanced degree in the United States today. This can be discussed and compared with the real world and how much social mobility is actually possible in the real United States.

SOCIAL CHANGE AND SOCIAL MOVEMENTS

Player Piano provides useful examples for social change and social movements. Social change is illustrated in the book with discussions and narratives that describe the war and the proliferation of technology that had a lasting and pervasive impact in Vonnegut's United States. This illustrates how technological advances act as a catalyst for social change (Lindsey and Beach). Additionally, the climax and resolution of the story involves the activities of the "Ghost Shirt Society," a revolutionary movement initiated by those dissatisfied and aggrieved characters in the novel. Many introductory-level books illustrate types and categories of social movements as well as their stages of development (Henslin). The Ghost Shirt Society can be examined in terms of these categories and stages, and it stands as a useful example of how collective action serves as a conduit for social change, particularly in times of growing dissatisfaction.

RACE, AGE, AND GENDER

The issues of race, gender, and age are almost nonexistent in *Player Piano*. In more than 300 pages, only about seven women are introduced and race is not mentioned. Vonnegut sometimes writes with a sexist tone, as the women are portrayed in an unmistakably negative light. He presents them as overemotional, shallow, and unintelligent. Paul Proteus's wife, Anita, is perhaps the most deplorable character in the novel. She is a controlling and manipulative former secretary who falsely leads Paul to believe she is pregnant to get him to marry her. In the story, we find that she lives vicariously through her husband's success and is more concerned with the advancement of his career than he is.

Despite the lack of commentary on racial, age, or gender inequality, I was able to incorporate these aspects by using an external structural approach to the sociology of literature by illustrating how their absence from the book may be a reflection of the social context in which Vonnegut wrote the book. He was a young white male writing in the early 1950s before the Civil Rights or Feminist Movements. I also addressed how women and people of color are absent within much of our popular culture, in general. Most of our heroes and main characters are white men. Furthermore, as part of class discussion and essays, we discussed how things have improved since the 1950s and whether these people are still decidedly underrepresented in not only our popular culture but also in other positions of prestige and visibility.

All these concepts addressed here are used as examples for lecture, discussion, and topics to write about. They are offered together with the raw explanation and empirical examples provided by the textbook and discussed in class. The induced salience of all the concepts addressed here provides a springboard for explaining the material covered in lecture and the textbook. All the students have common experience of the book, therefore when examples of the book are used for the class, everyone should able to relate to them and compare them to real life.

STUDENT EVALUATIONS OF THE SOCIOLOGY-THROUGH-LITERATURE TEACHING METHOD

Though others have written about and encouraged the use of the sociology-through-fiction approach in the classroom, few of the articles reviewed actually made an attempt to find out how the students evaluated this method. At the end of each semester, an anonymous survey was distributed to students to assess their perceptions and opinions regarding the assigned work of fiction. Questions were asked about the book in general, how relevant they thought it was to the class, and how well the instructor was able integrate it into class activities and assignments. Responses were formatted to a five-point scale ranging from "strongly agree" (five points) to "strongly disagree" (one point). The survey was administered to introductory sections over five semesters (at the two different schools). The data demonstrate a high level of reliability with an alpha score of 0.886, and the survey items were straightforward and easy to understand suggesting face validity.

Based on student responses, the reaction to the book and its use seems favorable. The first two items were intended to determine whether the students enjoyed the book and found it easy to read. If the novel was entertaining and easy to follow, the students may have been more likely to read it. Therefore, the first two items were about how the students viewed the book in general. Though most of the students agreed that the story was entertaining and also rated the language and writing style favorably, they were not among the highest mean scores in the survey (3.57 and 3.88, respectively). The second and third questions measure the book's perceived usefulness to the class. This was intended to determine whether the students thought the story was relevant to the course. Though they felt it related well to the class (mean score of 4.17), it appears as though they were less certain about whether this book actually *added* to their understanding of the material covered in the class (3.68). The fifth and sixth items were designed assesses how well the book was integrated into class activities and assignments. The first of those items, addressing the instructor's ability to integrate the book into the class, was quite positive (4.02). The majority of the respondents rated the item on the writing assignments favorably (3.7), although a third of them did not agree that the essays were useful. The sixth and seventh items look at their overall opinions regarding the use of fiction and its impact on learning. A large majority (73 percent, 3.98) liked the use of fiction in class. However, whether the use of fiction actually made a difference in what they learned was less certain (3.2), with nearly 58 percent of the respondents indicating that they were not sure whether it made a difference or that it made little difference at all.

In addition to the descriptive data addressed above, further analysis was conducted to find any possible relationships between the students' evaluation of this teaching method and independent variables such as gender, school of attendance (*State University* or *Liberal Arts*), and year in school. The students' majors were not measured, because the vast majority of these students were freshman and sophomores and had yet to pick a field of study. To simplify these analyses, a factor analysis (varimax rotation) was run to determine whether the eight evaluative variables could be reduced to fewer factors. Only one significant component (explaining 55.91 percent of variance) was extracted from the analysis with all the variables loading at 0.6 or above. With this in mind, an aggregate for those variables was computed to create an index labeled "Total Evaluation of the Teaching Method." The Total Evaluation variable was used in tests with the independent variables identified above. There were no significant differences between gender and year in school. There was a difference in the mean total evaluation scores when grouped by the schools of attendance. This will be addressed in some detail below.

Another issue considered was that of student reading habits. When I started to get some initial negative feedback from the *State University* students, I asked them how often they read novels or read recreationally. It seemed apparent that these students did not have a history of strong reading habits. Not having strong reading habits may make reading literature a new or perhaps even an uncomfortable experience for the students (Sullivan). I therefore decided to add items on the survey that assessed reading habits. Three items were added:

- How many novels do you read for recreation in one year?
- In general, how many hours do you spend per spend per week reading for personal enjoyment? (This includes ALL forms of reading: magazine, news papers, books: fiction and nonfiction.)

- In general, how many hours do you spend per spend per week reading materials related to your coursework?

There were no significant differences or correlations found between these reading variables and the total evaluation variable or any of the eight individual evaluative items. Reading habits apparently had little impact on student evaluations. Because these items were not included in the surveys distributed at the *Liberal Arts* school, a comparison of reading habits between the two groups of students was not possible.

A Change of Venue: The Findings of Student Evaluations Related to Setting

The only significant difference found among independent variables was school of attendance. This is an interesting result and warrants some discussion. The students at the *Private Liberal Arts University* rated the teaching method more favorably than those at the *Regional State University*. The mean scores for total evaluations of the method are 33.42 (average a response of 4.17) and 27.01 (average response of 3.38), respectively ($T = 8.42$, significance at 0.000). What exactly caused the difference in these evaluations can be examined from two perspectives: (1) the organizational structure of the respective institutions and (2) demographic differences between the students themselves.

Structural Differences

There were several structural differences between the two schools. The change from the *Private Liberal Arts* to the *Regional State University* brought with it a significantly different setting for this nontraditional teaching approach. The first had to do with the difference in the school calendars and course schedules. The *Liberal Arts* sections were four credit hours. The semesters were twelve weeks long with classes meeting Monday through Friday. At the *State University,* the courses were three credit hours and met Monday, Wednesday, and Friday over a fifteen-week semester. The drop in credit hours put class time at a greater premium, and it was difficult to devote the same amount of attention to the book. Additionally, the difference in class the schedule meant the *State University* sections met less frequently. It seemed as though there was a lower intensity level to the course compared with a class that meets daily.

Another issue related to school structure was that the *State University* employs a book rental program. Under this system, students pay a flat fee per semester that covers the rental of all primary textbooks. Supplemental books are not covered under the rental program requiring students to purchase them. Some at the school think this causes students to feel less obligated to purchase and read supplemental texts. In various classes, students sometimes expressed that they felt it was inappropriate to use supplemental texts because they were not covered by the rental system.

Demographic Differences

Another explanation for the difference in overall evaluations may be related to demographic differences in the two groups of students themselves. First, the difference between the students at the two schools may have been academic achievement. The average Scholastic Aptitude Test (SAT) score of the freshman class at the *Liberal Arts* school the year the data was collected was a 1260. The freshman class at the *State University* presented an SAT school of 1008. Highly achieving students may have a greater affinity for the use of fiction, thus evaluating the method more favorably. Also, such students may simply have a more positive attitude toward education and learning in general, leading to higher evaluations. Second, the interest areas of the students may also be a factor. Sobal, Hinrichs, Emmons, and Hooks (1981) and Sullivan (1982) theorize that the use of fiction has grown less effective with the decline of the number of liberal arts student in their classes. They are less likely to have a predisposed affinity for fiction if they are in school to earn more vocational degrees. This notion fits well when comparing the two schools included in this study: a liberal arts institution and one with a greater vocational-technical orientation. Students at a liberal arts school may expect a more liberal arts approach to their classes and may have a greater affinity for reading fiction.

Last, there were obvious socioeconomic differences between the students at the two schools. Surveys distributed to incoming freshman each year reveal that while the students at the *State University* are predominantly middleclass, the students at the *Liberal Arts* school tend to be upper middleclass and higher. At the *Liberal Arts* school, 47.5 percent of the students reported coming from households with income at $100,000 or above with 16.3 percent reporting $200,000 or more; the data at the *State University* reveal that only 17.5 percent of students come from households with incomes of $100,000 or greater. Conversely, 11.2 percent of the students at the *Liberal Arts* school come from households with incomes of less than $40,000, while 32.9 percent of those at the *State University* fall below that level. The education levels of the students' parents were quite different well. At the *Liberal Arts* school, 32.7 percent of fathers and 38.9 percent of mothers had an undergraduate degree, and those holding graduate degrees were 45.4 percent and 25.7 percent, respectively. The numbers at the *State University* were 21.9 percent of fathers and 24.2 percent of mothers for undergraduate degrees and 15.6 percent and 12.7 percent for graduate degrees. The various demographic differences between the students at the two schools may indicate that the difference in total evaluation may be a function of social class.

CONCLUSION

The intent is for students to gain a deeper and more lasting grasp of the material. Student data indicate that they like the use of the book in class, and some also felt it has added to their learning. However, given that the second-highest item response was that related to the instructor of the course, it is possible that the overall attitudes about the instructor could actually be what is influencing student attitudes toward this teaching method. The fact that the *Private Liberal Arts* students indicated a higher regard for the teaching technique points to some deeper questions about the possibility for innovative teaching techniques in various educational settings. For whatever reason (structural or demographic), the data suggest the *Liberal Arts* setting is more receptive to such nontraditional methods. Though it may still be effective and desirable to use such techniques at regional state universities, it may be less well received. There is much more to be considered and studied.

Nevertheless, the ultimate intent of this assignment is to achieve a greater retention of knowledge after students have moved on to other studies. This study does not actually confirm or refute this argument. In fact, sociology as a discipline may know little about any lasting knowledge of sociology after exposure to a general education class. As the purveyors of the discipline, we should not only be interested in recruiting "majors," but also have an interest in creating a lasting general understanding of the sociological perspective to those who choose other majors by demonstrating its applicability to students later in life. Additionally, it may serve to enhance the public image of the discipline if students see the perspective as relevant and meaningful. Exploring new ways to deepen the introductory-level experience can be a step in this direction.

WORKS CITED

Corbett, Ronald P. "'Novel' Perspectives on Probation: Fiction as Sociology." *Sociological Forum* 9 (1994): 307–14.

Cosbey, Janet. "Using Contemporary Fiction to Teach Family Issues." *Teaching Sociology* 25 (1997): 227–33.

Coser, Lewis A. *Sociology Through Literature: An Introductory Reader*. Englewood Cliffs, NJ: Prentice Hall, 1963.

Griswold, Wendy. "American Character and the American Novel: An Expansion of Reflection Theory in the Sociology of Literature." *American Journal of Sociology* 86 (1981): 740–65.

Hegvedt, Karen A. "Teaching Sociology of Literature Through Literature." *Teaching Sociology* 19 (1991): 1–12.

Henslin, James M. *Essentials of Sociology: A Down to Earth Approach*. Boston: Allyn and Bacon, 2000.

Hoffman, Thomas P. "The Theme of Mechanization in Player Piano." In *The Critical Response to Kurt Vonnegut*, edited by Leonard Mustazza, 5–14. Westport, NY: Greenwood Press, 1994.

Kendall, Diana. *Sociology in Our Times*. Belmont, CA: Wadsworth, 2001.

Las, Cheryl. "Science Fiction and Introductory Sociology: The Handmaid in the Classroom." *Teaching Sociology* 24 (1996): 54–63.

Lena, Hugh F., and Bruce London. "An Introduction to Sociology Through Fiction Using Kesey's One Flew Over the Cuckoos Nest." *Teaching Sociology* 6 (1979): 123–130.

Lindsey, Linda L., and Stephan Beach. *Sociology*. Upper Saddle River, NJ: Prentice Hall, 2002.

Lindstrom, Fred B. Review of "Teaching Sociology With Fiction: An Annotated Bibliography." *Sociological Inquiry* 68 (1998): 281–284.

Mills, C. Wright. *The Sociological Imagination*. New York: Oxford University Press, 1959.

Ritzer, George. *Classical Sociological Theory*. Boston: McGraw-Hill, 2000.

———. *The McDonaldization of Society*. New Century Edition. Thousand Oaks, CA: Pine Forge Press, 2000.

Sobal, Jeff, Donald W. Hinrichs, Charles F. Emmons, and Wade F. Hook. "Experimental Learning in Introductory Sociology." *Teaching Sociology* 8 (1981): 401–22.

Sullivan, Teresa A. "Introductory Sociology Through Literature." *Teaching Sociology* 10 (1982): 109–16.

Sullivan, Thomas J. *Sociology: Concepts and Applications in a Diverse World.* Boston: Allyn and Bacon, 2001.

Van De Poel-Knottnerus, Frederique, and David J. Knottnerus. "Social Life Through Literature: A Suggested Strategy for Conducting a Literary Ethnography." *Sociological Focus* 27 (1994): 67–80.

Vonnegut, Kurt. *God Bless You, Mr. Rosewater: Or Pearls Before Swine.* New York: Delta Fiction, 1965.

———. *Player Piano.* New York: Delta Fiction, 1952.

Wineapple, Brenda. "God Bless You, Mr. Vonnegut." *Current Perspectives in Social Theory* 2 (1981): 233–45.

Insights from the Novel: Good Citizens in Social Contexts

Janine DeWitt and Marguerite Rippy

INTRODUCTION

Encouraging our students to become global citizens calls for innovative approaches that capture the complexity of social life, including methods that stimulate ethical introspection and resist injustice. Novels provide a rich venue for students to examine situations from multiple viewpoints and grapple with what action they might take if confronted with these types of decisions. Students use novels to examine the process of determining the "right" course of action and to explore the moral boundaries of a given social situation. When articulating their intuitive response to literary dilemmas, students also reflect on the values and assumptions about social dynamics that help create their interpretations.

Novels enable students to analyze specific situations in which ethical decision making occurs. This process of examining narratives approximates the ethical dilemmas students encounter on a day-to-day basis. Instinctively, students identify the importance of social context to ethical decision making. They are acutely aware of the dialogues regarding what constitutes morality that result from divergent perspectives. Analyzing and discussing these divergent perspectives enables students to overcome the idea that it is impossible to determine a "best" course of action. Instead they are prompted to articulate a rationale for the course of action they deem "best"—all things considered. As such, novels provide an engaging way to develop ethical reasoning and offer sociologists a method to provide students with models to use their understanding of social context to support good citizenship and resist social injustice.

Using fiction to teach sociological concepts is not a new idea. In 1963, Lewis Coser published an "experimental" collection that illustrated key sociological ideas such as social control, stratification, and bureaucracy. In the introduction to his anthology, he notes that literature can offer "social evidence and testimony. It is a continuous commentary on manners and morals" (Coser "Sociology" 2). In fact, novels provide a rich medium for illustrating sociological concepts. Coser further explains:

[T]he trained sensibilities of a novelist or a poet may provide a richer source of social insight than, say, the impressions of untrained informants on which so much sociological research currently rests. There is an intensity of perception in the first-rate novelist when he describes a locale, a sequence of action, or a clash of characters which can hardly be matched by those observers on whom sociologists are usually wont to rely.[1] (Coser "Sociology" 3)

SOCIAL JUSTICE: THE COURSE FRAMEWORK

The activities described in this essay are based on activities in Marymount University's 300-level interdisciplinary course, Social Justice: Ethical Dilemmas in Social Context. This essay focuses on the use of two novels in that course, *Number the Stars* and *The Good German*, which depict ethical dilemmas associated with "good citizenship" during World War II.

In this course, students initially define social justice by synthesizing theoretical work of philosophers, sociologists, political scientists, and theologians. This traditional academic exercise in abstract reasoning provides the foundation for examining actual situations and is intended to convey the complexity of social justice. There is a great deal of disagreement over what constitutes social justice: some even contend that social justice is not possible. Through discussion, students begin their personal quests to understand social justice by situating specific ethical dilemmas within the interdisciplinary study of ethics.

We explore a range of scenarios portrayed in novels and on film that highlight ethical dilemmas or situations that result from conflicting value systems. Analysis of multiple situations requires students to apply abstract theories and transfer knowledge from one social context to another. Examining both real and fictional situations enables students to consider the social dynamics that construct views of a "good society." Throughout the semester, students study how the social context shapes our perspectives on ethical dilemmas, including how social justice is manifested in specific situations. An understanding of the role that key social institutions and dominant groups play in determining what is considered "good" or "right" results from comparing similar situations that occur in different social contexts.

The narratives analyzed also establish a connection between the past and present. Students reflect on the meaning of being a "good" citizen in the past as well as the role of global citizenship now. For example, how did being a "good" German during World War II differ from being a good German in post–World War II Berlin? How does being a "good" American today, in light of the War in Iraq or the Abu Ghraib prison scandal, differ from being a good American during the Truman era when the decision was made to drop the atomic bomb on civilian targets?

Gradually, a personal sense of social justice results from exploring a series of narratives. At the end of the course, students research a contemporary dilemma with the goal of determining how social justice can be achieved in this situation. The students examine this specific situation to reveal the role that social context plays in shaping competing definitions of "right." They discuss the key social groups and institutions involved, the role of dominant ideology, and the history of group relationships and social interactions as they concern their chosen topic.

To prepare students for their individual projects, the class looks at the Holocaust as a case study of ethical citizenship in crisis. The two novels below are particularly useful in their ability to address one of the clearest examples of failed ethical citizenship in the twentieth century. The Holocaust remains a searing example of the tangible consequences of social and individual moral failure. *Number the Stars* and *The Good German* present different perspectives—historically, aesthetically, and nationally—on this complex historical moment. These divergent perspectives allow students to process the Holocaust through multiple lenses, engaging in multicultural and interdisciplinary study of this historical moment.

TOWARD A SOCIOLOGY OF ETHICS: ETHICAL DILEMMAS AND MORAL DIALOGUES

Sociological contributions to the study of ethics can also provide valuable tools for developing ethical reasoning skills among our students. In the classroom, students often confuse the fact that there are conflicting definitions of morality with the notion that morality is simply a matter of personal opinion. By analyzing the types of moral claims made, as well as the social dynamics that generate these claims, students can transcend their individualized understanding of ethics to focus on the process of achieving social consensus, which necessarily guides moral action in any society.

To explain divergent perspectives on morality, sociologists examine the dynamics that create this moral fragmentation. Loseke suggests that morality is constructed by key actors using claims-making strategies. She contends that there are three types of moral claims: religious, organizational, and humanitarian. Central to this constructionist analysis is the interrogation of who determines what is defined as moral or ethical action. Religious claims are often based on scriptures or historical documents. While there may be differences of opinion on how to interpret those documents, moral judgments are not based on human claims. Secular claims made by organizations often are based on logic and appeal to common beliefs about what is good such as patriotism, free markets, individualism, family, or fair play. Finally, humanitarian claims usually target the elimination of pain and suffering by appealing to emotions (Loseke 50–56).

These competing claims produce an ethical dilemma or a situation in which value systems compete. Rushworth Kidder contends that dilemmas commonly reflect the juxtaposition of four core values systems: truth versus loyalty; individual versus community; short term versus long term; justice versus mercy. By selecting novels that highlight ethical dilemmas, literature offers a way to explore and discuss the social dynamics that generate these competing claims.

Resolving ethical dilemmas by moving toward a consensus about what constitutes a good life requires extensive discussion and, often, a broader appeal to common ground. Amitai Etzioni's work outlines ways of restoring moral order such that individual rights are balanced with social responsibility. Communities play a key role in this process. For Etzioni, a good society is one that supports "moral dialogues to determine the values that will constitute the shared cultures of its communities," rather than basing values solely on tradition ("The Good Society" 90).

Analyzing novels enables students to participate in a classroom version of a "moral dialogue" and develop the skills necessary for moral discourse. By discussing the ethical dimensions of the storyline with others, students gain an appreciation for approaching a situation from diverse perspectives and in some cases, by appealing to fundamental shared values, are able to reach consensus on the "right" course of action. This ability to grapple with ethical decisions is an essential element of a strong undergraduate education, but it is a difficult outcome to achieve.

Students are more likely to explore and redefine their ethical decision-making framework in the territory of fiction, where the ground may be less personal and their beliefs less fixed. According to Mark Johnson,

> Narrative makes it possible for us not only to explore the consequences of decisions and commitments over an extended period of time, but also to reflect on the concrete particularities that make up the fine text of our actual moral experience. It invites us to develop our perception of character, of what is important in a given situation, and of the subtly interwoven threads of our moral entanglements.... (197)

Thus students are able to develop insight not only into the novels presented in class, but into their own roles and responsibilities as citizens. The two novels used in this course, *Number the Stars* and *The Good German*, depict ethical dilemmas associated with "good citizenship" during World War II.

NUMBER THE STARS BY LOIS LOWRY

Number the Stars is often read as a morality tale by children in elementary schools. The virtues of bravery, honesty, and friendship are central to this portrayal of life in World War II era Denmark. "Good Danes" disobeyed the laws imposed by Nazi occupation and helped Danish Jews escape massive deportation. According to the U.S. Holocaust Museum, 7,200 Jews escaped to Sweden, and only 500 Jews were sent from Denmark to the Theresienstadt ghetto in Czechoslovakia.[2] While resistance efforts were relatively successful in Denmark, similar efforts in Germany, France, or Italy often meant death to those involved. We know there were heroes in all of these countries, but what made resistance efforts more successful in Denmark?

There were a number of social institutions that made resistance possible. At the highest level, the Danish government officials appeared to cooperate with the Nazis but seldom interfered with resistance efforts by Danish citizens. An underground newspaper provided most Danes with war accounts received from the BBC, so they were well aware of the atrocities that were under way elsewhere in Europe (*Denmark: Living with the Enemy*). Some accounts indicate that Young Danes, often students, were particularly active in resistance efforts, running underground newspapers or hampering the movement of German troops (Werner). Interestingly, both *Number the Stars* and the Disney version of the same historical event, *A Miracle at Midnight*—highlight family involvement in the resistance. Finally, most historical accounts indicate that Danish Jews were well integrated in their society, living as neighbors and known by their national rather than religious identity. This integration made it difficult for the Germans to exile Danish Jews (Jensen and Jensen).

Number the Stars illustrates how elements of the social context helped support social justice in Denmark during the Holocaust. The main character is Annemarie Johansen, a ten-year-old Danish girl who provides insights on the events that unfold when her family decides to hide her neighbor, Ellen Rosen. This decision to protect Ellen is motivated by friendship and a greater sense of social justice. As a result, the Johansen family must grapple with several decisions. First, the Johansens must decide whether to accept a greater risk of danger by helping the Rosens escape to Sweden. Transporting the Rosens increases the risk of being caught by the Nazis for both the Johansens and Rosens. Most students are reluctant to place family members in harm's way. Interesting dialogues ensue over what circumstances might warrant such risk. A second ethical dilemma occurs when Annemarie learns that she has not been privy to the complete truth. Her parents and Uncle Henrik had not been forthcoming about the extent of their involvement in resistance efforts, in part to protect the children. When confronted by a Nazi soldier, Annemarie was compelled to "lie" in an attempt to protect others. Since quite a few Danish families were involved with resistance efforts, the process of reflective analysis gives students an opportunity to uncover the social or contextual factors that help make heroic actions possible.

Ideas to Stimulate Informed Class Discussion

Exercise One: Situated Analysis

Students are given a series of questions to reflect on the ethical decisions made by the main characters in the novel. This reflection sets the stage for examining the role played by social institutions such as government, family, and religion. In addition, the questions are designed to prompt empathy by placing the student in the hypothetical position of the main characters. For example, the following questions are used to guide reading of *Number the Stars*:

1. Consider the decisions made by the Johansen family when hiding Ellen, and later helping the Rosens escape to Sweden. How did these decisions place the Johansen family in danger? Would you be willing to accept the same risks, if faced with this situation? Why or Why not? In what type of situations would you be more likely to accept such risks?
2. Annemarie was "protected" from the truth by her parents and Uncle Henrik. Later in the story she lies to protect others. When is lying an acceptable practice? Do you make such judgment calls on a case-by-case basis or do you believe that there should be some general rules that guide your decision making?
3. In this story, the Resistance Effort seems to be an acceptable endeavor—Why? What social factors made these "heroic" actions seem acceptable?

Subsequently in class, students explore the basis for ethical decision making (instinct versus reason) as well as the rationale accompanying those decisions (ends versus means, duty, common good, fairness, justice, and so on). Examining when certain actions are acceptable provides the foundation for situating ethical decision making in a specific social context. For example, the same events could be viewed as treason rather than heroic in a different context.

In *Number the Stars*, the contextual elements suggested in the novel such as the passive role played by the Danish government, resistance involvement of several Johansen family members, and integration of those practicing the Jewish religion in Denmark make it possible for students to situate the initial theoretical discussions within a specific historical and social framework. Discussion of the novel is supplemented with historical footage from the videos *The Danish Solution* and *Denmark: Living with the Enemy*, as well as online readings from Danish scholars who examine how collective organization facilitated resistance efforts (Jensen and Jensen).

Exercise Two: Experiential Learning Using the U.S. Holocaust Museum

Analysis of multiple situations requires students to transfer knowledge from one social context to another. After reading the online pamphlet, "Resistance during the Holocaust,"[3] students speculate about which elements of the social context are most likely to support resistance efforts. They then test their hypotheses by comparing the relative success of resistance efforts in countries other than Denmark using exhibits on the second floor of the U.S. Holocaust Museum. Upon return, students write a reflective essay analyzing how Annemarie's experience could have differed if she lived elsewhere in Europe.

While our own university's proximity to Washington, D.C., enhances the potential for experiential processing and application of topics discussed in class, the variety of resources available on the Internet offer many opportunities for students in any geographic location to test out the ideas raised in group discussion against their own individual experience of Holocaust primary sources. For example, the virtual exploration of Internet exhibits, such as critiques of the historical portrayal of Denmark as a nation of heroes are easily accessed.[4] These experiential assignments shift the emphasis from group consensus or interpretation of an event to individual application of ideas and knowledge generated in class. Students can test out, accept, or reject ideas that we have formulated together regarding ethical citizenship in Denmark and begin to develop their own framework for ethical decision making.

THE GOOD GERMAN BY JOSEPH KANON

The Good German[5] is used in this course to highlight contemporary social construction of good and evil, particularly as it relates to retrospective representations of the Holocaust. The understanding of how "good" people arrive at flawed moral choices has long been a topic of academic study.[6] Because the novel is set in the immediate aftermath of the war, students consider how quickly social definitions of "good citizenship" can change. Being a "good" German under the Nazi rule was quite different than being a "good" German once Allied forces occupied Berlin. This novel explicitly poses the problematic formulation of good citizenship in a shifting historical context.

The title itself provokes students to discuss just who might be the "good German," raising questions of the intersection between morality and national identity. Viewed from a feminist or multicultural perspective, the novel also invites questions about the coherence of national identity when defined against multiple matrices of gender, race, class, and religion.

Activity one, described below, asks students to construct various definitions of good citizenship as posed from the various perspectives of characters in the novel, allowing students to generate multiple viewpoints before moving on to analyze the potential strengths and weaknesses of each. We analyze characters' values and decision making from a literary perspective, asking which characters evoke sympathy or condemnation. More important, why do we sympathize with some characters and not others? Wartime survival requires characters to make a range of decisions that fuel student discussion. Activity two asks students to take a more structural approach to the novel, adapting Louise Rosenblatt's transactional reader response for the specific purpose of understanding *The Good German*.

By grounding the analysis of ethical dilemmas, the novel provides parameters for "moral dialogues"[7] in the classroom—affording students the flexibility to arrive at different conclusions based on the values that they deem most important, even if they disagree about the "right" course of action. These ethical dilemmas are fueled by characters' cultural points of view and selective use of historical detail. Similarly, in real life, key social institutions or dominant groups portray social definitions of "good" or "right" using selective techniques. Therefore, moral decisions made by Renate, a Jewish character accused of Nazi collaboration, may appear more negative than those of Gunther, a German police officer who is not accused of collaboration in the wartime aftermath, despite his entrenched position within a German institution directly implicated in the mechanisms of Holocaust destruction.

Ideas to Stimulate Informed Class Discussion

Exercise One: Character Analysis

In this exercise, we facilitate a class discussion and analysis of how each major character fits or fails to fit the title, *The Good German*. Names of major characters are placed on the board (Renate, Bernie, Gunther, Jake, Lena, Emile) and then students generate associations with what is "good" about each character, and in what way each is seen as or sees himself or herself as "German." In this way, the discussion opens as a value-neutral accumulation of ideas. Often, surprising associations emerge, and this approach creates an opening for dissent and discussion regarding the portrayal of characters, as well as about each character's defining traits. At times, the discussion has evolved into a deconstruction of national identities, with the argument leaning toward Jake's position as a multinational observer rather than an Americanized perspective. At other times, gender and ethnicity have emerged in the foreground of the discussion, with the controversial Renate positioned as either heroic maternal figure or self-loathing caricature, depending on the inflection of the reader's interpretation.

After these subjective viewpoints are raised, the class makes an effort to reconcile various interpretations of the characters by analyzing the values and criteria used to develop their interpretations. Often, these discussions result in a methodical deconstruction of one's own perspective, as the student retraces her interpretive steps. Positioning the values within an ethical framework like that of Loseke can help evaluate the implications and causes for individual character's actions, which in turn helps students see how they might develop their own framework for ethical decision making, and what the implications of their own choices and values might privilege or neglect.

Exercise Two: Reader Response and the Creation of Textual Meaning

This exercise shares much in terms of strategy with the first exercise in that it asks students to contemplate how their own positions as readers might inflect their interpretation of the novel. In contrast to the character analysis exercise, however, this approach asks students to start with an analysis of their own value systems and their implications, rather than asking them to arrive at the realization after character analysis and discussion.

By adapting Louise Rosenblatt's transactional reader response model of textual interpretation for group discussion, this exercise introduces students to literary theory as well as to ethical considerations.[8] The purpose of the exercise is to encourage students to locate possible meanings of the text, based on the intersection of specific personal/historical reading responses and textual clues. It applies the theory of transactional response specifically to *The Good German* and its reinterpretation of history in light of personal meaning. The discussion opens with a simple three-column diagram on the board. The columns are titled "Your Own Historical Context," "Meaning," and "Clues from the Text."

In the first column, students generate a list of factors they feel influence their own positions as a readers. Ethnicity, gender, historical moment, belief system, attitudes toward reading, and prior knowledge of novel's themes might all be listed in this column.

The instructor then asks the class to address the third column: "Clues from the Text." The instructor might ask students to consider a specific scene of the novel in terms of the suspense or detective genre—what "clues" does it give readers to steer them toward specific value-laden interpretations of characters or plot events? Students could work in small groups to consider several key scenes (Renate's trial, Jake's methods of discovering Lena, Gunther's revelation of his role in his wife's internment). Students comb through the text looking for clues that guide their interpretation of these moments. What actions were seen as problematic, or as laudable? Are some people depicted as more valuable than others? Why? Students fill the column with a list of these "clues" as a group. In the process, they may discover more personal factors that can be added to the left-hand column as well.

Finally, as a whole class, we fill in the middle column, where our own individual belief system intersects with the textual clues we located as a group to create meaning. One problem with this exercise can be that the class tends to gravitate toward the small-group portion of discussion before returning to what is usually an enlightening and fruitful whole-class discussion. Leave enough time for the whole-class construction of "meaning."

NOVELS FACILITATE MULTIPLE MODES OF ANALYSIS

Investigating how different groups in a society might view morality lays the essential foundation for an ability to advocate a specific moral perspective. In the classroom, this process of analysis can be achieved using works of fiction, particularly novels that highlight moral or ethical issues. As Johnson notes, studying literature offers insight into life through character analysis, historical discussion, ethical reasoning, and aesthetic appreciation:

We learn from, and are changed by, such narratives to the extent that we become imaginatively engaged in making fine discriminations of character and in determining what is morally salient in particular situations. We actually enter into the lives of the characters, and we perform acts of perception, decision and criticism. We find ourselves judging of a character that she shouldn't have done X, or wishing that he had seen a particular situation differently than he did. We want to stop the characters and tell the "Oh no, don't do that!" or "No, that's not what she meant." Just as in life, we find ourselves surprised by what happens, or disappointed in ourselves for not having seen something earlier. We explore, we learn, and we are changed by our participation in the fiction that creatively imitates life. (196)

The Good German lends itself to interdisciplinary analysis because of its journalistic approach to post–World War II Berlin, which contrasts its highly fictionalized use of character and plot; *Number the Stars* directly addresses choices that pit individual ethics against national identity in a style open to the most basic reader.

These novels, written for different audiences about divergent national perspectives on the Holocaust, allow students to develop a framework for ethical decision making within their own social contexts. The novels provide a foundation for considering "good citizenship" in the contemporary world. Students learn an interdisciplinary approach to the study of the social world that helps to define them and that they, in turn, help to define.

The Joint Task Force on Student Learning reports that learning takes place "in the context of a compelling situation that balances challenge and opportunity" rather than passively receiving "wisdom" from the expert in the front of the room. The research on effective strategies for moral and civic education is less prolific. A recent report on undergraduate moral and civic education conducted by the Carnegie Foundation compared the similarities and differences between teaching ethics and teaching in general and found that while teaching ethics is similar to teaching in general, there are particular challenges that complicate the process of teaching ethics (Colby). For example, moral education entails addressing ideas that are "multilayered, subtle, and often confusing. Many of these ideas conflict with students' preconceptions, making them even harder to grasp" (Colby 131). Not only are concepts of morality complex, but students also tend to work from "oversimplified explanations" even when presented with evidence to the contrary (Colby 132). The ethics classroom demands both a tolerance of difference and an assumption that not all choices can be "good"— assumptions that may seem to conflict with each other to many students.

Four factors in particular complicate the teaching ethics. First, students must move beyond moral relativism, that is, "the idea that no position can be considered any more or less valid than another" (Colby 15). Second, an effective ethics education must support "deep understanding" and enable students to make a "personal connection with ethical concepts" at both an intellectual and emotional level (Colby 134). Third, students must develop the skills of moral discourse, including the ability to state, research, and defend opposing viewpoints (Colby 145). Finally, for moral education to hold long-term value, students must be able to transfer learning to contexts beyond the classroom (Colby 142).

Our experience in teaching Social Justice: Ethical Dilemmas in Social Context suggests that novels can play an important role in ethical education. Novels can provide a forum for the discussion of ideas that students find relevant, but not predetermined, and can offer specific insights into the motivations and frameworks for ethical decision making. The novel, however, is only one in a series of strategies geared toward ethical education of the college citizen. Courses focused on ethical dilemmas need to offer students exposure to theories of ethical decision making, strategies for engaging in social justice, and opportunities to engage in individual exploration and creation of meaning. Our goal is for students to practice using knowledge in authentic contexts, thus maximizing the chance they will be able to continue their education even after graduation.

END NOTES

1. Although using fiction to teach outside the literature classroom may not be a dominant academic trend (yet), many professors teaching outside the humanities have used narratives to invigorate their classrooms. For further discussion of this practice in general, see Chrisler, Boyatzis, and Von Wright.

2. U.S. Holocaust Museum Web site http://www.ushmm.org/museum/exhibit/focus/danish/.

3. U.S. Holocaust Memorial Museum Web site http://www.ushmm.org/education/foreducators/resource/resistance.pdf.

4. For example, Jensen and Jensen, *Denmark and the Holocaust*.

5. Joseph Kanon has written a series of historical novels that focus on ethical dilemmas set during World War II (*The Good German, Los Alamos*) and during the Cold War (*The Prodigal Spy*).

6. For further reading on this topic, see Berger, Hughes, and Coser, "The Visibility of Evil."

7. This phrase is given fuller context in Etzioni's work, "Moral Dialogues in Public Debates."

8. For approaches to the integration of basic literary theory in the classroom, see Deborah Appleman's *Critical Encounters in High School English: Teaching Literary Theory to Adolescents*.

WORKS CITED

Appleman, Deborah. *Critical Encounters in High School English: Teaching Literary Theory to Adolescents*. New York: Teacher's College Press, 2000.

Berger, Ronald. "Constructing the 'Jewish Problem' in Nazi Germany." In *Social Problems: Constructionist Readings*, edited by Donileen Loseke and Joel Best, 272–77. New York: Aldine de Gruyter, 2003.

Boyatzis, Chris J. "Studying Lives through Literature: Using Narrative to Teach Social Science Courses and Promote Students' Epistemological Growth." *Journal of Excellence in College Teaching* 5, no. 1 (1994): 31–45.

Chrisler, Joan C. "Novels as Case-Study Materials for Psychology Students." *Teaching of Psychology* 17, no. 1 (1990): 55–57.

Colby, Anne, Thomas Ehrlich, Elizabeth Beaumont, and Jason Stephens. *Educating Citizens: Preparing America's Undergraduates for Lives of Moral and Civic Responsibility.* San Francisco: Jossey-Bass, 2003.

Coser, Lewis. *Sociology through Literature.* Englewood Cliffs, NJ: Prentice Hall, 1963.

———. "The Visibility of Evil." In *A Handful of Thistles: Collected Papers in Moral Conviction,* 28–35. New Brunswick, NJ: Transaction Books, 1988.

The Danish Solution: The Rescue of Jews in Denmark. Written, Directed, and Produced by Karen Cantor and Camilla Kjaerulff. Singing Wolf Documentaries, 2003.

Denmark: Living with the Enemy. Part of the series A Force More Powerful. Films for the Humanities & Sciences, 2004.

Etzioni, Amitai. "The Good Society." *Seattle Journal of Social Justice* 1, no. 1 (2002): 83–96. http://www.gwu.edu/~ccps/etzioni/A296.pdf.

———. "Moral Dialogues in Public Debates." *The Public Perspective* 11, no. 2 (March/April 2000): 27–30. http://www.gwu.edu/~ccps/etzioni/A271.html.

Hughes, Everett C. "Good People and Dirty Work." In *The Classical Tradition in Sociology,* edited by Jeffrey Alexander, R. Boudon, and M. Cherkaou, 81–91. London: Sage Publications, 1997.

Jensen, Mette B., and Steven L. B. Jensen. "Denmark and the Holocaust." Danish Institute for International Studies, 2003. http://www.diis.dk/sw12080.asp.

Johnson, Mark. *Moral Imagination: Implications of Cognitive Science for Ethics.* Chicago: University of Chicago Press, 1993.

Joint Task Force on Student Learning. "Powerful Partnerships: A Shared Responsibility for Learning." *American Association for Higher Education with the American College Personnel Association and National Association of Student Personnel Administrators,* June 2, 1998. http://www.myacpa.org/pub/documents/taskforce.pdf.

Kanon, Joseph. *The Good German.* New York: Picador, 2001.

Kidder, Rushworth M. *How Good People Make Tough Choices: Resolving The Dilemmas of Ethical Living.* New York: Fireside, 1995.

Loseke, D. R. "Constructing Moralities." *Thinking About Social Problems: An Introduction to Constructionist Perspectives.* New York: Aldine De Gruyter, 1999.

Lowry, Lois. *Number the Stars.* New York: Bantam Doubleday Dell Books for Young Readers, 1989.

"Resistance during the Holocaust." U.S. Holocaust Memorial Museum. http://www.ushmm.org/education/foreducators/resource/resistance.pdf.

Von Wright, M. "Narrative Imagination and Taking the Perspective of Others." *Studies in Philosophy and Education* 21 (2002): 407–16.

Werner, Emmy E. *A Conspiracy of Decency: The Rescue of the Danish Jews during World War II.* Cambridge, MA: Westview Press, 2002.

Using *The Autobiography of Malcolm X* to Teach Introductory Sociology

Brent Harger and Tim Hallett

INTRODUCTION

Sociologist Joya Misra has argued that the success of introductory sociology classes hinges on making concepts lively and "real" (346). This can be problematic, because many students find the textbooks that are associated with these classes to be intimidating and dull. Informal classroom polls and feedback on student evaluations support this contention, suggesting that students will avoid reading from textbooks if at all possible. A study by Jay Howard found that only 40 percent of students "Always" or "Usually" read a traditional survey textbook when paired with a reader featuring common articles (200), and Hu and Kuh have found that over 18 percent of college students are academically disengaged (555). Combined, these findings highlight the importance of using readings that engage students. Textbooks are unlikely candidates, and some scholars have argued that instructors and students would be better off if textbooks were abandoned altogether (Westhues 92).

In our introduction to sociology classes, we have found that applying sociological concepts to the events in a book that students are interested in reading and eager to discuss is an effective way to make sociology lively and real. While much of the sociological literature focuses on the use of novels, we argue that both novels and autobiographies can engage readers and provide students in a diverse classroom with a common ground for the application of sociological concepts. Novels and autobiographies also provide instructors with a level of flexibility that is lost in the constraining organization of a single textbook (Westhues 89–90). Moreover, learning to apply concepts to the characters and events in a book eases the transition to applying these concepts to the students' own lives and provides a basis for class discussion about topics that not all students have personally experienced. Not every student will have experienced poverty, for example, but all students can apply concepts relating to poverty to the experiences of a character in a book, and in doing so gain a better sense of the different social contexts that others face.

In this chapter, we make the case for using *The Autobiography of Malcolm X* to teach introductory sociology classes. While *The Autobiography of Malcolm X* is an autobiography and not a novel, we summarize the literature on using novels in sociology and compare this literature to our own experiences using autobiographies in the classroom. We then describe how autobiographies are particularly helpful for introducing students to the concept of the "sociological imagination" before highlighting this with an in-class exercise. Finally, we discuss student feedback and some of the drawbacks to using autobiographies and the extent to which these drawbacks can be mitigated.

THE USE OF NOVELS IN SOCIOLOGY

The idea of using novels to teach sociology is not new. Various authors have described using novels in courses ranging from introduction to sociology (Laz, Lena and London, and Hartman) to social theory (Gotsch-Thomson) and the family (Clear, Cosbey, and Hall). Recently, a novel titled *The Dancer's Gift: An Introductory Sociology Novel* has been written specifically for use as an introductory reading (Kennedy, Zusman, Schacht, and Knox). Given this body of literature, it is clear that one need not reinvent the wheel when deciding how to implement books like novels into course readings.

Importantly, the literature also notes some of the drawbacks associated with choosing a novel over a textbook. Chief among these drawbacks is the amount of time and labor involved (Westhues 90–91). Time is needed to read potential works before a selection can be made, and a considerable amount of effort is required to prepare lectures that tie into specific events in a book and to organize lectures so that each reading corresponds to a day of classroom lecture and discussion. Another downside is that students themselves will not have a desk reference for class concepts and definitions, necessitating that a portion of class time be dedicated to teaching, learning, and documenting them in note form. To alleviate this issue, we use a form of "guided notes" in our classes (Heward). Guided notes are essentially partial lecture notes that we make available to students before each class. These notes are partial in the sense that two or three words that are important to understanding each concept are omitted and replaced with blank lines. For example, our definition of human agency is "The actions of individuals or groups in society." In the guided notes that we provide to students, this definition is replaced with "The _____ of individuals or groups in _____." Students then bring these partial notes to class, where they complete definitions and add examples as concepts are discussed. By providing students with partial lecture notes, we allow students to spend less time copying word-for-word definitions and more time focusing on examples and class discussion, while ensuring that students who do not come to class will not have the same notes as those who do.

While using a novel may make class preparation more challenging (especially the first time), we feel that the benefits—such as increased student interest and the broadening of student horizons—outweigh the costs. Lena and London, for example, describe beginning their classes by having students read *One Flew Over the Cuckoo's Nest* as early as possible, helping generate "immediate interest and enthusiasm" among their students (125). In her family course, Hall uses the novel *A Thousand Acres* to connect course themes and allow her students to apply the knowledge they have gained about topics such as family violence (370–71). Fitzgerald argues that novels allow students to gain a greater understanding of other cultures, stating that students "can learn and understand the basic sociological concepts while discovering how a people live and why they make certain choices" (244). These types of benefits have prompted us to exclude textbooks from our own introduction to sociology classes. Because events in novels often build on one another, we feel that novels can help students better understand complex issues such as racism. Rather than a single example of racism, then, students can see the way that one instance of racism affects a character's opinion toward another instance of racism, helping students to see the way that the social structure of racism is affected by individuals and, at the same time, constrains the options available to those individuals.

BEYOND NOVELS: AUTOBIOGRAPHIES IN THE CLASSROOM

While much of the sociological literature on using novels in the classroom focuses on specific books that can be used with specific courses, Hill provides instructors with suggested criteria for choosing a "sociologically useful" novel (39–40). Instructors, Hill argues, should find books that describe an array of major social institutions; represent diverse groups through well-defined characters; illustrate processes of social change, cooperation, and/or conflict; and utilize actual historical situations and events. In light of these criteria, we argue that autobiographies, in addition to novels, can be highly effective teaching tools.

The use of autobiographies is not unprecedented. Clear, for example, provides a list of fictional, biographical, and autobiographical works that are useful for teaching the sociology of family (218). A footnote to this work states:

While technically biography is outside the field of imaginative literature, Professor Clear could not be persuaded to distinguish between novels and biographies except by asterisks, which he reluctantly added to nonfiction items in his reading list. Since the line between modern novels and highly moving autobiographies is indeed at times a fine one, editorial yielding on the point will perhaps be forgiven by our readers. (217)

Clear recognizes that autobiographies, like novels, present students with interesting characters whose lives can be examined from a sociological perspective.

We argue that autobiographies are ideal teaching tools because sociology requires students to examine the intersections of human behavior with large-scale social structures and institutions in a way that they have likely never considered. Reading about real people and events helps to provide a concrete basis for students to see the world through the lens of sociology and to increase their levels of understanding. Discussing the effects of poverty on a character in a work of fiction, however compelling, may lead students to dismiss the relevance of social structures such as the economy or the education system on the basis that it is just "made up" by an author. The autobiography of a noted historical figure that lived through poverty, on the other hand, provides a concrete connection to the topic and allows for further contextualization through other historical information such as newspaper and magazine articles or documentary films. This contextualization, coupled with autobiographical description, fits Misra's argument that we need to make concepts "real" to students.

Autobiographies and the Sociological Imagination

Making concepts such as class, race, and gender real is only a small part of what we hope to accomplish in teaching introduction to sociology. Our overarching goal is to teach students to think sociologically and become, by the end of the semester, elementary sociologists in practice. This involves getting them to see the connections between social structures and the actions of individuals in society, what C. Wright Mills calls the sociological imagination. To quote Mills:

> The sociological imagination enables us to grasp history and biography and the relations between the two within society ... It is the capacity to range from the most impersonal and remote transformations to the most intimate features of the human self—and to see the relations between the two. (6–7)

The sociological imagination is a recognition that an individual's outcomes in life are not based solely on that individual's qualities. Rather, individuals are shaped by social structures just as the actions of individuals shape social structures. Mills provides unemployment as an example, noting the difference between one unemployed citizen in a city of 100,000 and 15 million unemployed citizens in a nation of 50 million. While the situation of the former may rightly be due to individual qualities, the situation of the latter is much more likely to be the result of the structure of opportunities, such as the economic and political institutions in a society.

In our classrooms, we use autobiographies to help students see the interplay between social structures and the agency of individuals. Like Mills, we view this interplay as the heart of sociology. For many students, seeing things in this way is difficult. Because American society privileges the ideology of the individual over a holistic knowledge of the social whole, thinking with the sociological imagination often seems "unnatural" to students. Using autobiographies to prompt students to think about the social whole instead of individual parts is a useful means to make thinking with the sociological imagination more natural and "real." The goal of our introduction to sociology classes is to use autobiographies to help students acquire the sociological imagination by examining the lives, experiences, and social contexts of the authors.

THE AUTOBIOGRAPHY OF MALCOLM X

In our classes, we have found that *The Autobiography of Malcolm X* is an especially useful means to teach the sociological imagination. As a starting point, *The Autobiography of Malcolm X* is a captivating, well-written book. Even before the students turn a page, the book piques their curiosity because, though they often know that Malcolm X was somehow controversial and that Spike Lee made a movie about him, they know little or nothing about who he really was, what he did, and why. *The Autobiography of Malcolm X* is ideal for sociology because it is partly a story about individual transformation and change—Malcolm journeys from a rural hick to an urban hipster to a hustler, incarcerated criminal, minister in the Nation of Islam, pilgrim and follower of Orthodox Islam, and finally a Civil Rights leader—but it is also a story about the social structures that enabled and constrained this individual journey—institutional racism, the criminal justice system, religion, and social movements.

The actions and experiences of Malcolm X necessitate looking past the individual to see the social structures at work in the background, and the controversial nature of his life forces students to question their assumptions about society and their (typically privileged) positions in society. Early in the semester, we make a point of stating that students are not required to *agree* with Malcolm's worldview. Students are, however, required to think sociologically in an attempt to *understand why* Malcolm's experiences with social institutions prompted him to act and think as he did, and in turn, how his actions and thoughts transformed society.

To demonstrate the utility of *The Autobiography of Malcolm X*, we now discuss one of the (many) highly salient excerpts from the book and how we use it in class. During Malcolm's youth, one particular encounter with a teacher had a large impact on his life. Malcolm was in seventh grade at a school in Lansing, Michigan, where he was one of the only African American students. Nonetheless, Malcolm was among the best students in the school, was popular and well-liked, and was even voted class president. We quote this excerpt at length, as to best illustrate how we use it in class:

Somehow I happened to be alone in the classroom with Mr. Ostrowski, my English teacher ... I had gotten some of my best marks under him, and he had always made me feel that he liked me. He was, as I have mentioned, a natural-born "advisor," about what you ought to read, to do, or think—about any and everything ...

I know that he probably meant well in what he happened to advise me that day. I doubt that he meant any harm. It was just in his nature as an American white man. I was one of his top students, one of the school's top students—but all he could see for me was the kind of future "in your place" that almost all white people see for black people.

He told me, "Malcolm, you ought to be thinking about a career. Have you been giving it thought?"

The truth is, I hadn't. I never had figured out why I told him, "Well, yes, sir, I've been thinking I'd like to be a lawyer." Lansing certainly had no Negro lawyers—or doctors either—in those days, to hold up an image I might have aspired to. All I really knew for certain was that a lawyer didn't wash dishes, as I was doing.

Mr. Ostrowski looked surprised ... He kind of half-smiled and said, "Malcolm, one of life's first needs is for us to be realistic. Don't misunderstand me, now. We all here like you, you know that. But you've got to be realistic about being a nigger. A lawyer—that's no realistic goal for a nigger. You need to think about something you *can* be. You're good with your hands—making things. Everybody admires your carpentry shop work. Why don't you plan on carpentry? People like you as a person—you'd get all kinds of work."

The more I thought afterwards about what he said, the more uneasy it made me. ... What made it really begin to disturb me was Mr. Ostrowski's advice to others in my class—all of them white ... They all reported that Mr. Ostrowski had encouraged what they had wanted. Yet nearly none of them had earned marks equal to mine.

It was a surprising thing that I had never thought of it that way before, but I realized that whatever I wasn't, I *was* smarter than nearly all of those white kids. But apparently I was still not intelligent enough, in their eyes, to become whatever *I* wanted to be.

It was then that I began to change—inside. (Haley 43–44)

We begin the class exercise by having two students read this excerpt aloud in class. One student reads the dialogue from Malcolm, another student reads Mr. Ostrowski's dialogue, and the instructor acts as the narrator. (In the class exercise, we strike the offensive word "nigger" from the text, substituting it with "n—ger" and we refrain from saying it aloud. We also explain doing so to the class before the reading. This allows the class to recognize the historical context and the sensitive racial legacy of the word without using it in a hurtful way.) Next, we have the students form groups and discuss three questions: (1) Where in the excerpt can we see individual actions and decisions? (This is the class definition for "human agency.") (2) Where in the excerpt can we see the weight of society, things that are beyond one's immediate control but that exert a force on one's life? (This is the definition for "social structure" in the class.) (3) How can we understand the relationship between the two? (Thinking with the sociological imagination.)

The students are immediately able to recognize and discuss a number of individual actions and decisions in the excerpt, though they begin to do so from a limited perspective. They tend to focus on Malcolm and recognize the individual intelligence and hard work that led him to get some of his "best marks" in Mr. Ostrowski's class and to be one of the school's "top students." They also note Malcolm's effort and desire to succeed in school and become a lawyer. Finally, they note that, after this painful interaction, Malcolm "began to change." This interaction is prominent in the book, because afterward Malcolm decides to leave Lansing for Boston, embarking on a path that would lead him to a life of crime, incarceration, and eventually to the Nation of Islam and his controversial views on race before finally taking on the role of a Civil Rights leader.

At this point the classroom discussion slows until we ask, "Who *else* in this excerpt is acting in important ways?" Then the students begin to think beyond Malcolm and focus on Mr. Ostrowski. They note that Mr. Ostrowski belittles Malcolm by calling him a "nigger," and telling him to be a carpenter rather than a lawyer. The students are typically angered by this individual action, since Mr. Ostrowski supported the other (white) students, and since Malcolm *was* smart and hard working.

To prompt the students to think further about these individual actions, we ask, "What could Malcolm and Mr. Ostrowski have done differently?" The students comment that Mr. Ostrowski could have supported Malcolm as he had supported Malcolm's white classmates. They also comment that Malcolm, instead of leaving Lansing and embarking on a life of crime, could have stayed and continued to work hard to become a lawyer in spite of people like Mr. Ostrowski, or he could have decided that Mr. Ostrowski was "right" and tried to become a carpenter.

Once we have gotten the students to think beyond the actions of a single individual, we follow up with the question about the weight of society. In looking at the excerpt, the students recognize the social inequality that existed in the labor market at the time. Malcolm admits in his own words that Lansing "had no Negro lawyers—or doctors either—in those days." The jobs that were available for African Americans were menial ones, such as Malcolm's job washing dishes. These kinds of labor market effects were beyond Malcolm's (and Mr. Ostrowski's) immediate control. The students recognize that this entire excerpt took place in a school, and though Lansing was in the North, educational opportunities were still limited for African Americans, despite their best individual efforts. At the time, Malcolm could have gotten straight As and still been denied admission to a good college, making his effort to become a lawyer impossible, regardless of his own actions or Mr. Ostrowski's.

Finally, we talk about the connection between these individual actions and social structures. One of the interesting quotes in this regard is Malcolm's comment on Mr. Ostrowski: "I know that he probably meant well in what he happened to advise me that day. I doubt that he meant any harm. It was just in his nature as an American white man." By acting as he did, Mr. Ostrowski was acting under the weight of, and in accordance with, social structure. Mr. Ostrowski's words were cruel, and they reflected the cruel reality of society. In fact, it is through Mr. Ostrowski's actions that Malcolm *feels* the weight of social structure. By trying to become a lawyer, Malcolm was acting against the limited opportunity structure of that social era. However, in response to this negative interaction (and the social structure behind it), Malcolm gave up on the goal of becoming a lawyer. As he said, "I began to change." Ironically, though he did not decide to become a carpenter, by going to Boston and becoming a criminal, Malcolm was still acting in a way that reflected and maintained the limited opportunity structure that confronted African Americans. Fortunately, in the end, his actions as a Civil Rights leader went far in the effort to change this social structure for generations to come.

Once we have gotten the students to begin thinking with the sociological imagination, we use this excerpt to bring four additional concepts to life: prejudice, discrimination, racism, and institutional racism. The discussion involving these concepts and this excerpt is among the most lively and engaging of the semester. First, we define prejudice as "holding preconceived ideas about a person or group," literally to prejudge (Giddens 401), and we ask the students if they think Mr. Ostrowski was being prejudice. Because Mr. Ostrowski seems to hold onto a limited view of what African Americans can do ("A lawyer—that's no realistic goal for a nigger. You need to think about something you *can* be"), *despite* the fact that Malcom was a top student, the vast majority of the students in our class argue that Mr. Ostrowski did have preconceived ideas and was indeed prejudice.

Then we define discrimination as "behavior that denies the members of a group resources or rewards available to others" (Giddens 397), and we ask the students if Mr. Ostrowski was discriminating. The students soon realize that the key to this argument is the extent to which the support (in the form of "advice" and "encouragement") that Mr. Ostrowski gave the white students but not to Malcolm "counts" as an important resource or reward. Most students argue that this kind support *is* an important resource, the very type of thing that can help someone get into college and eventually law school. A smaller segment of the students argue that, because this support is "vague" and not material in nature (like giving or withholding an actual job), it is not discrimination. Throughout this discussion, what we are most excited to see is how the students use the concepts and the text to make arguments and think critically. We force them to be skilled in their arguments and to support their view, but we do not force them to interpret the excerpt one way or another.

Next we define racism as discrimination against the members of a racial group by a powerful other, or "a special form of discrimination based on race" (Henslin 210). The student's arguments in this regard usually flow from the earlier discussion of discrimination. If the students felt that Mr. Ostrowski was withholding important resources from Malcolm, the excerpt provides them with considerable ammunition to argue that this discrimination was based on race.

In discussing racism in relation to this passage, another interesting issue arises that involves "intent." Some students use the excerpt to modify the definition of racism to focus on intentional efforts. For these students, though they uniformly feel that Mr. Ostrowski was "wrong," they focus on Malcolm's comment "I doubt that he meant any harm." To these students, the larger issue is the limited opportunities provided to African Americans at the time, and not Mr. Ostrowski's painful advice to Malcolm. As instructors, we use this opportunity to introduce the concept of institutional racism, which we define as "patterns of discrimination based on race that have become structured into existing social institutions" (Giddens 401). The concept of institutional racism brings the class back to the earlier discussion of social structure, and the racial inequalities that had been built into the job market and the education system. Whether or not the students think that Mr. Ostrowski's actions were malicious, the students can see that Mr. Ostrowski's actions were indeed in response to, and effectively in support of, institutional racism.

Through exercises like these our students start to acquire the sociological imagination, and they are better equipped to read the rest of the book holistically. While this excerpt on its own does not reveal why Malcolm advocated the controversial views expressed later in the book, students can see this excerpt as one piece of a larger sociological puzzle that reveals how the social structures of racism and discrimination influenced Malcolm's thoughts and actions. By connecting Malcolm's experience as a child when his father was murdered by white supremacists with this interaction with Mr. Ostrowski and the examples of institutional racism throughout the book, students begin to see how social structures placed a limit on what Malcolm was able to become. They are better able to understand why Malcolm dropped out of school and gave up legitimate work for a life of crime. By making these connections, they are able to *understand why* Malcolm came to accept the Nation of Islam's teaching that "the white man is the devil" before he reversed his views in light of his experience with Orthodox Islam. They are also able to see how, over time, Malcolm's actions helped to change the structure of institutional racism, which limited his own life chances. Even though students do not have to agree with Malcolm's final view of the "race problem" in America, they are able to understand where that view came from and its implications for society.

It is through reading *The Autobiography of Malcolm X* with this kind of sociological imagination that students *become* sociologists. This interplay is developed further through the use of concrete examples from the 1950s and 1960s. Because Malcolm X was a real person, we are able to provide students with historical newspaper accounts of the events he describes in his autobiography and show video clips from his speeches. We are able to provide additional context to help students see how structure and agency intertwine not just for Malcolm X, but for all people, past and present. This approach is similar to those that Kaufman (309) and Hanson (235) advocate—that is, providing students with historical documents to demonstrate the impact of social structures on the lives of individuals—to help students understand the sociological imagination.

Once students have started to think sociologically, this thought process extends to essays, written exams, and papers where students further cultivate their sociological abilities. A short essay assignment, for example, might ask students to compare the social structures that Malcolm faced in the 1960s with those that African Americans face today, prompting students to make explicit connections between historical events, social change, and their own social worlds. This is reinforced when students take the first exam and answer essay questions asking them to examine a social structure such as the education system or the criminal justice system and discuss how it affects the actions and life chances of individuals. In a question like this, students may draw on Malcolm's negative and limited experience in the formal education system and compare this with how he educated himself during his time in prison, while reflecting that Malcolm's informal but extensive self-education was only possible after he had been moved to a medium-security prison that operated without bars and where Malcolm had constant access to an extraordinary library. In the final paper for the class, students are required to use course concepts as a means to think with the sociological imagination while comparing and contrasting their lives to the life of one of the main characters in one of the autobiographies that we read over the course of the semester. Despite the fact that the overwhelming majority of the students in our classes are white, most students choose to compare and contrast their lives to Malcolm X. The sociological imagination helps them to see that, although in many ways their lives are different from Malcolm's, everyone feels the weight of various social structures, and everyone acts in relation to those broader structures. Thinking this way helps students to uncover unexpected similarities to a radical black man living fifty years ago, and to think about their own lives in a richer, broader way.

STUDENT FEEDBACK

When asked informally at the end of the semester what they will take away from our classes, students commonly mention *The Autobiography of Malcolm X*. We have examined formal data from departmental student evaluations to determine whether students enjoy reading autobiographies as a part of the class. These evaluation data cover eleven class sections from the fall of 2003 through the summer of 2006 and contain responses from 560 students. In response to the open-ended question "What did you like most about this course?" 22.1 percent of students responded that they liked the readings most and an additional 6.1 percent noted that they liked not having a textbook. Comments in response to this question included one student who said, "I enjoyed the practical application—applying the sociology concepts to the real lives of different people across society." In line with this comment, another student noted that it was beneficial not having a textbook because students "could actually apply what we learned in class to readings and life." These comments support our contention that students prefer autobiographies to traditional textbooks as well as our belief that these books help students understand the sociological imagination.

In response to another open-ended question asking students to list any readings that they thought were valuable, 43.9 percent responded that they thought *The Autobiography of Malcolm X* specifically was valuable and another 15.1 percent responded that all readings were valuable. Combined, these responses indicate that 59.1 percent of students considered *Malcolm X* to be particularly valuable. Conversely, only 5 percent of students stated that they thought either *The Autobiography of Malcolm X* or all readings were unsatisfactory. In response to these questions about whether readings were valuable, one student stated that the "use of autobiographies [was] better than standard textbooks [and] made lectures more interesting." This student also noted that the use of autobiographies made it "easier to provide examples for terms." Another student wrote that *Malcolm X* was valuable "although I didn't agree about anything he said. It made me try to see things in other views." These comments also suggest that *The Autobiography of Malcolm X* is a particularly strong book for use in teaching introductory sociology despite the fact that students themselves might not agree with the words or actions of Malcolm X.

Considering how much student opinion tends to vary, with one student often enjoying an aspect of a course for each student who dislikes that same aspect, these results suggest that students do enjoy these kinds of readings and exercises. When coupled with the learning that we see in the essays, exams, and final paper, we are confident in our conclusion that *The Autobiography of Malcolm X* provides students with an excellent introduction to sociological thinking.

Drawbacks

While we believe that autobiographies are excellent tools to help introduce students to the sociological imagination, it would be naïve to think that there are no drawbacks, and it would be unfair if we did not discuss them. Among these is a problem related to the charge that novels are "just made up." While supposedly based on facts and actual events, we recognize that there is an amount of fictionalization involved in writing an autobiography. This fictionalization may involve condensing numerous secondary characters into one, changing information about individuals the author does not wish to identify, or simply fleshing out conversations that are only partially remembered. While we have never heard students use these criticisms, recent news stories surrounding James Frey's book *A Million Little Pieces* suggest that we may have to address them in the future.

To some extent this problem is mitigated by the fact that Malcolm X was a public figure, so book facts can be checked against those of newspaper reports and arrest records. In the classroom we acknowledge that Malcolm's perspective of certain events may be different than that of others at the time. By providing historical newspapers covering some of the same events, we invite students to examine differences in perspective without claiming that any view is "right" or "wrong." In many cases, students find that events in the book are depicted by Malcolm X in the same way as by reporters for the *New York Times*, supporting his credibility.

Another drawback to using autobiographies or novels is that some students simply do not enjoy reading. *The Autobiography of Malcolm X* is 523 pages and, though we break it up over a number of weeks, some students will lose interest. We try to decrease this problem by putting statements about the required reading in our syllabi and discussing it on the first day of class. We also note that reading fifty pages of an autobiography is generally more enjoyable than reading a thirty-page textbook chapter. Nonetheless, in a class of eighty students, it is not unusual to have ten students withdraw after seeing the required readings on the syllabus. Students who add the class late then face the challenge of catching up on these engaging but lengthy readings. And, like other more traditional classes, there are always students who stick with the course but react negatively to any sizable reading. For these students, we can only hope that our classroom examples and discussions will spark an interest that makes them want to do the required reading. We do believe that our classes have helped students who had not been "readers" to become so.

There are also drawbacks to using *The Autobiography of Malcolm X* in particular. Malcolm X continues to be a controversial figure and his statements are often offensive. Making disclaimers before embarking on the readings are helpful in this regard. However, there are always a handful of students who are unable to set aside their personal views about Malcolm X to see the bigger picture. Malcolm X's rhetoric puts the white students in our classes on guard. The defensiveness of the white students has the unfortunate unintended effect of making the minority students uncomfortable at times. We protect against this by emphasizing that minority populations are heterogeneous in their views, and as examples such as Martin Luther King Jr. attest, Malcolm X does not represent the views of all African Americans. Since minority students may be reticent to express their thoughts and feelings in this context, we do our best to informally gauge their feelings and to talk with them in less-intimidating contexts, for example, before and after classes and in office hours.

We do not want to overstate these challenges. They are real but infrequent, and if the benefits of teaching autobiographies did not outweigh the costs, we would have changed our approach long ago.

CONCLUSION

In sociology classes, the use of autobiographies provides the instructor with opportunities for increased flexibility and additional contextualization and provides students with a common ground for the application of course concepts and a potential bridge to the understanding of their own experiences through the sociological imagination. Class evaluations and informal conversations support our contention that students enjoy learning about sociology in this way. The added possibility for contextualization with autobiographies and the fact that they are based on a person's life experiences make them ideal for introducing students to sociology, because students in our classes are being introduced to ideas that may seem counterintuitive. In situations such as this, we believe that the more contextual information we can supply to support students' developing sociological imaginations, the better.

Autobiographies can help students take the first step toward thinking holistically about the interconnections of social structures and human agency in their own lives and those of others. And yet, in the literature about teaching sociology, autobiographies are largely ignored. One possible reason for the lack of attention given to autobiographies is their functional similarity with novels. Because many of the teaching methods, benefits, and drawbacks associated with novels also apply to autobiographies, instructors who use autobiographies can refer in part to the existing literature. Despite these similarities, the literature can benefit from further classroom experimentation and scholarship on the use of autobiographies and the similarities and differences between teaching novels and autobiographies.

Although we have discussed some of the drawbacks to using novels or autobiographies in the classroom, we believe that the included example of Malcolm's interaction with his teacher Mr. Ostrowski demonstrates the potential for learning that these books hold. At the same time, the detailed nature of this exercise shows the amount of time and work it takes to prepare class exercises without the support of a textbook. The question, then, is whether student engagement and learning are increased enough to justify the added time and effort spent on class preparation. For us, the answer comes both during the semester as we see students begin to apply the sociological imagination to the readings and at the end of the semester when students reflect on what they have learned. On evaluations and in informal conversations, students frequently cite *The Autobiography of Malcolm X* and the focus on applying concepts to real events as one of the highlights of the course, noting how beneficial these techniques are in developing their understanding of sociology. We have never heard a student describe a textbook as the highlight of a course.

WORKS CITED

Berg, Ellen. "An Introduction to Sociology Using Short Stories and Films: Reshaping the Cookie Cutter and Redecorating the Cookie." *Teaching Sociology* 20 (1992): 265–69.

Clear, Val. "Marriage Education through Novels and Biography." *Journal of Marriage and the Family* 28 (1966): 217–19.

Cosbey, Janet. "Using Contemporary Fiction to Teach Family Issues." *Teaching Sociology* 25 (1997): 227–33.

Fitzgerald, Charlotte D. "Exploring Race in the Classroom: Guidelines for Selecting the 'Right' Novel." *Teaching Sociology* 20 (1992): 244–47.

Giddens, Anthony. *Introduction to Sociology.* New York: W. W. Norton, 1996.

Gotsch-Thomson, Susan. "The Integration of Gender into the Teaching of Classical Social Theory: Help from *The Handmaid's Tale.*" *Teaching Sociology* 18 (1990): 69–73.

Haley, Alex. *The Autobiography of Malcolm X.* New York: Ballantine Books, 1992.

Hall, Kelley J. "Putting the Pieces Together: Using Jane Smiley's *A Thousand Acres* in Sociology of Families." *Teaching Sociology* 28 (2000): 370–78.

Hanson, Chad M. "A Stop Sign at the Intersection of History and Biography: Illustrating Mills's Imagination with Depression-Era Photographs." *Teaching Sociology* 30 (2002): 235–42.

Hartman, Cheryl J. "Enriching Sociology 100 Using the Novel *Things Fall Apart.*" *Teaching Sociology* 33 (2005): 317–22.

Henslin, James M. *Essentials of Sociology.* Boston, MA: Allyn and Bacon, 2002.

Heward, William L. "Guided Notes: Improving the Effectiveness of Your Lectures." The Ohio State University Partnership Grant Fast Facts for Faculty, 2003. http://telr. osu.edu/dpg/fastfact/notes.html (accessed August 9, 2006).

Hill, Michael R. "Novels, Thought Experiments, and Humanist Sociology in the Classroom: Muri Sandoz and Capital City." *Teaching Sociology* 15 (1987): 38–44.

Howard, Jay R. "An Examination of Student Learning in Introductory Sociology at a Commuter Campus." *Teaching Sociology* 33 (2005): 195–205.

Hu, Shouping, and George D. Kuh. "Being (Dis)engaged in Educationally Purposeful Activities: The Influences of Student and Institutional Characteristics." *Research in Higher Education* 43 (2002): 555–75.

Kaufman, Peter. "Michael Jordan Meets C. Wright Mills: Illustrating the Sociological Imagination with Objects from Everyday Life." *Teaching Sociology* 25 (1997): 309–14.

Kennedy, Meredith, Marty E. Zusman, Caroline Schact, and David Knox. *The Dancer's Gift.* Columbus, OH: McGraw-Hill Higher Education, 2002.

Laz, Cheryl. "Science Fiction and Introductory Sociology: The Handmaid in the Classroom." *Teaching Sociology* 24 (1996): 54–63.

Lena, Hugh F., and Bruce London. "An Introduction to Sociology through Fiction Using Kesey's *One Flew Over the Cuckoo's Nest.*" *Teaching Sociology* 6 (1979): 123–31.

Mills, C. Wright. *Sociological Imagination.* New York: Oxford University Press, 1959.

Misra, Joya. "Integrating 'The Real World' into Introduction to Sociology: Making Sociological Concepts Real" *Teaching Sociology* 28 (2000): 346–63.

Westhues, Kenneth. "Transcending the Textbook World." *Teaching Sociology* 19 (1991): 87–92.

Stories in Psychology: Sensation and Perception

Alexis Grosofsky

Psychology may be one of the first disciplines to come to mind when considering using literature in classes other than those one would find in an English department. It certainly seems to be a logical fit—what could be more appropriate than learning about human behavior by reading about it? A search of the literature, however, does not reveal much. This could mean that not many psychologists are using literature in their courses or it could mean that, while being incorporated into courses, few write articles detailing the pedagogical use of such material.

My review of the literature revealed approximately twenty articles or chapters devoted to the use of literature in psychology. Of those, over half were about the use of literature in clinical, personality, or psychiatry courses. This is consistent with the results of a survey of psychology and literature courses conducted by Lyle Grant (1987). Grant found that courses incorporating both fields tended to be offered by English departments, relied on psychoanalytic theory, and had the goal of teaching literary criticism and interpretation. I focused on psychology courses incorporating literature rather than English courses incorporating psychology.

Joan Chrisler (1990), for example, described a writing assignment in psychology that incorporated literature. Students examined the main character of a novel, autobiography, or biography dealing with mental illness. The students described the symptoms exhibited by the main character, discussed the diagnostic label they would apply and potential treatment options, and identified which theory they thought best described the character's illness. Thus, literature served as a sort of case study enabling students to apply the material they were learning.

A similar approach was used by William Tucker (1994) whose article is titled, "Teaching Psychiatry through Literature: The Short Story as Case History." Students in Tucker's class considered what conducting therapy with the character would be like (for example, identifying the transference and counter-transference issues that might arise). Four other articles reported various related approaches. Some students wrote poems about the experience of mental illness as a means both of fostering understanding of mental illness and increasing empathy for individuals with mental illness who often are portrayed derisively in popular culture (Chrisler). Other students viewed feature films about "madness" taught by a psychologist and film historian (Fleming; Hiam; Piedmont) to investigate the influences of the medium of film on people's attitudes and perceptions of mental illness. The focus, again, was on literature as case study.

Others focused very narrowly on a specific work or specific author. Dana Dunn (1999), for example, used two of Wallace Stegner's novels (*A Shooting Star* and *Crossing to Safety*) to explore the subjective nature of the self. Students focused on issues of stress and coping with *A Shooting Star,* while *Crossing to Safety* allowed them to explore issues of aging and the longitudinal meaning of self. Dinko Podrug (2003) used William Shakespeare's *Hamlet* but focused on how characters responded to one another, rather than focusing exclusively on one character and how that character portrayed psychological topics as is common with other assignments.

With the exception of the poetry-writing exercise, these approaches used literature more as a case study than anything else. The other area I found with multiple references was the introductory course. Two of these references are quite dated, Harvey Katz, Patricia Warrick, and Martin Greenberg (1974) and Lita Schwartz (1980). The final reference is more recent (Stoddart and McKinley). The point of these seems to be one of illustration of multiple concepts through literature.

It would seem, then, that literature is used at the most logical places in psychology and is used primarily to allow students to apply the skills (for example, diagnostic) they are learning. Providing examples of concepts is the third main use of literature based on the extant literature. One could argue that clinical areas are the easiest places in which to incorporate literature. Can it be incorporated in other topical areas or for different purposes? There is so much literature available that it seems some creative thinking could yield additional possibilities for its pedagogical incorporation.

I found a few articles describing courses that incorporated novels/literature into classes other than those that were within the clinical realm (for example, personality, psychiatry, abnormal/disorders) or that were introductory in nature. These approaches are more related to what I have done in the classroom. Two authors incorporated literature to help students learn about gender stereotypes. Hilary Lips (1990) used science fiction in which gender as we know it does not exist to help students learn about the gender-based assumptions they are often unaware they are making, while students in Mary Crawford's (1994) psychology of women course read romance novels to uncover gender stereotypes our culture holds. Other authors dealt with developmental topics. Andrea Zeren and Nancy Lusignan Schultz (1987) used literature to discuss identity formation, while Suzy Gattuso (1997) used literature to illustrate gerontological issues.

I wanted to incorporate literature into my Sensation and Perception course. This course is one of the courses more toward the "hard science" end of the psychological spectrum. As such, students often are not looking forward to taking it. Sensation and Perception includes a fair amount of anatomy and brain pathway detail as we talk about how the senses operate. This type of material is not always popular with psychology majors. It is, however, one way by which they can satisfy our experimental cluster requirement.

I have been incorporating literature into my Sensation and Perception course for over ten years now. I do so for some of the same reasons others have mentioned: (1) having a novel assigned as class reading, especially in a non-English class, is often a rare experience and students appreciate the change in pace it provides from a traditional textbook; (2) students are motivated to read such books because they tend to be more accessible than traditional textbooks; (3) such texts provide a mechanism by which students can come to empathize with the experiences of those who may perceive the world differently than they do; and (4) paired with a text-related assignment, the novels help students approach material from a different perspective that is engaging while, at the same time, is relevant to the course.

My course goals include, among others, students understanding how the senses operate (in both normal as well as disordered functioning) and being able to see links between the material covered in the course and other areas (both within psychology as well as outside of psychology). Using literature in class seemed like a natural way to accomplish these goals.

I like to actively engage the students in my classes, and I accomplish this by creating opportunities for the students to "get their hands dirty," so to speak. Students in Sensation and Perception experience a variety of demonstrations illustrating various concepts as well as complete laboratory exercises. Some labs allow students to experience classic phenomena in the field (for example, the just noticeable difference in psychophysics, the two-point threshold in tactile sensitivity), while others teach students about particular senses by having them test their own abilities (for example, vision, gestation).

It was an easy step to add literature to my course to expand student opportunities to be actively involved with the course material. I will describe four areas in which I incorporated literature to give my students a better appreciation for the related material.

LITERATURE USED FOR VISION AND AUDITION

When teaching the sections about our dominant senses—vision and audition—I give students several choices of literature to read. The themes of the novels, however, are the same. Each of the books I use deals with a person who has some sort of disability when it comes to the sense in question. Students self-select whether they would prefer to read about vision or hearing. The books I have offered as choices for my students for vision include John Hull's (1992) *Touching the Rock: An Experience of Blindnesss* or Hull's (1997) *On Sight and Insight*. Both of these are autobiographical accounts of the author's experiences with losing his sight.

Students who choose to focus on audition select from Henry Kisor's (1990) *What's That Pig Outdoors?* or Bonnie Tucker's (1995) *The Feel of Silence*. These are also autobiographical books, but they deal with audition rather than vision.

In addition to reading the selected novel, students have an accompanying activity in which they spend a minimum of one hour experiencing diminished sight or hearing coinciding with the sense they selected. I encourage students to engage in everyday tasks such as going to the store rather than sitting passively in a familiar place (for example, their dormitory room) during their "observation." I ask students to pay close attention to the information they are able to pick up with their other senses and to be aware of differences between what they normally sense and what they sense when their hearing or vision is unavailable/diminished. Needless to say, I emphasize safety issues by telling students they should have a friend with them at all times during this activity to help watch out for them. Students who choose hearing, for example, are often amazed at how much they rely on hearing to determine whether or not it is safe to cross the street.

After students have read the book and done their observation, they write about their experiences and compare them with those of the author. They are prompted, for example, to write about any differences they noted in their other senses while one of their dominant senses was diminished. They are also asked to talk about whether their views of blindness or deafness have changed as a result of the experience. This is followed by an in-class discussion in which students share their experiences and observations. Students have found this activity so enjoyable and intriguing that some want to repeat it with the sense they did not originally select.

LITERATURE USED FOR OLFACTION

Student's read David Suskind's (1985) *Perfume: The Story of a Murderer* in conjunction with this unit. *Perfume* is a unique literary work because the entire story revolves around the sense of smell. The main character, Jean-Baptiste Grenouille, is a man who has no odor himself, yet is incredibly sensitive and gifted with it comes to identifying and creating odors. His primary sense is olfaction. Students grapple with a character whose main sense is so very different from their own. Students follow up their reading with a two- to three-page response paper. I give them a number of jumping-off points to help them get started with their response. I ask them to consider, for example, (1) how the ideas in the book tie into theories and facts learned in class; (2) how the ideas in the book relate to other areas of psychology (or other disciplines); and (3) aspects (psychological) with which the student agrees or disagrees including an explanation of why the student feels as she or he does. Many students report becoming sensitized to smells while reading the book; some report that going to the dining hall becomes (temporarily) difficult.

I also recommend Chandler Burr's (2003) *The Emperor of Scent*. This is a novel about an olfactory researcher, Luca Turin, who is outside the mainstream. He proposes a theory of olfaction based on the vibrational properties of the constituent molecules (such a theory was proposed earlier and abandoned in favor of a lock-and-key theory). The book gives students an insight into the difficulties associated with research and publication. It is, in my opinion, a fascinating read (I may be biased, of course).

LITERATURE USED FOR INDIVIDUAL AND CULTURAL DIFFERENCES IN PERCEPTION

Edwin Abbott's (1992) *Flatland* is a time-honored classic first published in 1884. It describes the adventures of A. Square who lives in Flatland, a two-dimensional world. A. Square encounters Spaceland (three dimensions), Lineland (one dimension), and Pointland (no dimensions). In each of his encounters, he tries to understand the other world and to have the inhabitants of that world understand his world. Although the book is actually a work of science fiction about the dimensions of space, analogies can be drawn about how culture can influence perception. This exercise is similar to Hilary Lips's use of science fiction to explore concepts of gender. Students again write a response paper in which I want them to consider the perceptual assumptions they take for granted. Students learn about how the zeitgeist can influence work produced because the book contains Victorian ideas about the sexes, which some students find difficult to put aside.

LITERATURE USED FOR TIME PERCEPTION

I have assigned Alan Lightman's (1993) *Einstein's Dreams* in conjunction with this topic. *Einstein's Dreams* us a series of short vignettes about alternate ways time might work. The story is about Einstein as a patent clerk in 1905 Berne, Switzerland, and each vignette is a dream he has that describes a world in which time operates differently than we perceive it to operate. The small size of the book can deceive students, so I warn them that even though each vignette is short, each is dense and rich with possibility about what life would be like if time moved in that particular way (for example, circular, moves more slowly the closer you get to the center of town, and many other variations).

CONCLUSION

Student response has been overwhelmingly positive. Using literature in my Sensation and Perception class has met my goals. Students appreciate the change in pace; they are motivated to do the "nontextbook" reading, and they learn to appreciate and empathize with those whose experiences are different from their own. By pairing each novel with an assignment that ties the literature's content to the course material, the novel's content is made more explicitly relevant to the student. Students often acquire insight and perspective into their own sensory capabilities as a result of reading relevant works of literature.

WORKS CITED

Abbott, Edwin Abbott. *Flatland: A Romance of Many Dimensions*. New York: Dover Publications, 1992.

Burr, Chandler. *The Emperor of Scent: A Story of Perfume, Obsession, and the Last Mystery of the Senses*. New York: Random House, 2003.

Chrisler, Joan C. "Novels as Case-Study Materials for Psychology Students." *Teaching of Psychology* 17, no. 1 (1990): 55–57.

Crawford, Mary. "Rethinking the Romance: Teaching the Content and Function of Gender Stereotypes in the Psychology of Women Course." *Teaching of Psychology* 21, no. 3 (1994): 151–53.

Dunn, Dana S. "Interpreting the Self through Literature: Psychology and the Novels of Wallace Stegner." In *Activities Handbook for the Teaching of Psychology*, edited by Ludy T. Benjamin, Barbara F. Nodine, Randal M. Ernst, and Charles Blair Broeker, 4:362–65. Washington, DC: American Psychological Association, 1999.

Fleming, Michael Z., Ralph L. Piedmont, and C. Michael Hiam. "Images of Madness: Feature Films in Teaching Psychology." *Teaching of Psychology* 17, no. 3 (1990): 185–87.

Gattuso, Suzy. "Literature in the Teaching of Gerontology." *Australian Journal on Ageing* 16, no. 4 (1997): 186–87.

Podrug, Dinko. "Hamlet as Process: A Novel Approach to Using Literature in Teaching." *Psychiatry: Interpersonal and Biological Processes* 66, no. 3 (2003): 202–13.

Stoddar, Rebecca and Marcia J. McKinley. "Using Narratives, Literature, and Primary Sources to Teach Introductory Psychology: An Interdisciplinary Approach." In *Best Practices for Teaching Introductory Psychology*, edited by Dana S. Dunn and Stephen L. Chew, 111–28. Mahwah, NJ: Lawrence Erlbaum Associates, 2005.

Usefulness of *Lord of the Flies* in the Social Psychology Classroom

Douglas P. Simeone

As an assistant professor of psychology, I feel I am more fortunate than others who teach at the college level. My reason for this belief is that most of the material I cover in class is relevant to the lives of my students, making it more likely that students will be intrinsically motivated to learn the material. Still, as anyone who has taught can attest, teaching at any level is no easy matter.

Because of my background in educational psychology I am never completely satisfied with what I am doing in the classroom as it relates to teaching and assessing what students are learning. Like most instructors I am always looking for ways to improve. I believe in a pedagogy that goes beyond the use of traditional teaching techniques in an effort to enhance the learning experience of my students as a means to expand their overall knowledge of the course material. For example, instead of using a typical research paper in my abnormal psychology class, I require students to compose a story. Students are granted the freedom to be as creative as they desire when it comes to developing the storyline. Within the story, however, they must have at least four characters and each character must have a different psychological disorder. The students' grades mostly depend on how well they have integrated the symptoms of the disorders into their characters' behaviors.

It used to be that teaching at the college level meant an instructor, for the most part, came to class and presented the material in a purely lecture format. The instructor also answered questions posed by students and assessed what the students had learned. Over the course of time teaching became more of a challenge. Today's college students don't just want to learn; they want and expect to enjoy their learning experience (Lieberman, Knox, and Zusman). Okan suggests this can be problematic for some instructors, for obvious reasons. After all, most of us do not go into the field of education and become instructors with the goal of becoming an entertainer. Yet there is nothing wrong with finding and using techniques that keep the students interested and increase the likelihood that learning will occur as demonstrated through the use of various assessment techniques.

As such, it seems that more instructors at the college level are looking for ways to bring what might be considered nontraditional techniques into the classroom. One of these trends includes the use of novels in classes in which the only book typically used is the textbook chosen by the instructor. It should be noted that the use of novels as teaching and evaluative techniques seems to be on the rise. Today, in increasing numbers, teachers are using novels in a number of ways and at a variety of education levels, including the college level.

Some may wonder how the novel can be used as a tool outside of the English curriculum. Cantor suggests that novels, and other atypical books, can be used as a way to provide relevant material that increases experiential learning. Dressel's *Teaching and Learning about Multicultural Literature: Students Reading Outside Their Culture in a Middle School Classroom* has been used to help students learn about different cultures. Novels have also been used to help enlighten students about the act of bullying (Quinn et al.), as a means to opening dialogue about themes found in books that are relevant to students' lives, such as character identity and values (Bean and Moni). They have also been used as a means to make connections with mathematics (Wagner and Lachance), teach literary terms and techniques (Bucher and Manning), improve students' ability to better understand what they have read (Macy), and, increase student curiosity and their motivation to learn about topics relevant to that which they are being taught (Kostelecky and Hoskinson). Furthermore, novels have been used to help students gain insight into how science works (Herreid). Perry's *Teaching Fantasy Novels: From "The Hobbit" to "Harry Potter and the Goblet of Fire"* has been used as a means to address the Twelve Standards of the English Language Arts. The novel has even been used in medical schools for more than thirty years as a means "to 'humanize' the overstuffed, science-based curriculum ... [and to help in] translating critical reading skills to 'reading' the patient, obtaining moral knowledge, and acquiring patients' perspectives on illness" (Wear 169).

It seems clear that novels have a place in education outside of the English curriculum. I have found that novels can be used as a tool to help students learn about, and reflect upon, principles and concepts that are relevant to their classroom experience in an enjoyable way. I use one novel in particular, *Lord of the Flies*, in my social psychology class. It is used as a means of determining how well students have learned and understood the many social psychological concepts and principles that are found in this novel. This book contains numerous social psychological principles touching on, in one way or another, almost all aspects of social psychology. Because this is so, when used in an appropriate way, it is an excellent evaluative tool to use at the end of the semester in terms of measuring the degree to which students have succeeded in meeting the class course objectives. Some of these objectives in the social psychology class include understanding such concepts as perception, attitude formation, aggression, bystander apathy, attraction, altruistic behavior, prejudice, conformity, obedience, persuasion, and group dynamics. All of these concepts, and many others, can be found within the text of the book, some overtly and others covertly. In essence, I use the book to assess the student's ability to recognize where and how the various theories and concepts of social psychology are applicable within the text of the book.

Lord of the Flies is a fascinating study of human behavior. The story itself revolves around a group of young boys stranded on a remote island after their plane is shot down during a war. It tells the tale of the struggles they face to survive, their attempt to remain civilized and the ultimate failure of that attempt, and the subsequent reverting of many of the boys to a more psychologically primitive state. While fictional, the story explores many facets of real-life behavior as it unveils the darker side of the human psyche. Furthermore, the book explores the role one's psyche plays in helping to determine how one will act in a given situation. It is this look into the human psyche and behavior that makes *Lord of the Flies* a compelling novel to use in any social psychology class. Because the book contains numerous social psychological concepts that would be discussed over the course of the semester, I knew it could be used in some form as a comprehensive final exam for the class. The questions I had to ask myself were "How can I use this book as a final exam?" and "How do I present it to students in a way that doesn't overwhelm them?"

Interestingly, the idea to use this novel in class came to me as I was watching television. Though I was familiar with the story I never thought about using the book in my class until I came across the movie version. As I sat and watched, the plot of the story raced back into my mind. It was at that point that I realized there were almost too many social psychological principles and concepts within the story to count. It then dawned on me that the book would be a useful tool in class. I knew I wanted to use the book in such a way that students would be made to demonstrate their overall knowledge of the course material. I still, however, had to find a way for them to do so. Fortunately, my background in educational psychology helped me to resolve this issue.

Based on my knowledge of educational psychology, I knew that one of the most powerful things an instructor can do to enhance learning in the classroom environment is to develop a pedagogy that includes strategies that increase intrinsic motivation. I came to believe that this book could be useful in doing so. According to Harackiewicz and Tauer, intrinsic motivation "involves the desire to take part in an activity for its own sake" (851). Of course, students are also driven by extrinsic motivation; that is, motivation that is outside of the person, such as completing the class with a passing grade (Kostelecky and Hoskinson 438). Given that the vast majority of students who sign up for a class are hoping to complete it with a passing grade, I did not really have to worry about them being extrinsically motivated. The difficult part was finding ways to increase their level of intrinsic motivation. I did this by first having them complete a similar, yet different, project earlier in the semester; a project that would serve, in essence, as a test run for the final. This project is designed to increase the likelihood that students will ultimately understand why and how I am using the *Lord of the Flies* and how it is related to the goals and objectives of the social psychology class. This is important because, as Wlodkowski suggests in *Enhancing Adult Motivation to Learn*, people become more competent, develop greater degrees of confidence, and look forward to assessment procedures when the assessment is clearly related to the course's goals and objectives and when they are provided with feedback that is informative and helpful.

For the first project, a research paper, students are required to think back to a time when they were persuaded to do something that they did not want to do or that they knew they should not do. Students are then told that the paper is to involve discussion of the social psychological factors that led to their being persuaded to engage in the behavior they displayed. It is explained that they should discuss any and all relevant concepts and principles, such as the type of message that was used to persuade them, the role their self-concept/self-esteem played in allowing them to be persuaded, whether deindividuation played a role or if group think was involved. Students are required to research each specific concept they discuss, and to use their research as a means of explaining and supporting what they had written. It is stressed that the more connections students are able to make between the various social psychological concepts and their own personal experience, the better the paper would be, resulting in a higher grade.

At the time the assignment is given to the students, I also explain that this assignment is a precursor to what they will have to do for their final exam. I explain that for the final exam they will be required to read the *Lord of the Flies* and discuss as many of the social psychological principles and concepts that they can find within the story. I further explain that while the current project is an important part of their grade, as it will help demonstrate how much they learned up to that point in the semester, it is purposely being used as a way to better prepare them for what I will expect from them as it relates to the final exam.

More to the point, as it relates to increasing intrinsic motivation, the students are told that once they successfully completed the semester project and receive the appropriate feedback they will (1) have a better understanding of the social psychological principles and concepts they discussed; (2) see the relevancy of these principles to their own life; (3) have a better understanding, based on the feedback, as to what they could have done differently; (4) feel more competent and confidant about their ability to do well on the final because they already successfully completed a project that is similar in nature. Based on the comments students made after completing the project it is clear that some truly appreciated the assignment. They recognized that having completed the project they had a better understanding of what will be expected of them when they begin work on the final exam. While students tend to be concerned about the final exam when it is first assigned, many of them feel more at ease about it, and have more confidence in their ability to do well, because they already completed a similar project.

In reality, then, this project serves three major purposes. It increases intrinsic motivation for the reasons previously discussed. It also increases intrinsic motivation because it is a project that students see as being relevant to their own lives because it is about them and the experiences they have had. Just as important, it serves the purpose of being a preparatory task for the final exam.

As it relates to my use of *Lord of the Flies*, students are informed on the first day of class that their final exam will be comprehensive, and that it counts for 40 percent of their grade. More specifically, it is stated that after reading *Lord of the Flies* they will write an extended essay. Furthermore, the exam will encompass their ability to find and reflect on the numerous social psychological concepts and principles found throughout the book.

It is made known that there is a minimum of fifty-five different social psychological concepts or principles dispersed throughout the book. For each one they recognize, they must briefly mention the passage in the book to which they are referring, including the page number where the passage can be found. Students are required to cite the specific concept or principle that applies to the passage and explain or define those concepts. Lastly, students must discuss how it is relevant to the passage in the book. Student responses do not have to be written in the order described above. As long as the above is included in each of their responses, they will receive full credit for the particular concept to which they were referring.

Students are graded on the number of references made to social psychological concepts and principles and, more important, how relevant the concept or principle is to the passage to which it refers. They are also graded on how well they explain or define the concept they are discussing. They are told that if a principle does not meet any of the above criteria it will not count toward the total number of principles found. So while students might turn in a paper with thirty principles, it is possible that they would earn credit for less than that number. Students are also given the opportunity to turn in one entry ahead of time for feedback on what they have written. In doing so, they will know if what they are doing is acceptable. I have included, for clarification's sake, the following ideal responses:

The first principle I would like to discuss is called hostile aggression. Hostile aggression is the type of aggression that one displays when angry, and is done with the intent of inflicting pain of some sort. On page 71 Jack was guilty of displaying hostile aggression, using both physical and emotional forms. In the passage Piggy berated Jack for letting the fire go out. At this point, after others had already given Jack a hard time for letting the fire go out, Jack lashed out. He hit Piggy in the stomach and smacked Piggy's head, knocking his glasses off (physical). Also, Jack had every intention of humiliating (emotional) Piggy when he called him "Fatty!" Both of these, in my opinion, are clear examples of hostile aggression.

Another principle found within the text is social loafing. Social loafing can be described as the tendency for an individual to contribute less when in a group setting than s/he would if being held personally responsible for completing a task. Because it occurs in a group setting the person is able to do little, yet still benefit if the group gets rewarded in some way. This tends to occur because evaluation apprehension is low as it is the group's performance that is measured, not the individual's. Within the book social loafing occurs a number of times. On page 50, for example, Ralph is frustrated because, while he and Simon try to build shelters, everyone else keeps running off. He mentions how at the meeting everyone decided they would work hard until the shelters were built, but instead they all run off. Once the shelters are built the others sleep in them, reaping the reward of being out of the elements despite contributing nothing as it relates to building them. I believe this passage to be a clear example of social loafing.

Responses such as the two above will earn full credit because they meet all the necessary criteria. Both responses discuss a specific social psychological concept. They also mention the page number of the passage where the concept is found, as well as a brief description of the passage. Lastly, the response includes a discussion of why the concept is applicable to the passage cited.

Because I believe in using a comprehensive final exam as a means to measure students' overall knowledge of the course material, the final exam is worth 40 percent of their overall semester grade. I admit that the grading scale I use is still a work in progress. I continue to wrestle with what should constitute a grade of A, B, C, and so on, as it relates to the number of social psychological concepts found within the book. Currently, students are told that the paper they submit must contain concepts that are relevant to the passage they are discussing, and all concepts must being adequately described and defined. To receive an A grade on the final exam, students must submit a paper containing a minimum of thirty concepts. To earn a B grade, students must turn in anywhere from twenty-four to twenty-nice concepts. For a grade of C, the criteria is anywhere from eighteen to twenty-three, and for a D grade, it is from twelve to seventeen. Any paper with fewer than twelve concepts will earn a failing grade.

The use of *Lord of the Flies* has received positive feedback from many students who have taken the social psychology class I teach at Heartland Community College. Many of them find it to be a unique model for this area of study, while also understanding how relevant the book is to this course. While not asked to do so, students have written a number of positive comments about the final exam. I've included some evaluative statements made by students that are representative of their general perception. One student stated:

After reading the book *Lord of the Flies* by William Golding I was able to reflect back on my learned knowledge and terminology of social psychology and how it is displayed in the book. I found many places where different social psychological concepts and principles are defined by the actions, behaviors and attitudes by the characters in the book. The book is a good source for this exam because of the story told by the author and how clear the messages are presented in the text.

Other comments include the following: "I have noticed that there are near endless amounts of [social psychological] concepts." "This book shows how much social psychology relates to our everyday life. If there could be this many different events that have to do with social psychology in this 200 page book, just think of how much it can be found in everything that you do." "Something that I found interesting is that age does not play a role in social psychology. It does not matter whether or not you are a ten-year-old boy or a full grown adult; you can display any of these characteristics."

Perhaps these last two student comments provide the best evidence that the use of *Lord of the Flies* in the social psychology classroom is, in fact, an effective technique when used to demonstrate that student learning has occurred. One student said, "When I started rereading the book *Lord of the Flies* (after having read it previously for another class), I realized that I was reading it differently. I was noticing things that I had not noticed the first time I read it and I found it to be incredibly interesting. I really enjoyed this assignment because it forced me to understand all the topics I learned this semester and apply it to this book." Another student stated, "Although I have read and seen *Lord of the Flies* in a high school English course, it was way more enlightening and productive this time around. This book was soaked in social psychological concepts ... that emphasized one's overall comprehension of this course, and which I recommend for further final exam applications . . . fun but lengthy final."

My students are not the only ones to recognize the value of using novels as an evaluative technique. One of the college deans overheard a student talking about how I was using the book, and he made a point of complimenting me on what I was doing. Two division chairs also were impressed by the technique, as were a number of my colleagues. It is my hope that some of my colleagues outside the English department will also begin using novels in their classes as well.

To reiterate that which I believe to be most important, when used appropriately, Golding's *Lord of the Flies* can be an excellent tool to use in the social psychology classroom. It gives students the chance to demonstrate their knowledge of social psychology in a nontraditional way. When using a technique in this way, students can't rely on rote memorization as a means of demonstrating what they have learned. Instead, they have to apply what they have learned and demonstrate their ability to recognize the social psychological concepts at work in a way that shows how well they have integrated the material over the course of the semester. If students can demonstrate knowledge of social psychology in this way, I know that they have an overall understanding of the course material and can apply it to their own lives when relevant. By doing so, I know the course objectives for the class have successfully been met.

I would be remiss if I did not discuss why I feel it is important for students to read the *Lord of the Flies* as opposed to watching the movie. First, the book is the true version of the story. It is widely known that Hollywood has a way of taking liberties when it uses a book as the basis for a movie. Second, I believe that by reading the book students will inherently spend additional time reflecting on what they read in a way that allows them to make more sense of the material. Reading also gives them the ability to reread passages to gain a greater understanding. Last, it is much easier to make notes in a book for later review and use. For example, as students are reading the book they can write down the social psychological concepts that pertain to the passage they are reading. When working on the final, students will find it much easier to use these notes as opposed to fast forwarding and rewinding through a tape or DVD.

I plan to continue using *Lord of the Flies* in my social psychology class, though I will be using other novels as well. Some of the other novels I plan to use include Mark Twain's *The Adventures of Tom Sawyer* and *The Adventures of Huckleberry Finn*. Because of the success I've experienced using this technique, it is likely that I will attempt to incorporate novels into the curriculum of some of the other courses in psychology that I teach as well.

WORKS CITED

Bean, Thomas W., and Karen Moni. "Developing Students' Critical Literacy: Exploring Identity Construction in Young Adult Fiction." *Journal of Adolescent and Adult Literature* 46, no. 8 (May 2003): 638–48. *ERIC*. EBSCO. Heartland Community Coll. Lib., Normal, IL. http://search.ebscohost.com/ (accessed July 10, 2006).

Bucher, Katherine T., and Lee M. Manning. "Bringing Graphic Novels into a School's Curriculum." *Clearing House* 78, no. 2 (November–December 2004): 67–72. *ERIC*.

EBSCO. Heartland Community Coll. Lib., Normal, IL. http://search.ebscohost.com/ (accessed July 11, 2006).

Cantor, Jeffrey A. "Experiential Learning in Higher Education: Linking Classroom and Community." 1997. *ERIC* Clearinghouse on Higher Education. ED404948. http://www.eric.ed.gov (accessed July 10, 2006).

Dressel, Janice Hartwick. *Teaching and Learning about Multicultural Literature: Students Reading Outside Their Culture in a Middle School Classroom.* Newark, DE: International Reading Association, 2003. Abstract. *ERIC.* EBSCO. Heartland Community Coll. Lib., Normal, IL. http://search.ebscohost.com/ (accessed July 10, 2006).

Golding, William. *Lord of the Flies.* New York: Berkley Publishing Group, 1954.

Harackiewicz, Judith M., and John M. Tauer. "The Effects of Cooperation and Competition on Intrinsic Motivation and Performance." *Journal of Personality and Social Psychology* 86, no. 6 (June 2004): 849–61. *PsycARTICLES.* EBSCO. Heartland Community Coll. Lib., Normal, IL. http://search.ebscohost.com/ (accessed July 12, 2006).

Herreid, Clyde Freeman. "Using Novels as Bases for Case Studies: Michael Crichton's 'State of Fear' and Global Warming." *Journal of College Science Teaching* 34, no. 7 (July 2005): 10. Abstract. *ERIC.* EBSCO. Heartland Community Coll. Lib., Normal, IL. http://search.ebscohost.com/ (accessed July 10, 2006).

Kostelecky, Kyle, and Mark Hoskinson. "A 'Novel' Approach to Motivating Students." *Education* 125, no. 3 (Spring 2005): 438–42. *ERIC.* EBSCO. Heartland Community Coll. Lib. Normal, IL. http://search.ebscohost.com/ (accessed July 10, 2006).

Lieberman, Michelle, David Knox, and Marty Zusman. "Engaging College Student Interest." *College Student Journal* 38, no. 3 (September 2004): 477–81. *Academic Search Premier.* EBSCO. Heartland Community Coll. Lib., Normal, IL. http://search.ebscohost.com/ (accessed July 10, 2006).

Macy, Leonora. "A Novel Study through Drama." *Reading Teacher* 58, no. 3 (November 2004): 240–48. *ERIC.* EBSCO. Heartland Community Coll. Lib., Normal, IL. http://search.ebscohost.com/ (accessed July 10, 2006).

Okan, Zuhal. "Edutainment: Is Learning at Risk?" *British Journal of Educational Technology* 34, no. 3 (June 2003): 255–64. Wilson Select Plus. OCLC. Heartland Community Coll. Lib., Normal, IL. http://firstsearch.oclc.org/ (accessed July 10, 2006).

Perry, Phyllis. *Teaching Fantasy Novels: From "The Hobbit" to "Harry Potter and the Goblet of Fire."* Portsmouth, NH: Teacher Ideas Press, 2003. Abstract. *ERIC.* EBSCO. Heartland Community Coll. Lib., Normal, IL. http://search.ebscohost.com/ (accessed July 10, 2006).

Quinn, Kathleen Benson, Bernadette Baron, Janine Kearns, and Susan M. Swearer. "Using a Novel Unit to Help Understand and Prevent Bullying in Schools." *Journal of Adolescent and Adult Literacy* 46, no. 7 (April 2003): 582–91. *ERIC.* EBSCO. Heartland Community Coll. Lib., Normal, IL. http://search.ebscohost.com/ (accessed July 11, 2006).

Wagner, Meaghan M., and Andrea Lachance. "Mathematical Adventures with Harry Potter." *Teaching Children Mathematics* 10, no. 5 (January 2004): 274. Abstract. *ERIC.* EBSCO. Heartland Community Coll. Lib., Normal, IL. http://search.ebscohost.com/ (accessed July 10, 2006).

Wear, Delese. "Toward Negative Capability: Literature in the Medical Curriculum." *Curriculum Inquiry* 34, no. 2 (June 2004): 169–84. *ERIC.* EBSCO. Heartland Community Coll. Lib., Normal, IL. http://search.ebscohost.com/ (accessed July 11, 2006).

Wlodkowski, Robert. *Enhancing Adult Motivation to Learn.* San Francisco: Jossey-Bass, 1985.

Demystifying Social Capital through Zola's *Germinal*

Lauretta Conklin Frederking

INTRODUCTION

In Political Inquiry and Analysis, our undergraduate majors study different methods and tools for research in political science. While learning about the dominant theories within the discipline, and the application of particular tools to test theory, students consider the strengths and weaknesses of each technique. A prominent course goal emphasizes how political scientists select methods appropriate for different research questions. Within this goal context, students spend several weeks reading and discussing social capital as a current topic of interest in the social sciences. After exploring several alternative techniques to study social capital, and its relevance for political outcomes, students read *Germinal*. To understand social capital, literature provides a unique perspective that invites discussion of the merit of literature as a general methodological tool.

SOCIAL CAPITAL AND DEMOCRACY

Democracy is experiencing its zenith of popularity. Across political, economic, and social spheres the triumph of democracy, as a prescription for economic and political success, appears complete. The fall of communism introduced initial uncertainty, but then surprising convergence around transitions toward democracy. Former communist leaders embraced democratic institutions; competition between parties and the rise of organized opposition led to a rapid transformation from communism toward democratic capitalism. And more recent years reveal a globalized movement through the ongoing exercises of institutionalizing democracy in countries like Afghanistan and Iraq; countries where democracy and marketization seemed untenable given limited citizen and elite support. Certainly in the latter cases, the domination of U.S. policy in international circles has had a considerable and more transparent influence on the uniform direction of regime changes away from authoritarianism and toward democracy. However, whether following from or fostering a wave of democratization, the recent overwhelming and widespread acceptance of democratic ideals has occurred at the same time that the reality has remained little more than procedural democracy.

Participation is at the core of the democratic process. Through voting, organizing, and demonstrating, the democratic ideal maintains that political outcomes should be a reflection of citizens' preferences. While unable to reflect all interests, and even perhaps reflecting no one's particular interest, democracy supports the claim that people contributing to political decisions is a fundamental value and, most assert, a fundamental right. As so many countries approach the transition to democracy, there is increasing attention to the types or quality of participation most conducive to both sustainable, stable democracy and productive marketization. In this context, scholars as well as policy makers identify social capital as informal networks and bonds of cooperation—a type of participation that supports economic efficiency and political stability. Tarrow (1996) documents the pattern for policy makers and the countless comparative studies searching for social capital reinforces the pattern for scholars.

In terms of economic development, social capital enables individuals to forgo short-run gains in transactions. They can forgo contracts, avoid enforcement and measurement costs, and tap into extensive information networks. When competing against businesses compelled to incur such costs, social cohesiveness and subsequently the value of social capital (Putnam) increases; it brings a competitive edge that translates into higher profits and long-run success. Bonds between individuals sharing a culture can foster social capital and nurture this economic advantage. The literature on the relationship between culture and development is replete with studies focusing on informal connections and their impact on political, social, and economic development. Politically, social capital and its accompanying properties of cooperation foster participation, and primarily through this informal participation in the form of cooperation, democratic stability follows. With the explosion of countries making the transition to democratic capitalism, political scientists and economists renewed the study not only of laws, but also of cultures and communities potentially conducive to social capital that promotes democracy and at the same time maximizes economic efficiency and growth.

In sharp contrast with the overwhelming advocacy of social capital, there are the observations of its increasing absence, with predominant evidence coming from the United States in particular. In his more recent book *Bowling Alone*, Robert Putnam traces the alarming trends of nonparticipation. Altruism, volunteering, and philanthropy are decreasing simultaneously with a decline in civic participation, religious participation, connections in the workplace, and informal social interaction. Even beyond the United States and throughout the developed world, the percent who vote, participate in citizens' groups, volunteer, and organize is in sharp decline. Politicians, bureaucracy, media, schools, churches, and charities are not beyond the reach of a growing distrust in North America. Evidence suggests that the observation is sound for much of Europe and South America as well.

In response, social capital has become an extremely important area of academic study, with scholars approaching the comparative investigation of participation, community, and trust. While connected theoretically and empirically, there is an unresolved tension in the dominating literature between the prescriptions and observations about participation and democracy.

SOCIAL CAPITAL PUZZLE

Across the subdisciplines of American and Comparative political science, scholars share similar theoretical assumptions and observations of social capital. Political scientists studying American and Comparative politics also share a perceived importance of social capital for democratic and economic outcomes (for example, Bates, Figueiredo, and Weingast; Fukuyama; Levy and Spiller; Pagden). For Comparativists, measuring its presence or absence leads to generalizations about the possibility, stability, and sustainability of democratic transitions. Within American politics, studies monitor the decline of social capital as an indicator of the decline in democratic participation (authors addressing aspects of declining support for politics in United States include Lipset and Schneider; Teixeira; Rosenstone and Hansen). Both subdisciplines emphasize the positive qualities of social capital and its coinciding presence with thriving democracy. However, while Comparativists search for evidence of social capital and scholars of American politics document its decline, *how* social capital may rise and decline is strikingly absent from the conversation and weakens its explanatory purchase.

Identifying how social capital works requires study of individual motivation. Arguably, political scientists intentionally focus on the patterns of aggregate outcomes rather than explaining why individuals behave the way they do. In the history of the discipline we have settled on microlevel assumptions that permit our efforts to generalize outcomes beyond any one case. As with the discipline's dominant assumption of rational choice, for example, the merit of the assumption rests on its ability to cover the widest range of outcomes regardless of the particular preferences of individuals. However, it is precisely at this level of studying human connections underlying social capital that we are able to push beyond documenting the binary presence or absence of social capital. To explain the increase and decrease of social capital over time, within and across communities, it is necessary to incorporate the study of the causal mechanism creating and destroying it. Ultimately, motivation and preferences become central to any explanation, and fiction offers a unique perspective and the opportunity to address the issues through a different lens.

Literature is a methodological tool that sheds light on human behavior. In this case of social capital, Emile Zola's *Germinal* presents imaginary truths about both the emergence and decline of social capital. The observations carry relevance for understanding compatibility of social capital with particular economic and political systems. A study of *Germinal* unpacks the puzzle why social capital deteriorates, introducing limitations and possibilities of integrating social capital in democratic capitalist systems. Ultimately, the analysis suggests an alternative hypothesis and direction for future research. For students, this exercise of studying the novel to understand social capital provides a rich example of social science research: developing relevant concepts; exploring how other social scientists identify the concept; analyzing evidence to test the prevailing theories/ hypotheses about the concept; redefining concepts in light of new evidence; and developing new hypotheses.

POLITICAL INQUIRY AND ANALYSIS COURSE

Political science majors at University of Portland take a course that focuses on methods of inquiry and research. Students learn how to articulate debates surrounding different concepts, methods, and questions in political science as part of a requirement to write a survey of the research. Social capital is a teaching example in which students hear the debates, receive a model for organizing the debates (like the overview presented above), and then explore alternative ways to study its impact.

Political science has been built on an interdisciplinary foundation. The formal intellectual study of politics was born in sociology departments; and early scholars studied politics through a seamless web of historical evidence and philosophical possibility. Both theoretically and empirically, politics has always been inextricably tied to economics, and most recently, the discipline of political science borrows its dominant methodological assumptions and tools from economics.

Expanding on the interdisciplinary core, the American Political Science Association gives formal recognition to politics and literature as an annual participating subdiscipline at conferences. And increasingly, political science courses bring fiction into the study of political concepts, events, and possibilities. While lauded for its anecdotal narrative of political events and pithy insights, literature is invoked, though rarely as the central methodological tool for testing our social science explanations. To enhance its credibility literature needs to be subject to criteria defining the legitimacy of our other methodologies. Specifically, does literature provide the opportunity for analyzing existing explanations and can it produce new generalizable explanations in cases in which the analysis is testable? Because of its specificity of character, time, and place and because of its emergence dependent upon the imagination, literature poses a challenge. And because the particularities of any story are so dense, there is an immediate question whether social science should support literature as a tool for understanding political science.

A central question is whether literature provides insight and the possibility of generalization in a way that is at least as beneficial as other research methods. John Horton and Andrea Baumeister's edited volume *Literature and the Political Imagination* outlines the agenda for scholars who seek to integrate fiction into social science: "It is not merely that literature can provide more lifelike examples than the etiolated and simplistic illustrations typically employed by philosophers, but that it should help to shape and inform the very terms in which issues are conceived" (13). It is from this position that the conversation with fiction challenges existing claims about democracy, and social capital specifically.

Unique themes emerge from the imposed conversations between political science claims on the one hand and the novelists' observations on the other. Insights contrasting the assumptions or ideals of democracy, and the potential

290 THE SOCIAL, BEHAVIORAL, AND POLITICAL SCIENCES

realities of democratic institutions follow from the interplay between theoretical ideas and fictional examples. The novelists define, create, and capture preference formation in a way that emphasizes the universality of many of these preferences especially under different regime types, while simultaneously defining the particularities and contingencies of experience. A new perspective emerges from the conversation. Ultimately, the specificity of the particular characters, settings, and dialogues invites generalization rooted in the explication of human connections rather than political scientists' more typical generalization from observed patterns of behavior. The perspective of social capital challenges existing ideas of social capital in a way that is both generalizable and subject to further research, contributing to its conceptual value as a methodological tool.

A POLITICAL SCIENCE READING OF *GERMINAL*

In the introduction of *Germinal*, Tancock discusses the place of Zola as a scientific writer. According to his study of Zola, "Zola proclaimed that in the modern world the novelist, like everybody else, must be a scientist in the sense that like the experimental scientist he simply 'observes' phenomena" (6–7). As a self-proclaimed neutral and objective observer, Zola studied the relative influences of physiology on the one hand, and environment on the other. As part of what he called experimental novels, the truth of social problems can be portrayed only through self-conscious dispassionate presentation. Certainly, there remains the uniqueness of particular characters, but his ambition is to portray challenges and emotions in the most universal terms.

In *Germinal*, victims are more general than the exploited individual or group, and the guilty oppressors are within each and every one. In this way, Zola's novel is a story centering on the coal miners and the "hell on earth" that is their day-to-day existence with the industrialists who manage and exploit them. However, in his narrative, it is the humaneness of the industrialists that emerges simultaneously and in sharp contrast with their acts of exploitation and brutality over the miners. The miners are portrayed as vindictive, rapacious, and violent in their interactions with each other, making it difficult for the reader to embrace their victimization with empathy. Ultimately, a powerful theme arises, that of the universal entrapment of the capitalist oppressor and capitalist victim. Both groups are dominated, defined, and therefore limited by the "environmental" conditions of competition and inequality.

For understanding social capital the strength of the book is precisely its ability to capture the way in which human agency dissolves into this "environmental" condition that appears seamless and inescapable. It is this shift that depicts the destruction of human connection and social capital, into the condition of human domination and destruction of social capital. Although Zola is writing during the Second Empire and writing about the imaginary Montsou (Mount Penny), this time and space location is not central to the observations he makes. Indeed, at many points, he alerts the reader to the general pattern across rural France, which moves further, beyond France and French citizens confronting industrialization. From compassionate and cooperative connections rich with social capital, *Germinal* is a study of collective surrender to brutal, competitive, and inhumane interactions. An ineluctability becomes critical for understanding social capital. However, the inevitability highlights central and generalizable moments when humans surrender social capital for individuality. The complexity of the thesis on social capital emerging from Zola's *Germinal* rests in the fact that it is precisely at the height of social capital, in the form of political solidarity, that the process of destruction becomes inevitable. In other words, capitalizing or maximizing the human bonds that are the foundation for social capital sows the seed for undermining those very human bonds.

The novel opens with the Guillaume family, a family born and raised within the coalmine setting. In the early stages of puberty, Catherine works on the mine, carrying the coal from the seam along the haulage road. Miles below the surface, the workers are spread throughout the mine and like flies caught on sticky paper they hang precariously. Through Zola's narrative we visualize the tension of their existence. They are caught within the claustrophobic space of the mine. The conditions are deplorable, the work unforgiving, and it is within these conditions that the comradeship between workers is tenacious. While extensive and productive, Zola teaches us that the comradeship is not gratuitous. It is earned and learned. It is entirely self-serving as much as it serves others. It is contingent and conditional, and yet it is powerful enough to withstand many contingencies and conditions. In other words, the social capital exhibited by the miners is rational and it is the product of choice between and by human agents.

Circumstance and environmental conditions inform the self-interest underlying the choice. The choice of cooperation over competition is not inevitable and human agency is profoundly apparent. This is critical when it comes to later observations in the aftermath of social capital destroyed. Something about the new conditions after destroyed social capital suggests the inevitability of a choice of competition instead of cooperation. Indeed, something happens to make social capital impossible. Understanding the key to this transformation is the value of Zola's work in terms of our intellectual discussion of the theories and empirical possibilities of social capital today.

When a central character Etienne arrives from a neighboring village, he is half-starved and desperate for work. The Guillaume family accepts him into their team when it is clear that the grandfather can no longer work. Initially they are hostile toward Etienne for his inexperience and physical weakness. Their dependence on the amount of coal collected for their group pay compels them to consider firing him from the group at the end of the first day. But Catherine is the first to reveal the possibilities when "with her unembarrassed air of good comradeship" (56) offered him food, drink, and confidence to keep pushing through the misery and accepting "the brutal rule of the skilled over the unskilled" (55). Certainly, the relationship between workers and the company is uncomfortable, but nevertheless the criticism is tempered, "only held in check by the strength of the hierarchy—the military system which holds them down, from pit-boy to overman, by putting each in the power of another" (63). Discipline and familiarity keep them tied to the exploitative contracts. And desperation keeps Etienne hopeful for continued work.

Catherine's father immediately arranges for credit until payday and lodging, and then invites him into the community through the gatherings at the local pub.

During the first of many pub scenes, we see community in action and becoming manifest in social capital. Standing between village and the coalmine, everyone meets at the pub, and it is at this meeting place that the depth and breadth of connection between miners is apparent. Ma Brule curses the young man who impregnated one of the family's girls, and the pub keeper discusses financial stress of the coal miners and claims he has been giving away "more than six pounds of bread every day for the last month" (77). Within minutes Etienne is brought into the community. It is a community of endless gossip, but underlying the gossip between families is a form of accountability. No matter how severe the words, they serve to hold others to the consideration of community.

The next scene opens in the owner's home. And here too "the establishment was run on patriarchal lines, without formality, this little society lived together on friendly terms" (82). Though distinct, both are marked by similar comfort, support, and modesty. Monsieur Gregoire argues with his brother who sold out his mine shares. Since financial times are bad with the mine, the brother curses Gregoire for holding on in the face of cut-throat competition. In response to the accusations, Monsieur Gregoire summarizes his vision of the mine and its mission: "I like a quiet life, and it would be so silly to bother my head with business worries. As for Montsou, it may well go on falling, but it will always yield enough for our needs. We mustn't be greedy, you know!" (89)

It is clear that the Guillaumes live a continual cycle of dependency and urgency. Seeking charity Maheude travels to the Gregoire estate. Here she describes the crisis to Madame Gregoire: "You paid up regularly for fortnights on end, but one day you go late and that was that; you never caught up again" (100). Their plight is shared by the other miners and is sanctioned by the owner Gregoire, but it is created by the pervasive capitalist competition underlying the existence of them all. It is this competition that transforms shared beliefs of community into the social capital asset of cooperation, but in the process destroys community as the essential source of future cooperation.

Behind the initial comfort, support, and modesty of the parallel spheres, an underlying inequality defines the relationship between the two. Tensions between skilled and unskilled boil closely to the surface of all their interactions. Between miners, discussion of their circumstances becomes more common. It not long before Etienne, the newcomer, is speaking of contributing to a collective fund: "it would be wise to start off a mutual aid society that would be independent of their good pleasure, and at least we could rely on that for cases of urgent need" (153). As Etienne becomes resolved about the exploitation, he proclaims his goal throughout the community, promising that they can capitalize on their community bonds to create solidarity that will redress the inequities. "Like all recent converts who believe they have a mission, he was an untiring propagandist" (154) and, preaching the idea of a provident fund, he finds that almost everyone who listened soon joined his cause: "'Each member,' he was saying, 'could easily give twenty sous a month. With these twenty sous accumulated over four or five years we should have a nest-egg, and when you have money behind you are strong, aren't you, whatever happens . . .'" (154). References to justice provide legitimacy to begin formalizing the collective organization. In other instances as well, justice becomes the moral yardstick for decisions within the community: to encourage a difficult marriage take place, and to condemn the storekeeper who is reluctant to extend more credit. And so justice defines the fatal link between the community and the oppressors. Friendship evolves from a neutral value into a social capital asset to reach the miners' goal of overcoming the bourgeoisie. Etienne resolutely defines the new terms of friendship to a fellow miner: "'Yes, let's be friends. You see, I would give everything up, women and drink and everything, for the sake of justice. There's only one thing that warms my heart, and that is that we are going to sweep away these bourgeois" (162).

Whereas community had been defined by the overlapping of beliefs and connections, it is at this point that the connections between individuals become role defined and role separated. The shift is subtle but carries dramatic consequences. Between Catherine and Etienne, for example, there is an attraction. However, with Etienne's new convictions about exploitation and with his determination to mobilize the community toward the unified goal of overcoming the oppressor, their human connection becomes complicated: "he regarded her with a feeling of mingled comradeship and resentment which prevented his treating her as a girl to be desired" (163).

In the transition from community member to labor leader, Etienne's life gains focus. Actions and directions become almost entirely defined by his role as labor leader. And he begins to judge the community not as humans but as the necessary instruments for his mission. Their existence is no longer about the human connections, but rather affirming the oppression and exploitation of the bourgeoisie. "Their loyalty to each other was supplemented by this soldierly pride, the pride in the job of men who in the daily struggle against death have developed a spirit of rivalry in self-sacrifice" (250). With Etienne's growing popularity and the pressure on the owners to cut costs, a strike is the next step. And it is at this moment that the community transformed into social capital increases value, and it is at this moment that social capital begins to deteriorate the community, the very condition for its existence.

Conflict within the group corresponds to the organization of protest against the bourgeoisie:

In fact it was what always lies at the bottom of exaggerated dogmas: one man runs to revolutionary violence and the other, by way of reaction, to insincere moderation, and both get carried far beyond their genuine convictions simply because they find themselves cast for parts not of their own choosing. (236)

Roles replace people as the primary condition for interaction. Friends refer to each other as comrades and the quality of their relations both becomes more intense and less comprehensive. There is intensity of purpose and direction. Attention to each other beyond the defined goal, however, diminishes significantly. They have become instruments for each other by their own decision, and by their own determination it is in their self-interest. But self-interest has evolved from the goal of a life filled with interaction and social satisfaction toward a goal of overpowering the enemy. To be clear, the life condition was miserable and so the shift is entirely laudable. At the same time, there is inevitability to the sacrifice of community in the process of mobilization, and specifically mobilization through organization.

Just as the bourgeoisie have already reverted to blaming the competition for the worsening conditions, miners begin to blame the struggle for their violence toward the workers who refuse to strike. The need for solidarity becomes the lens that separates the man as worker from the man as friend. Friendship is now at the behest of the single purpose of solidarity, and solidarity as seen here is severely defined, limited, and ruthless.

The difference and consequences are profoundly illustrated by Catherine's will to provide for her starving family. Already the youngest has died, the grandfather is comatose, and another sibling is robbing to eat day to day. Catherine joins the scabs in spite of our knowing her most sincere, deep loyalty to the workers. Indeed, she is one of the most vocal and supportive community members. But weighing the survival of her family with the single cause of destroying the mining company, she chooses to help her family survive. In one of many wrenching scenes, Catherine is beaten brutally and publicly by her parents, as they essentially disown her. The strength of solidarity is demonstrated, but also the cost of that solidarity in terms of the human bonds that connected them all before the struggle. One must recognize that the community is at the height of its connectedness in terms of intensity and accountability, but the terms of that intensity and accountability are singularly defined, and therefore limited. Ultimately, capitalizing on solidarity means surrendering the multifaceted bonds that made the solidarity possible.

As a fascinating consequence of the emerging single dimension of interaction is that it makes legitimacy and morality less relevant except as it concerns the single goal. The miners care less and less what they do outside of the worker mission. Catherine is the single character holding onto the emotional connections as her barometer of virtue. All people and actions begin to be weighed by their contribution to the cause.

A final parallel scene with Monsieur Hennebeau sharpens the statement that interactions between people become more limited just as they become role defined. In one of the final scenes, Hennebeau realizes his wife's adultery. Knowing that his marriage for a long time has been a limited bond defined only by the commitment to live together, he nevertheless laments the betrayal by her sexual encounters. Connecting his marriage with the worker's struggle, he screams: "These starry-eyed revolutionaries could demolish society and build a brave new world if they liked, but they would not by so doing add one single joy to man's lot, not relief him of a single pain merely by sharing out the cake" (339). Instead, they will join the bourgeoisie in the clamor for a version of success that depends on the suppression of others. And in the process, they will surrender the joy of community for the joy of more bread, better wages, and power, albeit defined and limited, but nevertheless power over others.

In the final days, the miner's wife, who is most reluctant to combat the company, becomes a powerful illustration of the transformation:

She was so different that she did not seem the same woman; she had been so sensible and used to blame him for being violent, saying that one ought never to wish for

anyone's death, and now she was refusing to listen to reason and talking of killing people. Instead of himself it was she who was talking politics, wanting to sweep the bourgeois away at one blow, demanding the republic and the guillotine to rid the earth of
these wealthy robbers grown fat on the toil of the starving masses.... Her words fell like
axe strokes in the darkness. The closed horizon had refused to open for her, and the unre-
alizable ideal was turning to poison in this brain crazed by grief. (377)

As the mobilizing organizes around the principle of overthrowing the bourgeois,
it becomes increasingly clear that the miners do not want a new order, but much
more simply they want to reverse positions of the old order. The fight leaves
their single goal unaccomplished, but much more severely, the fight leaves their
humanity, their community "utterly broken" (421). The workers savagely dis-
member the owner and then destroy the mine itself, knowing that potentially
hundreds will die a slow suffocating death below.

RECONCEPTUALIZING SOCIAL CAPITAL AND DEMOCRATIC CAPITALISM

Guided class discussion with students encourages consideration of *Germinal*
within the context of social capital. While other scholars approach the study of
social capital in effective ways, there is a prevailing view of social capital as a
good thing, The novel captures a perspective of social capital by psychologically
and sociologically tracing its initial emergence from community and then
explaining its deterioration. As community begins to generate social capital, it
uncompromisingly begins to undermine the very community that is social capital's foundation. Study of the novel suggests complexity and challenges the prevailing assumption of positive outcomes attached to social capital. It is the shift
from community to social capital that transforms human relationships into
human utility, and community cooperation into labor solidarity. The shift from
community to goal orientation increases the value of social capital, but also
seems to destroy its source.

With the increase in social capital, as described in *Germinal*, there is a
simultaneous and inevitable deterioration of its foundation, community. Ultimately, capitalizing on social capital destroys its potential value in the future.
This generalized claim is counter to the interpretation that "those who have
social capital tend to accumulate more" (Putnam 169), and according to Cole-
man, that these are "resources whose supply increases rather than decreases
through use and which become deplete if not used" (as described by Putnam
169). Without defining a mechanism that explains its rise as well as its decline,
scholars may be settling on an incomplete version of social capital. Zola's narrative emphasizes the emergence of a collective goal and subsequently the role
definition and the role delineation of miners' interaction. This shift takes place
as soon as the miners decide to mobilize and specifically organize their mobilization against the oppressor. Defining an enemy, and sharing experiences of
oppression by the enemy, brought them together in community, but it is the decision to eliminate the enemy that brings them together in solidarity, newly
focused and newly defined into instruments of their goal rather than brothers and
sisters of their community.

Both democracy and capitalism incorporate the ideal of participation. However, for both democracy and capitalism the attainment, but even more profoundly the practice of participation, depends on organization. To the extent that either or both forces bring organization, they introduce clearly defined goals that become the organization's mission; the mission decides the focus for interaction between members or participants of the organization. It is this organization or institutionalization that more generally disaggregates the community, and the individuals within the community, into different roles for different activities. Within the institution, there is accountability; beyond the specific role and mission, however, individuals lose relevance to one another. As with Zola's miners, the purpose of their organizing can include intense solidarity, but it is a limited association. Indeed, just like Zola's characters, individuals in democratic institutions are much more like instruments for the particular political goal, rather than participants in a democratic community.

Another extension of Zola's insights is the relevance of authoritarianism or oppression for bringing individuals together in a cooperative way. The exploitative conditions experienced by the miners brought them together for mutual support both economically and socially. It is under the authoritarian system that community flourishes and it is at the moments of rebellion within the authoritarian system that social capital is at its zenith. This poses a critical challenge to all political scientists advocating social capital as the vehicle for fostering stable and sustainable democratic capitalism. And for political scientists who conflate solidarity as social capital, Zola highlights how at the very point when it becomes solidarity, social capital is being undermined by the erosion of community. Indeed, if democracy follows from rebellion against an authoritarian regime, for example, this new conceptualization of social capital suggests that the act of rebellion itself undermines social capital. And so it may be that social capital pushes the community away from authoritarianism and toward democracy, but this movement and then the consolidation of democracy, through institutions and formal mechanisms for participation, destroys community—the precondition for social capital. It may be unsettling, but also compelling, to consider a different perspective of social capital. The emerging claim that challenges both prevailing theoretical and prescriptive views of social capital is that social capital may create democracy. However, the very process of institutionalization through democratization and marketization undermines social capital.

From the analysis, students consider the claim that while authoritarian settings may limit formal participation in elections and limit participation in institutions that are part of the political system, they simultaneously can foster informal participation and cooperation more conducive to the benefits associated with social capital. When the value of social capital reaches its zenith in terms of cooperative outcomes, it simultaneously approaches its greatest challenges. It is here that social capital confronts an inevitable decline. From this perspective, the cultivation of social capital toward the goals of democracy and capitalism may be misdirected. Similarly, the scholarly search for social capital as the leading force of stable democratic capitalism is missing the crucial part of the explanation of social capital and its role in transitions.

CONCLUSION

Students complete this section of the course with an understanding of literature as a tool to analyze concepts and hypotheses in political science. More generally, they understand the process of social science research: craft hypotheses, survey existing research, develop concepts, collect evidence, analyze evidence, revisit hypothesis, and generate new hypothesis. Literature is particularly effective in providing evidence about human behavior and motivation. Social scientists can rigorously treat the fictional truths as evidence to test existing hypotheses and concepts. Another effective way to use the fictional material is through thought experiments, developing hypotheses and alternative ideas to counter existing claims. As with the example of social capital and *Germinal,* the analysis of fiction leads to new hypotheses, to different understandings of prevailing conceptualizations and relationships, and possibly to more accurate generalizations.

WORKS CITED

Bates, Robert H., Rui J. P. De Figueiredo, Jr., and Barry R. Weingast. "The Politics of Interpretation: Rationality, Culture, and Transition." *Politics and Society* 26, no. 4 1998): 603–42.

Fukuyama, Francis. *Trust The Social Virtues and the Creation of Prosperity*. New York: Free Press, 1995.

Horton, John, and Andrea T. Baumeister, eds. *Literature and the Political Imagination*. London: Routledge, 1996.

Levy, Brian, and Pablo R. Spiller, eds. *Regulations, Institutions, and Commitment*. Cambridge: Cambridge University Press, 1996.

Lipset, Seymour Martin, and William Schneider. *The Confidence Gap*. New York: Free Press, 1987.

Pagden, Anthony. "The Destruction of Trust and Its Economic Consequences in the Case of Eighteenth-Century Naples." In *Trust: Making and Breaking of Cooperative Relations,* edited by Diego Gambetta, 49–72. Oxford: Basil Blackwell, 1988.

Putnam, Robert. *Bowling Alone*. New York: Simon & Schuster, 2000.

———. *Making Democracy Work: Civic Traditions in Modern Italy*. Princeton, NJ: Princeton University Press, 1993.

Rosenstone, Steven J., and John Mark Hansen. *Mobilization, Participation and Democracy in America*. New York: Macmillan, 1993.

Tancock, L. W. Introduction. In *Germinal*, by Emile Zola. Baltimore: Penguin Books, 1954.

Teixeira, Ruy A. *The Disappearing American Voter*. Washington, DC: The Brookings Institute, 1992.

University of Pennsylvania Law Review. Symposium *Law, Economics, and Norms*. 1996.

Zola, Emile. *Germinal*, translated by L. W. Tancock. Baltimore: Penguin Books, 1954.

TEACHING THE NOVEL IN PROFESSIONAL STUDIES

The Use of Contemporary Novels as a Method of Teaching Social Work Micropractice

Pamela Black and Marta M. Miranda

INTRODUCTION

The profession of social work is rooted in liberal arts education; therefore, the novel genre is a likely vehicle for the pedagogical demands of integrating knowledge and skills in the provision of human services. The Council on Social Work Education (CSWE) is the accrediting body for social work education programs, and their educational standards are infused throughout the social work curriculum. The goal of social work education is to develop generalist practitioners who need a broad base of knowledge and a wide range of skills to address a variety of issues and problems. The social work curriculum practice sequence must identify the problems facing populations at risk and address social and economic justice issues. The authors use various contemporary novels to teach beginning social work practice at a regional comprehensive university.

The epistemology of social work theory and practice integrates theoretical frameworks from many disciplines, including biology and human development, behavioral sciences, sociology, psychology, anthropology, and political science. The professional social work curriculum also includes strong institutional and organizational components with specific focus on the assessment and intervention of social and economic justice issues. Social work practice is the application of knowledge and social work values and ethics to the processes of helping individuals, families, groups or communities (NASW 1). The primary practice components are assessment, intervention, and evaluation. Due to the professional nature of social work education, the practice sequence also has a strong skill development component. Therefore, the practice courses include both theoretical and methods/laboratory classes. The learning objectives and assignments discussed in this chapter are taught in the introductory practice theory course and its concurrent laboratory methods section.

The professional preparation of the students as generalist social workers demands the ability to apply critical-thinking skills to social and psychological problems at both private and public issue levels. The practice sequence challenges the students to move toward professionalism by encouraging self-awareness and self-understanding, the application of previous knowledge base, and the attainment of skills necessary to assist diverse client populations in a variety of settings. To accomplish this comprehensive set of learning objectives, the students must be able to identify the interactional factors within multidimensional systems. The narrative and characters in the novel give students their first exposure to the complex situations that affect clients. The characters become their first clients; their psychological characteristics, their social networks, and their communities bring the reality of human diversity, suffering, and resilience to the classroom.

The evidence of institutional and societal factors that interact and often serve to create or solve the client's problems is often a challenge for students to identify; the story allows for students to grapple with the multidimensional components of client situations and allows them to practice assessment and intervention in a nonthreatening and safe manner. Through the characters/clients, the students try on their hypothesis of the problems and solutions and experiment with possible interventions that may create positive change.

PURPOSE AND APPLICATION OF THE NOVEL

The novels expose students to different scenarios, situations, and characters that challenge their personal worldviews and demand that they address personal biases that may impede the helping relationship. We all have a certain worldview that has been shaped by our culture and background. The social worker's view of how problems are solved, who to go to for help, and how to begin the helping process may differ greatly from that of the clients. Social workers must recognize and understand how these differences may hinder or enhance the professional working relationship with their clients.

The following are specific examples of the content areas that are covered in the practice sequence by the inclusion of the novel and the rationale for using the novel to address crucial social work practice issues.

CULTURAL COMPETENCY AND DIVERSITY

The National Association of Social Workers has created standards for cultural competence in social work practice. These standards of practice charge social workers with the ethical responsibility to becoming cultural competent service providers (NASW 7). The increased population growth naturally creates a demand for social workers to be prepared to work in a diverse society and to infuse a global perspective in their service delivery. This starts with self-awareness of their culture and exploring possible cultural biases that may interfere in working effectively with other cultures. Becoming culturally competent is an ongoing process that begins with self-awareness, acceptance, and valuing diversity. Through the use of the novels, students are introduced to a diversity of clients. Students may live in areas with little diversity in regards to race, culture, and sexuality, but through the novels they learn about groups other than their own. In a study on assessing quality in social work education with a focus on diversity, eight abilities were identified as relevant to be effective social work practitioners (Gingerich, Kaye, and Bailey 4). These abilities included communication, practice, values and ethics, professional use of self, critical thinking, diversity, advocacy for social justice, and world of work (meaning valuing a diverse world).

The novels give students an opportunity to learn and understand the experiences of different cultures. In their exploration of learning about other groups, they develop a framework for culturally relevant practice. This framework integrates knowledge about the psychosocial effects of oppression on marginalized groups. Students learn to understand their client's experiences, assess effects of those experiences, use intervention methods suited to the client's culture, and evaluate the social work intervention and services (Van Voorhis 4).

List of readings include a diversity of issues, as well as, cultural diversity. Instructors encourage students to choose a novel that will increase their knowledge of a population or group that is different from their own. The assigned novels provide a challenge to students to motivate them to increase their personal and professional perspectives. In addition, the novel provides sociocultural and interpersonal knowledge that helps to build the practical skills necessary to work with multiple problems, clients, and settings.

For example in the novel *Clay's Quilt* by Silas House, a Kentucky author, the novel highlights the rich Appalachian culture of eastern Kentucky. House describes the mountainous setting and coal-mining practice of the region and how the characters relate to this cultural aspect. The story illustrates a traditional religious and family value system of some of the characters in the novel. *Clay's Quilt* helps students learn about a different area of the state and culture with which they may be unfamiliar even though they reside in the same state. This learning process not only helps to educate students on a different culture but also diffuses any myths and stereotypes they may have about individuals living in Appalachia areas. Students are exposed to a different religious belief system that may personally conflict with their own. Additional themes of the book include domestic violence, grief issues, and issues faced by newly married couples.

Here are additional examples of the novel reading list and their diversity of themes assigned to beginning social work practice students.

- *The Bean Trees* by Barbara Kingsolver: Book themes include Native American culture, adoption, poverty, child abuse, and single mother's issues.
- *The Book of Ruth* by Jane Hamilton: Book themes include rural culture, mental health issues, multigenerational family violence, newly married couple stages of family development, and substance abuse.
- *How the Garcia Girls Lost Their Accent* by Julia Alvarez: Book themes include Hispanic culture, acculturation, gender roles, and immigration.
- *Ryan White Story: My Own Story* by Ryan White, Ann M. Cunningham, and Jeanne White: Book themes include HIV/AIDS, community oppression, irrational fear of AIDS, family relations, development stages of adolescence, and death and dying issues.
- *The Secret Life of Bees* by Sue Monk Kidd: Book themes include spirituality, contemporary uses of adolescent development and self-identity, parental loss, sibling loss, child maltreatment, racism, and female power.

- *The Women of Brewster Place* by Gloria Naylor: Book themes include African American culture and urban culture, child neglect, urban poverty, community breakdown, institutional violence, and racism.

CONTEMPORARY SOCIAL ISSUES

The novels make the situations presented in class relevant to students by exposing them to contemporary social issues they may experience in practice. The students make a connection to the real world by examining the issues presented in the novels. They learn and practice the use of the skills in a safe, controlled environment by choosing a main character from the novel as their client. Some examples of issues that students address via the novel during the practice sequence include child abuse, domestic violence, mental health, racism, homophobia, and poverty—all of which are pertinent to the current practice of social work. Below are some in-depth examples of additional novels whose content is relevant to current social work practice.

The novel *Icy Sparks,* written by Gwendolyn Hyman Rubio, a Kentucky author, exposes students to the Appalachian culture and therefore is an excellent vehicle for addressing the specific issues inherent in rural social work practice. The main character in the novel, Icy, is a ten-year-old girl experiencing symptoms characteristic of Tourette syndrome, a neurodevelopmental disorder that typically appears in childhood or adolescence and is characterized by involuntary movements or vocalizations (Wilkinson et al. 477). The young character experiences the vocal and motor tics that are typical of the syndrome. The symptoms of the disorder become more noticeable in a classroom setting and it negatively affects her academic performance, social relationship with peers, and relationship with the primary classroom teacher. The novel also examines the issues surrounding the informal private arrangement of kinship care. Kinship care is the full-time parenting of children by kin or relatives. After the death of her parents, Icy goes to live with her elderly grandparents who live on a farm in eastern Kentucky. There are approximately 6 million children under the age of eighteen living with relatives other than their parents and 4.5 million being cared for by their grandparents (U.S. Bureau of the Census); this novel exposes students to a relevant social issue affecting children and families today. There are benefits and challenges to the practice of kinship care. A major benefit is the preservation and connection to the family; kinship care maintains the family connection and provides children with psychological and emotional stability (Crumbly and Little 1). Along with benefits are the challenges that grandparents, especially if elderly, experience in their commitment to maintain the child's safety and well-being. Icy's grandparents deal with role confusion, lack of institutional and societal support, issues of morbidity and mortality due to health and age, and their lack of education and understanding of Icy's behavior. The novel becomes a teaching tool for students to identify the lack of resources available in rural areas because of isolation and poverty as well as to showcase the resilience and strengths of rural families and the characteristics of kinship care.

In the novel *Rubyfruit Jungle* by Rita Mae Brown, students explore the themes of adoption, attachment issues, and homophobia. The main character of the novel is an adolescent/young adult who struggles with the negative views and acceptance of her self-identity. Ruby was adopted as an infant. As a child, she experiences abuse from her mother who seems to exhibit behaviors related to issues of attachment and loss because of her inability to have children. Ruby's mother has difficulty accepting and loving her child (who is independent, outspoken, intelligent), and throughout the novel their relationship becomes more strained. When Ruby leaves home to attend college, she becomes involved in an intimate relationship with her female roommate, which results in her expulsion from the institution.

This novel teaches the students the challenges experienced by adopted families, the psychological traumas of attachment disorders, and the personal, societal, and institutional consequences of oppression. The main character in the novel, Ruby, is struggling with the developmental challenges of adolescence and young adulthood while navigating the integration of a stigmatized identity. The particular content of this novel challenges student's traditional views of family and gender identity and it exposes them to the additional demands placed on members of oppressed groups as a result of societal and institutional discriminatory attitudes and practices.

CONTENT FOR ANALYSIS AND CRITICAL THINKING

The process of choosing the novels to be included in the reading list used for teaching social work practice involves the identification of novels with sufficient content for students to analyze and apply critical thinking. It is the role of educators to challenge, motivate, and provide students with the tools they need to become critical thinkers. "Critical thinking is defined as the intellectually-disciplined process of actively and skillfully conceptualizing, applying, analyzing, synthesizing, and/or evaluating information gathered from, or generated by, observation, experience, reflection, reasoning, or communication, as a guide to belief and action" (Scriven and Paul).

The stories and situations involving the characters in the novels lend themselves to the process of analysis for students to understand the biopsychosocial issues effecting everyday functioning. There should be enough material in the novels for students to be able to engage in the social work problem-solving process. The story provides the case history for the student and allows them to analyze, assess, intervene, and evaluate the client's problems and strengths. The social work problem-solving processes include the development of hypothesis and demands the evaluation of the evidence presented in the novel scenario. In addition, students learn to apply theoretical perspectives (such as systems theory, labeling theory, conflict theory, role theory, and so on) to the novel case to generate hypothesis, strategies, and methods that create personal and societal change. Theories are used to help explain or predict behavior (Robbins, Chatterjee, and Canda 5). In short, theories are tools that help us make sense of the situation or problems (Hutchinson 85).

Application of Conflict Theories

In *Clay's Quilt,* a conflict perspective can be used to explain some aspect of the identified problem and situation with one of the main characters in the novel. Earlier in the novel, students are introduced to Alma, a young adult female character who is experiencing physical and emotional abuse by her husband Denzel. As a consequence, she is struggling with the decision of whether to remain in the marriage or seek a safer alternative. Feeling hopeless, she seeks advice and safe refuge from her parents who have traditional religious beliefs of gender roles, believing that women should remain married even in abusive situations versus separation or divorce. She is encouraged to stay in the marriage and be a better wife, which results in her feeling responsible for his abusive behavior, going back to work on her marriage, and continuing to be abused. Conflict theories deal directly with concepts of oppression, inequality, exploitation, and coercion (Robbins, Chatterjee, and Canda 88). Conflict theories (Hutchison 56; Robbins, Chatterjee, and Canda 88) or value-conflict theory (Long and Holle 143) are used mostly to help us understand social, political, or economic conflicts between larger systems (groups, institutions, societal) and how these conflicts influence human behavior. Alma, who is representative of an oppressed group within society, is experiencing individual oppression and conflict caused by their husbands and partners but also influenced by the philosophical beliefs, pressures, and religious ideology of larger social systems.

The last step in the analytical process is the evaluative effort in which students develop outcome measures for their intervention. The novel provides the opportunity for students to develop desired outcomes for the intervention process. For example, what kind of behavioral changes would signal a successful intervention? How would you and your client measure success? Students begin the process of considering evaluative tools for the assessment of the tentative plan of intervention.

LEARNING OBJECTIVES AND CLASS ASSIGNMENTS

As previously stated, the instructor's teaching practice course must facilitate the integration of knowledge and skill by developing assignments that clearly meet the desired learning objectives. The course expectations are that students apply their previous knowledge base from various disciplines—such as biology, human behavior, the social environment, sociological and psychological theory, political science, and public policy—to the assessment, intervention, and evaluation of client's problems.

The pedagogical rationale for the order of the learning objectives is designed to address the students' developmental learning curve by teaching skill sets that complement and build on one other. Students first develop self-awareness and self-understanding, then describe the client situation addressing professional values and ethics, and then move toward analysis and evaluation. The expectation is that the student will develop higher-order thinking skills by evaluating the evidence apparent in the novel using critical-thinking skills to analyze the impact of societal and institutional oppression at the individual, institutional, and societal level. The tasks of creating an assessment and a tentative intervention plan are the capstone assignments for the class learning objectives. The following course objectives are met via the use of the novel.

Course Objectives in Social Work Practice I: Theory and Methods

Objective 1: Recognize and Develop the Effective Use of Self in Social Work Practice

Course assignments related to objective 1: Group discussion and written assignment addressing the use of self in social work practice. Students identify strengths, weaknesses, and hot buttons that will help or hinder their ability to function as a professional social worker. This assignment helps students bridge their personal selves to their professional social work role.

In social work practice the term "Use of Self" is one's ability to build a positive working relationship with others by understanding and examining the workers' personal values. Values are the beliefs, preferences, or assumptions about what is desirable or good (Zastrow 35). It also involves what we consider important or least important in making decisions (Kirst-Ashman and Hull 14). The stories and the characters are used as the background for students' exploration and use of self. They are asked to identify behaviors and attitudes expressed by the characters that create affinity or conflict for them. This process allows for rich classroom discussion and for the beginning of raising awareness of one's ability to establish helping relationships based on their personal strengths. It also alerts the students to the areas that may present problems for them in their professional helping role.

Objective 2: Apply Social Work Values and Ethics in the Helping Process

Course assignment related to objective 2: Develop a plan to establish a helping relationship. Apply social work values and ethics and design a plan to address any potential ethical dilemmas. This assignment is a short narrative with an action plan that incorporates the beginning social work skills of preparing for a working relationship with a client (Cournoyer 159). The identification of personal strengths, weaknesses, or challenges is a necessary process of self-understanding for the social work student. Students need to identify those areas or issues of social work practice with clients that may present personal and professional ethical dilemmas.

The Code of Ethics of the National Association of Social Workers provides a guide for students on their ethical conduct with clients and in the profession. When there is a conflict between personal and professional values, it is advisable to adhere to the values, principles, and standards of the profession (NASW 3). To meet this objective, students are engaged in a brainstorming session about contemporary social issues; they are asked to identify the ones that create the most incongruence with their personal values and experience. Students identify potential ethical dilemmas and are asked to make a plan for how they would manage the conflict that arises when one occurs. For example, in the novel *Geography of the Heart* by Fenton Johnson, the student works through the ethical dilemma of having a gay male client with HIV and how that client struggles to inform his partner and family, or not, of his HIV status. The situation in the novel is an opportunity for students to learn their ethical responsibility to their client versus their personal values, and how to establish a professional helping relationship with both the individual and his family. In addition to the management of the difficult diagnoses, the student must address his or her issues with alternative lifestyle choices, and irrational fear of AIDS and homophobia. Resolving ethical dilemmas is a problem-solving process. The student learns to conceptualize and address the dilemma via research and consultation. This assignment allows students to determine what distinguishes the issue as an ethical dilemma, meaning a problem with competing and imperfect solutions, or whether it is an actual ethical problem with clearer solutions (Kirst-Ashman and Hull 354). In this assignment, the role of advocacy and activism are explored as part of the professional social work role since this novel character is in obvious need of both.

Objective 3: Develop and Use Critical-Thinking and Analytical Skills

Course assignment related to objective 3: Critical issues debate. Students are assigned to debate teams on which they identify and research social issues present in the novels. They are asked to present a rationale for defending or opposing positions. Lindsay states that critical thinking is the use of intellectual and effective processes that evaluate statements, arguments, and experiences by judging the validity, or worth, of those statements, arguments, and experiences (Kirst-Ashman and Hull 26). During this assignment, students are taught the skills needed to engage in advocacy and activism as they engage in research and preparation for the debate of the identified social problem. For example, in the novel *Dead Man Walking* by Helen Prejean, the issue of the death penalty arises to create a germane discussion of the role of the state and the personal and family tragedy for victims and perpetrators of violence.

It is crucial that the students evaluate the available evidence and present their rationale for debating the pros and cons of the death penalty. The issues present in this novel clearly lend themselves to the use of higher-order thinking to arrive at a rationale position for defending or opposing the death penalty.

Objective 4: Develop Skills in Conducting Multidimensional Assessment and Planning Corresponding Interventions

Course assignment related to objective 4: Written multidimensional biopsychosocial summary assessment. This is the final assignment for the course and it incorporates all of the social work competencies needed to engage in the beginning stages of social work practice. Students are asked to identify a point of intervention in their novel case where a social worker could have intervened to promote a better outcome for the individual client system. After identifying their point of intervention, they develop an analysis of the problem, the strengths, resources, and social networks that assist in the problem-solving process. The assessment process in social work practice is the investigation and determination of variables affecting an identified problem or issue as viewed from micro-, mezzo-, and macroperspectives (Kirst-Ashman and Hull 28). The comprehensive methods of assessment are served well by the narrative form. The novel authors provide rich and diverse characters and vignettes that support the analysis of data and identification of the circumstances appropriate for social work intervention.

Social Work Competencies and Practice Skills

In addition to Social Work Practice I: Theory and Methods, students concurrently participate in a weekly two-hour skills laboratory/methods section. The atmosphere for the lab is relaxed, light-hearted, and conducive to learning by promoting risk taking and offering support to students as they learn and practice new skills. The theory and practice students are divided into small groups, no larger than ten per session. They engage in numerous role-plays and skills development exercises that simulate worker-client situations (these exercises are video taped). The students learn the basic social work competencies needed to engage in the interviewing and data collection process, as well as practice their ability to establish beginning relationship skills with their novel clients. In this setting, the novel characters come alive via the student role-plays. They are given lots of freedom in the character/client responses; therefore, various outcomes develop from the different novel scenarios.

Social Work Skills Objective Related to the Use of the Novel:
Facilitate Beginning Social Work Interactions

During the skills laboratory/methods section, the students engage in mock interviews with their novel client. Students prepare by developing three-by-five cards with the basic characteristics and issues present in their novel case. They alternate between the role of worker and client. All students participate in the role-plays and engage in evaluating themselves and their peers on the use of basic social work interviewing skills, such as the use of open-ended questions, evidence of respect for the client situation, physical attending skills, managing resistance, and so on. The role-plays are video taped and serve to further increase student awareness of their interpersonal skills, strengths, and weaknesses that can facilitate or hinder the establishment of helping relationships with future client systems. During the lab/method sections, the students are asked to display sensitivity to gender, class, race, ability, and sexuality, as well as engage in the professional use of self, identify client's strengths and weaknesses, and develop a plan for self-care and professional development. The learning of the social work competencies and skills through the use of experiential activities are strongly enhanced by the use of the novel case content.

SUMMARY

The novel character/client and their situation greatly serve the students by providing an opportunity to apply their theoretical knowledge base and to practice the beginning social work skills. In addition, students are able to develop the necessary experience of engaging in a helping relationship through role-plays based on the lives created in the story. The richness and diversity of human experience is readily available to the students via the novel narrative. The novel content assists in meeting the course learning objectives by providing fertile ground for analysis, assessment, intervention, and evaluation of contemporary issues that affect the professional helping relationships and are relevant to the practice of social work today.

The novel helps students to apply knowledge of biopsychosocial variables that affect individual development and behavior and to use theoretical frameworks to understand interactions among individuals and between individuals and social systems. The teaching and learning of social work practice via the novel integrates this knowledge, which deepens students' understanding of and informs their choices about issues of private and public importance to client systems.

The social work educational outcomes set by the CSWE (4) and the practice standards set by the NASW (5) are clear in reference to the need for students to be able to understand the forms and mechanisms of oppression and discrimination and the strategies for change that advance social and economic justice. By exposing students to the complicated lives of the novel characters, the societal and institutional forces that affect client's problems are made accessible and real to the students. They become engaged in the problem-solving process with their novel characters/clients and they become part of their learning experience. The students move from reading textbooks and theories to reading popular novels, which expands their horizons and motivates active learning. The social work practice students have offered consistent positive feedback on the use of the novels to their learning experience over the year, and the use of the novel has become an integrated and successful tool for meeting the practice learning objectives in the baccalaureate social work curriculum. The authors find the use of the contemporary novel an invaluable and creative tool in the professional development of beginning social work students.

APPENDIX: ASSIGNED NOVELS

Alvarez, Julia. *How the Garcia Girls Lost Their Accents*. New York: Plume, 1992.
Brown, Rita M. *Rubyfruit Jungle*. New York: Bantam Books, 1977.
Hamilton, Jane. *The Book of Ruth*. New York: Anchor Books, Doubleday, 1990.
House, Silas. *Clay's Quilt*. New York: Ballantine, 2001.
Johnson, Fenton. *Geography of the Heart*. New York: Washington Square Press, 1996.
Kidd, Sue M. *The Secret Life of Bees*. New York: Penguin Group, 2002.
Kingsolver, Barbara. *The Bean Trees*. New York: HarperCollins, 1988.
Naylor, Gloria. *The Women of Brewster Place*. New York: Penguin, 1983.
Prejean, Helen. *Dead Man Walking*. New York: First Vintage Books, 1993.
Rubio, Gwyn H. *Icy Sparks*. New York: Penguin Group, 1998.
White, Ryan, Ann M. Cunningham, and Jeanne White. *Ryan White: My Own Story*. New York: Penguin Putnam Inc., 1992.

WORKS CITED

Council on Social Work Education (CSWE). *Educational Policy and Accreditation Standards*. N.p.: author, 2001. http://www.cswe.org (accessed August 1, 2006).
Cournoyer, Barry R. *The Social Work Skills Workbook*. Belmont, CA: Brooks/Cole, 2005.
Crumbley, Joseph, and Robert L. Little. *Relatives Raising Children: An Overview of Kinship Care*. Washington, DC: Child Welfare League of America, 1997.
Gingerich, Wallace J., Karen Kaye, and Darlyne Bailey. "Assessing Quality in Social Work Education." *Assessment and Evaluation in Higher Education* (1999): 119–30.

Hutchison, Elizabeth D. *Dimensions of Human Behavior: Person and Environment.* Thousand Oaks: Sage Publications, 2003.

Kirst-Ashman, Karen K., and Grafton H. Hull. *Understanding Generalist Practice.* Belmont, CA: Brooks/Cole, 2006.

Long, Dennis D., and Marla C. Holle. *Macro Systems in the Social Environment.* Itasca: F. E. Peacock Publishers, Inc, 1997.

National Association of Social Workers (NASW). *Code of Ethics.* Washington, DC: Author, 1996.

———. *Standards for Cultural Competence for Social Work Practice.* Washington, DC: Author, 2001.

Robbins, Susan P., Pranab Chatterjee, and Edward R. Canda. *Contemporary Human Behavior Theory: a Critical Perspective for Social Work.* Boston: Allyn and Bacon, 2006.

Scriven, Michael, and Richard Paul. *Defining Critical Thinking.* Foundation for Critical Thinking. http://www.criticalthinking.org/aboutCT/definingCT.shtm (accessed July 12, 2006).

U.S. Bureau of Census. *Grandparents Living with Grandchildren: Census 2000 Brief.* Washington DC: Author: 2000. http://www.census.gov/population/www/socdemo/grandparents/html (accessed July 12, 2006).

Van Voorhis, Rebecca M. "Culturally Relevant Practice: a Framework for Teaching the Psychosocial Dynamics of Oppression." *Journal of Social Work Education* (1998): 121–34.

Wilkinson, Berney J., R. Douglas Shytle, Mary B. Newman, Paul R. Sanberg, Archie A. Silver, and David Sheehan. "Family Impact of Tourette's Syndrome." *Journal of Child and Family Studies* (2001): 477–83.

Zastrow, Charles H. *The Practice of Social Work: Applications of Generalist and Advanced Content.* Pacific Grove, CA: Brooks/Cole, 2003.

Multicultural Novels in Education
Elizabeth Berg Leer

When I began my career as a middle-school English teacher many years ago, I was struck by the vast differences among my students. Although they were all twelve or thirteen years old, some looked ten and some could have passed for sixteen. Some were loud and boisterous, and others were painfully shy. Some wore name-brand, expensive outfits, and others rotated three threadbare T-shirts. Some devoured books and read with fluent ease, while for others reading was a slow, arduous, even painful process. While most liked the social aspect of school, only some liked the academics, as well. I remember feeling continually challenged—and sometimes frustrated—trying to meet the needs of these unique individuals in my classroom. The irony of my situation was that in this small, rural school district in central Minnesota, the student population was not only racially homogeneous—every single student I taught there in my six-year tenure was white—but largely homogeneous in regard to ethnicity and religion, as well. Most of my students were from German Catholic families who had lived in that area for generations, and cultural diversity was an abstraction for them, something with which they had almost no personal experience.

To be honest, I admit that the concept of cultural diversity was still rather abstract to me, too. I grew up and attended high school in a predominantly white town and then went off to a small liberal arts college that was also overwhelmingly white. While I read a few African American authors as a literature major and took a required Human Relations course for my certification in education, I cannot recall ever formally discussing the concepts of race, diversity, or cultural pluralism, let alone institutional racism or white privilege, during my undergraduate career. Student-teaching in an urban high school constituted my only personal experience with cultural diversity before becoming a licensed teacher, and even this exposure was limited because only two of the five courses I taught were racially mixed. (My twelfth-grade general English classes had both black and white students, but the beginning German students I taught were all white.)

While I recognized that student-teaching in a diverse urban school was a valuable experience, at the time, I failed to see how it could be relevant to my employment in a rural, white, homogeneous school.

EDUCATION IN A DIVERSE SOCIETY

Today, demographics are rapidly changing in the United States. Although whites made up 69 percent of the population in 2000, this percentage is decreasing every year, and by 2050, whites are expected to become a plurality rather than the majority ("Racial Demographics"). As our country is becoming increasingly multicultural, most schools are gaining minority representation, and the challenge of effectively educating students from various cultural backgrounds is no longer restricted to urban areas. Teachers from many traditionally homogeneous schools in suburbs and rural areas are now finding themselves in teaching environments significantly different from years past. Like their urban counterparts, these teachers, too, have the obligation to meet the instructional needs of all of their students, those who share their own cultural background, ethnicity, religion, and so on, and those who do not. They must now examine their curricula to make sure that the diversity in their classrooms and in the larger society is reflected, and they must interrogate their pedagogy, questioning whether it is responsive to students from various backgrounds.

Diller and Moule assert that educators require "cultural competence," which they define as "the ability to successfully teach students who come from cultures other than your own" (2). They argue that only when teachers have the cultural knowledge, sensitivities, and skills to teach "culturally different" students will these students be able to achieve their full potentials. Although I largely agree with Diller and Moule, I would like to see their definition of cultural competence extended. Sixteen years after my first foray into a classroom in the teacher role, and from my new vantage point as a teacher-educator, I have come to realize that regardless of where new teachers accept employment, it is imperative that they are knowledgeable about issues of diversity and are able to teach with cultural competence. I argue that only when teachers are sensitive to cultural differences, are aware of the ways that race and power operate in society, and can guide their students to this knowledge through carefully chosen curricula, will *all* of their students be able to achieve their full potential.

Regardless of student population, schools have the responsibility to educate their students to live and work in a pluralistic society (Nieto). We cannot assume that students will remain in their insular communities for a lifetime (and neither can they, despite their adolescent assertions), nor that these communities will remain homogeneous for the next seventy years. Also, technological advances in both communication and commerce are rapidly shrinking the globe and decreasing the likelihood that students will interact only with people like themselves. Thus, even predominantly "white" schools need to expose students to the perspectives and intellectual and artistic contributions of people from a variety of backgrounds. English teacher Emily Style argues that school curriculum must "function both as window and as mirror, in order to reflect and reveal most accurately both a multicultural world and the student herself or himself" (150). In the literature classroom, this responsibility means not limiting the curriculum to the canon of white European thought, but including works of writers of color and giving voice to minority perspectives and experiences as well. Like teacher-educator Marilyn Cochran-Smith, I believe that teaching is an inherently political activity and that teachers have the power to influence society and make the world more socially just.

TEACHERS AND MULTICULTURAL LITERATURE

Multicultural literature is an excellent vehicle to foster understanding of others and to expand one's worldview, and an increasing number of teachers today seem to understand the value of teaching a diverse, inclusive curriculum to their students. However, teaching multicultural literature is a challenging and complex task for teachers, especially if those teachers are white and have had little experience with cultural diversity (Willis). For example, Saha's study of student-teachers teaching multicultural literature reveals that the teachers did not fully understand the literature itself, criteria for choosing it, or the purposes of teaching it. My own recent study of four white high school teachers teaching multicultural literature to predominantly white students seems consistent with Saha's findings. The teachers voice commitment to teaching diverse texts, but they seem unsure about how to go about this task—how to choose appropriate literature, how to explore relevant themes, how to structure discussions, and so on.

In addition, I discovered that despite teachers' stated beliefs about the importance of multicultural literature, inclusive curricula and teaching do not necessarily follow. All of the teachers in my study perceive value in teaching texts by people of color and choose to do so voluntarily. However, in the semester-long courses I observed, most of the curricula remained overwhelmingly white. Also, with one notable exception, the teachers in my study seem to be universalists, not pluralists. Focusing on similarities among cultures and individuals seems to be the top priority when studying texts by people of color (based both on stated beliefs and observed practices), while little attention is paid to fundamental differences in life experience for various groups and individuals and the underlying reasons for these differences. While the teachers all acknowledge difference in the classroom, they do not explore it with any depth, choosing to focus instead on "human" qualities like the feelings and emotions of characters of color. Rather than helping students to understand and grapple with difficult social issues like oppression, white privilege, and institutional racism, the teachers allow discussions to remain on a more benign, superficial level. Teacher-educator and activist Gloria Ladson-Billings contends that "white teachers wish to avoid race talk of any kind" and therefore often fail to take up racial issues even when authors are explicit about racism in the texts. This situation is problematic because if teachers fail to interrogate the concept of race or engage in antiracist pedagogy while simultaneously adopting a universalist stance toward the texts, students will continue to conceive of racism only as individual acts of discrimination and will remain blind to the systemic inequality that is still pervasive in society. Spears-Bunton argues that because of the strong emotional connections readers can develop toward literary characters, multicultural literature has the power to change attitudes and beliefs more effectively than discussions of cultural issues in the abstract. In addition, she sees diverse texts as natural openings for the discussion of important societal issues—like oppression, or the intersection of race, class, and gender—that would otherwise go unexplored in the curriculum. Thus, a tremendous educational opportunity is lost when multicultural literature is not used as a tool to help students learn how to critique society. Teachers rob diverse literature of its potential transformative power when they assign it to students but neglect to thoroughly address its themes, context, and social commentary. In Ladson-Billings's words, "great multicultural texts are not enough to disrupt performances of whiteness. Curriculum won't matter if teachers don't change."

Teachers can hardly be blamed, however, when their efforts to teach multicultural literature fall short. Instead, they should be applauded for their commitment to taking on and struggling with the challenging, sometimes frustrating work of teaching diverse texts (Vinz), despite almost no preparation for the task. The disconnect between theory and practice seems almost inevitable given teachers' lack of knowledge of multicultural texts (including texts appropriate for secondary school use), their lack of pedagogical knowledge relating to those texts, and their lack of academic discourse on racially charged themes like racism, oppression, and white privilege. In my study, for example, none of the teachers believed that their undergraduate teacher education programs adequately prepared them to teach multicultural literature. Beyond the reading of, say, a token African American text in a survey of American literature, three of the four recall no academic preparation at all. Not only were courses in multicultural literature not required, they were either seldom or never offered. All of the teachers indicate, however, that familiarity with a wide range of multicultural texts should be a top priority for English education majors, because teachers tend to teach what they know. The myriad of responsibilities demanded of teachers leaves little time for mastering a new academic area and developing the curricula to teach it. The teachers in my study also suggest that preservice teachers would benefit from specialized pedagogical knowledge tied to multiculturalism. All of them confess to feelings of uncertainty as they introduce their students to texts by people of color. Although they believe in the importance of exposing their students to a variety of perspectives and experiences, they lack confidence in their abilities to do the texts justice. Like me when I started teaching, they have had little personal experience with racial diversity or academic experience exploring social issues like race and oppression; therefore, approaching these sticky issues with students is disconcerting. As Bolgatz notes, "Few teachers are taught how to be racially literate, so we do not know how to help our students learn these skills" (12).

A RATIONALE FOR NOVELS IN (ENGLISH) TEACHER EDUCATION

Given teachers' lack of academic preparation for teaching students from an inclusive, multicultural perspective, a logical first step for English teacher education programs would be to require several courses in multicultural literature. Three additional components important to teacher education include pedagogical content knowledge (knowledge of how to teach multicultural curriculum), coursework in multiculturalism and race theory, and an immersion experience working with students from nondominant cultures. Ideally, this four-pronged diversity component should stretch across the college or university curriculum and be woven throughout the teacher education program; however, given institutional politics, the considerable time necessary to enact substantive change, and other constraints, I think it is not only practical, but also most beneficial to current students, for The Teaching of English to fill in the gaps and shoulder as much of this content as possible.[1] Weaving the theme of multicultural teaching throughout the program and involving multiple departments would certainly afford students a more comprehensive education and allow greater time for personal growth and reflection, but until that structure is in place, English methods must teach to the gaps and address the needs of teacher candidates.

Knowledge of Multicultural Literature

Because my own institution, like many others, requires little literature beyond the traditional canon,[2] I consider it my responsibility to provide teacher candidates with at least an introduction to texts that reflect and address the diversity of our society. My methods courses privilege multicultural narratives to increase students' exposure to the rich body of works written by people of color. Instead of just talking to my teacher candidates about the importance of teaching an inclusive curriculum in their own classrooms, I ask them to read and talk about multicultural literature themselves. I purposefully design assignments that require students to interact with multicultural novels and think about how they could use them in their future classrooms. They read novels, discuss them, engage in research to enhance their understanding of the cultural contexts, develop relevant teaching activities, and practice those activities with classmates. Although they will certainly need to continue seeking out and reading unfamiliar texts independently and finding supplementary materials on their own, it is important to provide teacher candidates with the time and guidance to begin this process as students. Because teachers' schedules are generally so full and their lives are so busy preparing for and teaching five classes every day, responding to students work, attending meetings, and helping with extra curricular activities, they find it challenging to do extensive reading and research on top of their regular daily activities.

Pedagogical Content Knowledge

In addition to knowledge about the content of multicultural literature, teachers also need knowledge of how to teach this specialized genre. Grossman identifies several components of pedagogical content knowledge. The first is the knowledge and beliefs about the purposes for teaching a particular subject at various grade levels. Teachers' goals for teaching multicultural literature will reflect these overarching beliefs. For example, if teachers believe that the primary purpose of teaching multicultural literature is to build bridges between cultures, they will most likely structure class activities and discussion to focus on human universals. In contrast, if teachers believe that multicultural literature should be a vehicle for cultural critique, their goals for student learning and therefore their pedagogy will look much different.

Another component of pedagogical content knowledge includes a sense of students' conceptions and misconceptions of a subject. To teach effectively, teachers must understand how students generally approach multicultural literature and where they most likely will experience difficulty. Teachers of multicultural literature need to understand, for example, that students often struggle when a novel deviates from the straightforward narrative structure that is most often employed in "white" literature. To cite a specific instance, because Native American stories often are told out of chronological order and because the boundary between myth and reality is often blurred, students can have difficulty following the plot. When teachers are able to anticipate potential student confusion, however, they can provide appropriate support and explanation before students are overly frustrated.

Pedagogical content knowledge involves knowing specific strategies, examples, analogies, and activities that effectively illustrate the subject matter for their students. For example, teachers need to know useful, productive ways to address topics like white privilege or the anger people of color can feel toward society. If these topics are not approached sensitively (and sometimes even when they are), students will resist the messages and tune out any potential learning. Teaching of English is the logical course to provide future teachers with this kind of pedagogical knowledge necessary to teach multicultural literature effectively. In the methods course, teacher candidates engage in discussion and shape their views about the purposes of multicultural literature study and build up an arsenal of ideas and strategies for teaching diverse texts. By including study of the novels themselves in the course, however, I provide my students with pedagogical models so they will be better able to make specific, concrete connections between the theory and practice of teaching. For example, I can talk generically about the importance of raising the issue of oppression in the classroom, but when the class is reading Mildred Taylor's Newbery Award-winning *Roll of Thunder, Hear My Cry*,[3] I can model questioning techniques for my students and engage them in actual activities that they can borrow for their own use later.

Knowledge of Multiculturalism and Race Theory

Possessing both in-depth knowledge of multicultural texts and knowledge and skills related to the teaching of them, while important, are not enough for teachers to be able to do the important cultural work of creating a more just society. To use multicultural literature as a tool for social justice in the classroom, teachers must also know how the institutions in our society work to the advantage of whites and the disadvantage of people of color, and they need to know that the problem of racism is deeply woven into the structure of our society. They need to understand what Delpit calls the "culture of power," the culture that maintains power and controls success. Because whites are part of this dominant culture, it is invisible to them, and they need explicit instruction about its workings (Rothenberg; Sleeter). We cannot expect white teachers of multicultural literature to go beyond a focus on human similarities or a surface treatment of cultural differences if they have no knowledge of race theory. Unfortunately, despite the tremendous amount of content to learn and the difficulty of learning to think in a new way, teacher candidates are rarely afforded much formal instruction in multicultural education. This situation underscores the importance of integrating as much of this instruction into methods courses as possible.

The study of multicultural novels can provide students with deeper understandings of racism, oppression, and white privilege. While certainly not a substitute for coursework focusing on multicultural education, including diverse novels in the English methods course provides a vehicle for discussing difference in society. Unless white teachers are able to understand that their experience in the world differs profoundly from the experience of students of color, they will be unable to teach all students optimally. Novels that reveal lived experience of people from minority groups, however, can help teachers throw off assumptions, gain empathy, and foster more welcoming, inclusive classroom communities.

MULTICULTURAL NOVELS IN ONE ENGLISH METHODS COURSE

As I structure my English methods course and decide how to weave in multicultural novels, I attempt to develop assignments that will help move teacher candidates beyond inclusive beliefs to the demonstration of those beliefs in practice. My lofty goal is to send teachers into society who cannot only articulate the importance of teaching diverse literature in their classrooms, but also who are able to take the next, far more challenging step, and align their actual teaching practices with their stated beliefs in a way that the teachers in my study could not. By focusing almost all of our allotted literature class time on diverse texts, I am attempting to provide teacher candidates with time and space to explore novels they would not otherwise encounter in college and help them to locate resources to further their individual exploration. While we do discuss common texts and specifically address inclusive teaching, most of my "teaching" of multicultural novels actually involves facilitating students' independent work and providing feedback on their ideas and pedagogy.

Multicultural Novel Teaching Packets[4]

Because I want my students to gain familiarity with literature they could use in their own future classrooms, and I want them to leave my class with some practical, ready-to-implement materials, I assign individuals or pairs of students to complete a multicultural novel teaching packet.[5] This major assignment invites students to choose a novel by a writer of color that would be appropriate to use with the grade level they plan on teaching. Students then work (with their partner) to make sense of the text, engage in research about the author and the historical context of the piece, and develop ideas for teaching the novel in their own classrooms. This assignment has been adapted from Willis and Palmer.

Before students begin, I approve their titles in advance to ensure that the books fit the assignment[6] and are appropriate for the desired age level. Although I do provide students with some possible book titles, they are largely free to choose whatever interests them. While they read their text, students also read the chapter in Willis's *Teaching and Using Multicultural Literature in Grades 9-12: Moving Beyond the Canon* that corresponds to the ethnicity of their novel's author. These chapters provide context for the literature and introduce students to some of the themes and issues that may have relevance in their own books. Because my students will be teaching a range of age levels, their novel choices reflect great variety in reading level and complexity; last semester's projects included, for example, Walker's *The Color Purple*, Alexie's *Indian Killer*, Myers's *Fallen Angels*, Chin's *Donald Duk*, Anaya's *Bless Me, Ultima*, Curtis's *The Watsons Go to Birmingham—1963*, and Carter's *The Education of Little Tree*. Upon completion, students share some of their findings orally, but I also share written copies of their packets with the rest of the class so that students have, at minimum, in-depth information and teaching ideas for six multicultural novels.

In addition to gaining exposure to multicultural novels and generating teaching resources, this assignment inevitably raises excellent topics for discussion. For example, when one student was researching *The Education of Little Tree*, she discovered that controversy surrounds the book's authorship. *Little Tree*, the well-received, heartwarming story of a young boy raised by his Cherokee grandparents in the mountains of Tennessee, is presumably based on the author's boyhood experiences. However, several years after its initial 1976 publication, Forrest Carter was discovered to be a pseudonym for Asa Carter, a member of the Ku Klux Klan and staunch segregationist who wrote speeches for George Wallace. Native Americans have since derided the book for its stereotyping and inaccurate depictions of Cherokee life. An obvious question that emerged was what would motivate an admitted racist to write this book? The more interesting and productive issue for our class, however, concerned questions of authenticity. If authors have done careful research, does it matter who tells the story? Can a white author speak for people of color and "get it right?" When teachers choose literature curriculum, should the author's identity influence text selection? How important is it for the curriculum to include literary contributions from a wide cross-section of society? Student inquiry into multicultural novels of their choice can promote rich discussion of these kinds of questions.

Multicultural Literature Unit Plan

A second major assignment that increases students' familiarity with multicultural novels and urges them to think about teaching these texts themselves involves creating a four- to six-week thematic unit that is grounded in multicultural literature. Teacher candidates, either individually or in groups of two or three, must select a theme that they could explore with their own students and a multicultural novel to "anchor" the unit. Then, they choose complementary literature that supports the unit's theme and they build a detailed plan for how they will teach the literature over the course of at least one month. The unit plan includes components like a rationale for the learning, instructional objectives, assessment instruments, and specific learning activities that engage the students. A major goal of this assignment is urging students to think about using a novel to explore an overarching theme, rather than teaching a text in isolation. Because students are required to bring in other multicultural literature—short stories, poems, and so on—they must think about what issues they would like to pull from the novels and foreground, instead of merely falling back on discussing elements like plot, characterization, and theme in a general sense. Common topics that teacher candidates have investigated through literature include civil rights, whether or not prejudice still exists, and coming of age in a diverse society. As with the multicultural novel teaching packets, I duplicate the unit plans for all members of the class so that students can use each other's work as resources in their own future classrooms.

Multicultural Literature Microteaching

As part of the unit plan assignment, students gain practice thinking about teaching multicultural texts and planning relevant learning activities. However, because translating plans into action can be challenging, students need the opportunity to practice their pedagogy in addition to planning for it. Because teacher candidates are limited to teaching a twenty- to thirty-minute lesson, and because their "students" (classmates) are unable to read lengthy works as homework, I do allow them to teach short stories or poems instead of novels if they choose. Regardless of the text, though, as students teach their lessons, they must incorporate ideas relevant to the text's multicultural underpinnings; they cannot ignore issues of race or ethnicity. In addition to receiving both written and verbal feedback from me after the teaching sessions, students receive written feedback from classmates, as well. Serving as a student for their classmates' teaching allows the teacher candidates to observe a range of teaching strategies, gain ideas for teaching activities, and reflect on what strategies seem most effective from the student's perspective. Practice teaching with peers allows students to discover, for example, that vague, open-ended questions can be hard for students to respond to and that teachers often need to prompt students to elaborate on their responses. They also discover that a teacher's plans do not always proceed as intended, and thinking on one's feet is a valuable classroom skill.

The House on Mango Street

While most of my teacher candidates' exploration of multicultural novels involves independent inquiry, on occasion we will study a common text. *The House on Mango Street* by Sandra Cisneros is one of my whole-class favorites because of its beautiful writing, its moving characters, and its appeal to a wide range of adolescent readers. Despite delving into complex themes, *Mango Street*'s brief chapters and straightforward language are accessible to reluctant and struggling readers, and the text can be used successfully with students from middle school through high school.

When the English methods class reads a common novel, I try to model several teaching activities that teacher candidates could use in their own classes to generate student response to the text. Often, I will ask students to keep a response journal as they read, instructing them about the difference between a "response" and a "report." At first, secondary students will want to "respond" only to plot details and whether or not they liked the book, but with some guidance, they soon get used to writing about, say, their predications based on the opening chapters, the author's literary techniques and their effectiveness, and their reasoned analysis of the book's quality. Responses can help students reflect more intentionally about a text, they can serve as a starting point for class discussions or formal papers, and they can show the teacher how well students are engaging with the text.

Common novel studies with teacher candidates are an ideal time for me to show students how jotting a written response to a question first and then discussing the question with a partner or small group before asking students to discuss it as a whole class[7] generates both higher-quality responses and better student involvement in discussion. When students have time to consider a response, write something down, and then verbalize their thoughts with one or two other people, they are much better prepared to share with the large group, and the experience is therefore much less threatening. When the English methods class reads the same novel, I can also model for students questioning that foregrounds cultural differences and deviates from the common pattern of focusing only on similarities and human universals. I might ask the following questions of *Mango Street*, for example: How would this story be different if the protagonist were white? How does Esperanza's ethnicity affect her sense of self? What cultural markers are evident in the text? What factor do you think influences Esperanza's coming-of-age most profoundly and why—her race, class, or gender? Questions like these can help (white, middle class) students think about the "invisible knapsack" of privilege (McIntosh) that they carry with them each day.

Other opportunities for response that I have demonstrated with my college students include reader's theater performance of the text and artistic response. An episodic novel like *Mango Street* is especially well-suited for a class collage, for instance. Each student can choose a chapter and create a visual representation of its main ideas and themes on a square piece of paper (or, if the teacher is ambitious, on a quilt square or a classroom ceiling tile). When students are finished with the art, they combine their squares into a collage that represents the novel as a whole. Students talk about their individual contributions and what their symbols mean, and the class discusses how all of the parts contribute to the beauty of the whole. Inevitably, students are impressed with their work, and the class period spent processing the finished product provides a satisfying sense of closure to the novel study.

FUTURE DIRECTIONS

Both research and my own practice teaching future English teachers have convinced me of the importance of steeping teacher candidates in multicultural education, and I agree with Darling-Hammond and Garcia-Lopez's summation:

Dealing with diversity is one of the central challenges of 21st-century education. It is impossible to prepare tomorrow's teachers to succeed with all of the students they will meet without exploring how students' learning experiences are influenced by their home languages, cultures, and contexts; the realities of race and class privilege in the United States; the ongoing manifestations of institutional racism within the educational system; and the many factors that shape students' opportunities to learn within individual classrooms. (9)

I have argued that multicultural novels can be an excellent vehicle for doing the important cultural work of "dealing with diversity." Through the study of multicultural texts, teacher candidates can explore issues like culture and race and privilege and enter their own classrooms better equipped to educate students to live in a diverse society, and simultaneously learn how to approach multicultural literature in their own classrooms with their own students. Ideally, colleges will respond positively and productively to the changes in society; for example, English departments will offer more inclusive curricula and education departments will infuse multicultural coursework throughout their teacher education sequences. However, even assuming for a moment these progressive moves, one English methods course cannot address multicultural literature adequately for future teachers of English.

Presently, to meet state Board of Education standards for initial teacher licensure, my Teaching of English course must include instruction in the teaching of writing, speaking, listening, and media studies in addition to literature. Thus, in one fifteen-week semester, I am forced to limit (multicultural) literature to just a few weeks of the syllabus, and realistically, I cannot include more than two to four novels on the syllabus. Although students do benefit somewhat, this thin exposure to multicultural novels provides inadequate preparation for future English teachers. My students would be much better served by devoting an additional methods course solely to multicultural young adult literature. Requiring this course would afford students the time and space to explore numerous texts representing a greater number of cultural and ethnic groups, delve into important themes, and reflect on appropriate pedagogy. Teacher candidates could become accustomed to "deliberately [putting] issues of race and oppression on the table" (Bolgatz 119) as they talk about literature. In addition, a separate course could provide more time for discussions about issues like text quality and evaluation, censorship, and specific pedagogical techniques, and students could take turns leading class discussions and gain experience actually practicing their pedagogy.

Teaching in the twenty-first century is a different endeavor than it was just a few decades ago. Because of the rapidly changing demographics of the United States, the knowledge and skill base required of teachers is much more extensive than ever before. An academic major in English that provides solid grounding in the traditional literary canon, but requires little reading beyond the "classics" of British and American literature, is no longer sufficient content knowledge for future English teachers. To teach effectively, English educators need to explore with their students a wide variety of age-appropriate literature that reflects the diversity of our society and addresses complex social issues in honest, thought-provoking ways, an important task that has historically been ignored by professors of English education (Smagorinski and Whiting). Unfortunately, many teachers find themselves ill-prepared to deliver curriculum in their middle and high school classrooms because they have not read or studied multicultural literature themselves and sometimes are not even aware of the possibilities.

Although I hope that English department reading lists will reflect increasingly diverse voices in the future, teacher education methodology courses must take the responsibility to step up and address this gap. I am fortunate to work at an institution that weaves a multicultural education theme throughout the entire teacher education curriculum, so by the time my students take the Teaching of English course just before student-teaching, they already have solid experience exploring issues of diversity, inclusiveness, and equity in education. Regardless of the teacher preparation program, however, infusing the study of multicultural novels into the English methods course ensures that teacher candidates will have, at the least, an introduction to diverse young adult literature and concrete strategies for teaching these texts in their own future classrooms.

APPENDIX

Multicultural Novel Teaching Packets

In *Teaching and Using Multicultural Literature in Grades 9-12: Moving Beyond the Canon*, Arlette Willis states that "preservice teachers need more than a list of multicultural books to read and discuss; they also need specific information about the historical, social, cultural, and ideological contexts in which to understand multicultural literature" (225). This assignment represents an opportunity for you to begin researching and learning some of this important information so that you are better prepared to teach multicultural texts in your own classroom. You (and a partner?) are responsible for creating a packet of information on a multicultural novel that you might consider teaching someday. These packets will be copied and shared with all members of the class, so that you will have in-depth background information on several novels by writers of color to use as future resources.

To begin, choose a text to read that would be appropriate for the young adults you plan on teaching someday (feel free to use Willis's lists on pp. 242–46) and tell me your choice. Then begin researching for your packet.

The novel packet must include the following components:

1. A summary of the novel.
2. A biography of the author.
3. Pertinent historical facts and events that occurred when the novel was written.
4. Pertinent historical facts and events that cover the time period discussed in the novel.
5. Cultural information that may improve understanding of the novel.
6. Two books reviews of the novel.
7. A teaching activity or idea to use with the novel. (Focus on multicultural themes, the experience of people of color, and so on.)

See pages 231–38 in the Willis text for an example of what some of these components might look like.

Thematic Multicultural Literature Unit Plan

Create a four- to six-week thematic unit that is grounded in multicultural literature. The literature may represent multiple cultures/ethnicities, or you may choose to focus all the literature on one culture/ethnicity. Choose to use a novel as a major part of the unit, but you must include other literature as well. As you plan the unit, think about how you can integrate several components of Communication Arts and Literature: reading, writing, speaking, listening, viewing, and using language effectively. You may work with one or two other people.

Your unit should include the following components:

Setting the Context for the Unit

Write a descriptive paragraph that answers the following questions: Who are your students? How many of them are there? What are their exceptionalities? How often does your class meet, and for how long? What is the course you are teaching? (NOTE: Envision a "regular" class, not twelfth grade Advanced Placement English; think of what you realistically may teach during student-teaching!)

Defining the Unit's Goals and Objectives

1. Identify a topic of the unit (and, while you're at it, give it a jazzy title).
2. Write a rationale for the unit, explaining the basic concepts and "essential understandings" that the unit will focus on, and explaining why this unit is appropriate for these particular students.
3. Outline or list the specific knowledge and skills that students will practice and acquire through this unit: the objectives. (What will students know and be able to do as a result of this unit?)
4. Indicate how the objectives specifically align with the Minnesota Language Arts Standards.
5. Indicate the appropriate assessments you will use to determine whether students understand the basic concepts for this unit. Describe both formal (projects, papers, tests) and informal (observations, journals) assessments you will be using.
6. List the materials (books, stories, poems, films) that will be used. These will, of course, reflect the multicultural focus of the unit.

Explaining the Unit Road Map

1. Describe the activities you will use to teach the students how to do the things they'll be assessed on, showing how all of the activities fit together. You may choose a day-by-day description of activities and lessons or a graphic representation of the unit, such as a table of daily work.
2. Describe how you will introduce the unit and the unit concepts to students.
3. Although the unit focuses on literature, make sure to integrate various strands of language arts: reading/literature, writing, speaking/listening, language use.
4. Include in your plan each of the following:
   a. One instrument to use in evaluating learning. This could be the rubric for a project, speech, or writing assignment; a checklist of the skills students are to demonstrate by the end of the unit; or some other evaluation instrument.
   b. One student handout that demonstrates how you design materials for your students to use.
   c. One formal lesson plan that is a part of the unit.

END NOTES

1. I will briefly discuss how teaching novels in English methods supports the first three diversity components: coursework in multicultural literature, pedagogical knowledge of multicultural literature, and coursework in race theory. Although completing a field experience in a diverse school environment would be a valuable part of an English

methods course, I will not discuss the diversity immersion component here. Reading multicultural fiction could certainly inform and complement a field experience in a diverse environment, but vicarious experience is no substitute for real interactions.

2. Currently, English majors at St. Olaf College are required to take one course with the designation Global Literatures in English, 1850–Present, which may or may not include works by writers of color. The reading lists for the required British and American literature surveys remain entrenched in the traditional white, male canon. The elective course American Racial and Multicultural Literatures is offered once each year. Due to increasing student interest, the class has grown from twenty to fifty students, but despite its growing popularity, no new sections have been added.

3. This historical novel, appropriate for middle-school readers, chronicles the life of an African American family in rural Mississippi during the Depression.

4. At the end of the article, I include assignment sheets for several of the activities I discuss in this section.

5. Only occasionally do students opt to work alone. I prefer partner work because I want to encourage the habit of collaboration with colleagues as a valuable professional development tool.

6. Before requiring that students gain approval for their novels, I encountered a situation in which a pair of students misunderstood the spirit of the assignment, and instead of choosing to study a novel by a writer of color, chose a text from the traditional, white, male canon of American literature because "it's about a black person."

7. This teaching technique is commonly referred to as "think/pair/share."

WORKS CITED

Alexie, Sherman. *Indian Killer*. New York: Warner, 1998.

Anaya, Rudolfo. *Bless Me, Ultima*. New York: Warner, 1994.

Bolgatz, Jane. *Talking Race in the Classroom*. New York: Teachers College Press, 2005.

Carter, Forrest. *The Education of Little Tree*. Albuquerque: University of New Mexico Press, 2001.

Chin, Frank. *Donald Duk*. Minneapolis, MN: Coffee House Press, 1991.

Cisneros, Sandra. *The House on Mango Street*. New York: Vintage, 1984.

Cochran-Smith, Marilyn. "Color Blindness and Basket Making are Not the Answers: Confronting the Dilemmas of Race, Culture, and Language Diversity in Teacher Education." *American Educational Research Journal* 32, no. 3 (1995): 493–522.

Curtis, Christopher Paul. *The Watsons Go to Birmingham—1963*. New York: Bantam Doubleday Dell, 1995.

Darling-Hammond, Linda, and Silvia Paloma Garcia-Lopez. "What Is Diversity?" In *Learning to Teach for Social Justice*, edited by Linda Darling-Hammond, Jennifer French, and Silvia Paloma Garcia-Lopez, 9–12. New York: Teachers College Press, 2002.

Delpit, Lisa. "Teachers, Culture, and Power: An Interview with Lisa Delpit." In *Rethinking Schools: An Agenda for Change*, edited by David Levine, et. al., 136–47. New York: The New Press, 1995.

Diller, Jerry V., and Jean Moule. *Cultural Competence: A Primer for Educators*. Belmont, CA: Thomson Wadsworth, 2005.

Grossman, Pamela L. *The Making of a Teacher: Teacher Knowledge and Teacher Education*. New York: Teachers College Press, 1990.

Ladson-Billings, Gloria. "Still Playing in the Dark: Whiteness in the Literary Imagination of Children's and Young Adult Literature Teaching." NCTE Assembly for Research Midwinter Conference. University of Minnesota, Minneapolis. February 2003.

McIntosch, Peggy. "White Privilege: Unpacking the Invisible Knapsack." *Independent School* 49, no. 2 (1990): 31–36.

Myers, Walter Dean. *Fallen Angels*. New York: Scholastic, 1989.

Nieto, Sonia. *Affirming Diversity: The Sociopolitical Context of Multicultural Education*. 3rd ed. New York: Addison Wesley Longman, 2000.

"Racial Demographics of the United States." *Wikipedia: The Free Encyclopedia*, August 8, 2006. http://en.wikipedia.org/wiki/Racial_demographics_of_the_United_States (August 14, 2006).

Rothenberg, Paula. "Integrating the Study of Race, Gender, and Class: Some preliminary Observations." In *The Feminist Teacher Anthology: Pedagogies and Classroom Strategies*, edited by Gail E. Cohee, et al., 135–49. New York: Teachers College Press, 1998.

Saha, Krishna. "Teaching Multicultural Literature: Five Preservice Teachers' Views and Practices." Dissertation, Columbia University, 2000.

Sleeter, Christine E. *Multicultural Education as Social Activism*. Albany, NY: SUNY Press, 1996.

Smagorinski, Peter, and Melissa E. Whiting. *How English Teachers Get Taught: Methods of Teaching the Methods Class*. Urbana, IL: National Council of Teachers of English, 1995.

Spears-Bunton, Linda. "All the Colors of the Land: A Literacy Montage." In *Teaching and Using Multicultural Literature in Grades 9-12: Moving Beyond the Canon*, edited by Arlette Willis, 17–36. Norwood, MA: Christopher Gordon, 1998.

Style, Emily. "Curriculum as Window and Mirror." In *Seeding the Process of Multicultural Education: An Anthology*, edited by Cathy L. Nelson and Kim A. Wilson, 149–56. Plymouth, MN: Minnesota Inclusiveness Program, 1998.

Tayor, Mildred. *Roll of Thunder, Hear My Cry*. New York: Puffin, 1976.

Vinz, Ruth. "Cautions Against Canonizing An(Other) Literature." In *Multicultural Curriculum: New Directions for Social Theory, Practice, and Policy*, edited by Ram Mahalingam and Cameron McCarthy, 127–54. New York: Routledge, 2000.

Walker, Alice. *The Color Purple*. New York: Pocket, 1990.

Willis, Arlette. *Teaching and Using Multicultural Literature in Grades 9-12: Moving Beyond the Canon*. Norwood, MA: Christopher Gordon, 1998.

Willis, Arlette Ingram, and Marlen Diane Palmer. "Negotiating the Classroom: Learning and Teaching Multicultural Literature." In *Teaching and Using Multicultural Literature in Grades 9-12: Moving Beyond the Canon*, edited by Arlette Willis, 215–50. Norwood, MA: Christopher Gordon, 1998.

Theories and (Legal) Practice for Teachers-in-Training

Colin C. Irvine

[A] literary critic, a term derived from two Greek words, krino, meaning "to judge," and krites, meaning, "a judge or jury person." (6)

Charles E. Bressler, *Literary Criticism:*
An Introduction to Theory and Practice

This essay presents a new twist on a somewhat familiar approach to teaching novels, especially those in American literature that tempt us into repeatedly taking biographical or historical approaches to the material and our teaching of it. By infusing the mock-trial approach with a heavy dose of literary criticism, I am hoping to answer these questions: How can we teach novels in a manner that makes each day in the unit essential and eventful? And how, moreover, can we use them to nurture ways of thinking that are critical, creative, and—from the students' perspective—relevant to the world beyond the books?

THE GREAT INTRODUCTION

Nearly all of us brash enough to teach novels seldom think in thick detail beyond that glorious first day or two of a given unit or novel—a fact especially apparent when we consider how we commonly approach teaching familiar and deceptively complex works such as *The Adventures of Huckleberry Finn* and *The Scarlet Letter*. When imagining the first day of a two-week unit on *Huck Finn*, for instance, I know that I have on more than one occasion envisioned any number of brilliant, original scenarios; and often these involve lavish costumes, life-size rafts, actual rivers, and scores of hands eagerly going up as my students clamor over one another in their eagerness to enter into the thrilling discussion that I trust will no doubt take place. And, in my active, all-too-literary imagination, I have even gone so far as to assume that the second and possibly even the third day of this splendid honeymoon phase of our collective, creative sojourn into the world of Huck and Jim will likewise be characterized by eventfulness and overwhelming, contagious enthusiasm.

Beyond the third or fourth day of my hypothetical undertaking, however, things often tend to get a bit blurry. What, exactly, the students will be doing in and out of class with and to the novel remains uncharted territory. Undaunted, I have nonetheless assumed all too often that, in any case, the students will after that second or third glorious day "continue to discuss the novel until we 'complete it,' at which time they take a test that, has," I cavalierly conclude for no apparent reason, "become a superfluous pedagogical convention."

And while this is the way many of us often envision how we will "teach" novels, the reality of what commonly occurs in the classroom is seldom inspired, enlightened, or even instructive. Lessons that burn hot on the first day tend to fizzle and sputter by the second and die by the third; and in the truly long run, students often find themselves writing perfunctory journals and taking equally meaningless tests to prove they read to the novel's final chapter. In short, the professor's sanguine vision is frequently something more momentous than the practice it precedes.

Thus, the question becomes, how can we effectively teach novels in a manner that makes each day in the unit essential and eventful? How, moreover, can we use novels to nurture ways of thinking that are critical, creative, and—from the students' perspective—relevant to the world beyond the books?

Although there are certainly countless first-rate answers to these questions, I will, nonetheless, offer one answer/lesson here that has worked wonderfully well in my literature courses. It is a method that combines a mock-trial approach to instruction with the introduction of various literary theories. It is also, to be sure, one that avoids the use of the seemingly obligatory journal. This combination of the formal and perhaps familiar mock trial with specific and scholarly literary theories commonly creates scenarios wherein, in most cases (pun intended), students interrogate texts and, in the process, become better readers of literature and of their own ways of thinking about literature. Furthermore, this approach to teaching novels ensures that each day of a two- or three-week unit is participatory and purposeful. Here, then, is how and why it works.

THE PRACTICE OF USING THEORIES

At the outset of the unit, I divide the students into three groups: prosecution team, defense team, and jury. The professor, who plays the part of the judge, would do well to wear his or her gowns on the days set aside for the trial and to insist that, during the coming days, the students "all rise" whenever she or he enters the classroom. And while this initial task of introducing the trial and assigning students to their respective groups often feels not unlike the opening day of any other original, and unusual unit—with the fireworks, the flowing rivers, and all the other regalia—in this case, the difference is that we are just beginning.

As is customary, the students receive a reading schedule at the outset; and included with this calendar is a list of literary theories and an agenda indicating when each theory will be introduced and discussed. Thus, as noted on the calendar, every second or third day (depending on when the course occurs during the week), the professor introduces a new literary theory and, in the process, breaks down that theory into its central tenets and its most important moves, or applications.

Based on what I have gathered through a process suitably described as a trial-and-error approach to pedagogy, I recommend beginning with formalism and outlining for the students specific tenets associated with this approach to reading and analysis before moving onto other theories. Following this plan of action, we read and discuss several essays by representative formalists such as Cleanth Brooks and W. K. Wimsatt and Monroe C. Beardsly, and we attempt to apply their ideas—in the form of questions—to very short stories, such as parables or equally short and concrete poems. I encourage the students to think of criticisms as collections of questions: New Critics, for instance, ask certain, specific (and, from the students' perspective, surprisingly familiar) kinds of questions. As outlined in *The Allyn & Bacon Guide to Writing*, these can be described as "turning-point starter questions," and include such customary inquiries as, "How do the metaphors and similes change? Is there a pattern to that change?" and, "How does the time or place depicted in the text change? How are other changes in the text related to these changes?" (352–53) Then, when attempting to build on this somewhat nonthreatening approach, I turn the students' attention to other forms of criticism, including feminism, Marxism, New Historicism, and, on occasion, deconstruction—the choice of what critical lenses is most relevant and potentially most useful for the prosecution and defense teams depends in many respects on the novel we are reading, and, as I tell the students, on how well they as readers use the theories to highlight relevant textual evidence before and during the impending trial.

Admittedly, the introduction of multiple theories in the context of a novel presents many potential challenges for students and teacher alike. So, to build in a kind of safety net, I rely in these lessons on the strategies of scaffolding and progression. Each time I introduce a theory, I, in conjunction with the students, apply it first to something familiar and second to the novel. It is critical, in my experience, that one follow this pattern of applying the new knowledge to the familiar before turning to the novel, which is—teachers and rereaders tend to forget—significantly complex and resistant, even to literary theories.

As an example of how one might build in progression to the lesson plan and larger unit, I will, when introducing Marxism, for instance, often invite the students to identify the power relationships on campus. I do this by reworking a particularly useful strategy that Deborah Appleman presents in her book *Critical Encounters in High School English: Teaching Literary Theory to Adolescents*. Following Appleman's lead, I draw five or six concentric circles on the board and invite the students to place the most authoritative players/groups/factions/figures in the center and the least powerful on the outer ring (almost without fail the students place the Board of Regents in the center and themselves on the outside). We then discuss what constitutes power in this place we call "college," how that power is represented, and how it is exercised. Interestingly, it seldom takes long for the students to conclude that, though they might inhabit the outer ring, they have power in numbers and can wield it in the way that they respond to teacher evaluations. The students are quick to conclude during these discussions that one of their most potent weapons in the classroom is the oppressive power of collective silence.

After checking to be sure the students understand and can apply the theory both to the familiar and the new/novel, I then instruct them to keep it in mind when answering a handful of theme-based, overriding questions for the unit. In this way, by returning repeatedly to the same set of questions after encountering each new literary lens, the students come to realize how, from either the standpoint of the prosecution or the defense, one literary theory might be more beneficial in a given case/question than another. This tactic also helps create coherence in the unit and keep the students focused on their primary objective: using theory in practical ways to succeed in the trial.

Meanwhile, outside of class, as we get closer to the date set aside for the showdown, the students meet in their respective groups and prepare/research. Those on the defense and prosecution teams must submit in a specific order a set of briefs; for the prosecution, these include the most important document/facet of the entire trial: the statement of the charges. It is in this written statement that we see the intersection of the theories and the practice of law.

As I make clear to the entire class, the statement of charges needs to be a carefully crafted document (1) because the wording in the statement determines what will and will not be admitted as evidence in the court, and (2) because the aspect, person, or persona being indicted must be guilty beyond a shadow of a doubt. The prosecution team has the power and privilege to declare what kind of literary trial will ensue: in other words, these students have the opportunity to state which literary lenses and what related evidence will be permitted and which will not. Accordingly, if a prosecution team in its statement of charges about *The Scarlet Letter* asserts that this will be a formalist trial, biographical information about Nathaniel Hawthorne and New Historic information dealing with the book's setting or its publication date are inadmissible. The onus is on the prosecution to object when and if the defense attempts to use evidence deemed outside the scope of formalism.

After the prosecution submits its opening statements, each side then presents relevant materials and witness lists via Moodle or Blackboard two or three days in advance of the date of the trial. The defense team then has time to construct its case and complete its research accordingly. Concurrently, those in the jury are charged with the task of preparing to take the stand and play whatever bit part from the novel that either the prosecution or the defense has assigned to them. This is a challenge, because it means that jury members must participate fully as witnesses/characters and simultaneously (when not on the stand) as objective jurors. Then, during the first day of the trial, after the prosecution and defense have read their opening statements, the prosecution calls its witnesses. In accordance with mock trial conventions, the defense, in turn, has the option to cross-examine the witnesses, while the prosecution can afterward, if it elects, redirect. During the succeeding class, the routine remains but the roles switch.

One particularly effective prosecution team outlined in its statement of charges related to *The Adventures of Huckleberry Finn* that Huck is guilty of aiding and abetting a criminal (Jim). And because that team explicitly allowed biographical details about Twain and historical information dealing with the narrative's setting or the book's publication as admissible evidence, the onus was on both the prosecution and the defense to find and use the best of such support during the trial.

After the final day of the trial and before the next class, both the prosecution and defense submit their closing statements via e-mail to the jury. The members of the jury meet outside of class, discuss the case and the closing statements, and then agree upon a verdict, which they render at the beginning of the next class. A week or so after the dust has settled, the members of the legal teams submit a reaction paper, while members of the jury submit a group paper (a summary of the trial and the group's deliberation) and an individual essay (an explanation/justification of their vote within the group).

Almost without exception, the best teaching experiences I have had as an English professor occurred on the days that my students enacted these trials in my American literature courses. I have witnessed otherwise reticent students rise to the occasion as well-spoken, confident attorneys who know both the theory and the text; I have witnessed similarly reserved students become emboldened when playing a part when taking the stand; and I have witnessed with wonder the sight of students paging frantically through their texts and their research materials in search of evidence in an effort to make or defend a particular point. All of this happens not on the first day but somewhere near the end, and not during a test for points but during a trial for proof. I have, moreover, told countless colleagues the story of the student in my American literature class who proclaimed passionately, "Objection, your Honor! The defense is posing a New Historic question, and the prosecution, in its opening statement, expressly forbade any evidence coming from outside the book."

Most excitingly, though, are those unanticipated moments during trials when issues arrive that professors cannot help but become excited about. As a case in point, I was thrilled when—during a trial in which, appropriately and *finally*, Roger Chillingworth took the stand—a spontaneous debate erupted regarding the reliability of the narrator as a witness and authority. The prosecution, having declared that this would be a formalist literary court of law, was caught off guard when the defense convincingly established for the jury (and the judge) that, in the Custom House chapter, the narrator proves himself to be biased and thus unreliable. Hardly stoic and far from appropriate in my role as judge, I was giddy.

THE VERDICT

What is at stake in this approach to teaching novels? What do the students learn? How does this way of learning better serve them? Why, if at all, would a professor take the time and make the extra effort to approach instruction in this much more painstaking and, admittedly, time-consuming manner?

To begin, students often discover that they already have formulated not only opinions about literary texts but also the inchoate beginnings of their own literary theories. As Charles Bressler points out in the fourth edition of his book *Literary Criticism: An Introduction to Theory and Practice*, "every reader espouses some kind of literary theory" (8). What most students and teachers tend to forget, though, is that, in Bressler's words, "Each reader's theory may be conscious or unconscious, whole or partial, informed or ill informed, eclectic or unified." The benefit of forcing the issue and making literary theories both public and relevant in a mock-trial unit is that doing so significantly decreases the likelihood that students will construct "illogical, unsound, and haphazard interpretations" (8).

Students likewise learn that literary theories have practical implications and applications. In this poststructural age when a text is a text is a text, students often find it exhilarating to apply their new-found ways of reading to such familiar things/topics/texts as commercials, clothing, and cartoons. Furthermore, when dealing for instance with such theories as feminism and ecocriticism, students realize that theories have real-world relevance. To appreciate how and why, from an ecocritical perspective, certain individuals and institutions define "the land" or how they determine something's supposed "value" is to begin to comprehend why certain policies should be called into question.

The students learn, moreover, when participating in these mock trials that they can *use* literary theories rather abuse them or feel abused by their often-esoteric and sometime condescending authors. More to the point, the students learn that every facet of novels, even supposedly sacred, canonical works, is open for debate. In this regard, ironically, the introduction of theories in this context facilitates what Mikhail Bakhtin might describe as the novelization of the novel. The mock trial makes requisite that, via these various lenses, the novel under investigation be taken down from its supposed pedestal and placed squarely in the center of the classroom, a now "novelistic zone," which, appropriately, is characterized by immediacy, equality, open-endedness, and, if you are lucky, humor (30–32).

Finally, for the teacher, this approach to instruction has many unexpected and startling side effects: the classroom becomes a forge in which new readings emerge and old, familiar ones are challenged. What's more, it becomes a place characterized most notably by fairness, inquiry, and democracy. In such a place, as one scholar of the classroom argues, teachers are able to resist the urge to dominate and, as a consequence, they in turn allow their students to expand and develop as intellectuals and as individuals (Martin 43).

WORKS CITED

Appleman, Deborah. *Critical Encounters in High School English: Teaching Literary Theory to Adolescents*. New York: Teachers College Press, 2000.

Bakhtin, Mikhail. *The Dialogic Imagination: Four Essays*, translated by Caryl Emerson and Michael Holquist, edited by Michael Holquist. University of Texas Press Slavic Series, No. 1. 1981. Austin: University of Texas Press, 1992.

Bressler, Charles E. *Literary Criticism: An Introduction to Theory and Practice*. 4th ed. Upper Saddle River, NJ: Prentice Hall, 2007.

Martin, Rachel. *Listening Up: Reinventing Ourselves as Teachers and Students*. Portsmouth, NH: Boynton/Cook Publishers, 2005.

Ramage, John, John Bean, and June Johnson. *The Allyn & Bacon Guide to Writing*. 4th ed. New York: Pearson Longman, 2006.

Selected Bibliography

Alkana, Joseph. "'Do We Not Know the Meaning of Aesthetic Gratification?' Cynthia Ozick's *The* S*hawl,* the Akedah, and the Ethics of Holocaust Literary Aesthetics." *Modern Fiction Studies* 43, no. 4 (1997): 963–90.

Appleman, Deborah. *Critical Encounters in High School English: Teaching Literary Theory to Adolescents.* New York: Teacher's College Press, 2000.

Arnett, Ronald C., and Gordon Nakagawa. "The Assumptive Roots of Empathic Listening: A Critique." *Communication Education* 32 (1983): 368–78.

Bakhtin, Mikhail. *The Dialogic Imagination: Four Essays*, translated by Caryl Emerson and Michael Holquist, edited by Michael Holquist. University of Texas Press Slavic Series, No. 1. 1981. Austin: University of Texas Press, 1992.

———. *Problems of Dostoevsky's Poetics*, translated by R. W. Rotsel. Ann Arbor, MI: Ardis, 1973.

Barthes, Roland. "Longtemps, je me suis couche de bonne heure." In *The Rustle of Language*, translated by Richard Howard, 277–90. New York: Hill and Wang, 1986.

———. "Theory of the Text." In *Untying the Text*, edited by Robert Young, 31–44. Boston: Routledge, 1981.

Beauvoir, Simone de. *The Second Sex*. Relevant excerpts can be found in various source readers, for example in *Sources of the West: Readings in Western Civilization*, Vol. II, edited by Mark A. Kishlansky. 4th ed. New York: Longman, 2001.

Berg, Ellen. "An Introduction to Sociology Using Short Stories and Films: Reshaping the Cookie Cutter and Redecorating the Cookie." *Teaching Sociology* 20 (1992): 265–69.

Bolgatz, Jane. *Talking Race in the Classroom*. New York: Teachers College Press, 2005.

Booth, Wayne C. "Why Banning Ethical Criticism is a Serious Mistake." *Philosophy and Literature* 22, no. 2 (1998): 366–93.

Boyatzis, Chris J. "Studying Lives through Literature: Using Narrative to Teach Social Science Courses and Promote Students' Epistemological Growth." *Journal of Excellence in College Teaching* 5, no. 1 (1994): 31–45.

Broome, Benjamin J. "Building Shared Meaning: Implications of a Relational Approach to Empathy for Teaching Intercultural Communication." *Communication Education* 40 (1991): 235–49.

Burke, Kenneth. "Linguistic Approach to Problems of Education:" In *The Yearbook for the National Study of Education*. Chicago: University of Chicago Press, 1955.

Chaffee, John. *Thinking Critically*. 8th ed. Boston: Houghton Mifflin, 2006.

Clear, Val. "Marriage Education through Novels and Biography." *Journal of Marriage and the Family* 28 (1966): 217–19.

Cochran-Smith, Marilyn. "Color Blindness and Basket Making are Not the Answers: Confronting the Dilemmas of Race, Culture, and Language Diversity in Teacher Education." *American Educational Research Journal* 32, no. 3 (1995): 493–522.

Colby, Anne, and Thomas Ehrlich, Elizabeth Beaumont, and Jason Stephens. *Educating Citizens: Preparing America's Undergraduates for Lives of Moral and Civic Responsibility*. San Francisco: Jossey-Bass, 2003.

Collier, Mary Jane. "An Introduction." In *Transforming Communication about Culture*, edited by M. J. Collier, xi–xix. Thousand Oaks: Sage, 2001.

Condon, John. "Exploring Intercultural Communication through Literature and Film." *World Englishes* 5 (1986): 153–61.

Corbett, Ronald P. "'Novel' Perspectives on Probation: Fiction as Sociology." *Sociological Forum* 9 (1994): 307–14.

Cosbey, Janet. "Using Contemporary Fiction to Teach Family Issues." *Teaching Sociology* 25, no. 3 (1997): 227–33.

Coser, Lewis A. 1963. *Sociology Through Literature: An Introductory Reader*. Englewood Cliffs, NJ: Prentice Hall.

Crawford, Mary. "Rethinking the Romance: Teaching the Content and Function of Gender Stereotypes in the Psychology of Women Course." *Teaching of Psychology* 21, no. 3 (1994): 151–53.

Dace, Karen Lynnette, and Mark Lawrence McPhail. "Crossing the Color Line: From Empathy to Implicature in Intercultural Communication." In *Readings in Intercultural Communication*, edited by Judith N. Martin, Thomas K. Nakayama, and Lisa A. Flores, 344–51. 2nd ed. New York: McGraw-Hill, 2001.

Darling-Hammond, Linda, and Silvia Paloma Garcia-Lopez. "What Is Diversity?" In *Learning to Teach for Social Justice*, edited by Linda Darling-Hammond, Jennifer French, and Silvia Paloma Garcia-Lopez, 9–12. New York: Teachers College Press, 2002.

Denmark: Living with the Enemy. Part of the series A Force More Powerful. Films for the Humanities & Sciences, 2004.

DeVault, Marjorie L. "Novel Readings: The Social Organization of Interpretation." In *Liberating Method,* edited by Marjorie L. DeVault, 109–38. Philadelphia: Temple University Press, 1999.

Diller, Jerry V., and Jean Moule. *Cultural Competence: A Primer for Educators*. Belmont, CA: Thomson Wadsworth, 2005.

Dunn, Dana S. "Interpreting the Self through Literature: Psychology and the Novels of Wallace Stegner." Vol. 4, *Activities Handbook for the Teaching of Psychology*, edited by Ludy T. Benjamin, Barbara F. Nodine, Randal M. Ernst, and Charles Blair Broeker, 362–365. Washington, DC: American Psychological Association, 1999.

Felder, Richard M., and Rebecca Brent. "The Intellectual Development of Science and Engineering Students. Part 1: Models and Challenges." *Journal of Engineering Education* (October 2004): 269–77.

Fiero, Gloria K. *The Humanistic Tradition*. 3rd ed. 6 vols. New York: McGraw-Hill, 1998.

Fitzgerald, Charlotte D. "Exploring Race in the Classroom: Guidelines for Selecting the 'Right' Novel." *Teaching Sociology* 20 (1992): 244–47.

Fleckenstein, Kristie S. "Inserting Imagery Into Our Classrooms." In *Language and Image in the Reading Writing Classroom: Teaching Vision*, edited by Kristie S. Fleckenstein, Linda T. Calendrillo, and Demetrice A. Worley, 3–26. Mahwah, NJ: Lawrence Erlbaum Associates, 2002.

Fleming, Michael Z., Ralph L. Piedmont, and C. Michael Hiam. "Images of Madness: Feature Films in Teaching Psychology." *Teaching of Psychology* 17, no. 3 (1990): 185–87.

Frost, Susan H., and Paul M. Jean. "Bridging the Disciplines: Interdisciplinary Discourse and Faculty Scholarship." *The Journal of Higher Education* 74, no. 2 (2003): 119–49.

Hall, Stuart. "Introduction." In *Representation: Cultural Representations and Signifying Practices*, edited by Stuart Hall. London: Sage and Open University, 1997.

Hanson, Chad M. "A Stop Sign at the Intersection of History and Biography: Illustrating Mills's Imagination with Depression-Era Photographs." *Teaching Sociology* 30 (2002): 235–242.

Hartman, Cheryl J. "Enriching Sociology 100 Using the Novel *Things Fall Apart.*" *Teaching Sociology* 33 (2005): 317–22.

Hawthorn, Jeremy. *Studying the Novel.* 5th ed. London: Hodder Arnold, 2005.

Hegvedt, Karen A. "Teaching Sociology of Literature Through Literature." *Teaching Sociology* 19 (1991): 1–12.

Henslin, James M. *Essentials of Sociology.* Boston: Allyn and Bacon, 2002.

Hill, Michael R. "Novels, Thought Experiments, and Humanist Sociology in the Classroom: Muri Sandoz and Capital City." *Teaching Sociology* 15 (1987): 38–44.

Hobbs, Catherine L. "Learning From the Past: Verbal and Visual Literacy in Early Modern Rhetoric and Writing Pedagogy." In *Language and Image in the Reading-Writing Classroom: Teaching Vision*, edited by Kristie S. Fleckenstein, Linda T. Calendrillo, and Demetrice A. Worley, 27–44. Mahwah, NJ: Lawrence Erlbaum Associates, 2002.

Howard, Jay R. "An Examination of Student Learning in Introductory Sociology at a Commuter Campus." *Teaching Sociology* 33 (2005): 195–205.

Izevbaye, Dan. "The Igbo as Exceptional Colonial Subjects: Fictionalizing an Abnormal Historical Situation." In *Approaches to Teaching Achebe's Things Fall Apart*, 45–51. New York: The Modern Language Association of America, 1991.

Johnson, Mark. *Moral Imagination: Implications of Cognitive Science for Ethics.* Chicago: University of Chicago Press, 1993.

Kaufman, Peter. "Michael Jordan Meets C. Wright Mills: Illustrating the Sociological Imagination with Objects from Everyday Life." *Teaching Sociology* 25 (1997): 309–14.

Kirst-Ashman, Karen K., and Grafton H. Hull. *Understanding Generalist Practice.* Belmont, CA: Brooks/Cole, 2006.

Koskimaa, Raine. "Digital Literature: From Text to Hypertext and Beyond." University of Jyväskylä. http://www.cc.jyu.fi/~koskimaa/thesis/thesis.shtml (accessed June 15, 2006).

Laz, Cheryl. "Science Fiction and Introduction to Sociology." *Teaching Sociology* 24, no. 1 (1996): 54–63.

Lindstrom, Fred B. Review of "Teaching Sociology with Fiction: An Annotated Bibliography." *Sociological Inquiry* 68 (1998): 281–84.

Loseke, D. R. "Constructing Moralities." In *Thinking About Social Problems: An Introduction to Constructionist Perspectives*, 47–68. New York: Aldine De Gruyter, 1999.

Martin, Judith N., and Thomas K. Nakayama. *Intercultural Communication in Contexts.* 2nd ed. New York: McGraw-Hill, 2004.

Mills, C. Wright. *Sociological Imagination.* New York: Oxford University Press, 1959.

Misra, Joya. "Integrating 'The Real World' into Introduction to Sociology: Making Sociological Concepts Real" *Teaching Sociology* 28 (2000): 346–63.

Montrose, Louis. "New Historicisms." In *Redrawing the Boundaries*, edited by Stephen Greenblatt, 393–418. New York: The Modern Language Association of America, 1992.

Moran, Timothy Patrick. "Versifying Your Reading List: Using Poetry to Teach Inequality." *Teaching Sociology* 27, no. 2 (1999): 110–25.

Nussbaum, Martha C. "Exactly and Responsibly: A Defense of Ethical Criticism." *Philosophy and Literature* 22, no. 2 (1998): 343–65.

———. "The Literary Imagination." In *Falling into Theory: Conflicting Views on Reading Literature,* edited by David H. Richter, 355–365. 2nd ed. New York: Bedford/St. Martin's, 2000.

Ross, Susan M., and Janet McNeil Hurlbert. "Problem-Based Learning: An Exercise on Vermont's Legalization of Civil Unions." *Teaching Sociology* 32 (January 2004): 79–93.

Sanders, Mark. "Ethics and Interdisciplinarity in Philosophy and Literary Theory." *Diacritics* 32, no. 3–4 (2002): 3–16.

Sleeter, Christine E. *Multicultural Education as Social Activism.* Albany, NY: SUNY Press, 1996.

Spears-Bunton, Linda. "All the Colors of the Land: A Literacy Montage." In *Teaching and Using Multicultural Literature in Grades 9-12: Moving Beyond the Canon,* edited by Arlette Willis, 17–36. Norwood, MA: Christopher Gordon, 1998.

Stock, Brian. "Ethics and the Humanities: Some Lessons of Historical Experience." *New Literary History* 36, no. 1 (2005): 1–17.

———. "Reading, Ethics, and the Literary Imagination." *New Literary History* 34, no. 1 (2003): 1–17.

Style, Emily. "Curriculum as Window and Mirror." In *Seeding the Process of Multicultural Education: An Anthology,* edited by Cathy L. Nelson and Kim A. Wilson, 149–156. Plymouth, MN: Minnesota Inclusiveness Program, 1998.

Templeton, Alice, and Steven B. Groce. "Sociology and Literature: Theoretical Considerations." *Sociological Inquiry* 60 (1990): 34–46.

Trilling, Lionel. "Manners, Morals, and the Novel." In *Essentials of the Theory of Fiction,* edited by Micheal J. Hoffman and Patrick D. Murphy, 77–91. 2nd ed. Durham, NC: Duke University Press, 1996.

———. "On the Teaching of Modern Literature." *Beyond Culture: Essays on Literature and Learning.* New York: The Viking Press, 1965.

Unsworth, Len. *Teaching Multiliteracies Across the Curriculum: Changing Contexts of Text and Image in Classroom Practice.* Buckingham, United Kingdom: Open University Press, 2001.

Van Engen, Abram. "Reclaiming Claims: What English Students Want From English Profs." *Pedagogy: Critical Approaches to Teaching Literature, Composition and Culture* 5, no. 1 (2005): 5–18.

Van Voorhis, Rebecca M. "Culturally Relevant Practice: a Framework for Teaching the Psychosocial Dynamics of Oppression." *Journal of Social Work Education* 34 (1998): 121–34.

Von Wright, M. "Narrative Imagination and Taking the Perspective of Others." *Studies in Philosophy and Education* 21 (2002): 407–16.

Westhues, Kenneth. "Transcending the Textbook World." *Teaching Sociology* 19 (1991): 87–92.

Willis, Arlette. *Teaching and Using Multicultural Literature in Grades 9-12: Moving Beyond the Canon.* Norwood, MA: Christopher Gordon, 1998.

Zastrow, Charles H. *The Practice of Social Work: Applications of Generalist and Advanced Content.* Pacific Grove, CA: Brooks/Cole, 2003.

Zunshine, Lisa. *Why We Read Fiction: Theory of Mind and the Novel.* Columbus: Ohio State University Press, 2006.

About the Editor and Contributors

Colin C. Irvine is an assistant professor of English at Augsburg College in Minneapolis, Minnesota. He earned his bachelor's degree from Carroll College in Helena, Montana, his master's degree from the University of Notre Dame and his doctorate from Marquette University. He teaches courses in environmental literature, American literature, secondary education methods, and composition; his research interests focus on the intersections of literature and life, with an emphasis on how novels inform and influence thought and behavior. He is currently at work on a project that entails annotating Aldo Leopold's *A Sand County Almanac*.

Pamela Black is an associate professor of social work education at Eastern Kentucky University. She holds a master's degree in social work. Her favorite part of teaching is the active engagement she values with students and being a part of their professional development to the practice of social work. Her scholarship interest includes the scholarship of teaching, child welfare, social justice, and diversity issues. As a social worker, her service interest and continuous commitment to social justice involves working with organizations at the community level to improve services and outcomes for women and children. She is also an avid summer reader.

Amy C. Branam is an assistant professor of English at Frostburg State University in Frostburg, Maryland. She received her doctorate in English from Marquette University. In addition to courses on nineteenth-century transatlantic literature, she teaches courses on women and literature. She has presented at numerous conferences on feminist issues in literature and contemporary culture; she has published articles on Edgar Allan Poe, Native American literature, and pedagogy.

John Bruni is an assistant professor of English at the South Dakota School of Mines and Technology, where he teaches literature, composition, and humanities. He holds a doctorate in English from the University of Kansas. He is the author of an article on Edith Wharton and evolution and a forthcoming article on Jack London and biological kinship. He is currently working on a book on popular science and evolution in early-twentieth-century U.S. literature and culture.

Ricia Anne Chansky is a doctoral candidate at Illinois State University, where her research focuses on feminist applications of visual literacy as humanist pedagogy and as a tool for reading verbal-visual rhetorics. Prior to her enrollment, she taught rhetoric, literature, and media studies at George Washington University and led seminars in visual literacy at the Smithsonian Institution, the National Gallery of Art, and the National Museum of Women in the Arts. She has published her research on visual literacy in *a/b: Auto/Biography Studies* and *The Journal of Popular Culture*.

Alan Ramón Clinton has spent the past two years helping to move Northeastern University's Advanced Writing in the Disciplines program in a more experimental direction, one that activates the powers of writing to extend disciplinary boundaries and make various disciplines communicate in new ways. This push has resulted in two other essays, both forthcoming: "Writing Is Against Discipline: Three Courses" in *Writing Against the Disciplines* (Lexington Books, Pedagogy and Activism Series) and "Discontinuity Editing: Exquisite Corpse, Control Revolution, and Radical Research" (University of Nebraska Press). He is the author of *Mechanical Occult: Automatism, Modernism, and the Specter of Politics* (Peter Lang 2004).

Janine DeWitt is an associate professor of sociology at Marymount University in Arlington, Virginia, where she has developed a series of courses that use narratives to blend sociological analysis with ethical decision-making skills. Her current scholarship applies this approach to the field of computer security education. She has presented and written about teaching ethical reasoning, cyberethics, and modeling the analysis of social, legal, and ethical contexts for computer security decision-making. She holds a doctorate in sociology from Duke University.

Lan Dong is an assistant professor of English at the University of Illinois at Springfield, where she teaches Asian American literature, world literature, and composition. She received her doctorate in comparative literature from the University of Massachusetts at Amherst. She has published articles on Jeanne M. Lee's *The Song of Mu Lan*, Gish Jen's *Typical American*, David Mura's *Turning Japanese: Memoirs of a Sansei*, Joseph Conrad's *Heart of Darkness*, Asian American films, and Chinese queer cinema. Her book chapters on D. W. Griffith's *Broken Blossoms*, Gish Jen, and food in Asian American childhood are forthcoming. She is working on a book manuscript on the cross-cultural transformation of Mulan.

Christine M. Doran is an assistant professor of English and Communication at Potsdam College, State University of New York, where she teaches English and gender studies courses. Her doctorate is from the University of Notre Dame and focuses on middle-class women's labor in the public sphere in late-nineteenth- and early-twentieth-century Britain. Her essay on Vera Brittain's autobiography, "Vera Brittain: The Work of Memorial in an Age of War," appeared in the inaugural issue of the *Journal of Interdisciplinary Feminist Thought*.

Lauretta Conklin Frederking is an assistant professor of political science at University of Portland in Portland, Oregon. She teaches comparative politics, political economy, and research methods. She holds a doctorate in political science from Washington University, a master's degree in political science from Columbia University, and a bachelor's degree from University of Toronto. She is the author of a book on immigration, several articles on immigrant neighborhoods, and articles on the arts and government entrepreneurship. She is the editor of the forthcoming book *The American Experiment: Religious Freedom*.

Alexis Grosofsky is a professor and former chair of the Department of Psychology at Beloit College in Beloit, Wisconsin. She earned her bachelor's degree in psychology from State University of New York (SUNY) College at Buffalo and her master's degree and doctorate in experimental psychology (memory and cognition) from SUNY–Binghamton (now University Center at Binghamton) with minors in perception and statistics. She teaches a variety of courses in psychology, including Introduction to Psychology, Sensation and Perception, Statistical Applications in Psychology, and Research Methods and Design. Alexis is interested in research about olfaction and pedagogy.

Tim Hallett is an assistant professor in the Department of Sociology at Indiana University, where he teaches Introduction to Sociology and Social Psychology. In addition to using *The Autobiography of Malcolm X*, he also uses *Catch Me if You Can* by Frank Abagnale, *Mankiller* by Wilma Mankiller, *Almost a Woman* by Esmeralda Santiago, *The Accidental Asian* by Eric Liu, and *Faith of My Fathers* by John McCain to introduce students to the sociological imagination and to teach them sociological concepts. Tim's research interests lie at the intersections of social psychology, organizations, and culture. He has published research on "inhabited institutions," symbolic power and organizational culture, and how emotions "blow up" in organizations. His current research examines institutional recoupling and turmoil in urban elementary schools.

Brent Harger is a doctoral student in the Department of Sociology at Indiana University, where he teaches Introduction to Sociology, Social Psychology, and Research Methods. In addition to the scholarship of teaching and learning, Brent is interested in issues related to childhood, adolescence, education, and social psychology. His previous research has examined the use of sarcasm and gossip in school staff meetings, and he is currently working on a paper that examines images of professors in popular film over the past twenty years. In his dissertation, he plans to examine bullying and teasing in the lives of preadolescent children.

Yuko Kawai is an associate professor of communication in the Department of English at Tokai University, Kanagawa, Japan, where she teaches intercultural communication, communication theory, and English as a foreign language. She completed her undergraduate education in Japan and received postgraduate degrees in the United States. She holds a doctorate in communication from the University of New Mexico. Her research interests focus on analyzing communication of globalization, nationalism, and race relations. She is the author of articles on racial representations of Asian Americans and also discursive intersections of Japanese nationalism and globalization.

Peter Kratzke is an instructor with the Program for Writing and Rhetoric at the University of Colorado–Boulder. He earned his doctorate from the University of Kentucky, and he has published articles on various American writers, including Sarah Kemble Knight, Mark Twain, Edgar Wilson ("Bill") Nye, Ambrose Bierce, and Jack London. Along with Carol Hamilton, he coedited *Short Stories in the Classroom* (NCTE 1999); more recently, he edited a double issue of the College English Association's *The Critic*. A longtime bicycle mechanic, Kratzke is presently studying "the wheel" in American literary history.

Elizabeth Berg Leer is an assistant professor of education at St. Olaf College in Northfield, Minnesota. She holds a Ph.D. in curriculum and instruction with an emphasis in English education from the University of Minnesota and an M.A. in English literature from Northern Illinois University. At the college level she has taught courses in general instructional methods, English methods, children's and adolescent literature, and educational psychology. She also has six years of experience teaching middle school and high school English and German. Elizabeth's current research interests focus on teaching multicultural literature and teaching in a diverse society.

John Lennon is an assistant professor of English at St. Francis College in Brooklyn, New York. Receiving his doctorate from Lehigh University in American Literature, he teaches a wide range of courses in American Literature, American Studies, and Film and Popular Culture. While his research interests are wide ranging, the main thrust of his scholarship examines manifestations of mobility and agency among the working and nonworking classes from the nineteenth century to the present. Currently coediting an anthology about trash cinema, John is also in the process of writing a book, *Boxcar Politics*, which examines the political history of the hobo in the United States.

Stephanie Li is an assistant professor of English at University of Rochester. She received both her doctorate in English language and literature and her masters of fine arts in fiction writing from Cornell University. Her current project, "Something Akin to Freedom": The Politics of Sexual Agency in Narratives by African American Women, is a historical study of black women in antebellum slavery and a literary analysis involving such authors as Harriet Jacobs, Hannah Crafts, William Faulkner, and Gayl Jones. She has published in such journals as *Callaloo*, *American Literature,* and *Legacy*.

Michelle Loris is the associate dean of the College of Arts and Sciences at Sacred Heart University in Fairfield, Connecticut, where she teaches both literature and psychology. She holds a doctorate in American Literature from Fordham University and a doctorate in Clinical Psychology from Antioch/New England Professional School of Psychology. She is the author of a book on Joan Didion, coeditor of a book on Gloria Naylor, and author of articles on Saul Bellow, Toni Morrison, and Willa Cather. She is also the author and coauthor of articles on post-traumatic stress.

Rachel McCoppin is an assistant professor of literature at the University of Minnesota, Crookston, where she teaches literature, humanities, and ethics courses. She holds a doctorate from Indiana University of Pennsylvania. She has published an article entitled "Creating American Literature" in the journal *Teaching American Literature: A Journal of Theory and Practice.* She coauthored an article entitled "Being Actively Revised by the Other: Opposition and Incorporation" in the book *Teaching Ideas for the Basic Communication Course.* She has authored articles on existentialism and modernism.

Marta M. Miranda is an associate professor of social work and the director of the Women's Studies Program at Eastern Kentucky University. She has thirty years of direct clinical and organizational social work practice experience. She has been designing and teaching social work practice courses for the last fifteen years. Her research, service, and activism focus is social justice.

Peter P. Nieckarz, Jr., is an associate professor of sociology at Western Carolina University in Cullowhee, North Carolina. He teaches several courses, including sociological theory, popular culture, social movements, the Internet and society, and race and minority groups. He has actively attempted to engage students by using innovative teaching methods in both general education and upper-level sociology courses. His recent research has focused on the commercialization of public radio, the emergence of virtual community, and the presence of human resistance and creativity within mass culture. He earned a doctorate in sociology from Western Michigan University.

Marguerite Rippy is an associate professor of literature and languages at Marymount University in Arlington, Virginia. She received her doctorate in English and performance studies from Indiana University, and her master's degree in Shakespeare from Vanderbilt University. She publishes on contemporary American cinema, focusing on topics such as Shakespeare on film, sexuality and race in classic Hollywood, and intertextual performance. She is currently completing a manuscript on Orson Welles's unfinished RKO film projects.

Gregory F. Schroeder is an associate professor of history at St. John's University in Collegeville, Minnesota, and its partner institution, the College of St. Benedict in St. Joseph, Minnesota, where he teaches modern European history. He earned his doctorate in history from Indiana University–Bloomington and has published works on postwar German history. His other research interests include the culture of memory in Austria and Germany, and he often directs the St. John's University/College of St. Benedict study abroad program in Salzburg, Austria.

Stephen E. Severn is an assistant professor of English and director of the Technical Communication Program at West Texas A&M University in Canyon, Texas. He holds a doctorate in English from the University of Maryland and a bachelor of science in engineering from the University of Pennsylvania. His research focuses on late-Victorian narrative fiction, film, and W. H. Auden. He has published pieces on Martin Scorcese, Thomas Hardy, Katherine Mansfield, and Elizabeth Gaskell. Dr. Severn also served for five years as an officer in the United States Navy and worked as a technical writer at the Department of Education.

Douglas P. Simeone is an assistant professor at Heartland Community College in Normal, Illinois, where he teaches various courses in psychology. He holds a master's degree in educational psychology from Northern Illinois University. To enhance student learning, he developed nontraditional projects for his students, including creative writing and reflective analysis as well as the opportunity to volunteer at mental health agencies. He also created a monthly campus talk show focused on diversity topics. He is currently involved in developing an emotional intelligence initiative at the college.

Eric Sterling is Distinguished Teaching Professor of English at Auburn University Montgomery (in Montgomery, Alabama), where he has taught since 1994. He holds a doctorate in English from Indiana University. He has published essays on using literature circles in the college classroom, on working with adjuncts, and teaching writing and literature. Professor Sterling has also published essays on Shakespeare, Spenser, Jonson, Moulsworth, Albee, O'Connor, Malamud, Jurek Becker, and Arthur Miller. He has also published three books: *The Movement Towards Subversion: The English History Play from Skelton to Shakespeare*, *Life in the Ghettos During the Holocaust*, and *Dialogue: Arthur Miller's Death of a Salesman*.

Marshall Toman teaches various humanities courses at the University of Wisconsin–River Falls. His degree is in twentieth-century American literature, with interests in Nabokov and Willa Cather, and in Central European literature and international film.

Monique van den Berg holds a B.A. in humanities with an English literature emphasis from Loyola Marymount University and an M.F.A. in poetics and writing from New College of California in San Francisco, where she was the editor of the literary magazine *Prosodia*. Ms. van den Berg has taught literature, composition, and creative writing at New College and at St. Norbert College in De Pere, Wisconsin. Her poetry has been published in numerous literary journals, and she is touring the country through 2008 as part of the Visual Verse project. She currently teaches English at the College of San Mateo in San Mateo, California.

Kristina B. Wolff is an assistant professor of sociology at the University of Maine at Farmington, specializing in social inequalities, public policy, and social change. She holds a doctorate in sociology and a master's degree in public administration from Syracuse University. Her publications include "To Protect and To Serve? An Exploration of Police Conduct in Relation to the Gay, Lesbian, Bisexual and Transgender Community" in *Sexuality and Culture* (coauthored). Her current research focuses on issues of inequality and militarism in the U.S. education system.

Index